INSIGHT GUIDES

asia's Best Hotels & Resorts

APA PUBLICATIONS
Part of the Langenscheidt Publishing Group

Editorial

Project Editors
Ed Peters
John Chan
Publisher
Jon Stonham

Distribution

UK & Ireland
GeoCenter International Ltd
The Viables Centre, Harrow Way
Basingstoke, Hants RG22 4BJ
Fax: (44) 1256-817988

United States
Langenscheidt Publishers, Inc.
46–35 54th Road, Maspeth, NY 11378
Fax: (1) 718 784-0640

Canada
Thomas Allen & Son Ltd
390 Steelcase Road East
Markham, Ontario L3R 1G2
Fax: (1) 905 475 6747

Australia
Universal Press
1 Waterloo Road
Macquarie Park, NSW 2113
Fax: (61) 2 9888 9074

New Zealand
Hema Maps New Zealand Ltd (HNZ)
Unit D, 24 Ra ORA Drive
East Tamaki, Auckland
Fax: (64) 9 273 6479

Worldwide
Apa Publications GmbH & Co.
Verlag KG (Singapore branch)
38 Joo Koon Road, Singapore 628990
Tel: (65) 6865-1600. Fax: (65) 6861-6438

Printing

Insight Print Services (Pte) Ltd
38 Joo Koon Road, Singapore 628990
Tel: (65) 6865-1600. Fax: (65) 6861-6438

©2003 Apa Publications GmbH & Co.
Verlag KG (Singapore branch)
All Rights Reserved
First Edition 2003

CONTACTING THE EDITORS
We would appreciate it if readers
would alert us to errors or outdated information by writing to:
11/D Ho Lee Commercial Building
38-44 D'Aquilar Street
Central, Hong Kong
e-mail: **guidebook@asia-hotels.com**

www.insightguides.com
www.asia-hotels.com

ABOUT THIS BOOK

Published by asia-hotels.com in association with Insight Guides, this is a unique guidebook as the hotels reviewed were chosen by guests with first-hand experience. A team of expert travel writers subsequently researched and compiled the entries, and as the guide deliberately contains no hotel advertising, they were free to write exactly what they felt and liked. Independent, authoritative, original and entertaining, this guide is essential reading for anyone who loves good hotels. But let us start from the beginning.

To be frank – choosing a hotel can be a nightmare. Whilst a dud flight is usually over in a couple of hours, spending hard-earned vacation time or a week on business in a lousy hotel is a different story. With more than 15,000 hotels and resorts in Asia the selection is vast and variable – and finding the right place for your needs is by no means easy.

Of course the hotels will tell you they are the biggest, best, nearest, quaintest, most romantic, etc ...which, to be fair, is their job. The wonderful prose we read both in hotel literature and on websites is a sales pitch. Invariably we turn to a trusted agent, the travel consultant – but therein lies a

choices for this book. The final result is 300 hotels across 21 countries ranging from the iconic to the rather less well-known boutique properties.

The guide is structured to make it easy for you to select a hotel. Grouped by country, each hotel has a short description which hopefully captures its true essence, and is supported by photographs and a list of facilities. Unfortunately, there is only so much room in a book, so if more information is required look up the hotel at www.asia-hotels.com where you should find more details. Reservations can also be made through this website.

Contributors

A decade in Asia has done nothing to dampen **Jon Stonham**'s passion for travel. Driven by a total lack of quality information on hotels in Asia, he co-founded asia-hotels.com in 1996 and is the motivating force behind this guide. An engineer by training, arithmetic and calculus are not a problem (with the help of a calculator) but for the life of him he cannot string two words together. Fortunately help was at hand in the form of Ed Peters and John Chan.

Ed Peters first set foot in Asia 25 years ago, and has been travelling the region ever since, variously disguised as a backpacker, serving officer with the Gurkhas and more recently as an award-winning journalist and travel writer. He has dossed down in a number of unusual venues when more regular accommodation proved unavailable, including on beaches, a police cell and in the bed of a most hospitable Nepalese

problem, as they cannot know about every destination and every hotel. To be honest, the best source of information comes from someone who has actually been there – tried the beds, sampled the food and been served by the staff.

This guide is based on just that. In 2002 over 42,000 customers of asia-hotels.com, Asia's leading independent hotel website, voted on-line for their favourite hotels across the Asia Pacific region, from Australia to India. In all 3,813 hotels received nominations. Our editors and hotel inspectors sifted through the 115,000 comments and scores to select the most popular

manager (who slept on the floor, in case you are wondering) – however he is not averse to slumming it in a five-star resort from time to time. He is based in Hong Kong, but also maintains a home in Phuket, and is usually to be found somewhere between the two.

Fleeing the British recession of the mid 90s, **John Chan** decided to backpack his way around the worst accommodation the world had to offer. With much foresight he eventually made booming Hong Kong his base – just in time for the 1997 economic crash. A writer of travel articles and educational textbooks he spent the past two and a half years inspecting and reviewing hundreds of hotels as the chief editor of asia-hotels.com.

Additional research and support was provided by **Adeline Mercier, Ana Suhaili, Cecile Cedo, Daydee Villarma, Don Angelico, Joanne Cabotaje, Mary Garlicki, Michelle Chow, Morens Semana, Nick Dover, Paul Robinson, Riyaz Moorani, Vivian Wong** and numerous others of the asia-hotels.com team.

Thanks go to **Jo Lote** for sub editing and proofing, **Harry Llufrio** of Gingerbreadman Multimedia for meticulously laying it out and **Graeme Wilson** of GWA Consultants and the team from Insight Guides for designing and producing the book. The photographs have been principally supplied by the hotels and supplemented by Insight Guides, freelancers and various national tourist associations.

Maps

Picture Credits
Front cover, back cover and page 2:
Banyan Tree Maldives Vabbinfaru
Page 4:
Mandarin Oriental Majapahit
Page 186:
Glyn Genin
Back cover:
Hilton Hanoi Opera

The national tourism bodies of
Australia (page 8), Hong Kong (page
44), South Korea (page 119), Macau
(page 132), Malaysia (page 136),
Philippines (page 192), Singapore
(page 208), Taiwan (pages 230/231)
and Thailand (page 237)

CONTENTS

Hotels by country

Indexes

Facilities

- Babysitting
- Beach
- Business Centre
- Casino
- Disabled Facilities
- Diving
- Golf Course
- Gymnasium
- Kids' Club
- In-room Computer Ports
- Nightclub
- Restaurants
- Room Service
- Satellite / Cable TV
- Spa
- Indoor Swimming Pool
- Outdoor Swimming Pool
- Tennis Court
- Tour Desk
- Water Sports

About the ratings

Guests with first-hand experience have essentially selected the hotels in this book. In 2002 asia-hotels.com polled its customers on their favourite hotels. Over 42,000 from 162 countries responded, nominating 3,813 properties covering nearly every country in Asia Pacific. Each hotel was rated on seven criteria using a scale of 1 – 10 (10 being best). The 'bellhop rating' was calculated from these scores using an asia-hotels.com formula. Our team of inspectors and independent travel writers then reviewed the ratings and number of votes to come up with 300 hotels across the main countries in the region. To be included hotels had to receive a minimum number of votes and an excellent overall rating. Our experts have added a few hotels that they feel merit being in the book to give it a broader coverage. These hotels are generally small and less well known, have opened in the last two years or are in countries where visitor numbers are low (eg Laos). These hotels have 'n/a' for their scores and ratings, although all have been personally inspected by one of the team. The end result is a mouth-watering selection from top-end 5-star hotels right down to some inexpensive but well-run boutique-type establishments. Note that the star rating has generally been supplied by the hotel; in some cases we have changed them (always down) where we feel it is clearly misleading. Where hotels have not supplied a star rating, we have given them one based on the experience of our inspections. Rates are as current as they can be but do fluctuate. Check www.asia-hotels.com or the hotels' own websites for the latest rates. Finally, we make every effort to get our information right, but hotels do change. If we have something wrong please do not hesitate to let us know.

Jon Stonham
stonham@asia-hotels.com
Co-founder & CEO, asia-hotels.com

Rates from: **US$ current price**
Star rating: ★ ★ ★ ★ ★
Bellhop rating:

Value:	1-10	Facilities:	1-10
Staff:	1-10	Restaurants:	1-10
Location:	1-10	Families:	1-10
Cleanliness:	1-10		

AUSTRALIA

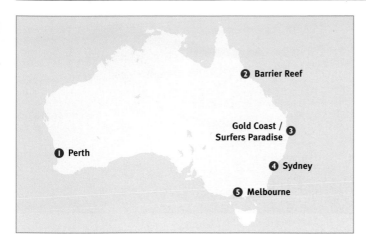

The traditional image of a dinki-di Aussie – whether a gleaming, muscled Bondi lifesaver or laconic, bush-hatted sheep shearer – has gradually been shouldered aside over the past few decades. Nowadays the iconic 'ocker' could easily be one of the prancing entrants in the annual Gay and Lesbian Mardi Gras parade. Or perhaps even one of the many recent Asian immigrants – from Vietnam, China or further afield – who have done much to add to the cosmopolitan melange of the 'Lucky Country'. But the essence of Australia remains unchanged.

This vast continent (7,686,848 square kilometres) ranges between desert and tropical rainforest, sophisticated urban areas with sprawling suburbs and isolated townships in the bush, stunning mountains and lush pasture. Australians enjoy a magnificent outdoor lifestyle, with a play-hard, work-hard (well, sometimes, mate) attitude that makes the most of its natural bounty. German immigrants planted the vineyards that have granted Barossa Valley wines world renown, the waves of Italian and Greek settlers did much to promote Australian cuisine beyond meat pies and beer, while Japanese finance helped to open up the Gold Coast. In other words, some of the best that the world has to offer is distilled into Australia.

With the possible exception of the purpose-built and rather soulless capital, Canberra, all the Antipodean metropoli exude their own character and allure to the casual visitor. Sydney is first port of call for many, and indeed where the first British convicts were dumped in the 18th century. The whole city is inspired and refreshed by its raison d'etre, the harbour. Overlooked by the architectural masterpiece of the Opera House, it acts as a focal point for dining and relaxation, and is the centre of attention during major events such as the annual Sydney-Hobart yacht race. Melbourne has always seen itself as a rival, and while it lacks the spectacular location it has as much charm and sophistication, especially when it comes to theatre and cuisine, and is equally devoted to sports, horse-racing and 'footy' to name but two. Adelaide, long known as the place for culture, has shaken off its previously staid image, and Brisbane, once derided as an overgrown country town, has become increasingly cosmopolitan after hosting a string of international events like the Commonwealth Games. Even Darwin, with a certain amount of cinematic assistance from *Crocodile Dundee*, has some claim to 'cool', although the weather is as hot as ever. Perth claims to be the sunniest of Australian cities, and even rain cannot damp its bright and breezy ethos. Cairns acts as the jumping off point for most of northern Queensland, notably to the stunning beauties of the Great Barrier Reef and the

rainforests of Cape Tribulation. Alice Springs, more or less in the centre of the continent, would probably not feature on any itinerary but for the proximity of Uluru, otherwise known as Ayers Rock – the outback's ultimate landmark and a sacred site for Australia's original inhabitants, the Aborigines. Mention should also be made of Australia's offshore islands, from the slightly other-worldly Tasmania to the hedonistic Hayman in the Whitsundays, which is also a prime venue for whale watching and scuba diving.

Most of Australia's 18 million inhabitants live in the coastal areas, so it follows that this is where the best hotels are. For location – right under the Harbour Bridge and looking on to the Opera House – it would be hard to better the Park Hyatt in Sydney, and up on the Gold Coast the Palazzo Versace is an intriguing jeu d'esprit of very modish accommodation. Head inland, and the main places to lay your head are bland motels or beery country pubs, where service echoes the old Australian ethos of 'I'm as good as you are, mate'. Between these two stellar stools is a range of decent resorts well placed to make the best of Down Under's natural assets of sun, sand and sea.

The weather varies immensely over such a vast continent, but all of Australia is hot in the summer between December and February, and the north is especially humid. It is best to time visits to the 'Top End' during the cooler winter (June – August) and this is also when the snowfields of Victoria and New South Wales open up. In spring, large stretches of the outback are carpeted with wildflowers. Hotels are often booked solid over Easter, Christmas and other school holidays.

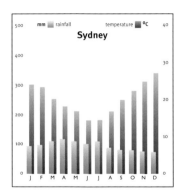

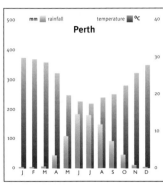

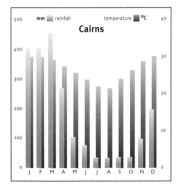

ANA Harbour Grand Hotel Sydney

176 Cumberland Street, The Rocks, Sydney, NSW 2000, Australia
T: +61 2 9250 6000 **F:** +61 2 9250 6250
http://www.asia-hotels.com/hotelinfo/ANA_Harbour_Grand_Hotel_Sydney/

The Rocks was the first part of Sydney to be settled by British convicts, so it is a fitting site for one of the city's premier hotels. Look out from one the 561 rooms and – wallop – it is sea-to-sky Miramax with all the classic symbols of Sydney thrown in for good measure. The superlatives continue inside, where the talents of more than 50 Australian artists are on display. High points of the ANA include its 'double double' rooms, with two double beds, and the Corner Suites with 270-degree views. The high life is available in the 36th-floor cocktail lounge, Horizons, and high jinks back at ground level in the solidly Australian Harts Pub. The Aylsium spa and health club include a gym, indoor pool, and puzzlingly – given Sydney's climate – a solarium. Stretch out here and you might well hear the First Fleet convicts jeering. At the time of writing this hotel was in the process of being taken over by the Shangri-La Group, so expect a name change soon.

Rates from: **US$ 171**
Star rating: ★ ★ ★ ★ ★
Bellhop rating: 🔔🔔🔔🔔 ½

Value:	7.78	Facilities:	8.36
Staff:	8.36	Restaurants:	7.95
Location:	8.87	Families:	6.31
Cleanliness:	8.69		

Burswood Resort Hotel

Great Eastern Highway, Burswood, WA 6100, Australia
T: +61 8 9362 7777 **F:** +61 8 9470 2553
http://www.asia-hotels.com/hotelinfo/Burswood_International_Resort_Casino_Perth/

It is tempting to think of the 417-room Burswood as 'Perth in a Packet'. On the banks of the Swan River, it may not be everyone's idea of beautiful architecture, but it does offer just about all the fun and frolic that seems to be automatically associated with the capital of Western Australia. There is a park, tennis courts and 18-hole golf course right next to the resort; a spa, pools indoor and out, and a health and fitness centre; the wheels spin 24 hours in the casino, or you can bet on the TAB in Champions sports bar; some 11 other bars and restaurants proffer international cuisine and wine, beer and spirits; rock your socks off in the Ruby Room nightclub, catch a play at the theatre or a concert in the Dome which seats up to 20,000. Without doubt, this is a place with something for everyone.

Rates from: **US$ 123**
Star rating: ★ ★ ★ ★ ★
Bellhop rating: 🔔🔔🔔🔔 ½

Value:	7.95	Facilities:	8.63
Staff:	8.25	Restaurants:	8.41
Location:	7.97	Families:	7.14
Cleanliness:	8.59		

Crown Towers

8 Whiteman Street, Southbank, Melbourne, VIC 3006, Australia
T: +61 3 9292 6666 F: +61 3 9292 6380
http://www.asia-hotels.com/hotelinfo/Crown_Towers/

The banks of the Yarra River, Melbourne's central aquatic artery, have undergone a transformation in recent years. They are now distinguished by such landmarks as the Exhibition and Convention Centre, the city aquarium, the Southgate restaurant and gallery complex, Federation Square and the Victorian Arts Centre. Right in the middle is the Crown Entertainment Complex, on the opposite bank from the central business district and home to the Crown Towers.

It is a somewhat unusual hotel, not least as on the doorstep is the country's largest 24-hour casino (350 tables and 2,500 gaming machines), as well as a host of nightclubs, cinemas, virtual reality interactive game venues and a bowling alley. The fun continues within the hotel, with a 3,000-square-metre spa dispensing 60 different Eastern and Western health and beauty treatments, a 25-metre indoor heated pool, a hi-tech gymnasium and two rebound ace championship tennis courts.

Fun, too, are the Crown's 'villas' – not the bungalow plus garden that the name might lead you to expect, but penthouses with dining and living areas, a butler at your beck and call and a choice of up to three bedrooms. The hotel's other rooms and suites may not be so large, but they are all framed by richly toned fabrics and warm timbers, with a facsimile machine, private safe, separate dressing room and marble-lined bathroom. And if the entertainment in the surrounding complex seems insufficient, there are some 40 channels on the TV.

Equally appealing for leisure or business travellers (there are 26 meeting and function rooms), the Crown complex sports more than 40 different restaurants, bars and snack outlets. Of note are Breezes, serving a blend of Australian and Mediterranean cuisines, the Japanese Koko, Chinese at Silks and all-day dining at the Conservatory.

The Crown will be joined by a new sister hotel, the 465-room Crown Promenade, in late 2003.

Rates from: **US$ 173**
Star rating: ★ ★ ★ ★ ★
Bellhop rating: 👍 👍 👍 👍 ½

Value:	7.90	Facilities:	8.78
Staff:	8.32	Restaurants:	8.69
Location:	8.85	Families:	7.03
Cleanliness:	8.85		

Four Seasons Hotel Sydney

199 George Street, Sydney, NSW 2000, Australia
T: +61 2 9238 0000 **F**: +61 2 9251 4745
http://www.asia-hotels.com/hotelinfo/Four_Seasons_Hotel_Sydney/

rock oysters on the shell early one evening in the Bar; gently bronzing by a private cabana at the heated free-form pool; and ingesting the aroma of a frangipani wrap in one of the spa's six soothing treatment rooms. Delivered with the traditional Four Seasons service and style, it is not surprising repeat guests come back asking for more.

Adopting the not overly absurd metaphor that the Four Seasons is an extensive, sunlit gourmet picnic, some of the morsels that the more sagacious might be inclined to savour would include: the 100 per cent ocker view over The Rocks to the Opera House, Botanical Gardens and Harbour Bridge; the rich silks, exotic Honduras mahogany and Italian marble bathrooms in the 531 rooms and suites; the sweet onion-dusted Victorian beef tenderloin at Kable's restaurant, complemented by one of its cellar's boutique wines; Sydney

Rates from: US$ 156
Star rating: ★ ★ ★ ★ ★
Bellhop rating: 🛎 🛎 🛎 🛎 ½

Value:	7.88	Facilities:	8.55
Staff:	8.78	Restaurants:	7.88
Location:	9.21	Families:	6.40
Cleanliness:	9.07		

Grand Hyatt Melbourne

123 Collins Street, Melbourne, VIC 3000, Australia
T: +61 3 9657 1234 **F**: +61 3 9650 3491
http://www.asia-hotels.com/hotelinfo/Grand_Hyatt_Melbourne/

order meals from around the globe. Evenings here tend to start with cocktails at Bar Deco, move on to one of the restaurants and finish at Monsoon's nightclub, with the R&B Thursdays proving especially popular. The usual roll-call of fitness facilities – pool, gym, tennis courts – is enlivened by the addition of a hotel nutritionist.

The Grand Hyatt is the point-and-click of hotels for corporate travellers. Its curved gold tower is right in the CBD, and the 549 rooms all have king-sized beds, window-side desks and the revolutionary Inter-touch Internet connection system. A techno butler stands ready to deal with set-ups, hang-ups and straightforward computer cock-ups round the clock, and there are two ballrooms and a host of function rooms for gatherings.

For corporate entertaining, Plane Tree Cafe offers a stylish but casual buffet, while the Hyatt Food Court provides freshly made-to-

Rates from: US$ 127
Star rating: ★ ★ ★ ★ ★
Bellhop rating: 🛎 🛎 🛎 🛎 ½

Value:	7.81	Facilities:	8.68
Staff:	8.40	Restaurants:	8.42
Location:	9.00	Families:	7.39
Cleanliness:	8.81		

Hayman

Hayman, Great Barrier Reef, QLD 4801, Australia
T: +61 7 4940 1234 **F:** +61 7 4940 1567
http://www.asia-hotels.com/hotelinfo/Hayman/

Hayman, the most northerly of the Whitsunday group, is not so much a resort island as a chimera. It is also a sublime tribute to millennia of creation by the tiny coral polyp, which formed the Great Barrier Reef that runs for 2,300 kilometres along the outer edge of Australia's continental plate. Staggering in both its natural beauty and its extraordinarily diverse recreations, Hayman has few equals in the whole of Asia Pacific.

Anyone landing here for the first time is beset by twin temptations. Do you just stay put on the 1,000-acre island, rejoicing in the ice-block white crescented accommodation curving round the twin hexagonal 'pools within a pool' by the beach – all embraced by 30 acres of lush gardens, beyond which lies thick woods of Moreton Bay ash, hoop pine and Whitsunday kurrajong inhabited by white cockatoos, painted lorikeets and Bhraminy kites? From May to November, myriad butterflies

swarm in gullies feasting on the nectar of eucalyptus blossom, and besides the main beach there are three others, two of which can only be reached by boat. As might be expected, there is a superlative spa here too.

Or, when Whitsunday wanderlust takes hold, do you plunge into that reality cliché – the wide blue yonder? A speedboat can take you to an outlying island and drop you off for the day with a picnic – or just the evening for a champagne sunset. Drop in on the reef itself for a bit of diving or snorkelling, courtesy of the Reef Goddess cruiser, or get up close in the semi-submersible Reef Dancer. Romantics may prefer a trip out to

Heart Reef, shaped by nature and cupid, and yes, Hayman also handles weddings. The 12.5-metre Sun Aura has a spacious deck for easy access to tackle for game and bottom fishing trips. You can skim the waves behind a 225hp ski boat, or aboard a windsurfer or one of the resort's catamarans. Humpback whales can be spotted during their stately migration to the Whitsundays between July and September. Seaplanes and helicopters handle flightseeing trips year-round. Guests can also mix and match their excursions, for example, packing a helicopter ride to the world famous Whitehaven sands, a snorkelling trip to the inner reef and a slug of champers

at sundown into a single seamless day. As the man said, three days here is good, a week better, a month – still not enough.

The choice of where to go and what to do around Hayman is mimicked in the resort, with the option of bedding down in anything from regular rooms (complete with balcony and breathtaking views) to the recently finished Beach Villa – with a private infinity pool and outdoor entertainment area. Other options include the Retreat Rooms with their extended open patios and outdoor showers, and the Penthouses, which have varied themes including Greek, Oriental and English.

Hayman's restaurants are pretty international too, both in cuisine and outlook. La Fontaine is French and formal, La Trattoria rustic and Italian, the Beach Pavilion casual in the extreme with extremely good seafood.

Of course, Hayman is Utopia for children. A special crèche handles ages six weeks to five years, while kids up to 12 can be safely and entertainingly corralled at Hernando's Hideaway. Intriguingly, Hayman also offers an etiquette class, teaching youngsters deportment, behaviour skills and the correct use of cutlery. If nothing else, the mere threat of being dispatched for an afternoon's P&Q minding should be enough to keep even the most mischievous in line.

Rates from: US$ 290
Star rating: ★ ★ ★ ★ ★
Bellhop rating: ♗ ♗ ♗ ♗ ♗

Value:	8.00	Facilities:	9.10
Staff:	9.14	Restaurants:	8.67
Location:	9.79	Families:	6.36
Cleanliness:	9.21		

Inter-Continental Sydney

117 Macquarie Street, Sydney, NSW 2000, Australia
T: +61 2 9253 9000 **F:** +61 2 9240 1240
http://www.asia-hotels.com/hotelinfo/InterContinental_Sydney/

There is no other word for it – the Inter-Continental is just so Sydney. It incorporates the former Treasury Building – built in 1851 but now gorgeously renovated – and is backed by a modern state-of-the-art skyscraper. Stand on the open-air terrace of the Australia Suite (complete with grand piano and a bathroom more like a mini spa with Bang & Olufsen providing the background music) and the city and harbour are laid out below like a feast. The views from the other – somewhat smaller and less luxuriously appointed – 503 rooms may not be quite so evocative, but there is no denying this is an eminently comfortable hotel. The Cortile – a courtyard right in the heart of the original building – is a hugely popular meeting and eating venue, as is Cafe Opera with its seafood-laden buffets. Unquestionably the most exciting venue though is 30 Something – unsurprisingly it is on the 31st floor and the views are quite mouth-watering (as is the Mediterranean cuisine).

Rates from: **US$ 147**
Star rating: ★ ★ ★ ★ ★
Bellhop rating: ♪ ♪ ♪ ♪ ½

Value:	8.13	Facilities:	8.39
Staff:	8.36	Restaurants:	8.10
Location:	8.99	Families:	5.58
Cleanliness:	8.89		

Marriott Sydney Hotel

36 College Street, Sydney, NSW 2010, Australia
T: +61 2 9361 8400 **F:** +61 2 9361 8599
http://www.asia-hotels.com/hotelinfo/Marriott_Sydney_Hotel/

The Marriott provides a wealth of choice right in the heart of Sydney's city centre. Take in breakfast, lunch or dinner (to say nothing of the view) at Windows on the Park, or fix yourself something courtesy of the in-room microwave and toaster. Dip into the rooftop pool and spa, or check into one of the suites with a corner spa bath. Settle down to work at the specially designed desk with high-speed Internet access ports, or take some time off – the hotel is planted directly overlooking Hyde Park and is only minutes away from the city's shopping and nightlife districts. Mix yourself a drink from the 'wet bar' in your room, or prop up Archibald's Bar and let the staff do it for you. With 241 rooms and suites packed into its 23 floors, the Marriott is compact and extremely convenient.

Rates from: **US$ 136**
Star rating: ★ ★ ★ ★ ★
Bellhop rating: ♪ ♪ ♪ ♪ ½

Value:	8.38	Facilities:	8.48
Staff:	8.63	Restaurants:	8.04
Location:	8.96	Families:	7.00
Cleanliness:	8.93		

Marriott Surfers Paradise

158 Ferny Avenue, Surfers Paradise, QLD 4217, Australia
T: +61 7 5592 9800 F: +61 7 5592 9888
http://www.asia-hotels.com/hotelinfo/Marriott_Surfers_Paradise/

It is big, it is bold, it is brash, it is the Marriott – and what else could you expect from Surfers Paradise, Queensland's number one centre for carefully manufactured fun?

Towering 28 storeys with 330 rooms and suites, the Marriott fronts the Nerang River, is surrounded by lagoons, ponds and waterfalls and is a short stroll to the main beach.

Plenty of aquatic fun is on hand right at the hotel, with a heated saltwater swimming pool, a lava tube waterslide and spa pools, while youngsters from four to 14 years can find ample amusement in their own Kids' Klub. Man-made sandy beaches and even a coral reef complete with tropical fish are surrounded by lush gardens.

The theme here is very much to entertain yourself how you will – sweat away in an aerobics class, pound around the two floodlit tennis courts or along the jogging track, or relax into a yoga or tai chi session. Lay back for an hour or two's pampering in the spa, or set out for some sailing or scuba diving. And on any given day, there will be rideable waves on the 26 beaches along the 42 kilometres of coast.

The Marriott's sunny rooms are especially comfortable, with TVs and VCRs as standard and CD players in the suites, a separate bath and shower, and tables and chairs out on the balconies. The smallest room is a generous 42 square metres and nearly half have two double beds – great for

families. The alfresco Lagoon Restaurant offers informal buffet and a la carte dripping with seafood, however there is also the Benihana Japanese Steakhouse inside. Unusually for an Australian hostelry, there is no real place to party in the resort, an omission that the area's plethora of bars and clubs do their best to redress.

Finally, the real 'you-beauty' of Surfers is its treasure trove of attractions. The Marriott lies within easy reach of 27 golf courses, clay pigeon and rifle ranges, four-wheel drive circuits and bushwalks, horse riding, a performing arts centre and a bird sanctuary. And if it just happens to be raining (yes it does happen), there is always the 24-hour casino.

Rates from: **US$ 146**
Star rating: ★ ★ ★ ★ ★
Bellhop rating: 🔔🔔🔔🔔 ½

Value:	7.72	Facilities:	8.24
Staff:	8.11	Restaurants:	8.13
Location:	8.41	Families:	7.28
Cleanliness:	8.54		

The Observatory Hotel

89-113 Kent Street, Sydney, NSW 2000, Australia
T: +61 2 9256 2222 **F**: +61 2 9256 2233
http://www.asia-hotels.com/hotelinfo/Observatory_Hotel_Sydney/

In the 10 years since it opened, The Observatory has rapidly become the pied-a-terre for Sydney insiders. Inspired by the historic 1850s Elizabeth Bay House, it glows with the warmth of a grand Australian home and its 100 rooms are luxuriously furnished with antiques, oil paintings and tapestries.

From the dome-shaped atrium of the entry foyer to the antique

fireplace and polished walnut furniture of the guests' exclusive drawing room, there is much to admire here. Colonial-style sash windows and period balconies give the rooms a sense of history, while CD players, fax/modem facilities and four telephones bring them bang up to date. The 22 Junior and Executive Suites are each designed slightly differently, and some have four-poster beds and a private terrace.

Both the Globe Bar and Galileo restaurant are well worth repeat visits, the former for its voluminous library, the latter for its Italian-tinged modern Australian cuisine. But the Observatory spa is somewhere you could linger indefinitely, not least because of the amazing subterranean pool. Its roof is ingeniously lit by fibre optics, which turn it into a vast firmament of twinkling stars.

Perhaps the chief delight of the Observatory is its unending devotion to detail. There is a complimentary weekday city limousine service for starters. Beds

are made up according to personal preferences – be it a particular sort of linen or non-allergenic pillows. The 'specs box' contains a variety of reading glasses for the shortsighted who are also absent-minded. In-room companionship can be provided in the form of a goldfish or two. If you are feeling under the weather, staff deliver a get-well-soon kit – a bowl of broth, herbal teas and dermatology products together with a selection of CDs and magazines. And youngsters automatically receive a personalised choc-chip dinosaur and pint-sized bathrobes. After all, there is nothing like getting brand loyalty off to an early start.

Rates from: **US$ 206**
Star rating: ★ ★ ★ ★ ★
Bellhop rating: ♙ ♙ ♙ ♙ ½

Value:	8.24	Facilities:	8.96
Staff:	9.14	Restaurants:	8.58
Location:	8.60	Families:	5.92
Cleanliness:	9.40		

Park Hyatt Melbourne

1 Parliament Square, Melbourne, Victoria 3002, Australia
T: +61 3 9224 1234 **F**: +61 3 9224 1200
http://www.asia-hotels.com/hotelinfo/Park_Hyatt_Melbourne/

The interior designers obviously gave their imaginations free rein when it came to drawing up the plans for the Park Hyatt. It is modern, intriguing, stylish without being over the top or painfully trendy and a lot of the time real fun as well.

A wall of vibrant blue, hand-sculptured glass signals your arrival at the art deco-themed, five-level Radii restaurant and bar. The guestrooms also carry a hint of art deco, where the use of warm-toned fabrics blends together beautifully with walls panelled with Madroña wood and richly coloured soft furnishings. The domed ceiling and colonnaded sandstone interior of the indoor 25-metre, edgeless aquamarine pool is offset by a striking Grecian mural. And contemporary works of art from local and international artists are displayed throughout the hotel, with the attention to detail usually reserved for a private collection.

Not that style triumphs over substance – this is very much a hotel for executives with a job to do. All rooms enjoy dedicated high-speed Internet access and interactive television, while the studios on the club floor have a fetching open-plan design with king-size beds. The suites in particular have a distinctive design that captures the very essence of the city, with outstanding views of the historic cathedral, the enchanting gardens and century-old elm trees that surround the hotel.

Away from work, there is a great deal to enjoy at the Hyatt. Extensive health and spa facilities border the pool, including a personal training studio, a tennis court and a sun deck. While Radii remains the hotel's chief dining and entertainment venue, right next door is Cuba, an exquisitely furnished cigar lounge hung with some arresting artworks. An open fire blazes here in winter in what is the only smoking venue in an otherwise 'smoke-free' environment – very much a sign of the times.

Rates from: **US$ 150**
Star rating: ★ ★ ★ ★ ★
Bellhop rating: 🔔 🔔 🔔 🔔 🔔

Value:	8.54	Facilities:	9.12
Staff:	9.03	Restaurants:	8.88
Location:	9.17	Families:	5.98
Cleanliness:	9.44		

Park Hyatt Sydney

7 Hickson Road, The Rocks, Sydney, NSW 2000, Australia
T: +61 2 9241 1234 **F:** +61 2 9256 1555
http://www.asia-hotels.com/hotelinfo/Park_Hyatt_Sydney/

You cannot get more Sydney than The Rocks, and you cannot get more Rocks than the Park Hyatt, one of the city's most stunning boutique hotels. It is not simply the location – practically reflected in the sails of the Opera House and occasionally specked by waves from the harbour. There is a real sense of occasion here – it is not a hotel you drop into casually merely to get a night's rest or have a hurried lunch, but one that should be approached with mounting anticipation and glee.

The senses are indulged completely at this 158-room hotel – or should that be resort? The concept of a grand mansion by the water is expressly fulfilled, with personalised butler service for each guest, luxurious interior design and unique artworks. There is a choice of regular rooms, studios or suites, all with a private harbour-facing balcony and many with the premium view of Jorn Utzon's masterpiece of 'frozen music'. Each room is spacious, elegant and equipped with walk-in wardrobes, remote control curtains, marble bathroom, CD player and Internet television access. There is also access to Playstation, though much more imaginative entertainment is to be found elsewhere in the Park Hyatt.

This could be at the spa, where a rooftop pool is joined by a gym, sauna and steam rooms, and such exclusive treatments as the Vichy Shower, which deliciously combines high-pressure jets with a light rain effect. Similarly salubrious, the Harbourkitchen is a waterfront restaurant where a wood-fired oven, rotisserie and chargrill integrate the flavours of seasonal and mainly Australian produce. There is also a walkabout wine cellar containing over 600 mainly domestic wines. Drinking still ranks high on Sydney's list of favourite recreations. The Club Bar, with its wood-panelling, armchairs and fire warmth, serves rare malts and vodkas, while the Harbourbar is divided into three sections – Champagne, Draft Beer and Martini, the last with an impressive 60-item menu. But shortage of choice is never really an issue at the Park Hyatt.

Rates from: **US$ 262**
Star rating: ★ ★ ★ ★ ★
Bellhop rating: 🔔 🔔 🔔 🔔 ½

Value:	7.56	Facilities:	8.33
Staff:	8.35	Restaurants:	8.28
Location:	9.02	Families:	6.39
Cleanliness:	8.70		

Sheraton Mirage Gold Coast

Sea World Drive, Main Beach, QLD 4217, Australia
T: +61 7 5591 1488 **F:** +61 7 5591 2299
http://www.asia-hotels.com/hotelinfo/Sheraton_Mirage_Gold_Coast/

There is live music in Breakers Cocktail Lounge, but the party really gets going at weekends in Rolls, the hotel's swish nightclub. For those needing to venture out, Marina Mirage's boutiques and restaurants are adjacent to the hotel; Sea World is a gentle stroll away and Surfers Paradise a 10-minute walk up the beach.

Situated on the Gold Coast's Broadwater Peninsula, the Sheraton packs some of the very best of this holiday region into its 293 comfortable rooms and 40 acres of lush palm gardens. Low-rise and well spread out, the resort features a 2.5-acre seawater lagoon pool, a spa and fitness facility, tennis courts and a unique beach fronting location. The pick of the rooms are the Ocean Premium with stunning sea vistas and the 35 fully equipped home-style villas. The restaurants make the most of Australian cuisine with the laid-back Oyster Bar in the garden, seafood buffet overlooking the pool and fine dining available in Horizons.

Rates from: **US$ 179**
Star rating: ★ ★ ★ ★ ★
Bellhop rating: ◑ ◑ ◑ ◑ ½

Value:	7.76	Facilities:	8.87
Staff:	8.47	Restaurants:	8.21
Location:	8.81	Families:	7.10
Cleanliness:	8.95		

Sheraton On The Park

161 Elizabeth Street, Sydney, NSW 2000, Australia
T: +61 2 9286 6000 **F:** +61 2 9286 6686
http://www.asia-hotels.com/hotelinfo/Sheraton_On_The_Park/

One of the most satisfying activities offered by the Sheraton has the added inducement of being absolutely free. Slip into the top-floor heated pool first thing in the morning, and chances are that you will have it, and the view of the breaking dawn through the arched roof and eye-level windows, all to yourself. The pool's limpid surface and the general air of calm here allow a little time to reflect on the diverse attractions of the hotel beneath which has undergone significant renovations in 2002/03.

For starters, there are 510 rooms and 48 suites, smartly decorated, well up to speed with technical accoutrements, with roomy bathrooms and – in case anyone was wondering about the hotel's name – cracking views over Hyde Park, central Sydney's 'lungs'. Two floors are dedicated to the Sheraton's executive club. Down on the first floor, the relaxed Botanica Brasserie is open seven days a week for breakfast, lunch and dinner, providing extensive buffets with extra special seafood at the weekends. The Conservatory is an elegant lounge serving traditional high tea, snacks and cocktails, while I'm Angus on the Park serves tantalising steaks.

The Sheraton's meeting facilities include a grand ballroom that can hold up to 1,000, and a substantial array of smaller rooms suitable for banquets or conferences. An on-site event-staging company can assist with audio-visual equipment, computer data display and sound and lighting as well as other expert techno back-up. Returning to the pool on the 22nd floor, the health club includes a fully equipped gym, massage rooms, saunas and steam rooms, a solarium and a team of personal trainers.

The Sheraton, apart from its obvious proximity to the park, is also only a short hop from downtown and has a covered walkway to the Monorail.

Rates from: **US$ 143**
Star rating: ★ ★ ★ ★ ★
Bellhop rating: 🛎 🛎 🛎 🛎 ½

Value:	7.85	Facilities:	8.39
Staff:	8.45	Restaurants:	8.09
Location:	8.97	Families:	6.75
Cleanliness:	8.90		

Sofitel Melbourne

25 Collins Street, Melbourne, VIC 3000, Australia
T: +61 3 9653 0000 **F:** +61 3 9650 4261
http://www.asia-hotels.com/hotelinfo/Sofitel_Melbourne/

Since its opening in 1996, the Sofitel has closely allied itself with Melbourne's arts scene, and the hotel's own consultant oversees the exhibitions that regularly grace the walls of Sofi's Lounge, the lobby, the Atrium and Cafe La. So there is a fair amount to look at inside the hotel, while the views from the 363 rooms and suites – which start on the building's 36th floor – are equally appealing across Melbourne and Port Phillip Bay. The rooms, suspended around a stunning atrium, are conveniently set up with broadband and other business-friendly accessories, while meetings and conventions are covered by a pillarless ballroom and an auditorium seating 380.

Right in the centre of Melbourne on trendy Collins Street, the hotel is surrounded by stylish boutiques, restaurants and cafes, and is just a short tram ride from theatres, the Melbourne Cricket Ground and the beautiful Treasury Gardens.

Rates from: **US$ 139**
Star rating: ★ ★ ★ ★ ★
Bellhop rating: ♭ ♭ ♭ ♭ ½

Value:	7.96	Facilities:	8.57
Staff:	8.81	Restaurants:	8.53
Location:	9.17	Families:	6.40
Cleanliness:	9.13		

W Sydney

The Wharf Woolloomoolo, 6 Cowper Wharf Road, Sydney, NSW 2011, Australia
T: +61 2 9331 9000 **F:** +61 2 9331 9031
http://www.asia-hotels.com/hotelinfo/W_Hotel_Sydney/

Thoroughly, utterly, gloriously hip, W claims to be for the executive but it is hard to see how anybody could concentrate on work here – although the business centre is open 24 hours a day. The 104 sophisticated rooms are divided between nine different designs, ranging from Zs (no view but skylights instead) to Ultra Lofts with an unimpeded lookout from the downstairs lounge and a bedroom upstairs. Breakfast at the W Cafe, or whet your whistle at the W Bar. Further choice of eating is available in the vicinity as W is part of the Wharf Woolloomooloo integrated retail complex. Oh, and W also stands for wellness of course, so you can sweat or swim or simply spa it at the Chakra where services are holistic – naturally.

Rates from: **US$ 166**
Star rating: ★ ★ ★ ★ ★
Bellhop rating: ♭ ♭ ♭ ♭

Value:	7.53	Facilities:	8.05
Staff:	8.47	Restaurants:	8.44
Location:	8.56	Families:	5.72
Cleanliness:	8.91		

The Westin Melbourne

205 Collins Street, Melbourne, VIC 3000, Australia
T: +61 3 9635 2222 **F**: +61 3 9635 2333
http://www.asia-hotels.com/hotelinfo/Westin_Melbourne/

At first blush, the modernistic Westin might seem to sit oddly with the redoubtable architecture of the nearby St Paul's Cathedral and city square. But in fact its grand public spaces and spacious balconied rooms have a timeless quality, plus a very Melbourne brio. The dedicated workstation in all 262 guestrooms – multi-function copier/printer/fax and ergonomic chair – means few headaches for executives, and the soft tones, timbers and classical furnishings have a soothing effect. Roving concierges are on hand to sort out any service problems, and you can relax over a glass or two at the elegant Martini Bar. Dining at Allegro is best done alfresco, weather permitting, with views down over cosmopolitan Collins Street, a shining emblem of millennium Melbourne. And even if gyms and suchlike make you shudder, drop into the basement wellness centre where the pool is a delirious exercise in Zen chic.

Rates from: **US$ 147**
Star rating: ★★★★★
Bellhop rating:

Value:	8.14	Facilities:	8.64
Staff:	8.80	Restaurants:	8.14
Location:	9.50	Families:	6.88
Cleanliness:	9.36		

The Westin Sydney

No. 1 Martin Place, Sydney, NSW 2000, Australia
T: +61 2 8223 1111 **F**: +61 2 8223 1222
http://www.asia-hotels.com/hotelinfo/Westin_Sydney/

The Westin – a combination of 19th-century general post office and 20th-century tower block – is a delightful hotel that makes the most of its historical antecedents while ensuring guests do not want for modern conveniences. The old GPO's telegraph and telephone exchanges have been converted into a ballroom and health club respectively, and the Grand Stair leading up to the first floor under the landmark clock tower has been painstakingly restored. The 416 guestrooms – which reinterpret the classical designs of the 1950s – are split between old and new wings, the former with high ceilings and antique fittings and the latter with floor-to-ceiling windows. The public areas are concentrated in the old GPO, with a potpourri of upmarket restaurants, bars and cafes as well as a food emporium. Would that Australia had more buildings like this to convert into hotels.

Rates from: **US$ 163**
Star rating: ★★★★★
Bellhop rating: ½

Value:	7.73	Facilities:	8.44
Staff:	8.33	Restaurants:	8.02
Location:	9.08	Families:	6.11
Cleanliness:	9.04		

CAMBODIA

Cambodia is a small country with incredible depth. It is easy to overlook little Cambodia on the map, but this is a land of extremes and far from anonymous. The glorious extreme is the historic ruined city of Angkor at Siem Reap. The ancient Khmer remains are among the most incredible sites on the planet. This great civilisation reached its flamboyant zenith between the 9th and 14th centuries, their architectural feats culminating in the magnificent Angkor Wat, deservedly one of the Seven Wonders of the World. Some 100 temples survive and are generally being sensitively restored, although recently concerns have been voiced about the damage tourism is inflicting on these stunning ruins. Still, without doubt Angkor is the defining reason to go to Cambodia.

But Cambodia has known more sinister extremes. Regional instability in the 1970s saw civil war sweep Pol Pot's Khmer Rouge to power and his introduction of an ultra-Maoist policy. Coined 'Year Zero' he intended to wipe out the existing Cambodian way of life and start afresh, but ultimately the end result was appalling genocide. More than two million died amid atrocities of unimaginable cruelty, and the educated classes were almost entirely lost.

The Vietnamese forced out the Khmer Rouge. Political chaos continued until the late 1990s when some stability returned and saw the battered country finally getting back on its feet. A stroll around Phnom Penh reveals a poor but lively city with Buddhist temples and French architecture. Reminders of the recent savage past are clearly visible – the Killing Fields and the Genocide Museum have become ghoulish yet compulsive tourist attractions. Today Cambodia wrestles with some big modern problems below its remarkably cheerful surface. The sex trade is massive with grim statistics for AIDS and paedophilia. And you realise just where Cambodia is today when recreational activities available to tourists include hurling grenades into ponds, or for US$200 you can fire a rocket launcher and blow up a live cow.

The recent stability has led to a tourist boom and some very good hotels are springing up. The infrastructure is evolving and Cambodia is easier now than it has ever been. Siem Reap and Phnom Penh remain the only viable places to visit, although the beaches around Sihanoukville may emerge soon as there is a good strip of coastline. Temperatures remain fairly constant and typically nudge above 30°C, with the dry season running from December to April. At other times of the year it can be uncomfortably humid – not the best time for clambering around the awesome but slippery temples.

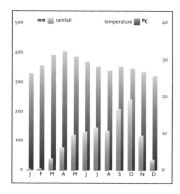

Angkor Village Resort

Wat Bo Street, Siem Reap, Cambodia
T: +855 63 963 563 **F**: +855 63 963 363
http://www.asia-hotels.com/hotelinfo/Angkor_Village_Resort/

The intimate Angkor Village is an architectural pioneer in Cambodia and has influenced other hotel projects in the area. Designed and built in 1995 by owner and French-trained architect Olivier Piot, the aim was to introduce guests to aspects of Khmer culture on as many levels as possible. The structure is built predominantly from teak, and Mr Piot and Vattho Tep, his equally talented Cambodian wife, have incorporated mainly local products in the construction and finish. The result is one of Siem Reap's most enjoyable and characteristic boutique hotels.

Set on four acres of lush green gardens, the hotel is an assortment of wooden bungalows nestled among tropical ponds and gardens that help elevate the relaxed but slightly exotic mood, and a high, surrounding red-brick wall offers seclusion from the street hustle and bustle. The two-storey bungalows are connected by slightly raised wooden walkways and incorporate 52 rooms. The Standard Rooms are somewhat basic apart from the wooden surrounds, whereas the Deluxe Rooms, being twice the size, are a perfect retreat from the heat after a hard days temple trekking. This recommended category features glossy polished floors you can skate on in your socks, and large windows that flood the rooms with light. Simple yet cosy interiors include bamboo fittings and local fabrics; clean polished white tiled bathrooms with simple lines and chrome fittings complete the picture.

This is no chain hotel, so the facilities are also simple and in keeping with both nature and the local character. This is a polite way of saying that they are basic, but again the property's personality seems to be only enhanced by this. The Angkor Village has succeeded in incorporating Khmer culture through the pleasant restaurant, which is better described as enhanced home cooking rather than fancy international dining, and through traditional dance shows on the small stage theatre over the road. The small bar is also a wonderful oasis to unwind in over an Angkor Beer, the local brew. The pool has recently been improved but is still very modest. The quaint resort also has a nearby elephant farm offering treks through the temples. Service is friendly and warm but occasionally just a tad innocent. But the deficiencies are forgivable and with the hotel being a gentle stroll into the local town, it makes an excellent home for seeing Siem Reap and its main attractions.

Rates from: **US$ 66**
Star rating: ★ ★ ★
Bellhop rating: ♙ ♙ ♙ ♙ ½

Value:	8.35	Facilities:	7.98
Staff:	8.81	Restaurants:	8.21
Location:	8.64	Families:	5.65
Cleanliness:	8.73		

Raffles Grand Hotel D'Angkor

1 Vithei Charles De Gaulle, Khum Svay Dang Kum, Siem Reap, Cambodia
T: +855 63 963 888 **F:** +855 63 963 168
http://www.asia-hotels.com/hotelinfo/Raffles_Grand_Hotel_DAngkor/

Owned and run by the Raffles Group, the Grand Hotel D'Angkor is the finest hotel in Siem Reap. Originally built in 1928, the black and white photographs reveal it was once very grand indeed. As the century passed the building slowly faded into obscurity and malaise. It was finally rescued in the late 1990s by the Raffles salvage team and beautifully restored. The property is grand again in many ways, the broad and proud chateau-like facade sitting majestically before the 60,000 square metres of gardens. The property's plush colonial roots have been rediscovered and augmented and are clearly visible throughout.

On entering the wonderfully aloof lobby you come face to face with a beautiful original fitting, the antique cage elevator. A descending spiral staircase leads to the renowned Elephant Bar, a sophisticated cocktail bar with iron railings, wicker furniture, huge tusks and a pool table. The dining choices are all luxurious and refined, although some are more casual than others. The candlelit Restaurant Le Grand offers Khmer flavours and fine dining in regal surrounds. The Cafe D'Angkor and Poolside Terrace share similar urbane themes with delicious international selections, but if there was to be a criticism it would be that there is not quite enough variety on the menu.

The hotel's new wing houses the State Rooms and Cabana Rooms. The rooms are modestly proportioned but decorated in homely European style with ample half-tester beds. They offer a choice of garden views or the infinitely preferable pool views. Landmark Rooms and Suites lie in the old wing and are larger and steeped in history. Interior features include free-standing cast iron baths and a fine selection of Cambodian art and memorabilia. Remarkably, next to the pool, you will find two luxurious private villas for those who really want to push the boat out, right down to the private wine cellar and 24-hour valet service.

For those worn-out temple gazers, the spa at the Grand provides a wonderful respite while the 35-metre lap pool, modelled on the ancient royal bathing pools of Angkor Thom, is a refreshing escape from the heat.

The hotel is expensive, immensely so if you consider the local economy. But it is the centrepiece of Siem Reap and lies a little closer than most to the thrills of ancient Angkor.

Rates from: **US$ 223**
Star rating: ★ ★ ★ ★ ★
Bellhop rating: ⌂ ⌂ ⌂ ⌂ ½

Value:	7.80	Facilities:	8.60
Staff:	8.83	Restaurants:	8.42
Location:	8.88	Families:	5.38
Cleanliness:	8.91		

Raffles Hotel Le Royal

92 Rukhak Vithei Daun Penh, Sangkat Wat Phnom, Phnom Penh, Cambodia
T: +855 23 981 888 F: +855 23 981 168
http://www.asia-hotels.com/hotelinfo/Raffles_Hotel_Le_Royal/

Le Royal is without question the top address in Phnom Penh. The sister to the Grand Hotel D'Angkor in Siem Reap and in the same elite class, Le Royal is probably the better of the two overall, although there are some obvious advantages to the Grand, primarily its proximity to Angkor Wat. Phnom Penh seems an unlikely setting for such an opulent property. Being in the centre of this rough and ready city is a double-edged sword – the location is wonderfully convenient for tourists or business travellers but it is besieged by the surrounding moped madness. Stepping inside provides a refreshing upper-crust respite. This classy hotel feels every inch a proud colonial heirloom from 1929, despite the upheavals the building has witnessed. After sliding into decay the building was respectfully restored and its 208 rooms were reopened in 1997.

The interior is majestic in both elegance and proportion, the historic grace radiating through the dignified chequered tiled corridors, robust European archways and cigar rooms. The three connecting wings of the hotel cover a complete city block and enclose an attractive and leafy pool. State Rooms revisit the historic theme and are set in the newer courtyard wings. In the original main building, splendid Landmark Rooms and Suites sumptuously present old world charm with touches of Khmer art and original antiques. Personality Suites are dedicated to the distinguished figures with close links to Le Royal such as Charles de Gaulle, Somerset Maugham and Jacqueline Kennedy.

The eight restaurants and bars never stray from the grand theme, Restaurant Le Royal offering a rich Khmer experience both for the eyes and palate, while the alfresco Cafe Monivong dishes out more casual Asian and continental fare. Service is courteous throughout the hotel and the Amrita Spa is a perfect place to shut out Phnom Penh and take in the sauna, jacuzzi or therapeutic massage treatments. The property has a capable business centre and good meeting rooms, and the regal ballroom is certainly fit for royalty. Being a Raffles property though this is not really a business hotel – Le Royal is really an experience.

Rates from: US$ 156
Star rating: ★ ★ ★ ★ ★
Bellhop rating: ♪ ♪ ♪ ♪ ½

Value:	7.98	Facilities:	8.65
Staff:	8.98	Restaurants:	8.29
Location:	8.87	Families:	6.48
Cleanliness:	9.12		

Sofitel Angkor

Vithei Charles de Gaulle, Khum Svay Dang Kum, Siem Reap, Cambodia
T: +855 63 964 600 **F**: +855 63 964 611
http://www.asia-hotels.com/hotelinfo/Sofitel_Angkor/

Opened in late 2000, the Sofitel Royal Angkor is a recent addition to Siem Reap and a very welcome one for travellers. It is an excellent 5-star hotel snapping at the heels of the previously untouchable Grand Hotel D'Angkor. Siem Reap still has plenty of rough edges but this hotel has all the trappings of modern international comfort. Spread liberally over large and immaculately trimmed gardens, there is an orderly and sedate contrast here to the lovable chaos of the country.

The calm, red tiled resort keeps a low profile in height terms with its trim 2-storey layout. The three wings are connected by covered boardwalks in case the heavens open, meandering past kept lawns and ponds. The interior, however, certainly does not keep a low profile – it is smart, stylish and feels every bit of a top hotel. The decor incorporates subtle French and Khmer influences and throughout is airy and bright.

Plenty of mock bass reliefs and statues remind you exactly where you are – just a few kilometres from the stunning temples of Angkor and almost as close as any hotel is permitted to be.

Facilities again fly in the face of what you would expect from a hotel in Siem Reap. The three restaurants are astutely captained by overseas chefs and put out food well above the rather mediocre standards offered just about everywhere else in town. The Sofitel Royal Angkor certainly has a credible claim for offering the best international buffet in Cambodia. Mouhot's Dream, named after the French botanist explorer and stilted on Sala Lake, offers fine dining with matching wine list and choice cigars, all with a view. The hotel also has a fine lagoon pool, which can make all the difference to a trip out here. The pool is an enticing alternative to sweaty temple trekking, whether or not you are templed out. And the spa's eight treatments rooms refresh those weary limbs with a wide selection of massages and treatments.

The 238 light and spacious rooms are thoughtfully designed and a pleasure to return to. The teak floors and uplifting continental bathrooms are inspired by the French, and there are local flecks such as reproduction Khmer stone artistry. In a land of ancient splendour, the Sofitel Royal Angkor delivers modern 5-star comfort and relaxation with chic and style.

Rates from: US$ 147
Star rating: ★ ★ ★ ★ ★
Bellhop rating: 🔔 🔔 🔔 🔔 ½

Value:	7.79	Facilities:	8.53
Staff:	8.72	Restaurants:	8.58
Location:	8.88	Families:	5.70
Cleanliness:	8.95		

CHINA

MONGOLIA

BEIJING ❶

SOUTH
KOREA

Suzhou ❷ ❸ Shanghai
❹ Hangzhou

NEPAL

Guangzhou ❺ ❻ Shenzhen

MYANMAR   VIETNAM

Lauded for its progress since its establishment in 1949, courted for its economic potential, excoriated for its human rights record, China is Asia's sleeping giant – the world's most populous country (1.25 billion and counting) but still one which has a fair way to go before it takes its true place on the international stage.

The prodigious leaps from feudalist to communist to capitalist have greatly enhanced the PRC, and for much of the past half century, China has been the world's fastest-growing economy. Yet it remains poor in many parts – there are sharp divisions between rural areas and the cities, the rich coast and the poor interior, and schisms within the political elite. But just as staging the Olympics in Seoul catapulted South Korea to prominence, so the 2008 Olympic Games should give Beijing the necessary fillip to show that it too can host the planet's most prestigious sporting event with requisite efficiency and panache.

As might be expected from a country with 9,561,000 square kilometres at its disposal, there is an enormous amount to see and do in China (too much to mention here), whether showcasing thousands of years of culture or something that was only built last year. Beijing's attractions lie not merely in trophy sights like the Great Wall, the Forbidden City and Tiananmen Square, but also in its 'hutongs', the maze of residential streets just out of the centre that are gradually being swept away in the name of development. Tianjin, to the east of the capital, is a former treaty port and hosts one of the country's most intriguing antique markets. A former German concession, Qingdao was Mao Zedong's favourite seaside holiday spot, and Chinese still flock to its beaches – backed by statuesque and very Germanic mansions – every summer. Shanghai is widely touted as China's 'Next Big Thing', a hotchpotch of new energetic capitalism and construction, with an exotic and varied nightlife. Slightly inland, Hangzhou caught Marco Polo's eye when he passed through in the 13th century ('one of the most splendid cities in the world') and, despite the onslaught of tourism, its lakes and temples are still utterly picturesque.

Shenzhen, on the border with Hong Kong, has gone from 99 per cent paddy fields to 99 per cent concrete in the space of 20 years, a Special Economic Zone that could be a metaphor for the new China. Inland, there are panoramic vistas in Guilin, the Terracotta Warriors in Xian, Tibetan highs in Lhasa and seemingly a different country altogether in the far western city of Umurqi.

Gone are the days of staying in grubby, Soviet-style dormitories, an alarming prospect that greeted China's first foreign visitors when the country started to open up in the late 1970s. True, some of its lesser hotels are behind when it comes to basic requirements like hot water and clean sheets, but nowadays all the major cities host a crop of 5-star – or at least some very acceptable 4-star – properties. Boutique hotels are making their first appearance around Beijing, and properties like the Grand Hyatt Shanghai (the tallest hotel in the world) are setting a trend that other cities can only hope to emulate.

Gone too are the days of foreign visitors being stared at as if they were on day release from some anthropological zoo. You are likely to attract some attention at tourist spots – if only to be included in a friendly souvenir photograph – and if you wander off the beaten track you can expect to be quizzed enthusiastically. Many young Chinese are keen to practise their English and other languages, and Beijing – in the run-up to the Olympics – is making a concerted attempt to drum some basic foreign words and phrases into its public officials.

China's borders embrace sub-tropical islands and frozen deserts, so it is difficult to recommend precise times to visit. The best rule of thumb is to avoid the sticky summers and chilly winters if possible. Spring, from March to April, and autumn (September to October) are more climatically welcoming. Lunar New Year, which falls in late January or early February, sees much of the populace uprooting and returning home for family celebrations, so expect hotel beds and rail and air tickets to be in short supply.

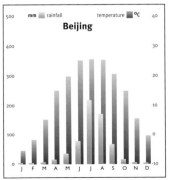

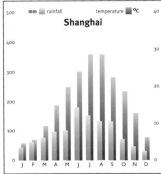

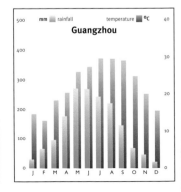

China Hotel by Marriott

Liu Hua Road, Guangzhou 510015, China
T: +86 20 8666 6888 **F**: +86 20 8667 7288
http://www.asia-hotels.com/hotelinfo/China_Hotel_By_Marriott/

The China Hotel has thrived from being next to the China Trade Fair Exhibition Centre, home of the huge spring and autumn Canton Fairs. This chunky and stately block consists of an office tower, serviced apartments and the 1,013-room hotel alongside a shopping arcade lined with the world's leading brand names. The facilities are very good and especially tailored to those on business – dataports and voicemail in the rooms, a hi-tech business centre with bi-lingual assistants, private meeting rooms and a 1,500-person capacity ballroom with 15 adjoining function rooms. Supporting leisure facilities include a manageable pool and a good basement entertainment centre, Catwalk. The Hard Rock Cafe adds an international dimension. Professional service and being just 20 minutes from the airport helps make the China Hotel by Marriott one of Guangzhou's most popular business hotels – with the Canton Fair rumoured to be moving venue soon, it will be interesting to see if it remains this way.

Rates from: US$ 77
Star rating: ★ ★ ★ ★ ★
Bellhop rating: ♗♗♗♗ ½

Value:	7.78	Facilities:	8.24
Staff:	8.12	Restaurants:	8.34
Location:	8.48	Families:	7.01
Cleanliness:	8.37		

China World Hotel Beijing

1 Jiangguomenwai Avenue, Beijing 100004, China
T: +86 10 6505 2266 **F**: +86 10 6505 0828
http://www.asia-hotels.com/hotelinfo/China_World_Hotel_Beijing/

Flush from a renovation programme that has seen its 716 rooms (including the Horizon Club rooms), health club, coffee shop and lobby given a complete makeover, the China World is now better equipped than ever to cater to visiting executives. This is primarily a business hotel, not least because it sits right next to the China World Trade Centre with its two 38-storey office towers and extensive exhibition facilities. The rooms – in particular the new 50-square-metre Premium Rooms – are spacious, designed to be somewhere you can sleep, work and relax without undue hassle, and of course electronic connectivity is a given. Apart from its location, the China World's biggest plus is its exceptional sporting facilities. Squash and tennis courts, golf simulators, driving range and putting course, an ice rink and an aerobics studio all back up regulars such as the fitness centre and an indoor swimming pool.

Rates from: US$ 128
Star rating: ★ ★ ★ ★ ★
Bellhop rating: ♗♗♗♗ ½

Value:	7.67	Facilities:	8.48
Staff:	8.58	Restaurants:	8.28
Location:	8.70	Families:	6.18
Cleanliness:	8.72		

Grand Hyatt Shanghai

Jin Mao Tower, 88 Century Boulevard, Pudong, Shanghai 200121, China
T: +86 21 5049 1234 **F:** +86 21 5049 1111
http://www.asia-hotels.com/hotelinfo/Grand_Hyatt/

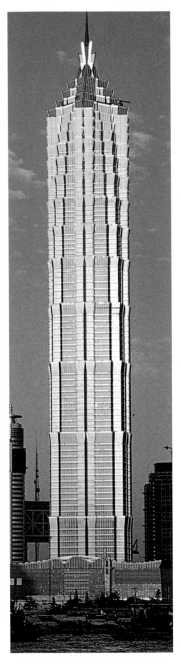

The Grand Hyatt is more than just a hotel. It is a glistening emblem of modern-day Shanghai – innovative, technologically advanced, ultra-luxurious and shaping the way forward for the new China. The entire structure is a catalogue of superlatives. Set in Pudong between the 53rd and 87th floors of the 421-metre, pagoda-like, US$540 million Jin Mao Tower (China's tallest building), the views over the city are stupendous, whatever the weather. The atrium soars a neck-craning 31 storeys, the 555 rooms average 40 square metres making them some of the largest in the city, and the Sky Lounge bar, fitness centre and the hotel itself are all rated as the highest on the planet.

The hotel sits above 52 floors of offices and is capped by an observatory on the 88th floor, traditionally an exceptionally lucky number in China. While the building's foundations are sunk deep into the ground, strong winds can sway its pinnacle by as much as 75 centimetres. Wandering the Hyatt's art deco-style floors is like exploring a space ship. Blast off from the ground floor via the elevators, and once your ears have popped a couple of times the public areas unfurl themselves like a blossoming flower. The hotel is always a hive of activity with diners crowding the tables, smartly suited executives scurrying to and from meetings, awed holidaymakers treading gingerly along the corridors and fashionably dressed emissaries from Shanghainese society lingering over drinks and the latest tidbits of metropolitan gossip.

There are nine restaurants and bars, and their gourmet sophistication and ambience is summed up by On Fifty Six, which embraces Japanese, wood-fired pizza, a grill room and the atrium lounge. Elsewhere the Grand Cafe's show kitchen is a tempting array of haute cuisine sights and aromas, Club Jin Mao enjoys a well-deserved reputation as the city's most exclusive Shanghainese restaurant and Food Live is an innovative concept offering favourite dishes from nine different Asian and Chinese food stalls.

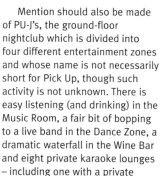

Mention should also be made of PU-J's, the ground-floor nightclub which is divided into four different entertainment zones and whose name is not necessarily short for Pick Up, though such activity is not unknown. There is easy listening (and drinking) in the Music Room, a fair bit of bopping to a live band in the Dance Zone, a dramatic waterfall in the Wine Bar and eight private karaoke lounges – including one with a private terrace – all of which act as a magnet to Shanghai's jeunesse very-dorée partygoers.

The accommodation – if that is not too pedestrian a term – includes 45 suites (Executive, Diplomatic, Presidential and Chairman's) and the 73-room Grand Club with its own 2-storey lounge. Individually decorated, the rooms would be hard to improve on; all feature interactive TV, dimmable lighting, high-speed modem lines, electronic sensor reading lamps, double-sided wardrobes that can be accessed from bed or bathroom, a tower shower with three showerheads and a heated mirror that will not mist up. While the Hyatt was designed by an American company, enormous care was taken to include Chinese elements. The hotel's furniture was all locally made, from the ceramic ice buckets to the carpets and the artwork that decorates the walls.

As an endnote, the hi-tech Jin Mao's car park has space for 2,000 bicycles, still the primary mode of transport in China! There is however parking for a 1,000 or so cars as well.

Rates from: **US$ 178**
Star rating: ★★★★★
Bellhop rating: 🛎🛎🛎🛎 ½

Value:	7.79	Facilities:	8.72
Staff:	8.35	Restaurants:	8.58
Location:	8.32	Families:	6.59
Cleanliness:	9.04		

Lu Song Yuan Hotel Beijing

22 Banchang Lane, Kuanjie, Beijing 100009, China
T: +86 10 6404 0436 **F**: +86 10 6403 0418
http://www.asia-hotels.com/hotelinfo/Lu_Song_Yuan_Hotel/

In a rapidly changing world there are few hotels left that provide a genuine snapshot of days gone by. Most heritage hotels across Asia have been swept aside and replaced by stereotype tower blocks as cities economically blossom with ugly concrete. Usually, only the luxury period pieces scrape through the metamorphoses, and even these undergo extensive restoration that can compromise their authenticity. The Lu Song Yuan is one of a dying breed – an affordable and unspoiled 2-star hotel, straight from the residential neighbourhoods of the 19th century. The term 'hotel' can only be loosely employed here as while the Lu Song is one of the most characteristic properties in Beijing, it branched off from the evolution of hotels well before the advent of what today would be considered standard facilities. There is no pool, no gym, no doorman, a business centre of sorts (with Internet access) and a simple restaurant – but you can hire a bicycle.

Hidden away down a little alleyway among the capital's hutongs (Mongolian for water well), the hotel can be hard to track down among the maze of charming backstreets, but this lends an air of seclusion and secrecy, plus bags of personality. Being built in traditional Chinese style it remains basic. The 57 rooms are set in the low buildings flanking a series of courtyards and quadrangles. They are generally small and spartan, but decorated with memorable Ming-style furnishings such as the hard yet ornate beds. Larger rooms, opening directly on to timeless courtyards, are especially popular making them difficult to book. The sweeping roofs, chunky red beams and pillars and lanterns are vaguely reminiscent of the Forbidden City just two kilometres south, but immeasurably more modest! It has to be said that the hotel is not built for comfort or for those in a rush. It is all about style and character and is a top pick for the more adventurous traveller wanting to experience a piece of China that is fast disappearing.

Rates from: **US$ 38**
Star rating: ★ ★
Bellhop rating: 🛎 🛎 🛎 🛎

Value:	9.05	Facilities:	7.38
Staff:	8.38	Restaurants:	7.13
Location:	8.39	Families:	4.58
Cleanliness:	8.25		

The Palace Hotel Beijing

8 Goldfish Lane, Wangfujing, Beijing 100006, China
T: +86 10 6559 2888 **F:** +86 10 6512 9050
http://www.asia-hotels.com/hotelinfo/Palace_Hotel_China/

The ancient city gate towers of Beijing were characterised by a massive base supporting a middle section and topped by a colourful penthouse under overhanging eaves. Their design is successfully replicated in Peninsula Group's Palace Hotel which also features a podium for its restaurant and banquet facilities, a main body of guestrooms and special accommodations on the top floors. Such historical echoes fit extremely well in the Palace, one of Beijing's older 5-stars set in the Forbidden City cultural district on the quaintly named Goldfish Lane.

But it would be a mistake to think that this hotel is a musty tribute to times gone by. Its 530 rooms and suites carry thoughtful details like mist-free mirrors in their marble bathrooms and computerised controls for lighting and air-conditioning. Naturally,

residents of the three Palace Club floors can enjoy their own lounge, but there is also a satellite business centre. The Duplex Suites probably enjoy some of the hotel's best views, while the Wangfujing and Presidential Suites come with two bedrooms, a kitchen, butler, whirlpool and private lift.

And it would be difficult to get more contemporary than Jing, with glass-walled, walk-in wine cellars, open kitchens and two private dining areas where you can feast on Western cuisine with distinctive Asian overtones. More traditionally, you can eat Cantonese in the Fortune Garden, where the

emphasis is on fresh fish and seafood, served to the accompaniment of live traditional Chinese music.

On the recreation side, the health club includes a gym, steam rooms and saunas, and an indoor swimming pool surrounded by tinted glass as well as an outdoor sun terrace for the summer months. And even non-shoppers should take a gander at the Palace's three-floor shopping arcade, populated by fashionistas such as Christian Dior, Hugo Boss, Bruno Magli and Louis Vuitton and heavily patronised by trendy local Beijingers, who once – it is hard to believe – all wore unisex Mao jackets.

Rates from: **US$ 125**
Star rating: ★ ★ ★ ★ ★
Bellhop rating: 🛎 🛎 🛎 🛎 🛎

Value:	8.27	Facilities:	8.69
Staff:	8.69	Restaurants:	8.54
Location:	9.16	Families:	6.80
Cleanliness:	9.14		

Peace Hotel Shanghai

20 Nanjing Road East, Shanghai 200002, China
T: +86 21 6321 6888 **F:** +86 21 6329 0300
http://www.asia-hotels.com/hotelinfo/Peace_Hotel/

Creaky though the service and facilities may be at this celebrated septuagenarian, it is difficult to confront the 12-storey Peace Hotel without a rush of affection. It has yet to be gobbled up and deluxed by an international chain, so what you get is pretty much China 1929. The 'Gothic Chicago' exterior – with its hallmark 77-metre-high, copper-sheathed pyramid roof and milky yellow granite walls – would not cause founder Victor Sassoon to break step. Inside the portentous grand entrance, the chandeliers, marble floors and rather dimly lit corridors are similarly unaltered.

The Peace Hotel's claim to fame is its Jazz Bar, with a venerable, showy six-piece jazz band thumping out the hits of the 30s and 40s – numbers that were current when the musicians (yes the very same ones) were in their teens. The bartenders make a mean Irish coffee, so this is an especially charismatic place to wind down after dinner. And for typically modern Shanghainese evening entertainment, there is the inevitable karaoke bar on the roof.

Far from disavowing its colonial past, the Peace Hotel has – somewhat surprisingly – embraced it with a will. Of its 363 rooms, eight suites are decorated with international themes – Indian, British, French, Italian, American, Italian, German and Spanish, and Sassoon's Room, the one-time opium trader's old private bedroom, is now available for private banquets. The rooms are slightly eccentrically appointed – with SOS buttons and hydrotherapy tubs in the suites – but also make a gesture to the millennium with modem jacks and IDD phones.

While the cuisine at the Peace is good, it is bettered by its locations. The Peace Banquet Hall is billed as a 'typical British palace', and the private rooms in Nine Heaven Hall have magnificent views over the Bund, while the French menu at the Peace Grill is augmented by dark brown patterned walls and Lalique lamps that present a highly apposite, old-fashioned ambience.

Rates from: **US$ 83**
Star rating: ★ ★ ★ ★ ★
Bellhop rating: 🐾🐾🐾🐾

Value:	7.76	Facilities:	7.68
Staff:	7.67	Restaurants:	7.82
Location:	9.23	Families:	6.31
Cleanliness:	8.05		

The Portman Ritz-Carlton Shanghai

1376 Nanjing Xi Road, Shanghai 200040, China
T: +86 21 6279 8888 **F**: +86 21 6279 8800
http://www.asia-hotels.com/hotelinfo/Portman_Ritz-Carlton/

The 564-room Portman Ritz-Carlton is like a city within a city within a city. As part of the Shanghai Centre on Nanjing Xi Road, it is in easy reach of a host of business and leisure facilities which augment what the hotel itself has to offer. This includes a half-dozen restaurants and lounges; sporting facilities that embrace squash and racquetball courts as well the more regular gym and pool, and a 24-hour business centre. Small wonder the Ritz regularly hosts royalty and US presidents.

The latter naturally head up to the Portman's quartet of Presidential Suites, but there is a range of other accommodation here with fewer zeroes on the price tag.

All the rooms and suites are decorated with a traditional oriental motif but graced with a touch of modern flair, and they range in size from 37 to 69 square metres. Club-level guests can make free with five different servings of snacks and beverages throughout the day in the lounge, and also have a dedicated concierge. And guests in any of the hotel's rooms can enjoy little complementary services that add a certain frisson to their stay – newspapers are delivered daily as a matter of course, shoes left out for cleaning come back glossily shined and the airport shuttle is free too.

Elsewhere in the hotel you can eat exceptionally well, and it is especially worth dropping in on the

Tea Garden, particularly at Sunday brunchtime when the Moet & Chandon flows freely. And the Ritz-Carlton Bar has an exceptional range of cigars and malt whiskeys, a walk-in humidor with private lockers, and live jazz playing nightly.

Setting the seal on the Ritz-Carlton's exclusivity is its one-of-a-kind sightseeing tour. It is not exactly cheap, but where else in the world can you be piloted around the city aboard a limited-edition Chang Jiang 750cc motorcycle with the hotel general manager as your personal chauffeur? Loyal guests get the trip for free on their 100th visit – plus the small matter of a Presidential Suite upgrade.

Rates from: **US$ 153**
Star rating: ★ ★ ★ ★ ★
Bellhop rating: 🛎 🛎 🛎 🛎 ½

Value:	8.10	Facilities:	8.72
Staff:	8.70	Restaurants:	8.34
Location:	8.95	Families:	6.71
Cleanliness:	8.95		

Pudong Shangri-La Shanghai

33 Fu Cheng Road, Shanghai 200120, China
T: +86 21 6882 8888 **F**: +86 21 6882 6688
http://www.asia-hotels.com/hotelinfo/ShangriLa_Hotel_Pudong/

The executive-friendly Shangri-La is pretty much Pudong personified. It is in spitting distance of the swizzlestick Orient Pearl TV Tower, and handy for the nearby Lujiazui commercial district while a couple of minutes ferry ride across the Huangpu River leads directly to the Bund.

The 606 rooms all come with a full-size writing desk, voicemail and dataports, while the Horizon Club rooms are equipped with high-speed Internet access. The Grand Ballroom and adjacent function rooms have previously hosted such events as the World Economic and Fortune global forums and the business centre, IT support team, gym, laundry, hotel service centre and of course room service all operate 24 hours a day, 365 days a year.

Finally, to wind down, the basement entertainment centre BATS is a fun mix of Western cuisine and live music with private dining rooms also available.

Rates from: **US$ 156**
Star rating: ★ ★ ★ ★ ★
Bellhop rating: 🛎 🛎 🛎 🛎 ½

Value:	8.02	Facilities:	8.66
Staff:	8.53	Restaurants:	8.22
Location:	8.31	Families:	6.76
Cleanliness:	8.91		

Shangri-La Hotel Hangzhou

78 Beishan Road, Hangzhou 310007, China
T: +86 571 8797 7951 **F**: +86 571 8707 3545
http://www.asia-hotels.com/hotelinfo/La_Hotel_Hangzhou/

One of China's premiere domestic tourist attractions is the scenic West Lake of Hangzhou. The best hotel of the region is no doubt the Shangri-La Hangzhou, the group's first property in China. Sitting pretty on the northern banks of the lake, the low-rise hotel is surrounded by 40 acres of tranquil wooded countryside. Being five minutes from the centre of town, the setting is supreme and removed from the sometimes intrusive mass tourism, and the lake views can be sublime. In two wings, the guest rooms are warm and homely, and some of them have the bonus of balconies. The interior design, five restaurants and bars and facilities are certainly up to Shangri-La's high standards, especially the indoor swimming pool and sauna. In China, 5-star can often be a gamble, but you certainly get the international interpretation here.

Rates from: **US$ 78**
Star rating: ★ ★ ★ ★ ★
Bellhop rating: 🛎 🛎 🛎 🛎 ½

Value:	7.91	Facilities:	8.13
Staff:	8.17	Restaurants:	7.98
Location:	8.93	Families:	6.43
Cleanliness:	8.37		

Shangri-La Hotel Shenzhen

East Side Railway Station, Jianshe Road, Shenzhen 518001, China
T: +86 755 8233 0888 **F:** +86 755 8233 9878
http://www.asia-hotels.com/hotelinfo/Shangrila_Hotel_Shenzen/

One of the first things you will see after crossing the main Hong Kong border into China is the Shangri-La.

Within sight of the Lo Wu customs post, the location is ideal for trans-border travellers doing business in Shenzhen's industrial economic zone, and also very handy for those on bargain shopping expeditions. Having exhausted one's credit card, there are plenty of recreational facilities, including a decent pool and sauna plus some popular restaurants to recharge the batteries. By Shangri-La standards the 553 rooms are a tad ordinary

but their service is well above the usually poor local levels. The Shangri-La Shenzhen as a whole is not as good as other hotels of this stylish chain but still deserves every one of its 5 stars. It is fittingly crowned with a pleasant revolving restaurant – Tiara – with commanding views of the city and Hong Kong beyond.

Rates from: US$ 71
Star rating: ★★★★★
Bellhop rating: 🛎🛎🛎🛎

Value:	7.68	Facilities:	7.98
Staff:	8.01	Restaurants:	7.90
Location:	8.30	Families:	5.76
Cleanliness:	8.08		

Sheraton Suzhou Hotel & Towers

388 Xin Shi Road, Suzhou, Jiangsu 215007, China
T: +86 512 6510 3388 **F:** +86 512 6510 0888
http://www.asia-hotels.com/hotelinfo/Sheraton_Suzhou_Hotel_Towers/

When so many hotels being raised in China nowadays are mere lumps of concrete and glass, it is a pleasure to discover one that takes its architectural cue from its 2,500-year-old surrounds. Only a couple of storeys high, the Sheraton is all local stone, winged roofs and

canals, while the entrance is modelled on the nearby Panmen Gate, the last vestige of the walls that once surrounded the city. So the hotel is a sort of Suzhou in miniature, but without the crowds and the noise.

Ancient on the outside, the 328

rooms within are all acceptably modern, with voicemail, dataports and the like while the long-stay rooms incorporate a kitchen. If you are not self-catering, there is Cantonese at the Celestial Court, Asian and Western at the Garden Brasserie or wood-fired oven pizza at the very art deco Riva's.

Rates from: US$ 99
Star rating: ★★★★★
Bellhop rating: 🛎🛎🛎🛎½

Value:	8.36	Facilities:	8.41
Staff:	8.42	Restaurants:	8.12
Location:	8.17	Families:	6.49
Cleanliness:	8.74		

The St Regis Beijing

21 Jianguomenwai Dajie, Beijing 100020, China
T: +86 10 6460 6688 **F**: +86 10 6460 3299
http://www.asia-hotels.com/hotelinfo/St_Regis_Beijing/

It is pretty much the number one address in China's premier city and first choice for many local and visiting executives – so the St Regis definitely has its location right. The diplomatic district is in hailing distance and the main business quarter only a few minutes drive away. HQ for CEOs? For sure.

More than half of the St Regis' 273 rooms are suites, spacious, subtly lit, furnished with deep sofas, easy chairs, weighty beds and DVD players throughout. It is the sort of place, in short, you can settle into with consummate ease and ideally set up a small business meeting, work alone or simply rest and relax, helped of course by the 24-hour butler service.

Elsewhere in the hotel there is a choice of nine places to eat and drink, including the Cigar Bar with its batteries of MonteCristos and Cohibas and other first-class stogies. The Astor Grill is noted for fine dining, while the Garden Lounge is more of an intimate fireside dining affair, and the Celestial Court serves up faultless Chinese cuisine drawing its dishes from all over the country. Keep your eyes peeled for long enough, and you will see a Who's Who of Beijing bent low over the menus and lingering over coffee and cognacs. Socialites should note that the Press Club Bar – patronised by a large number of professionals apart from journalists – is especially convivial.

In free moments, it is rewarding to take a dip in the 25-metre indoor pool, an impressive Romanesque affair with an adjacent fitness facility filled with the latest weights and the like. The range of treatments at the spa is equally inspiring, while the hotel bowling alley allows a window into one of Beijing's most popular indoor pastimes. It is not difficult to see why the city's upper echelons favour the St Regis. It is said that power is the greatest aphrodisiac, in which case this hotel is pretty damn sexy.

Rates from: **US$ 178**
Star rating: ★ ★ ★ ★ ★
Bellhop rating: ♪ ♪ ♪ ♪ ½

Value:	7.70	Facilities:	8.47
Staff:	8.57	Restaurants:	8.13
Location:	8.70	Families:	5.89
Cleanliness:	8.99		

The St Regis Shanghai

889 Dong Fang Road, Pudong, Shanghai 200122, China
T: +86 21 5050 4567 **F:** +86 21 6875 6789
http://www.asia-hotels.com/hotelinfo/St_Regis_The/

Anyone travelling to Shanghai for the first time since the 1980s or before is in for a dose of culture shock when they hit the St Regis. Garbed in tails, a multi-lingual butler, savvy in the ways of the city and fluent in IT, will be waiting to escort you to your room. The gloomy dormitories of 20 years ago, watched over by harridans who regarded being asked to unlock your room as a personal affront, have long been demolished. In their place is the likes of the St Regis, whose standards of service and comfort should make similar establishments in London and New York look to their laurels.

The butlers, or butleresses even, remain on call 24 hours a day, happy to unpack luggage or advise on and make restaurant reservations. The 318 rooms, decorated with soft-toned rich fabrics, are at least 48 metres square – some of the most spacious in Shanghai. The desk chair is ergonomic, the bed is custom designed with 900-coil mattresses, Internet is broadband, the sound system is BOSE and the TV is cable. Floris soap and shampoo are stacked on the shelf of the bathroom's 'rainforest' shower. And all guests are automatically invited to evening 'wind down' cocktails in the Executive Lounge.

Cocktail downed, there is a medley of Chinese and Italian restaurants to sate the appetite. Danieli's rests on the top floor with stunning views over the city complemented by an innovative, modern interior design and similar cuisine. Carrianna serves southern Chinese, with the emphasis on fresh seasonal dishes, while Saints comes marching in all day with international fare.

Executives staying here – and the St Regis is very much positioned with them in mind – can also take advantage of the 600-seater Astor Ballroom and nine adjacent, if rather smaller, meeting rooms. It has been said that, even though it is in Pudong, the St Regis is a little remote, however with a hotel this good that is not really a valid criticism.

Rates from: **US$ 120**
Star rating: ★ ★ ★ ★ ★
Bellhop rating: ♗ ♗ ♗ ♗ ½

Value:	8.64	Facilities:	8.70
Staff:	8.97	Restaurants:	7.94
Location:	7.85	Families:	5.64
Cleanliness:	9.18		

White Swan Hotel

1 Southern Street, Shamian Island, Guangzhou 510133, China
T: +86 20 8188 6968 F: +86 20 8186 1188
http://www.asia-hotels.com/hotelinfo/White_Swan_Hotel/

Guangdong's provincial capital Guangzhou is a writhing and sprawling city filled with typically grim and functional business hotels. But luckily it has the sanity and luxury of the White Swan Hotel, set on the tiny river island of Shamian, a quiet and quaint pocket of the city renowned for its colonial architecture where the earliest French and English traders originally set up shop. The location is ideal for those looking to escape the frantic city streets, with the hotel sitting on the banks of the Pearl River and enjoying a peaceful tree lined neighbourhood. Presidents and royalty including Queen Elizabeth, Richard Nixon, Deng Xiaoping and nearly every European premier have dropped in to enjoy the hotel's quiet sophistication since it opened in 1983.

The bright lobby – with its high ceiling and cascading rockeries – gazes straight out on to the river and gives a grandness that sets the scene for the whole hotel. The 843 spacious and well-maintained rooms and suites (half with river views) including two executive floors complete with broadband access and private lounge, a first-class business centre and extensive conference facilities, means the business visitor is more than adequately catered for. These are complemented by an impressive array of leisure offerings from the two indoor and eight outdoor tennis courts, two squash courts, a golf driving range, two free-form swimming pools, health club and spa.

With nine restaurants and bars, the international range of food is broad to suit the hotel's clientele, from the French cuisine of the Silk Road Grill Room to the authentic sushi and teppanyaki of Hirata, from the Sichuan Provincial Restaurant to the elegant tea ceremonies and dim sum of the Jade River Garden. Each of the restaurants has as strong focus on the river, many with stunning views. For the ultimate, sit in the hotel's gardens and enjoy alfresco barbeque at the River Garden or take a cruise (weekends only) on the hotel's tour boat.

Rates from: **US$ 74**
Star rating: ★ ★ ★ ★ ★
Bellhop rating: 🛎 🛎 🛎 🛎 ½

Value:	8.33	Facilities:	8.67
Staff:	8.56	Restaurants:	8.48
Location:	8.44	Families:	7.25
Cleanliness:	8.68		

HONG KONG

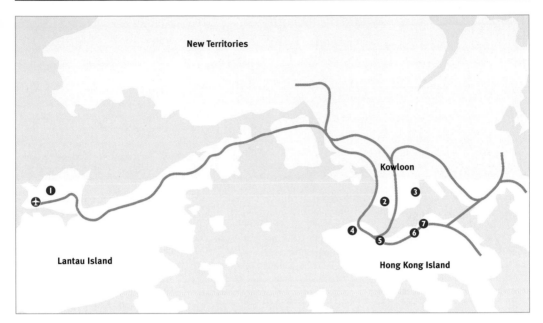

Something happens to people when they arrive in Hong Kong. All those previously lethargic sloths you shared the plane with become suddenly animated. As if activated by remote control, the easy-going crowd that lazily sauntered on to the plane decides to disembark in a desperate clamber. It is rush hour before you even clear customs. One of the first signs you will see is a huge banner proclaiming 'Relax. Train will arrive in three minutes.' Welcome to Hong Kong, city of life, and one of the most energetic places in the world.

Many Asian cities have developed along similar timescales, encountered the same waves of growth and bust, and tend to resemble one another. Hong Kong had a head start on the rest of the region, the former British colony booming as the only gateway to the vast, untapped

resources of China. A motley crew of fishing junks and an assortment of paddy fields blossomed into one of the major cities of the Far East, in only a few generations. Today Hong Kong harbour bristles with sky-scraping success, and even with the economic wobbles since

the 1997 handover the skyline changes noticeably every year.

Hong Kong is tiny by international standards, a crowded and jumbled city with layer upon layer of development and urban clutter, mostly squashed around that incredible harbour. In an effort

to stop some of it falling in, land has been reclaimed. A core of land only a few square metres across may have office space, hotel rooms, a shopping plaza, a car park and an underground railway line, all stacked on top of each other. Given its history as a trading outpost it is not surprising that the territory remains an international business centre, and you will see plenty of suits nipping back and forth. But there is an optimistic spring in their steps, not the depressed plod you find elsewhere.

For tourists, Hong Kong is a major travel hub and it is a traditional jumping off spot for shopaholics. There can be few places with more shops per square metre than Hong Kong – they are absolutely everywhere. And everyone is at it. Where do Hong Kongers find room to stash it all in their compressed flats? For visitors, Tsim Sha Tsui is often the first port of call, but try diving into vibrant Causeway Bay for brand-named goods and shopping plazas. The malls of Central and Pacific Place in Admiralty are lined with fancy upmarket apparel. At the other end of the scale are the grungy street markets and

bargains of counterfeit capital Mongkok. For arty types, the shops of Cat Street in Sheung Wan offer a treasure trove of quality Chinese antiques.

When it comes to restaurants little needs to be said – the dining is predictably excellent. Yet it can also be very cheap and whatever your budget the food is good. The Cantonese may be a tolerant bunch, but not when it comes to poor cuisine. Hotel restaurants are right up there, their menus bulging with world-class culinary indulgences. The hotels themselves are a reflection of Hong Kong – modern, compact, energetic and efficient – with service just a bit too rushed. Expect staff to be hurried and doing several things at once. Be warned that rooms in the territory tend to be half the size of those in other cities. Some can be comically small with not enough room to swing a spring roll, let alone a cat.

Hong Kong is a place that loses nothing with the seasons, but it can get uncomfortably humid in the summer months, and the monsoons between July and September can put a dampener on things. September through April is

the time to come although it can get a tad chilly in January and February.

The touristy circuit is fairly limited but it is best to submerge yourself in the many enjoyable low-key diversions, all of which are close at hand. Museums are generally educational and presentable. Incense wafts through the temples that provide interesting pockets of culture among the modern progress. And then there is the pungent whiff of various unidentifiable shrivelled roots and creatures in the traditional medicine shops and wet markets. Hong Kong is an intriguing place to absorb. There is just so much going on.

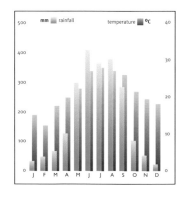

The Excelsior Hong Kong

281 Gloucester Road, Causeway Bay, Hong Kong Island, Hong Kong
T: +852 2894 8888 **F:** +852 2895 6459
http://www.asia-hotels.com/hotelinfo/Excelsior_The/

Marking its 30th anniversary in 2003, the Excelsior provides a grandstand for all the classic Hong Kong icons. Look north from its 34 storeys, and there is Noel Coward's Noon Day Gun out in the midday sun, the (still) Royal Hong Kong Yacht Club, Victoria Harbour and the peaks of Kowloon in all their glory. And a few steps from the back of the hotel leads straight into the manic heart of the island's busiest upmarket retail district, so it is the perfect carrier bag offloading point for the compulsive shopper.

Hong Kong's reputation for hyperefficiency and good food is borne out in the accommodation and half-dozen restaurants. The 884 rooms and suites are mines of solid comfort, and perked up with broadband, voicemail and the like. The 270-degree views from the top-floor ToTT's Asian Bar and Grill are fantastic, while the underground Dickens pub pulls a good beer-swilling, sports-cheering crowd from the buzzing environs, especially when big matches are on.

Rates from: **US$ 115**
Star rating: ★ ★ ★ ★
Bellhop rating: ⌂ ⌂ ⌂ ⌂

Value:	7.90	Facilities:	7.86
Staff:	8.08	Restaurants:	7.97
Location:	8.91	Families:	6.63
Cleanliness:	8.34		

ASIA'S BEST HOTELS & RESORTS

Grand Hyatt Hong Kong

1 Harbour Road, Wan Chai, Hong Kong Island, Hong Kong
T: +852 2588 1234 **F:** +852 2802 0677
http://www.asia-hotels.com/hotelinfo/Grand_Hyatt_Hong_Kong/

It is easy to get bogged down trying to find which of the reams of 5-star city hotels lives up to the inevitable claim as the best in town. The Grand Hyatt – right next to the Convention and Exhibition Centre – has a good shot at the Hong Kong title and is constantly rated near the top by those in the know, as it is simply a cut above the usual 5-star format. The soothing design and style is one of the key factors, the Grand Hyatt managing to conjure a professional and classy atmosphere that is simultaneously relaxed and not overly formal. A big, broad, black marble lobby with sweeping staircases invokes a corporate air, but this is softened with trickling fountains, greenery and the gentle golden glow from the lighting.

Other areas of the Grand Hyatt, from the restaurants to the rooms, are more contemporary. Local artistry is incorporated to lend a modern yet distinctly Asian angle. The John Morford-designed rooms are light and crisp with a sprinkle of Zen about them – lots of pale angular woods and beige tones, with designer fittings. The good thing about the Grand Hyatt is that standards are maintained throughout – each room category is essentially the same in ambience, upkeep and facilities – there are no low-category rooms with unpleasant surprises. Each room is extremely well equipped and includes a fax and broadband Internet access. Suites vary with sumptuous additional living space, kitchenettes and superior electrical appliances. Oh, and the taps are gold-plated. Around 70 per cent of the rooms overlook the harbour – some of the views are sublime. With full business amenities, a splendid range of tasteful top restaurants including one of Hong Kong's favourites – Grissini – and groovy JJ's Nightclub there is little reason to be unhappy. At the time of writing, the scenic landscaped pool area and roof gardens shared with the Renaissance next door was in the process of being renovated, with the addition of a spa slated to open in late 2003.

Rates from: **US$ 260**
Star rating: ★★★★★
Bellhop rating: 🐾🐾🐾🐾 ½

Value:	7.67	Facilities:	8.56
Staff:	8.51	Restaurants:	8.66
Location:	8.45	Families:	6.85
Cleanliness:	8.94		

Harbour Plaza Hong Kong

20 Tak Fung Street, Hunghom, Kowloon, Hong Kong
T: +852 2621 3188 **F:** +852 2621 3311
http://www.asia-hotels.com/hotelinfo/Harbour_Plaza_Hong_Kong/

This shiny blue block juts out into the famous harbour, giving the impression of almost being afloat. Smooth and well appointed the modern Harbour Plaza takes full advantage of its Kowloon-side position with bay windows flooding the interior with light – especially in the bright lobby with its point-blank harbour views, marble staircase and hint of Italian flair. There is space, a rare Hong Kong commodity, and the immediate neighbourhood emits an equally smart air rather than the usual frantic clutter. Spacious and smart harbour-view rooms comprise 70 per cent of the total, and the outstanding glass-walled rooftop pool is a beauty. Being 10 minutes drive from Tsim Sha Tsui is considered a minor inconvenience in international terms, but well off the beaten track for local residents. First-rate dining includes the local novelty of a breezy alfresco cafe (an almost impossible feature in the heart of the city) and an original Pit Stop Formula One bar. A brave and original Hong Kong hotel.

Rates from: **US$ 99**
Star rating: ★ ★ ★ ★ ★
Bellhop rating: 🛎 🛎 🛎 🛎 ½

Value:	8.19	Facilities:	8.48
Staff:	8.42	Restaurants:	8.19
Location:	7.65	Families:	6.80
Cleanliness:	8.79		

Holiday Inn Golden Mile Hong Kong

50 Nathan Road, Tsim Sha Tsui (W), Kowloon, Hong Kong
T: +852 2369 3111 **F:** +852 2369 8016
http://www.asia-hotels.com/hotelinfo/Holiday_Inn_Golden_Mile_HK/

If Hong Kong ever needed acupuncture, they would probably stick one of the needles in Nathan Road – Hong Kong's Golden Mile. The sheer energy and brio of this neon-swathed strip of shops, clubs and pubs can be mesmerising – so sidestepping into the Holiday Inn is an exercise in calm. The hotel is never going to win any awards for its views, but the 600 ultra family-friendly 28-square-metre rooms are among the largest in the city and are big enough to accommodate two double beds. The innovative European creations in the Avenue restaurant and the 18 flavoured vodkas in Hari's Bar are two other major pluses. Opened in 1975 but well maintained, the Holiday Inn Golden Mile has always been owned by the Harilela family who regard it as a personal trophy. A lot of regular guests feel the same.

Rates from: **US$ 126**
Star rating: ★ ★ ★ ★
Bellhop rating: 🛎 🛎 🛎 🛎

Value:	7.80	Facilities:	7.86
Staff:	7.95	Restaurants:	7.92
Location:	8.71	Families:	6.64
Cleanliness:	8.22		

Hyatt Regency Hong Kong

67 Nathan Road, Tsim Sha Tsui (W), Kowloon, Hong Kong
T: +852 2311 1234 **F:** +852 2739 8701
http://www.asia-hotels.com/hotelinfo/Hyatt_Regency_Hong_Kong/

Nothing much to look at, the Hyatt Regency is a functional number filling a niche quite nicely. If it were an airplane it would be a Boeing 747, an unspectacular but reliable (and very successful) workhorse. A ramp way tucked behind the hotel off Peking Road accesses the unusually placed 1st-floor lobby. In fact, much of the interior layout is a little awkward and slightly ageing, but the hotel staff are very attentive and courteous. Average rooms are straightforward and predictable with a dark oriental theme. Restaurants and other facilities are adequate, and the live sports broadcasts at the Chin Chin Bar always pull a good crowd. The location in Tsim Sha Tsui's Nathan Road is key, and the MTR station is on the doorstep, putting the bulk of Hong Kong's major districts within a comfy 15-minute radius. This ageing jumbo may not be a beauty but it still maintains attentive service in a first-class location.

Rates from: **US$ 113**
Star rating: ★ ★ ★ ★
Bellhop rating: 🛎🛎🛎🛎 ½

Value:	8.01	Facilities:	8.28
Staff:	8.56	Restaurants:	8.37
Location:	9.15	Families:	6.61
Cleanliness:	8.84		

Inter-Continental Hong Kong

18 Salisbury Road, Tsim Sha Tsui (W), Kowloon, Hong Kong
T: +852 2721 1211 **F**: +852 2739 4546
http://www.asia-hotels.com/hotelinfo/InterContinental_Hong_Kong/

All of Hong Kong's best hotels, by definition, have views of one of the world's most scenic harbours, with the lesser ones straining on tip-toe for a glimpse. When it comes to harbour views then the Inter-Continental is number one – period. The views from Tsim Sha Tsui looking towards the magnificent island skyline are preferable to the reverse, and the Inter-Continental has the most central and balanced view. Being the only hotel wrapped by the waterfront promenade and built quite literally on top of the harbour, the waters are totally unobstructed from any floor. For a room with a view, this is it. This side of the glass the rooms are spacious, well equipped and classic with thick, rustling, brass-coloured curtains and bed covers. The bright, open lobby has been remodelled since the hotel changed hands from the Regent in 2001. The business-like and stark atmosphere is softened with the odd leaf and attentive service.

There are leaves galore around the pool, and the jacuzzi overlooking the harbour is another highlight, and a success in that the horrendous Salisbury Road traffic nearby is effectively shut out. It is also here that the more visible evidence of feng shui is seen with the stone, circle-square energy portal – a consideration that heavily influences the design and layout of this smart property. Comprehensive business facilities plus its location across the road from the MTR station pull many business guests (and again, there are those harbour-view boardrooms). The late closing times and 24-hour nature of many of the facilities is convenient for the jet-lagged traveller. With a soothing spa, international-scale conference facilities and the obligatory top restaurants, there is little missing from the checklist. If there is a criticism it is that the Inter-Continental's split-layered layout feels a bit like an exhibition centre or has echoes of the nearby public museums.

Rates from: US$ 207
Star rating: ★ ★ ★ ★ ★
Bellhop rating: 👍 👍 👍 👍 ½

Value:	7.85	Facilities:	8.77
Staff:	8.72	Restaurants:	8.72
Location:	9.02	Families:	6.81
Cleanliness:	9.05		

Island Shangri-La Hong Kong

Pacific Place, Supreme Court Road, Central, Hong Kong Island, Hong Kong
T: +852 2877 3838 **F:** +852 2521 8742
http://www.asia-hotels.com/hotelinfo/Island_ShangriLa_Hong_Kong/

Deservedly ranked as one of Hong Kong's best, the Island Shangri-La avoided many of the disadvantages of earlier hotels in the territory when it was built in 1992. The major impact is space. Whereas many Hong Kong hotels are compact and bunched up in the jumble of city streets, the Island Shangri-La was constructed halfway up a wooded hillside overlooking the financial district and therefore had more room to play with. A large airy lobby lets you know what you are in for, it is modern and sharp but rooted in classic styling. High windows allow sunlight to fall upon the pastel marble. And just to really show off, they dared to hollow out its core to form an atrium almost from the base up to the 56th floor. This bright pillar of nothingness is utter decadence in space-conscious Hong Kong, and they pushed the boat out further by draping the backdrop of the shaft with the world's largest silk painting.

Rooms are once again classical yet fresh and new, with deep, refined shades plus chandeliers, and are thoroughly equipped. Since rooms follow the contours of the

arcing structure, the floor plan is slightly wedge-shaped and dimensions are wide. There is little difference in between each category, the harbour-view rooms being slightly larger but that is all. Views sweep across the financial district below and span most of the harbour. The side-facing rooms catch plenty of green hillsides and the skyscrapers poking towards them. The facilities are top rate – a dignified library, classy function rooms and sleek business facilities all tell of a property chiefly attracting corporate guests. The trendy open kitchen restaurant, Cafe TOO, departs from this theme and is incredibly popular with Hong

Kong's gourmet junkies, as are the Shangri-La's other six restaurants. The hotel has a great location atop the upmarket shopping mall of Pacific Place, a few minutes walk to the MTR at Admiralty and just down the road from the big bucks of Central.

Rates from: US$ 192
Star rating: ★★★★★
Bellhop rating: ♝♝♝♝ ½

Value:	7.75	Facilities:	8.65
Staff:	8.57	Restaurants:	8.55
Location:	8.87	Families:	6.91
Cleanliness:	8.95		

JW Marriott Hotel Hong Kong

Pacific Place, 88 Queensway, Central, Hong Kong Island, Hong Kong
T: +852 2810 8366 **F**: +852 2845 0737
http://www.asia-hotels.com/hotelinfo/JW_Marriott_Hotel_HK/

hospitality – well above Hong Kong's usual service levels – and the enormous restaurants stuffed with patrons that are their own advertisement. Tidy business facilities and a good heated outdoor pool complete the picture. Grade A minus across the board.

A superior jack-of-all-trades, the JW Marriott is simply a fine 5-star property that has successfully managed to marry a string of slight advantages. The location above the classy Pacific Place shopping mall and MTR station in Admiralty is the first – Hong Kong's premier business and shopping districts are one station in either direction. The hillside elevation ensures harbour views from the multi-layered lobby and front-facing rooms. Reverse rooms enjoy mountain views of Victoria Peak – not bad either – and all 602 rooms are crisp, light and warm. Other big pluses include the Marriott

Rates from: **US$ 194**
Star rating: ★★★★★
Bellhop rating: 🛎🛎🛎🛎 ½

Value:	7.92	Facilities:	8.52
Staff:	8.59	Restaurants:	8.43
Location:	8.93	Families:	6.97
Cleanliness:	8.87		

The Kowloon Hotel

19-21 Nathan Road, Tsim Sha Tsui (W), Kowloon, Hong Kong
T: +852 2929 2888 **F**: +852 2739 9811
http://www.asia-hotels.com/hotelinfo/Kowloon_Hotel_The/

Right behind that grande old dame the Peninsula in the core of Tsim Sha Tsui, the Kowloon Hotel is the rather newer dame opened in 1986 and the accommodation of choice for the budget-minded single executive. Both hotels have the same owner, so expect the same top-notch service, but without the history and with substantially lower room rates. Included in those rates in each of the Kowloon's 736 smart if very cramped rooms is a tri-lingual, multi-functional computer-cum-satellite television – a tad slow connection-wise but still very workable. If you can drag yourself away from it, of the hotel's quartet of restaurants, the crowds of Hong Kongers feasting on Cantonese delicacies in Wan Loong Court are the best recommendation any chef could wish for. On the downside, the Kowloon lacks exercise facilities, but entrance to the California gym just across the street is available for a nominal fee.

Rates from: **US$ 72**
Star rating: ★★★★
Bellhop rating: 🛎🛎🛎🛎

Value:	8.02	Facilities:	7.69
Staff:	7.83	Restaurants:	7.53
Location:	8.98	Families:	5.99
Cleanliness:	8.30		

Mandarin Oriental Hong Kong

5 Connaught Road, Central, Hong Kong Island, Hong Kong
T: +852 2522 0111 **F:** +852 2810 6190
http://www.asia-hotels.com/hotelinfo/Mandarin_Oriental_HK/

The Mandarin Oriental is pungently characteristic of Hong Kong. When it first opened it was the city's tallest building, an accolade that now seems almost risible. Yet although it is now 40 years old, and dwarfed by surrounding skyscrapers, its extraordinarily high standards of service ensure that it remains the doyenne of Hong Kong hotels with a reputation that far exceeds the bounds of the SAR. The Mandarin successfully captures a classic and traditional air, liberally spread with such Chinese touches as intricately carved screens, bygone era porcelain and robust furniture. The 1960s block-style architecture means there are no floor-to-ceiling windows but a formal and intimate interior is reinforced by the black marble backdrop and bright gold trimmings.

Equally adept at catering to both upper-echelon business and leisure travellers, the Mandarin is unique in Hong Kong in offering a balcony with almost all its 541 rooms, and harbour-view rooms even come with binoculars. Extravagantly furnished, the rooms are particularly comfortable and care is taken to provide everything from designer toiletries to high-speed Internet access, while the suites come equipped with a mini business centre.

Just as guests can pick and choose their accommodation, so a manifold range of restaurants and bars wait to satisfy their appetites. The Chinnery is a cosy bar serving bangers and mash plus an exhaustive range of single-malt whiskies, while Vong is cutting-edge trendy Franco-Asian cuisine. Man Wah presents the acme of Chinese cuisine, and the menu at the Mandarin Grill comprises 300 dishes. The ground-floor Captain's Bar is wall-to-wall suits, with senior and junior captains of industry

making free with the grain and the grape. Breakfast at the Cafe is good opportunity to watch the myriad pedestrians scurrying the streets of Central, afternoon tea at the Clipper Lounge a time to relax with scones and the hotel's signature rose petal jam.

Finally, the Health Centre comes as a minor surprise, with its centrepiece a pool in the style of a Roman spa with a domed roof and Doric columns. In Hong Kong's competitive market it is worth noting that this stellar hotel maintains a strong loyal following and has seen quite a few others come and go.

Rates from: US$ 200
Star rating: ★ ★ ★ ★ ★
Bellhop rating: ◖◖◖◖ ½

Value:	7.78	Facilities:	8.32
Staff:	8.81	Restaurants:	8.72
Location:	9.08	Families:	6.63
Cleanliness:	8.96		

The Marco Polo Hong Kong Hotel

3 Canton Road, Harbour City, Tsim Sha Tsui (W), Kowloon, Hong Kong
T: +852 2113 0088 **F:** +852 2113 0011
http://www.asia-hotels.com/hotelinfo/Marco_Polo_Hong_Kong_Hotel/

With a back door that opens straight out on to the Star Ferry pier at Tsim Sha Tsui, this is the best of the three Marco Polos along Canton Road. The 4-star hotel has just put the finishing touches on an extensive renovation which saw the lobby spruced up, the ballroom given a facelift and the coffee shop streamlined into the swish Cafe Marco. The rooms are a major asset – giants by Hong Kong standards, and although there is something of the 1980s about them, they are airy, welcoming and relaxing, and many enjoy good unobstructed harbour views. A decent little outdoor pool is handy and the restaurants compete well with the countless others in the adjoining shopping centres of Harbour City and Ocean Terminal. Nice trimmings, well maintained, friendly and helpful staff, and a great stepping off point for the ferries across the harbour or up to mainland China.

Rates from: **US$ 127**
Star rating: ★ ★ ★ ★
Bellhop rating: ♪ ♪ ♪ ♪ ½

Value:	8.28	Facilities:	8.19
Staff:	8.17	Restaurants:	8.02
Location:	9.05	Families:	7.11
Cleanliness:	8.57		

Novotel Century Harbourview

508 Queen's Road West, Western, Hong Kong Island, Hong Kong
T: +852 2974 1234 **F:** +852 2974 0333
http://www.asia-hotels.com/hotelinfo/Novotel_Century_Harbour_Hotel/

You have heard of instant noodles – the Novotel Century Harbourview is instant Hong Kong. Unlike

Central, Western district could not be more Chinese – its shops, cafes and offices rattle to the click of the abacus and are infused with the aromas of traditional apothecaries. Not that this is in any way a backwater. The MTR, ferry terminals and cross-harbour tunnel are a modest taxi ride away, and the hotel itself – with some of the best rates on the island – is well endowed with mod cons. Its 274 rooms all carry voicemail and dataports, the Waterfall Cafe functions smartly under the aegis of head chef Popeye Yeung, and cocktails slip down easily at Moons on the 28th floor by the rooftop swimming pool. This is a cheap, cheerful and very Hong Kong hotel.

Rates from: **US$ 54**
Star rating: ★ ★ ★ ½
Bellhop rating: ♪ ♪ ♪ ♪

Value:	8.28	Facilities:	8.04
Staff:	7.96	Restaurants:	7.04
Location:	7.90	Families:	5.94
Cleanliness:	8.48		

The Peninsula Hong Kong

Salisbury Road, Tsim Sha Tsui (W), Kowloon, Hong Kong
T: +852 2920 2888 **F**: +852 2722 4170
http://www.asia-hotels.com/hotelinfo/Peninsula_Hong_Kong/

Wander where you will through the Peninsula and you always end up with the same conclusion: the term '5-star hotel' is a woefully inadequate description for your surroundings. You might be touching down on the rooftop helipad, peering majestically at the harbour through the telescope in the Marco Polo Suite, lingering over the signature braised veal shank in Gaddi's, day-dreaming while lazing in the Graeco-Roman pool, or simply taking a mildy cheeky, air-conditioned short cut through the lobby where you will be greeted by a chorus of

immaculate pageboys at the main door. Whether it is the Pen's style, service or downright sophistication, the oldest of Hong Kong's hotels is not so much a grande dame as a newly crowned empress.

The Pen marks its 75th anniversary this year (2003), a celebration anticipated especially keenly by Mr Chan Pak, who started as a dollar-a-month pageboy in July 1928 and now combines the roles of hotel totem and honorary elder statesman at all the Pen's more superior functions. An integral part of the

hotel, Mr Chan's long years of service have embraced its opening, the pre-war years when the Japanese barber eavesdropped on British top brass while cutting their hair and – to the amazement of some of the older members of the board – the inauguration of the city's first discotheque ('Scene') in 1966.

The Peninsula underwent a spectacular renaissance in 1994, when a 30-storey tower was grafted on to the existing building. The Duke and Duchess of Kent flew in from Britain for the grand opening, where they were joined by thousands of Hong Kongers anxious not to miss the party of the decade, and quite of few of whom had actually been sent an invitation.

The Pen was built opposite what at the time was the main railway station, bringing passengers from as far away as Europe to its doorstep. Guests are more likely to arrive nowadays from the international airport in one of the hotel's 14 Rolls-Royces, although some land around the corner at Ocean Terminal at the end of a cruise. But the unique frisson of arrival at the Pen is the

same even if you have just stepped off the MTR (Tsim Sha Tsui, Exit E).

Once inside the rarefied air of the Pen, there is a huge amount to discover. The renovation gave the old hotel the space to expand its inventory to 300 rooms and suites, each decorously fitted out to be equally adaptable to the high-flying executive or high-class holidaymaker. The top of the new tower was made over to Felix, a restaurant that soon became equally celebrated for its eclectic

cuisine and Philippe Starck design – to say nothing of the panorama of Kowloon from the gentlemen's bathroom. The spa grew as well, embracing a sun terrace and grooming treatments under the eye of expert trichologist Wing Tan. But the cornerstone of the Pen has always been its lobby, with gilded pillars and an equally gilded air that lends itself naturally to an elegant high tea – delicate pastries and scones and a strainer by the pot – over tidbits of the latest gossip. Very little has changed here since the Pen opened all those years ago – which is precisely why the vast majority of guests like it so much.

Rates from: **US$ 305**
Star rating: ★ ★ ★ ★
Bellhop rating: ♗ ♗ ♗ ♗ ♗

Value:	7.76	Facilities:	8.79
Staff:	8.91	Restaurants:	8.90
Location:	9.09	Families:	7.16
Cleanliness:	9.20		

Regal Airport Hotel

9 Cheong Tat Road, Hong Kong International Airport, Chek Lap Kok, Lantau, Hong Kong
T: +852 2286 8888 **F:** +852 2286 8686
http://www.asia-hotels.com/hotelinfo/Regal_Airport_Hotel/

The words 'airport hotel' usually conjure up images of dreary corridors lined with shoebox rooms bearing disturbing traces of previous occupants. But when they built the Regal Airport they cut a brand new template. Its airy, modern design makes it more like a resort than somewhere to spend a hurried night between flights. And many of the Regal's regular guests make it their Hong Kong base, using the express train service to commute into Central, which is only 23 minutes away.

A short trolley-push via covered walkway from the terminal, the Regal's 1,100-plus rooms make it the largest hotel in Hong Kong. Yet there is no sense of being dwarfed by its 12 storeys, thanks largely to a crisp interior design. Combining a wealth of colour with chrome and plain wood finishes, the rooms –

regular, suite or club floor – are universally habitable. Double glazing shuts out the whine of distant turbines, thick pile deadens passing footfalls, so this is somewhere you can sleep, work and rest in peace.

Built around a central courtyard containing a swimming pool, the Regal serves up a thoughtfully crafted cocktail of business and leisure. Sort out secretarial or translation services via the business centre, or fax and surf from your room. The basement games centre caters to seven-year-olds of all ages, with a menu embracing darts, billiards, pool and a host of electronic games. There are 17 function rooms, stacked to the brim with state-of-the-art audio-visual kit and a 1,000-square-metre ballroom (also the largest in Hong Kong). And the China Coast Wine

Bar – one of seven spots within the Regal where you can browse and sluice – is a focal (and very social) point for the local community rather than just another hotel bar. Guests focusing on food should head for Cafe Aficionado and its sumptuous 24-hour buffet. Plus, if you have some time before your flight, Lantau Island's beaches and the Big Buddha at Po Lin are both in easy reach.

Rates from: US$ 140
Star rating: ★ ★ ★ ★ ★
Bellhop rating: ♦ ♦ ♦ ♦ ½

Value:	8.01	Facilities:	8.46
Staff:	8.31	Restaurants:	8.10
Location:	8.78	Families:	5.93
Cleanliness:	8.91		

Renaissance Harbour View Hotel

1 Harbour Road, Wan Chai, Hong Kong Island, Hong Kong
T: +852 2802 8888 **F:** +852 2802 8833
http://www.asia-hotels.com/hotelinfo/Renaissance_Harbour_View/

The Renaissance Harbour View meets a need rather than a desire. If transplanted away from its enviable location it must be considered very ordinary, but the benefits of sitting on the fringe of Hong Kong harbour and being quite literally only a stone's throw from the Hong Kong Convention and Exhibition Centre cannot be underestimated. The Centre, shopping arcades and Wan Chai MTR station are all accessible by covered walkways so everything is close at hand, with the hotel blending into the busy surroundings. The Renaissance itself is now dated, with 1980s hangovers such as the uncomfortable purple leather panelling behind the reception desk and the imposing glass-piped light fitting dangling before it. Some of these echoes persist in underlying design and layout of the rooms, but they have been renovated well in reserved, deep brown tweeds. The huge landscaped pool shared with the Grand Hyatt next door is a superior option, but is currently under renovation until mid-2003. Comfy enough, the big bonus is surely in the harbour rooms where you can admire the endless to and fro of boats and helicopters.

Rates from: **US$ 126**
Star rating: ★ ★ ★ ★ ½
Bellhop rating: 🛎 🛎 🛎 🛎 ½

Value:	7.88	Facilities:	8.43
Staff:	8.15	Restaurants:	8.08
Location:	8.68	Families:	6.09
Cleanliness:	8.72		

The Ritz-Carlton Hong Kong

3 Connaught Road, Central, Hong Kong Island, Hong Kong
T: +852 2877 6666 **F:** +852 2877 6778
http://www.asia-hotels.com/hotelinfo/Ritz_Carlton_Hong_Kong_The/

The cosy Ritz-Carlton is not a patch on her award winning Singaporean sister, and is one of the more modest efforts of this outstanding chain. In some ways this is just another 5-star property, but there are a few little details that help it stand out. The decor is somewhat regal and refined with gentle shades, and sometimes suggests you should have packed a bow tie or evening dress. Almost exclusively European, there is little to remind you of the Far East apart from the odd vase, not that it matters. There is no big swanky lobby. Proportions in the public areas are rather small and the interior layout is irregular, lending an air of intimacy rare in 5-stars, and especially so in Hong Kong. Homely and rather mumsy rooms are equally soothing, and unobstructed views over the harbour or towards Hong Kong's stunning modern architecture are big pluses, as is the excellent location just minutes stroll from Central MTR station. With recent renovations the food and beverage outlets are steering away from fine dining to broaden their choice and appeal. Still, Toscana, with its northern Italian cuisine remains a firm favourite for many in Hong Kong.

Rates from: **US$ 205**
Star rating: ★ ★ ★ ★ ★
Bellhop rating: 🛎 🛎 🛎 🛎 ½

Value:	7.97	Facilities:	8.37
Staff:	8.94	Restaurants:	8.51
Location:	9.04	Families:	6.98
Cleanliness:	9.09		

The Royal Pacific Hotel & Towers

33 Canton Road, Tsim Sha Tsui (W), Kowloon, Hong Kong
T: +852 2736 1188 **F**: +852 2736 1212
http://www.asia-hotels.com/hotelinfo/Royal_Pacific_Towers/

The golden cuboids located right on top of the Macau Ferry Terminal in Tsim Sha Tsui flank the shopping and entertainment district, and are only a few minutes walk from the MTR through pleasant Kowloon Park. The Royal Pacific has a small but capable business centre and is ideally placed for business hop offs by sea to Macau and major cities in China, or much closer to home of course. But it is mainly aimed at tourists, and offers good and tidy albeit rather small rooms, some with pleasing views. The hotel is compact, cramming in practical and active facilities. Space is well utilised, and the staff are warm and friendly. The older block is perhaps of good 3-star stock and the newer one more like a 4-star. Decent, trustworthy and very competitively priced, it dominates its particular niche in the market.

Rates from: **US$ 71**
Star rating: ★ ★ ★ ½
Bellhop rating: 🛎🛎🛎🛎

Value:	8.00	Facilities:	8.05
Staff:	8.17	Restaurants:	7.49
Location:	8.67	Families:	5.99
Cleanliness:	8.58		

Sheraton Hong Kong Hotel & Towers

20 Nathan Road, Tsim Sha Tsui (W), Kowloon, Hong Kong
T: +852 2732 6843 **F**: +852 2367 5097
http://www.asia-hotels.com/hotelinfo/Sheraton_HK/

Smart and sleek, the Sheraton is no more than a good 5-star hotel, but certainly no less. The location is tough to better for tourists, or indeed business travellers, enjoying a unique spot on tourist Mecca – Nathan Road. It also enjoys splendid harbour views from many of its unfussy and predictably smart rooms. The vista from the Sky Lounge is really quite superb, especially at night. The food and beverage is a particular pull, with a full range of flavours on offer. The popular basement bar Someplace Else is one of the area's prime singles' joints. Plus the outdoor heated roof pool and jacuzzi make for an excellent recreational space. The underlying bones of the hotel are several decades old, but the newly applied gloss following recent renovations bring it all up to date. Nothing fancy, but the Sheraton is a good and trustworthy all-rounder.

Rates from: **US$ 131**
Star rating: ★ ★ ★ ★ ★
Bellhop rating: 🛎🛎🛎🛎 ½

Value:	7.76	Facilities:	8.18
Staff:	8.28	Restaurants:	8.06
Location:	8.85	Families:	6.50
Cleanliness:	8.56		

YMCA - The Salisbury

41 Salisbury Road, Tsim Sha Tsui (W), Kowloon, Hong Kong
T: +852 2268 7000 F: +852 2739 9315
http://www.asia-hotels.com/hotelinfo/YMCA_-_The_Salisbury/

This fantastic budget hotel is not some murky and dingy dormitory smelling of old socks. It is exactly what a budget hotel should be and a product well above what one expects from a YMCA. The first draw is the unbeatable location overlooking Hong Kong harbour and very close to the Star Ferry in Tsim Sha Tsui – it is difficult to be more centrally placed than this. It is not a hotel in the true sense of the word and not surprisingly there are no bellhops or fancy extras, it is strictly a no-frills affair. Whereas 'no-frills' often means low standards and a level of frustration, the opposite is true here. Standards are delivered, and maintenance is impressively high. The atmosphere is definitely youthful with bright adolescent colour combinations and notice boards plastered with details of

local educational courses and outdoor activities. Groups of kids, rather than executives, drift around.

The indoor facilities are comparable to any pocket-sized leisure centre in standard and appearance. An indoor pool, rock climbing wall, aerobics classes and squash courts are just some of the sports on offer and guests are welcome to join in. A small chapel also holds services, a unique and welcome option for churchgoers, but the Christian element only gently filters through for non-believers. Bright rooms are excellent and stupendous value. Recently renovated with more than a hint of IKEA, they are spick-and-span and equipped with useful bits and bobs such as kettles and in-room safes. They are reasonably sized too, a bonus in a town where many cheaper hotel rooms make

you feel like a battery hen. In addition to all of this the upper front-facing rooms have some of the best views in Hong Kong, spanning out over one of the world's great harbours. The YMCA guest enjoys an even better angle than at the posh Peninsula next door. The restaurants are so-so and personal service is absent but staff are all friendly. And anyway, who cares? There is so much else going for this budget beacon.

Rates from: US$ 77
Star rating: ★★★ ½
Bellhop rating: 👍👍👍👍 ½

Value:	8.57	Facilities:	7.91
Staff:	8.11	Restaurants:	6.59
Location:	9.04	Families:	6.54
Cleanliness:	8.52		

INDIA

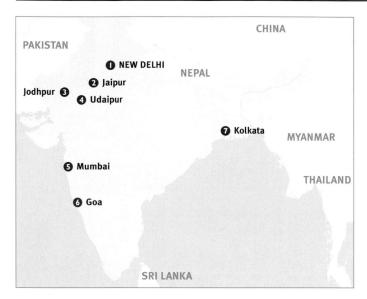

Awesome India is one of the ultimate travel experiences. Surely no other country possesses the diversity and depth of this mesmerising land. The engrossing culture is stunningly exotic and rich. The land varies wildly, from sweltering tropics to the unforgiving icy extremes of the mighty Himalayas. And the turbulent wake of ethnic variation, eventful history and political strife has led to an equally disparate people, filling every possible niche of human existence. India overflows with beauty and toil. The sights, sounds, smells and tastes will push your senses to their very limits.

India as we know it was born of the legacy of British colonial rule. Formerly a patchwork of feuding princely states, the subcontinent became the jewel in the crown of the British Empire. The independence movement led by world-shaker Mahatma Gandhi

sounded the death knell for European colonialism around the globe, and the partition that accompanied the forced British withdrawal still drags on today. The largest democracy on the planet is barely holding together a most complicated nation, and the traditional caste system, although formerly outlawed, has ingrained the social strata. The miniscule elite's vast wealth is contradicted

by overwhelming poverty. Age-old religious tensions are fuelled by fundamentalism and irresponsible elements in the political arena.

Although immensely rewarding, travelling around India is hard going. The nation grapples with widespread illiteracy, poor infrastructure and a distinct lack of services. Unless backpacking (and India is one of the most fascinating backpacking destinations), then

colonial structures. Spirituality courses through the nation's veins, not surprising as India gave rise to both Hinduism and Buddhism. Sprawling Delhi and Mumbai (Bombay) are traditional gateways but both are worth escaping for the jewels that lie within. Agra hosts the exquisite white marble Taj Mahal, one of the Seven Wonders of the World, and to the south are the striking spires of Sri Meenakshi temple in Madurai. The golden shores of Goa were first colonised by the Portuguese, then later by long-haired hippies, and although it is slowly heading upmarket it retains much of its original appeal. Rajasthan, though, is most visitors' highlight – Jaipur, Jodhpur, Jaiselmer, Udaipur and Puskar provide an enthralling variety of palaces, forts, havelis and bazaars.

flying is the only comfortable and practical way to traverse the subcontinent. The rail network takes most of the strain, but has seen slow modernisation. Car provides an acceptable alternative but take a driver, as the roads will test even the steeliest nerves.

With a population of more than a billion, India is second to China as the most populous country on earth. Yet you will hear few investors referring to India as 'the world's second-biggest market' with the same salivating optimism as with China. Business practices can be frustrating with corruption undermining what ought to be an industrial powerhouse. International hotel chains often invest in new properties only to

have local partners sneakily edge them out. Standards inevitably slip and the result is that the quality of the hotels varies wildly. Star ratings are not always reliable and, relative to the rest of Asia, are typically inflated, so it pays to do your research before you check-in. Generally speaking Indian hotels are bad (some are horrendous!) but glowing exceptions do exist. A few prominent chains are fittingly represented and India's better heritage hotels possess a magic that you just cannot get elsewhere.

Despite the challenges and head-scratching contradictions, the country is laden with wondrous sights to captivate the visitor. It is liberally dressed with incredible temples and forts and inspired

The Indian climate is as diverse as the country itself, from the searing heat of Chennai (Madras) to the cool hill stations of Shimla. The seasons are loosely divided into the hot (February to May), the wet (June to October) and the most temperate season, the cool (November to January). With a slice of humour, adventurous travellers who are willing to invest a little time and effort will find India to be one of the pinnacles of travel. And the gentle, unflappable Indians, with their alternative outlook on life have the inane ability to make you laugh, or at other times, cry.

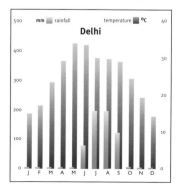

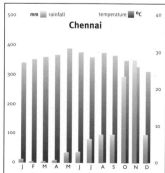

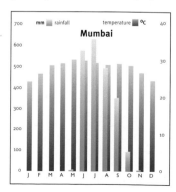

Ajit Bhawan

Jodhpur 342006, Rajasthan, India
T: +91 291 510 410 F: +91 291 510 674
http://www.asia-hotels.com/hotelinfo/Ajit_Bhawan/

The engaging subcontinent can sap your strength but the Ajit Bhawan is an absolute oasis for weary travellers. This unusual hotel is a refreshingly unique and comfortable abode and a thoroughly enjoyable experience. The major appeal must lie in the Ajit Bhawan's rich heritage and personal charm. The century-old property is robustly built from brick and stone and topped with Mughal-style domes. Within its fortified walls lie well-tended gardens – a sharp contrast to the dusty arid plains around Jodhpur.

The initial feel is more like an inn than a hotel. The small lobby and public areas are caught in an enchanting time warp. Stately woods are omnipresent. When sinking into the comfy chairs in the Gol Kamra Lounge or the Prince's Bar you become aware of faces peering from the black-and-white photos and noble paintings of the past. Stuffed animal heads also eye you up.

Outside is an entourage of lovingly restored vintage cars, some of which are available for hire. Lining a winding path are charismatic igloo-style bungalows. Each follows a different theme, whether it is fading occupations such as the Weaver Room, or more socially elevated settings like the Warrior or Princess Rooms. The cylindrical shape and authentic individual decor is truly arresting. Each room is decked out with corresponding handicrafts and family curios and chunky traditional furniture. Some even have trees growing right through them, while others sport stained glass windows and clanking arched wooden doors, but all maintain spotless bathrooms. Outside you can chill out on your terrace or drift off on the lawn in a hammock. The Heritage Building houses the Deluxe Rooms set around the attractive and refreshingly cool pool, and are a little more up to date and include TVs.

Beyond the pool and restaurant there is very little in the way of hotel facilities. There is the bonus of well-done entertainment put on in the evenings with a pleasant buffet. Staff are especially friendly even if some do muddle things at times. The hotel also has the additional benefit of being just a few minutes from the town centre. Blending heritage, personal service and a fantastically low price, the Ajit Bhawan is a regular favourite for those who really know India.

Rates from: **US$ 42**
Star rating: ★ ★ ★ ½
Bellhop rating: **Editor's pick**

Value:	n/a	Facilities:	n/a
Staff:	n/a	Restaurants:	n/a
Location:	n/a	Families:	n/a
Cleanliness:	n/a		

Imperial Hotel New Delhi

1 Janpath, New Delhi 110011, India
T: +91 11 2334 1234 **F:** +91 11 2334 2255
http://www.asia-hotels.com/hotelinfo/Imperial_/

The Imperial is a perfect blend of the nostalgic elegance of historic New Delhi and the modern requirements of today's hotels. Built in 1931 as part of Delhi's rejuvenation, the hotel maintains much of its original aesthetics but constant restoration keeps it very functional. Located centrally on Janpath, the Imperial is just a short stroll from the tourist heartland, Connaught Place. The area is somewhat chaotic but the hotel is intelligently set well back. The Imperial is as stately and proud as its name would suggest, with plenty of historical throwbacks. Ceilings are high, paintings abound and little touches include brass fittings and historic photos. Spacious rooms split into four wings echo this colonial ambience, but have Internet ports to bring you up to date. One striking aspect of the Imperial is the outstanding food. Restaurants are lavish and the food first-class – check out the wood-carved interior and menu of the Spice Route – it is no surprise the likes of Gandhi, Nehru and Kipling dined here.

Rates from: **US$ 189**
Star rating: ★ ★ ★ ★ ★
Bellhop rating: 🛎 🛎 🛎 🛎 ½

Value:	8.17	Facilities:	8.14
Staff:	8.56	Restaurants:	8.47
Location:	8.64	Families:	5.89
Cleanliness:	8.56		

The Leela Kempinski Hotel

Sahar, Andheri, Mumbai 400059, Maharashtra, India
T: +91 22 5691 1234 **F:** +91 22 5691 1212
http://www.asia-hotels.com/hotelinfo/Leela_Kempinski_Hotel_The/

Mumbai has three or four hotels with international clout, and one of these is the Leela Kempinski. The Leela is a bold angled block with two flanks opening out like welcoming arms. It is situated 25 kilometres away from the city centre and lies round the corner from both the domestic and international airports, making it most convenient for those wanting to avoid the rather odorous trip into town. Given the location it has more space to play with and the 11 acres of exterior grounds are more like those of a resort than a city hotel, with a huge palm-fringed swimming pool and a jogging track. The 423 rooms and suites are functionally modern with nice touches of Indian decor; and the business, dining and leisure facilities are extensive, making the hotel a popular choice for those arriving late at night or transferring through.

Rates from: **US$ 183**
Star rating: ★ ★ ★ ★ ★
Bellhop rating: 🛎 🛎 🛎 🛎 ½

Value:	7.78	Facilities:	8.30
Staff:	8.36	Restaurants:	8.36
Location:	7.93	Families:	7.45
Cleanliness:	8.33		

Lake Palace Udaipur

Pichola Lake, Udaipur 313001, Rajasthan, India
T: +91 294 252 8800 **F:** +91 294 252 8700
http://www.asia-hotels.com/hotelinfo/Lake_Palace_Udaipur

The James Bond movie *Octopussy* was partially set in India with much of the filming taking place in the delightful historic Udaipur. The closing scene saw Bond with requisite damsel in the splendour of a sumptuous floating palace. The location chosen for this scene was none other than the Lake Palace, one of the highlights of this romantic lakeside city.

The Taj Group's Lake Palace is one of the world's most celebrated concept hotels. The 17th-century pleasure retreat was originally built for royalty and is spectacularly set in the middle of Lake Pichola. Various Maharajas would impress their ladies here, and the old magic still works. The Lake Palace has a reputation that precedes it, and when drifting towards it on the hotel shuttle boat it is hard not to picture a majestic feast of Rajasthani indulgence.

Now for a small reality check. The compact property is actually a little weathered and worn in places, and there is more than a hint of the 1970s about the interior. It is not a disappointment (so long as your imagination has not run away with you) but it is quite ordinary in service, facilities and maintenance, although renovations are under way. People come here for its historic depth, lake views and the architecture – there are characteristic twisting Indian pillars, ornate windows, intricate inlay archways and whitewashed walls.

The 85 rooms fall into two categories – the ordinary and the out-of-the-ordinary. Ordinary rooms, or standard, are cosy and come with views of the central lily pond or terrace, and for the next category up, lake views. The out-of-the-ordinary rooms, or suites, are the highlight of the Lake Palace, massive cool and airy with stained glass windows and bright tiled floors – some even have antique swings. There is a small pool and the main restaurant is good – certainly not always a prerequisite even in top Indian hotels. Despite the droughts which can shrink the lake, the location plus cultural depth makes this one of the most fascinating hotel experiences on the subcontinent.

Rates from: US$ 271
Star rating: ★ ★ ★ ★ ★
Bellhop rating: 🔔 🔔 🔔 🔔 🔔

Value:	8.54	Facilities:	8.34
Staff:	8.96	Restaurants:	8.56
Location:	9.70	Families:	6.61
Cleanliness:	8.96		

The Leela Palace Goa

Cavelossim, Mobor, Goa 403731, India
T:+91 832 871 234 **F:** +91 832 871 352
http://www.asia-hotels.com/hotelinfo/Leela_Palace_Goa_The/

The Leela Palace encapsulates some of the very best that India has to offer – history, hedonism, extensive gourmet dining, an intriguing menu of Ayurvedic spa treatments, naturally beautiful landscapes and luxurious accommodation that is a blend of styles both ancient and modern.

Set on a peninsula wedged between the River Sal and the Indian Ocean, fringed by a 22-kilometre beach and set in 75 acres of landscaped grounds, the Leela's centrepiece is an extensive free-form artificial lagoon. Taking its architectural cue from Portuguese colonial days and the

13th-century Vijayanagara Palace, the resort's rooms, one- and two-bedroom suites are supremely comfortable, decorated with richly textured Indian fabrics and all come with spacious marbled bathrooms and full balcony or private terrace. The more expensive accommodation includes a private pool.

The resort, of course, is not the popular Goa of hippiefied raves, but a much more rarefied locale. A 300-metre strip of beach is reserved for guests, who can also play a round or two on the Leela's par-three, 9-hole golf course. A trio of floodlit tennis courts and a

gaming room offers further diversion, but the resort's trump card is its spa. Free consultations are provided by the resident Ayurvedic doctor – but can anyone doubt the wisdom of self-prescribing something along the lines of the Pizhichil treatment, in which two therapists pour warm oil all over your body in a special rhythmic pattern while simultaneously massaging? Other stellar offerings include a medicinal rice pudding scrub and an oil massage done solely with the therapist's feet.

Some or all of the above are bound to work up an appetite, and while Riverside's Italian fare and views of the trawlers at anchor are excellent, it is really the Indian specialties at Jamavar that excel. Late-night action is provided in abundance by Aqua, the lounge-cum-discotheque, which has an extensive range of cognacs and cigars over which Goa's famed sunsets can be enjoyed.

Rates from: US$ 222
Star rating: ★ ★ ★ ★ ★
Bellhop rating: 🛎 🛎 🛎 🛎 ½

Value:	7.92	Facilities:	8.65
Staff:	8.51	Restaurants:	8.45
Location:	8.31	Families:	7.75
Cleanliness:	8.84		

Maurya Sheraton Hotel & Towers

Diplomatic Enclave, Sadar Patel Marg, New Delhi 110021, India
T: +91 11 2611 2233 **F:** +91 11 2611 3333
http://www.asia-hotels.com/hotelinfo/Maurya_Sheraton/

India's 5-stars are very much hit and miss, but this one is certainly one of Delhi's best and holds its own internationally. The location, halfway between the airport and city centre, in the green diplomatic district definitely helps to mellow the ambience of this rugged choking city. Opened in 1978 but well maintained, this spacious hotel is bright and open, with a large lobby. Of the 515 rooms, the new ITC One Wing is a class apart; pitched as '7-star' by the hotel it is aimed at the very top-end traveller with 76 private residence-style rooms including personal butler and exclusive lounge with a range of state-of-the-art facilities. Not to be confused with the separately housed 107-room Tower Club or the 55 Executive Club rooms in the main hotel. Of the very good facilities, the North Indian restaurant Bukhara is perhaps the best known with many guests raving about its sensational menu and cosy setting.

Rates from: **US$ 90**
Star rating: ★★★★★
Bellhop rating: 🐾🐾🐾🐾

Value:	7.71	Facilities:	8.21
Staff:	8.17	Restaurants:	8.55
Location:	7.83	Families:	6.71
Cleanliness:	8.24		

Oberoi Grand Kolkata

15 Jawaharlal Nehru Road, Kolkata 700013, India
T: +91 33 2249 2323 **F:** +91 33 2249 1217
http://www.asia-hotels.com/hotelinfo/Oberoi_Grand_Calcutta/

This classic property is generally regarded as the best in Kolkata and, therefore by definition, Eastern India. The Oberoi Grand is indeed grand in the flesh. The noble architecture and design draws on its Victorian past. The hotel's dignified marble lobby with green palms and leather sofas leads on to a healthy range of first-class facilities. In the 213 rooms, DVD/laser disc are standard as are dataports, voicemail and Internet connections. Outside, the 24-hour business centre and conference rooms are excellent. Leisure facilities include a fine courtyard pool and the local rarity of a genuinely inviting health club. The Thai, Indian and international restaurants are certainly among the best in town, offering superb decor as well as tantalising flavours, with a wheelbarrow load of vegetarian options on each menu. Set in central Chowringhee district, the Oberoi Grand is well located for business or visiting the city's places of interest.

Rates from: **US$ 100**
Star rating: ★★★★★
Bellhop rating: 🐾🐾🐾🐾 ½

Value:	8.62	Facilities:	8.41
Staff:	8.57	Restaurants:	8.67
Location:	8.43	Families:	6.62
Cleanliness:	8.52		

Oberoi Towers

Nariman Point, Mumbai 400021, India
T: +91 22 5632 4343 **F:** +91 22 5632 4142
http://www.asia-hotels.com/hotelinfo/Oberoi_The/

The Oberoi Towers is a bit of a conundrum. It is actually just half a hotel rather than an independent entity. The Oberoi and the Oberoi Towers are effectively two wings of the same hotel, split in half supposedly for tax purposes. The Oberoi, with its cavernous atrium and butler service tends to act as the executive wing of this benchmark complex, and be the residence of choice for international dignitaries, while the bigger and taller Oberoi Towers is the more affordable choice of business travellers. But this semi-detached existence in no way diminishes Mumbai's top business hotel and facilities in both wings are readily available to the Towers' guests.

Perched on Nariman Point, the hotel is situated perfectly for business as it overlooks the CBD. It also has the bonus of flanking Back Bay and gazes out across the Arabian Sea. Both the tourist and entertainment areas of Colaba and the Churchgate Railway Station

district lie also within a convenient radius.

The Oberoi Towers offers Superior Rooms with city outlooks, Premium Rooms that oversee the harbour and Deluxe Rooms with wonderful ocean views. The 575 rooms are not all that different from those in the other half of the hotel, but are sedate and certainly designed with the business traveller in mind. Each room has gentle colours, generous space and a large bathroom and is fitted with

practical extras such as fax machines (on request) and dataports.

The lobby is filled with activity as scores of business people engage in casual meetings or tap away at their laptops. Taking both wings together, facilities are broader and more up to date than just about any other hotel in the city. Importantly, business amenities come out tops with a first-class 24-hour business centre. The choice of restaurants is varied and aimed squarely at the international guest – in total there are six serving a mix of Indian, Italian and continental cuisine. There is a good health club to burn off any excess intake while two outdoor pools take advantage of Mumbai's typically hot weather.

Rates from: **US$ 124**
Star rating: ★ ★ ★ ★ ★
Bellhop rating: ♙ ♙ ♙ ♙

Value:	7.15	Facilities:	8.17
Staff:	8.19	Restaurants:	8.32
Location:	8.44	Families:	6.76
Cleanliness:	8.39		

Rajvilas Jaipur

Goner Road, Jaipur 303012, Rajasthan, India
T: +91 141 268 0101 **F**: +91 141 268 0202
http://www.asia-hotels.com/hotelinfo/Rajvilas_Hotel_The_Oberoi/

At some stage or another just about everyone has fantasised about living in a palace, waited on hand and foot in opulent surrounds, the monarch of all they survey. Rajvilas turns the fantasy into reality, and even if the 'king (and/or queen) for a day' has to checkout and pay the bill sooner or later, the experience is unforgettable.

Rajasthan is India at its most exotic and colourful best, a one-time cluster of principalities infused with a proud martial history and bedecked with ancient palaces. Rajvilas is just one such former stately home, converted into a conglomeration of four very different sorts of accommodation set in 30 acres of beautifully manicured gardens. For the ultimate regal vision, you need to stay at one of the trio of villas, each with an outdoor dining pavilion and a private swimming pool that is heated in winter. Inside, four-poster beds draped with mosquito nets, metre-thick walls and latticed windows imbue a heartening feeling of security. The 13 luxury tents are rather more Rajasthan. Forget camping – these are fitted out with teak floors, air-conditioning, and beautifully appointed interiors while the bathroom is centred around the magnificent colonial-style free-standing cast-iron tub. A combination of these two accommodations is provided by the single-tented villa, which has a four-seater dining table and its own garden. However, the main body of Rajvilas' accommodation comes in the 54 Deluxe Rooms, clumped in groups of four or six around a central courtyard. There is a king-size bed, dressing room and walk-in closet and the ensuite

marble bathroom has a sunken tub as well as a separate shower overlooking a private walled garden. And steeped in history though Rajvilas may be, wherever you are staying in the hotel there is satellite TV, CD and laser disc players and connections for the Internet.

While Rajasthan waits outside Rajvilas' gates – be it rides in a horse-drawn buggy, watching polo matches or absorbing the palaces, forts and bazaars of the nearby Pink City of Jaipur – it is worth spending some time in the hotel simply to revel in the atmosphere. You can comfortably while away the hours in the Rajwada Library and Bar, where there are scores of books lined up on teak shelves, a white Italian marble fireplace and board games like chess and backgammon. Similarly, it would be a pity to rush meals in the Surya Mahal dining room, a study in Rajasthani decor with sculpted sandstone pillars, scalloped arches and handcrafted brass doors. Local culinary delights are served in silver thalis, but the kitchen can also whip up light fusion cuisine with elements from Asia and Europe. You can also eat alfresco in the adjoining courtyard, with entertainment laid on by traditional folk dancers.

For active types, the Rajvilas has two floodlit tennis courts and an immaculate croquet lawn, as well as an outdoor swimming pool and jacuzzi. Just by the pool, the hotel's spa is contained in a restored haveli whose walls are adorned with hand-painted frescoes and whose therapists are skilled in a wide range of holistic treatments. One of the most relaxing activities is to take part in a yoga session in the precincts of a nearby centuries-old Shiva temple. This ancient philosophical exercise was devised in India, and it perfectly encapsulates the gracious recreation that is found everywhere at Rajvilas.

Rates from: **US$ 274**
Star rating: ★ ★ ★ ★ ★
Bellhop rating: 👍 👍 👍 👍 👍

Value:	8.38	Facilities:	9.20
Staff:	9.28	Restaurants:	8.80
Location:	8.64	Families:	6.90
Cleanliness:	9.57		

Rambagh Palace Hotel

Bhawani Singh Road, Jaipur 302005, Rajasthan, India
T: +91 141 238 1919 **F:** +91 141 238 1098
http://www.asia-hotels.com/hotelinfo/Rambagh_Palace_The/

The Rambagh Palace is an Indian heritage hotel in the grandest and most palatial form. This distinctive property, which graces the Rajasthan capital of Jaipur and revels in the city's beautiful history and architecture, is impressive in both scale and presentation. Lying a few kilometres from the walled Pink City, it is built from white marble and sits in 47 acres of manicured gardens abloom with ashoka, bougainvillea and lantana trees and preening peacocks.

The Rambagh started out as a subtle four-room pavilion built for Maharani Chandrawatji's lady-in-waiting back in 1835. It was expanded into a hunting lodge in 1887 and was officially named as a

palace in 1925 when Maharaja Sawai Man Singh II decided to move in. 1957 saw it become an elite hotel which the prestigious Taj Group started to manage in 1972. The graceful Rajasthan architecture was built in royal proportions and to lofty standards. The sweeping tiled floors, ornate columns and arches and regal domes took skills and craft to assemble.

Standard and Superior Rooms are comfy and themed, but quite spartan as far as luxury hotels go – however the suites are anything but standard. The four which formerly housed the royal family: the Prince's Suite, Maharani Suite and brace of Maharaja Suites are stunning in their grandeur and grace. Picture opulent Victorian wood-panelled rooms or elegant white marble chambers complete with a trickling fountain. The remaining Historical Suites and Luxury Rooms lie somewhere between these suites and the Superior Rooms, each is uniquely decorated and filled with character.

Service here is very idiosyncratic – most staff do a magnificent job

but with others it comes with outstretched hand. The facilities though can draw few complaints. The grandeur of the Suvarna Mahal dining hall makes a wonderfully majestic dinner setting, the intricate decor of the Neel Mahal 24-hour restaurant is equally pleasing to the eye and the palate and the Polo Bar is one of the most upmarket places to relax in Jaipur. Tennis, squash and an indoor pool, with leaded windows, panelled walls and delicate carvings, are some of the recreational pursuits on offer. And in true Rajasthan tradition, horse riding can be arranged or, having visited Jantar Mantar, the remarkable stone observatory in Jaipur, map your own destiny with the in-house astrologer.

Rates from: **US$ 109**
Star rating: ★ ★ ★ ★ ★
Bellhop rating: 🛎 🛎 🛎 🛎 🛎

Value:	8.59	Facilities:	8.78
Staff:	9.19	Restaurants:	8.52
Location:	9.33	Families:	7.41
Cleanliness:	9.11		

Taj Bengal

34B Belvedere Road, Alipore Kolkata 700027, India
T: +91 33 2223 3939 **F**: +91 33 2223 1766
http://www.asia-hotels.com/hotelinfo/Taj_Bengal/

One of the best hotels in East India, the Taj Bengal sits comfortably in green surroundings a little south of the Maidan, and just a few kilometres from Kolkata's CBD. Though not particularly spectacular the Taj remains a true respite in a mad city. The exterior is modest and angular, but inside is a trim and tidy luxury hotel with a striking 1,100-square-metre atrium lobby full of tall palms, marble floors and elegant chandeliers. Business travellers mainly frequent the hotel attracted by the international-class facilities and services. The broad outdoor pool is perhaps the centrepiece, with a popular poolside barbeque sizzling away from November to March. The other restaurants offer quality, variety and in the case of the Hub, 24-hour flexibility. Incognito is one of the city's top discos. Rooms are fair with Internet access and dataports but the service levels are very high, as one would expect from the Taj Group.

Rates from: US$ 133
Star rating: ★ ★ ★ ★ ★
Bellhop rating: 🐾 🐾 🐾 🐾 ½

Value:	7.64	Facilities:	8.26
Staff:	8.46	Restaurants:	8.46
Location:	7.60	Families:	7.68
Cleanliness:	8.30		

Taj Mahal Hotel New Delhi

1 Mansingh Road, New Delhi 110011, India
T: +91 11 2302 6162 **F**: +91 11 2302 6070
http://www.asia-hotels.com/hotelinfo/Taj_Mahal_Hotel/

The well-established Taj Mahal is one of Delhi's best hotels. It is primarily aimed at business travellers, focusing on comfortable practicality. Hugely welcome is the fully equipped 24-hour business centre. All the predictable yet very presentable 300 rooms have dataports for modems and PCs, and in-room faxes. With roaming wireless connectivity and a cyber butler, you can be online just about anywhere in the hotel. The higher-floor Taj Club offers additional perks including transfers, private check-in and further business facilities including valet service and meeting rooms. Celebrated restaurants are centred mainly on Indian and Chinese themes, but there is the 24-hour international outlet, Machan, especially useful for the jet-lagged guest. The Taj also has the advantage of a central location near New Delhi's most famous landmark, India Gate, so is well positioned for tourists as well. For those taking time out, the hotel offers a decent fitness centre and a very generous outdoor pool.

Rates from: US$ 100
Star rating: ★ ★ ★ ★ ★
Bellhop rating: 🐾 🐾 🐾 🐾 🐾

Value:	8.23	Facilities:	8.73
Staff:	8.88	Restaurants:	8.80
Location:	8.76	Families:	7.25
Cleanliness:	8.93		

Taj Mahal Hotel Mumbai

Apollo Bunder, Colaba, Mumbai 400001, India
T: +91 22 5665 3366 **F:** +91 22 5665 0300
http://www.asia-hotels.com/hotelinfo/Taj_Mahal_Mumbai/

Opened in 1903, the Taj Mahal Hotel Mumbai is the grandest hotel in the city. The stunning Edwardian architecture is a distinctive landmark – the classic Mumbai postcard portrays the colonial Gateway of India archway aside this majestic hotel. It was built by local tycoon J.N. Tata who, so the story goes, indignant at being turned away from a top hotel on racist grounds, decided to build his own. True or not, the end result is a superb example of the architecture of the day, not to mention a fitting raspberry at the British Raj.

The Taj is gracious and distinguished inside and out. Some areas such as the lobby are sleek, businesslike and modern, offering contemporary luxury and comfort. Other areas bask in the glory of the Taj's portentous past – the beautifully ornate iron staircase is of particular note. Palatial yet tasteful banquet rooms could potentially mingle with the royal residences of Europe. The Harbour Bar is Mumbai's oldest licensed bar and offers a superior venue for a tipple, albeit with a stiff upper lip. Souk, the new West

Asian rooftop restaurant serves a mix of Lebanese, Greek and Moroccan with some fine views. With the exception of the more casual Shamiana, all the restaurants are elegant and highly refined. The Zodiac Grill with its domed astrological ceiling, full grand piano and white-gloved butler service is one of the city's more exclusive (and pricey) establishments.

The business and leisure facilities are world-class, but if one had to be picky the rooms are a tad

below par in places (although many have been recently upgraded). The comfy Heritage rooms are all different with varying touches in decor and furniture but feeling at times old rather than historical. The 1973 addition of the Tower Wing slightly blemished the exterior grace of the hotel, but the rooms within are more modern and many enjoy the same superb sea views as the original Heritage Wing.

There is no doubt that the illustrious Taj is one of the most characteristic hotels in India and goes a long way toward meeting its founder's objective of conceiving Bombay's (as it was then), if not Asia's, finest hotel.

Rates from: **US$ 129**
Star rating: ★★★★★
Bellhop rating: 🛎🛎🛎🛎 ½

Value:	7.54	Facilities:	8.24
Staff:	8.27	Restaurants:	8.42
Location:	8.52	Families:	7.09
Cleanliness:	8.32		

INDONESIA

The ebb and flow of troubles that have washed over the Indonesian archipelago for much of the last five years reached their apogee with the terrorist bombings in Bali in October 2002. In the wake of the financial crash of the late 1990s, governmental shenanigans in Jakarta and unrest in the remainder of the country, the attack was the last thing that Indonesia needed.

At the time of writing, international advisories still warned against non-essential travel to Indonesia, and the decision to go there remains very much a personal choice. That this is a source of regret cannot be overstated, as the country's 13,000-plus islands, strung from Sumatra in the west to Irian Jaya in the east, make up one of the most fascinating parts of Southeast Asia.

More than 1,000 years ago traders from as far away as China were sailing to the spice islands of Indonesia, and the same

commodity drew Europeans as early as the 16th century. Dutch colonialists subsequently gained a strong foothold in the country, and

– after the Japanese occupation during World War II – Indonesia only finally achieved independence in 1949 after several years of

and many of the intermediate hotels can be guaranteed to provide extremely comfortable stays. Perhaps the best value of all, Indonesia's guesthouses, or losmen, are often family run and very hospitable.

Straddling the equator, Indonesia has two main seasons – wet between October and April, and dry for the rest of the year, with slight geographical variations. The wet season is by no means unbearable, as storms tend to come in sudden bursts and once they have subsided it will be dry for the rest of the day. The Christmas holiday season traditionally attracts a horde of visitors from Australia and the rest of the world. Still, the political climate is what will really be affecting visitors' plans and it is only to be hoped for that it will stablise soon.

armed struggle. The decades that followed were marked by a gradual prosperity, interspersed with some domestic upheavals, and tourism only started to take off in the late 1960s, with Bali leading the way, as it has done ever since.

First port of call for many visitors is the capital, Jakarta, a maelstrom of a metropolis which acts as a magnet for Indonesians from all over the country who have come to look for work. Bandung, a lovely art deco city which the Dutch planned as an alternative capital, sits in the hills to the east, while further across Java are stunning man-made wonders like the 1,100-year-old Buddhist temple of Borobudur and natural marvels like the dormant volcanic Mount Bromo. The Hindu enclave of Bali, most tellingly described as 'The Morning of the World', remains perhaps the most picturesque and intriguing of all the Indonesian islands, while further east Lombok and Flores are less developed but still hold many attractions for holidaymakers. Komodo is famed for its giant lizards, cunningly marketed as 'dragons', while divers tend to flock to Sulawesi, and in particular to Manado, where Bunaken Island is ranked as one of the top underwater sites in the world. More difficult to get to, the

Bandas also have some superb coral reefs as well as a number of statuesque colonial forts. Sumatra, whose oil, rubber, pepper and coffee contribute largely to the Indonesian economy, has one of the country's most diverse ethnic populations. Irian Jaya remains very much the 'wild east', however its trekking opportunities through the little travelled hinterland cannot be matched.

With a wealth of culture, natural beauty and marine sporting facilities, Indonesia has all the potential to become one of the region's top tourist destinations. Families travelling here will find their children are greeted with especial warmth, providing an instant entrée to the local community.

The phrase 'paradise resort' has been used so frequently it has almost lost its currency, but it really does apply to some of Indonesia's top-flight accommodation. Aman is the name that most obviously springs to mind, with three properties in Bali and two elsewhere, and the country's major destinations all host some very acceptable 5-stars. Not that you always need to shell out top dollar, as inexpensive labour leads to high staffing levels

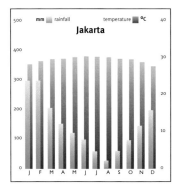

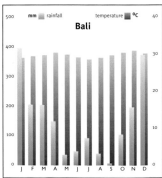

Alila Ubud

Gianyar 80572, Bali, Indonesia
T: +62 361 975 963 **F**: +62 361 975 968
http://www.asia-hotels.com/hotelinfo/Alila_Ubud/

It used to be called the Chedi, and it used to be one of the most popular hotels in Bali's arts and culture capital. Now re-emerging in a new incarnation as the Alila Ubud, old friends (and they are many) of this stunning hotel will heave a sigh of relief to hear that very little has been altered. You still wind your way through rice paddies and past stately banyan trees to get down to the hotel from the main road, an intermission between everyday life and the nigh delirious seclusion of the Alila. The swimming pool still looks like a slab of polished basalt perched above the forested slopes leading down to the Ayung River. The 56 Deluxe Rooms and seven villas, clustered together like local village houses, still revel in panoramic views and intimate interiors, with a design that melds traditional Balinese with modern geometry:

smooth plaster walls and concrete support thatched roofs, terrazzo tiles blend with gravel and crushed rock, wood meets glass. The brasserie-style Western, local and oriental dishes served up beneath the towering coconut pillars of the Restaurant are just as mouth-watering as ever they were. You can stand and be sluiced beneath the spa's waterfall showers that burst forth like a jungle cataract before

and after an outdoor treatment. In sum, the Alila is the new face of an old friend.

Remarkably for a hotel in this day and age, guests will search their accommodation in vain for a television. The inference of course is that there is so much else to do here other than goggle, and that this is meant to be an escape from the intrusions of the modern world. Plus, you only need to look out of the window for a 24-hour entertainment channel.

Rates from: **US$ 215**
Star rating: ★ ★ ★ ★ ★
Bellhop rating: 🛎 🛎 🛎 🛎 ½

Value:	8.02	Facilities:	8.48
Staff:	9.05	Restaurants:	8.76
Location:	9.11	Families:	6.09
Cleanliness:	9.18		

Amandari

Ubud 80571, Bali, Indonesia
T: +62 361 975 333 **F**: +62 361 975 335
http://www.asia-hotels.com/hotelinfo/Amandari/

For as long as anyone in Kedewatan can remember, every six months the villagers have donned full temple dress and walked a sacred path that leads to the Ayung River gorge, where they pay their respects to the spirits that live there. The path leads straight through Amandari, but nothing was built over it so as to avoid offending local sensibilities.

While the resort's 30 free-standing suites were under construction, workmen uncovered a tiger carved in a rock above a sacred spring. A sculptor made a fair copy of it, which was placed in a sea of grass in the colonnaded courtyard across from Amandari's entrance. Shortly after, a night watchman swore he saw the stone tiger move, so now a village temple keeper places a canang – offerings of flowers and a

sandalwood incense stick – by the statue every morning.

Ubud could almost be described as the soul of Bali, and Amandari – meaning Peaceful Spirits – is one of its most evocative locales. With its entrance designed like a wantilan, or community meeting place, it could really be just another earth-toned village, spread among the rice

fields. Each suite has a private swimming pool or courtyard. They are connected by river-stone walkways and lined with high walls of soft volcanic rock. Only coconut and teak woods are used in the villas, which are redolent with the smell of natural thatch. The suites are delightfully polarised between bed and bath – the former a four-poster covered by a cotton

Kamasan-style painting, and the latter the last word in alfresco ablutions, with a tub that is totally open to the sky framed by stone planters of ferns and bonsai bamboo. The Amandari Suite includes an outdoor dining bale of teak and bamboo surrounded by tropical gardens and a private swimming pool with views of the rice terraces and valley. A recent arrival at Amandari is a single 3-bedroom villa, set slightly apart from the main resort in its own coconut and teak wood compound and a 2-tier swimming pool. As an added bonus, two staff are on call at all times.

Breakfast, lunch and dinner at Amandari are served at the Restaurant, a casual, 2-storey affair set above the green tiled pool, whose curving sweep of lightly salted water mimics the rice terraces that tumble down towards the gorge. After dusk, gamelan players wearing the bright red headcloths, called destar, strike up from the nearby music pavilion, merging their rhythms with the night.

To work up something of an appetite here, guests can make use of the floodlit tennis court, or try out the fitness centre, whose state-of-the-art equipment contrasts vividly with an adjacent lotus pond. Less energetic, but equally entertaining, the library is crammed with newspapers, magazines and rare books. And to take the best advantage of the glorious surrounding countryside, Amandari has its own private bale across the gorge from the resort. An early morning hike, plunging down to the bank of the river, crossing the swaying suspension bridge and then climbing up the other side, is an exhilarating way to start the day. And at the top, with cold towels, chilled water and a continental breakfast, stands a waiter looking for all the world as if he was wafted across the ravine by magic. Which given the spiritual nature of Amandari, may just be possible.

Rates from: **US$ 625**
Star rating: ★ ★ ★ ★ ★
Bellhop rating: 🛎 🛎 🛎 🛎 ½

Value:	7.70	Facilities:	8.67
Staff:	9.08	Restaurants:	8.46
Location:	8.79	Families:	6.02
Cleanliness:	9.24		

Amanjiwo

Borobudur, Magelang 56501, Central Java, Indonesia
T: +62 293 788 333 **F**: +62 293 788 355
http://www.asia-hotels.com/hotelinfo/Amanjiwo/

To Amanjiwo's complement of butlers, chefs, managers and other virtuoso staff, add the Artist In Residence whose studio is open to guests who are welcome to make use of the easel and paints on hand. There is also a watercolour set in each suite, and regular guided expeditions to the countryside for a morning's charcoal sketching. This part of Java is regarded as the island's cultural and spiritual heart, so what better way to ease yourself into the surroundings than to dabble with a brush or pencil for a while?

There could scarcely be a more inspirational subject than the nearby landscape. Amanjiwo (Peaceful Soul) is cradled in a natural amphitheatre with the horizon punctuated by a quartet of volcanoes. And in the middle of the lush rice fields of the Kedu plain rises Borobudur, the largest Buddhist sanctuary in the world. At the resort's heart is a spherical limestone monolith centred by a soaring, bell-shaped rotunda; this is flanked by two crescents containing 36 free-standing suites, 15 of which have their own pool. All the suites include an outdoor kubuk, or pavilion, for private dining or lolling, and the interiors are characterised by typical Yogyakarta style – lofty ceilings, wooden screens, batik pillows and glass paintings – all concentrated around the centrepiece four-pillar bed set on a terrazzo platform.

Java is renowned for its age-old massage, called pijat, which is both hedonistic and healing, and Amanjiwo's therapists can also deliver facials, cream baths and beauty treatments within the privacy of your suite. Supper at Amanjiwo is usually taken to the strains of a gamelan orchestra in the antique-finished, silver-leaf ceilinged, theatre-like Dining Room which serves Indonesian and Western cuisine, or on the Terrace overlooking the Kedu plain. And the Bar – built about the rotunda which is the highest point of the resort – is the consummate place for a nightcap.

Rates from: **US$ 625**
Star rating: ★ ★ ★ ★ ★
Bellhop rating: 🔔 🔔 🔔 🔔 ½

Value:	7.21	Facilities:	8.04
Staff:	9.04	Restaurants:	8.17
Location:	8.83	Families:	5.75
Cleanliness:	9.25		

Amankila

Manggis 80871, Bali, Indonesia
T: +62 363 41333 **F:** +62 363 41555
http://www.asia-hotels.com/hotelinfo/Amankila/

Time tends to float off toward the horizon at Amankila; but every day, at 4pm or thereabouts, two Balinese women dressed in bright sarongs and gauzy blouses, known as kebayas, lay out tea on the steps of the library. Guests wander by in ones and twos to pick up glutinous rice cakes and cups of Indonesian tea, and then retire to their poolside bales, beach chairs and books. Such is the pace of life at the resort whose name means Peaceful Hill.

Set on a cliff in the Karangasem Regency in the east of the island of Bali, Amankila's 34 free-standing suites with their alang alang thatched roofs incorporate a series of inwardly curving shapes. The motif is visible right the way through the suites, from the paras-stone moulding around the entrance doors to the floor-to-ceiling mirror between the bedroom and the bathroom. Canopied, king-sized beds, deep soaking tubs, cozy divans, double terrazzo vanities and seashell-finished taps complete the interior decor. Each suite has an outdoor terrace and nine have their own pool.

An elevated walkway leads from the suites to Amankila's heart, a trinity swimming pool that flows down toward the sea like a rice

terrace. At the beach itself, reached by a winding stone pathway, a 45-metre turquoise tiled lap pool lies secluded by a throng of coconut palms and shaded by a stately frangipani tree.

Come evening, the Restaurant up by the main pool opens for dinner, but for the acme of private dining, book the single candlelit table on the flower-strewn sand. Supper is prepared and served by a dedicated chef and waiter, who discreetly retire at the end of the

meal, leaving you to digest in the adjacent lounging bale fitted with cushions and bolsters, and lit by flaming bamboo torches.

Rates from: **US$ 625**
Star rating: ★ ★ ★ ★ ★
Bellhop rating: 🔔🔔🔔🔔🔔

Value:	7.68	Facilities:	9.19
Staff:	9.53	Restaurants:	8.99
Location:	9.28	Families:	6.18
Cleanliness:	9.54		

Amanusa

Nusa Dua 80363, Bali, Indonesia
T: +62 361 772 333 **F:** +62 361 772 335
http://www.asia-hotels.com/hotelinfo/Amanusa/

Sometimes, some people somehow feel the need to say that Amanusa is not quite as stellar as some of the other inhabitants of the Aman galaxy. Call it caviling, but they insinuate that its 35 thatched-roof suites are merely an extension of the rest of Nusa Dua, rather than a mini palace in its own exclusive location. Not so.

Couples staying here (and to check-in alone is an exercise in self-mortification) can take part in an exhilarating romp through all the inimitable diversions that are utterly – and there is no other word for it – Amanesque. Take, for example, the ride down to the Bali Golf and Country Club (with

preferential tee times for guests, of course) or the adjacent beach, where Amanusa maintains nine private bales, each with their own pot of frangipani water to wash off sandy feet. Your transport is an open-topped Volkswagen, which swoops and putters along the tree-hung lanes as if it was bearing visiting royalty. At the resort's pool, bordered by unglazed batik pots, the attendants proffer bathers sweet orange slices in a bowl of ice. Pause between sets during a floodlit game of tennis on one of the hardcourts, and there is a pot of chilled chrysanthemum tea waiting to refresh you.

All Amanusa's suites embrace a

four-poster bed and a mahogany desk and table for private dining. The light-filled bathroom is blessed with a marble-tiled tub enclosed in a glass wall recessed into a reflection pond. There is also an outside shower dripping with bougainvillea, and eight suites have private swimming pools.

Besides offering dining at the beach, Amanusa has two main restaurants – the Terrace with commanding views down toward the sea, and the Restaurant, an Italian extravaganza where you eat inside or out by the pool. Nusa Dua means two Islands; Amanusa means Peaceful Isle. You can not get more apposite than that.

Rates from: **US$ 625**
Star rating: ★ ★ ★ ★ ★
Bellhop rating: ♗ ♗ ♗ ♗ ♗

Value:	7.94	Facilities:	9.03
Staff:	9.50	Restaurants:	8.81
Location:	9.03	Families:	7.28
Cleanliness:	9.41		

The Balé

Nusa Dua 80363, Bali, Indonesia
T: +62 361 775 111 **F**: +62 361 775 222
http://www.asia-hotels.com/hotelinfo/Bale_The/

There is a simple rule at the Balé – no under-16s. So the resort provides a tailor-made excuse for dumping the kids with the grandparents, chucking a few essentials in a bag and jetting to this hillside resort in Nusa Dua. Assuming a break at this ultra-sexy resort is to rekindle some long-dormant passions, you will not need to bring too many clothes. The high walls surrounding the 20 very contemporary pavilions keep even the personal butlers' prying eyes away from the pool, verandah and the daybed in the secluded tropical garden, all of which seem to make skinny dipping imperative. If you have a spare moment to venture out (preferably clothed), the menu at Faces restaurant is kept deliberately short as the emphasis is on total freshness, while the range of spa treatments is rather longer but just as enjoyable.

Rates from: **US$ 395**
Star rating: ★★★★★
Bellhop rating: **Editor's pick**

Value:	n/a	Facilities:	n/a
Staff:	n/a	Restaurants:	n/a
Location:	n/a	Families:	n/a
Cleanliness:	n/a		

Bali Hyatt

Jl Danau Tamblingan, Sanur, Bali, Indonesia
T: +62 361 281 234 **F**: +62 361 287 693
http://www.asia-hotels.com/hotelinfo/Bali_Hyatt/

Smarter than harassed Kuta, but less park-like than Nusa Dua, Sanur incorporates a refined beach resort with a slightly rugged Balinese edge. The town's white sand beach ensured this was one of the first areas to be developed for tourism, and it is a relief to report that the seaside is as glorious as ever. Pretty much in the centre of Sanur Beach, the Bali Hyatt was built in 1973 (and renovated in 1994) and so the 600 different species of flowers and shrubs that grow in its 36 acres have had time to mature into a stunning labyrinth of pathways full of tropical colour. The 390 rooms and suites with thatched roofs, natural wood finishes and batik trimmings, are divided between three courts – Hibiscus, Frangipani and Bougainvillea – each with views over the sea or gardens. The Hyatt is nothing if not faithful to its antecedents – there may be more modern hotels in Bali but this certainly has an endearing charm.

Rates from: **US$ 83**
Star rating: ★★★★★
Bellhop rating: 🛎🛎🛎🛎 ½

Value:	8.20	Facilities:	8.74
Staff:	8.77	Restaurants:	8.40
Location:	8.71	Families:	7.46
Cleanliness:	8.81		

Bali Inter-Continental Resort

Jl Uluwatu 45, Jimbaran 80361, Bali, Indonesia
T: +62 361 701 888 **F**: +62 361 701 777
http://www.asia-hotels.com/hotelinfo/Inter-Continental_Resort_Bali/

By far the largest of the three mainstream Jimbaran Bay beachfront hotels, the 425-room Inter-Continental (each with private balcony) is the sort of resort where a family can divert itself for an entire holiday without ever having to leave. It is a mammoth, fortress-like building split into six wings, beautifully decorated with fine artwork and handicrafts, and contains a comprehensive assortment of recreational and gustatory facilities, all by the edge of the sea and amid leafy tropical acres – a sort of 'Bali on a plate' concept but not one that feels in any way artificial. Yet, while the hotel is huge, the scale is balanced by intimate corners such as the Bale Bengong. A romantic private dining pavilion on a raised platform set back a little from the beach, dinners a deux here naturally lead to 'The Question' being popped over coffee.

Rates from: **US$ 125**
Star rating: ★ ★ ★ ★ ★
Bellhop rating: 👍 👍 👍 👍 ½

Value:	7.99	Facilities:	8.76
Staff:	8.80	Restaurants:	8.35
Location:	8.53	Families:	6.99
Cleanliness:	8.83		

Bali Padma Hotel

Jl Padma No 1 Legian, Kuta, Bali, Indonesia
T: +62 361 752 111 **F**: +62 361 752 140
http://www.asia-hotels.com/hotelinfo/Bali_Padma_Hotel/

Rijsttaffel dinner to a tropical beach party, with events varying from kampung village style to wild jungle raves. The 1,000-square-metre pool is a great draw whether you are staying for pleasure or a pleasurable sort of business, and all guests will appreciate the facilities which include water sports on the beach, a spa, squash and tennis courts.

While Bali is generally associated with the antithesis of work and the office, it is also a popular destination for business boondoggles more properly described as incentives and conventions. Smack on the beach in Legian, with 405 rooms running the gamut from Presidential Suite down to specially equipped Family Rooms, each with private balcony, the Bali Padma is no slouch at hosting corporate events. Combining its exotic location with the richness of Balinese culture and a wide variety of cuisine, the hotel can serve up themed events from a

Rates from: **US$ 102**
Star rating: ★ ★ ★ ★ ★
Bellhop rating: 👍 👍 👍 👍 👍

Value:	8.30	Facilities:	8.54
Staff:	8.93	Restaurants:	8.52
Location:	8.81	Families:	7.86
Cleanliness:	8.65		

Banyan Tree Bintan

Site A4, Lagoi Tanjong Said, Bintan Island, Indonesia
T: +62 770 693 100 **F:** +62 770 693 200
http://www.asia-hotels.com/hotelinfo/Banyan_Tree_Bintan/

The Banyan Tree Bintan is in Indonesia, but only just. The island of Bintan is a quick 45 catamaran minutes from Singapore. A further 15-minute drive transports you to the picturesque Banyan Tree. On the peaceful northwest tip of this lush tropical island, the resort is big on luxurious ambience and leafy green tranquillity. It is spectacularly laid out and dramatically photogenic. A choice of secluded luxury villas are perched at intervals among the wooded hillside, and march right down to the rocks by the sea. Each is spacious and airy with private jacuzzis or pool and delightful verandahs with some quite amazing views of the thriving canopy, the sapphire bay or the sandy beach cove. Villa themes are closely linked to their environment and include Valley Villa, Seaview Pool Villa and Villa-on-the-Rocks.

A feeling of romance and the privacy is maintained throughout the resort. The Banyan Tree is renowned for its spas, and this one enjoys the added bonus of a hillside elevation and sweeping views. The restaurants offer a wonderful selection of Southeast Asian specialties at the Saffron, Mediterranean cuisine at the Cove or seafood alfresco at Crossroads,

although prices are more in line with top Singapore hotels rather than top Indonesian ones. Generally, facilities are low-key to keep the resort in that idyllic spa mode. Apart from the two tennis courts and various beach and water sport activities there are no energetic facilities such as a gym,

and there is not even a bar. However, nearby is the Greg Norman-designed 18-hole Laguna Bintan Golf Course, one of three courses on Bintan.

As you would expect from Banyan Tree the staff really are a magnificent crew, and even with its top-end price tag the resort proves incredibly popular, and not just with weekending Singaporeans.

Rates from: **US$ 330**
Star rating: ★★★★★
Bellhop rating: ♬♬♬♬ ½

Value:	7.37	Facilities:	8.44
Staff:	8.85	Restaurants:	8.04
Location:	8.48	Families:	6.01
Cleanliness:	8.79		

The Dharmawangsa

Jl Brawijaya Raya 26, Kebayoran Baru, Jakarta 12160, Indonesia
T: +62 21 725 8181 **F:** +62 21 725 8383
http://www.asia-hotels.com/hotelinfo/Dharmawangsa_The_/

Being met at Jakarta's airport, as far as the Dharmawangsa is concerned, means meeting you before you get anywhere near Immigration. Chauffeur-driven Bentleys speed guests to the hushed residential area of Kebayoran Baru. No one ever checks in at the lobby. Butlers unpack, pack, and pack a whole lot of other services into the 24-hour-a-day service. Exclusive? Answer that one with a multi-starred 'yes'. The Dharmawangsa's 64 rooms and 36 suites make up not so much a boutique hotel as a graceful Indonesian mansion, with the interiors reflecting the grace and beauty of the country's culture and heritage. The hotel's restaurants blend the finest elements of Indonesian and international cuisines. There are swimming pools (indoor and out), tennis and squash courts for the energetic and a supremely luxurious spa for the sybaritic. Expensive? Answer that one with a multi-dollar signed 'yes'. But it is worth every cent.

Rates from: **US$ 210**
Star rating: ★ ★ ★ ★ ★
Bellhop rating: 🔔 🔔 🔔 🔔 ½

Value:	8.23	Facilities:	8.96
Staff:	9.29	Restaurants:	8.58
Location:	7.98	Families:	6.35
Cleanliness:	9.35		

Four Seasons Resort Bali at Jimbaran Bay

Jimbaran 80361, Bali, Indonesia
T: +62 361 701 010 **F**: +62 361 701 020
http://www.asia-hotels.com/hotelinfo/Four_Seasons_Resort_Bali_Jimbaran_Bay/

To begin – slightly controversially – with the end, there is something everyone should do at Four Seasons Jimbaran two hours before they check out. Pick up the phone, call one of Executive Chef Marc Miron's team and ask for a picnic to eat aboard the plane as an alternative to dreary in-flight food. Chilled grilled prawn cocktail with roasted tomato sambals is a favourite choice, closely followed by the house smoked Tasmanian salmon, but you can choose anything off the in-villa dining menu. It is not simply a 30,000-feet gourmet treat, rather a temporary souvenir from a heavenly holiday location.

Such bravura, forethought and attention to detail really sets the Four Seasons apart. Other resorts have villas with plunge pools and thatched roofs, gamelan-toned dining under the stars and gentle, caster-footed staff with frangipani tucked behind their ears. But here they pull it off with such subtle panache it is almost indiscernible. For example, it is rare for hotels to admit it is possible to eat anywhere but in their own restaurants, but Four Seasons leaves a list of the island's most popular bars and eateries in every villa to add to its own five offerings. And on the subject of food, the resort's specially designed cooking school embraces a holistic menu embracing the art of Balinese entertaining, Asian dishes drawn from the resort's herb and spice garden and health-conscious spa cuisine. Children staying here, rather than being sidelined, are encouraged to roam around the 35 acres that include 1,500 hand-carved stone sculptures framed by lush plants, flowers and trees. Their own club is housed in a charming beachside Pondok, where they can learn Balinese dance, listen enthralled to Balinese legends or make kites.

And so to the resort proper. Four Seasons employed indigenous building materials and styles, and the vast majority of the coralline limestone rock used for many of the walls was quarried on site, individually chipped and put into place by hand. The result is 147 secluded walled villas, the majority with one bedroom, but there are also six doubles and two extra-large Royal Villas complete with staff quarters, sauna and jacuzzi. These are arranged in groups of approximately 20 around a village square with a circle of staff on duty around the clock. Jimbaran junkies tend to insist on one of the beachfront villas, but all of them have ocean views. On top of the regular accommodation offerings, a short stretch down the road and opposite the Four Seasons' beachside restaurant Pantai Jimbaran (universally known as PJ's) stand the Private Estates. The original plan was that these would be sold as private homes, but a change of heart saw them added to the room inventory. Comprising four-, three- and two-bedroomed villas, they literally beg to be filled with friends and family for a highly memorable celebration, wedding or party.

Finally, Four Seasons Jimbaran is distinguished by an exceptional spa, with nine treatment rooms spread over 930 square metres, dispensing the likes of rainshower massages and side-by-side massages. And for anyone in need of a little extra Balinese culture, the Ganesha Art Gallery presents four curated shows every year with a revolving collection of additional work by local artists.

The Four Seasons is built into a gently terraced hillside called Bukit Permai, which descends gracefully down to a broad sandy beach. You do not need to reach for a dictionary to work out that it means Beautiful Hill.

Rates from: **US$ 575**
Star rating: ★ ★ ★ ★ ★
Bellhop rating: 👢 👢 👢 👢 ½

Value:	7.66	Facilities:	8.96
Staff:	9.15	Restaurants:	8.60
Location:	8.83	Families:	7.03
Cleanliness:	9.13		

Four Seasons Resort Bali at Sayan

Sayan, Ubud, Gianyar 80571, Bali, Indonesia
T: +62 361 977 577 **F:** +62 361 977 588
http://www.asia-hotels.com/hotelinfo/Four_Seasons_Resort_Bali_Sayan/

Discard any ideas of conventional design and execution, all ye who enter here. For everything at Sayan conspires to startle and amaze. Starting at the entrance – a long teak platform bridging a roaring chasm that leads to the lobby – this is a resort that seems to have been turned on its head. The main building is no pseudo-Balinese thatchery, but a boldly contemporary circular structure that could almost be a flying saucer that has fortuitously landed in Ubud.

Pillars, ponds, hanging vines and a wealth of shrubs and trees help blend the Four Seasons into the surrounding rice terraces. Overall, it is an astonishing architectural achievement, and the 18 suites and 42 villas merely emphasise this. The bulk of the villas are within a few steps of the Ayung River, and are so tucked into the hillside that each entrance is via stairs leading from the roof that has its own deck and lotus garden. Down the circular stone stairway, there is a private plunge pool, a second deck, indoor and outdoor bathing facilities, handmade Indonesian furniture and a euphoric sense of peace and privacy.

This sense is mirrored in the spa, with its 180-degree view of the valley and four treatment rooms where rejuvenation programmes focus on using elements from the earth such as clay, mountain botanicals and warming spices. While the oval-shaped Ayung Terrace offers top-class dining with a view, the Four Seasons' triumph here is its pool, a 2-tier affair almost within arms reach of the river perfectly melding human creation with nature. And on the subject of human creation, children are actively discouraged from coming here, so the loudest noises you are likely to hear are the birds calling from the trees.

Rates from: **US$ 575**
Star rating: ★ ★ ★ ★ ★
Bellhop rating: ♫ ♫ ♫ ♫ ♫

Value:	7.91	Facilities:	9.10
Staff:	9.49	Restaurants:	8.90
Location:	9.33	Families:	5.75
Cleanliness:	9.47		

Gran Melia Jakarta

Jl HR Rasuna Said Kav X-0, Kuningan, Jakarta 12950, Indonesia
T: +62 21 526 8080 **F**: +62 21 526 8181
http://www.asia-hotels.com/hotelinfo/Gran_Melia_Jakarta/

This is Sol Melia's Asian flagship and it shows. The architecture Emilio de Nadal employed is distinctive and bold, the exterior being tiled in blue glaze and muscling in on the Jakarta skyline. The impressive lobby is vast, cavernous and representative of the ambition of the hotel. Within the enormous atrium, trickling water and a giant silver globe make a further grandiloquent statement – in such a crowded metropolis few hotels have a comparable luxury of space and scale.

The hotel has a total of 426 rooms and suites with extensive facilities to match. The European-style rooms are smooth, calm and well fitted. In keeping with the hotel's dimensions they are especially generous in size, and business travellers will be pleased to find the desk is located sensibly next to the data and phone ports, rather than across the room as in other local hotels. The 60 executive-floor Royal Service rooms are exceptional and the associated club lounge especially well done. One memorable feature here is the incredibly thick and rich carpets. You virtually need a combine harvester to carve through them.

The restaurant choice is suitably wide and follows the expected Asian cuisine norms of local, Chinese and Japanese, and of course fine Mediterranean dining with a heavy Spanish influence. The quality of food is high, from casual to fine dining. The business guest is catered to fully, and corporate facilities include 11 meeting rooms and a giant pillarless ballroom with a capacity of 3,000. On the leisure side, there is a very pleasant outdoor pool, a 24-hour gym and a brace of tennis courts.

The location is not bullseye central, but it is convenient being in the rapidly developing Golden Triangle area of Kuningan. The business district is 15 minutes away and the immediate area is populated by embassies. Overall, this is a top 5-star hotel with more than a dash of flair and high standards throughout.

Rates from: **US$ 95**
Star rating: ★ ★ ★ ★ ★
Bellhop rating: 🔔 🔔 🔔 🔔 ½

Value:	8.12	Facilities:	8.32
Staff:	8.49	Restaurants:	8.61
Location:	8.34	Families:	7.22
Cleanliness:	8.56		

Grand Hyatt Bali

Kawasan Wisata, Nusa Dua, Bali, Indonesia
T: +62 361 771 234 **F:** +62 361 772 038
http://www.asia-hotels.com/hotelinfo/Grand_Hyatt_Bali/

The humungous Grand Hyatt stretches along a substantial part of the beach on the eastern side of Nusa Dua, looking out toward the isolated promontory of Pura Bias Turgal and its solitary shrine. This is a mainstream tourist resort, for sure, embracing 750 rooms, villas and suites, yet the ambience is solidly Balinese. Designed along the lines of one of the island's traditional water palaces, the accommodation is grouped into four self-contained 'villages' so guests are not overawed or disoriented by their surroundings, which are spread over 40 acres. Landscaped gardens, two free-form pools and a host of other water features connected by meandering pathways complete a picture that is near idyllic. Kids – and this resort was built with them uppermost in mind – should love to hare around exploring. There is also the specially equipped Camp Nusa for 3 to 13-year-olds to keep youngsters occupied in fun, hands-on activities that range from fish feeding to squash clinics, from painting and pottery to kite flying and cooking.

The Hyatt's rooms themselves might be air-conditioned and fitted with satellite television, but such modern accessories do not detract in any way from the decor – muted batik fabrics, graceful bamboo furnishings and Balinese handicrafts. And you only have to step outside to balcony or garden to admire the island's nature in the raw.

Although guests can tuck in at any of the resort's eight restaurants and bars, two – the Watercourt and the Night Market – especially ooze local character. The Watercourt is surrounded by statues of the Garuda, the winged gods of Indonesian mythology, and serves Balinese cuisine in a courtyard overlooking a pond teeming with carp. And the Pasar Senggol market brings together a conglomeration of food stalls and dance performances while artisans create puppets and carve, weave or paint as they would in their home villages.

Rates from: **US$ 148**
Star rating: ★★★★★
Bellhop rating: ♢♢♢♢♢

Value:	8.28	Facilities:	9.04
Staff:	8.95	Restaurants:	8.57
Location:	8.72	Families:	7.72
Cleanliness:	8.91		

Grand Hyatt Jakarta

Jl MH Thamrin Kav 28-30, Jakarta 10230, Indonesia
T: +62 21 390 1234 **F:** +62 21 390 6426
http://www.asia-hotels.com/hotelinfo/Grand_Hyatt_Jakarta/

The magnificent lobby of the Grand Hyatt makes a vigorous introduction to this hotel that is part executive headquarters, part retreat from the city and all pleasure. Sturdy columns soar three floors to the ceiling, and a double staircase and escalators lead down to ground level flanked by a series of ponds set about with palm trees and greenery. The whole harks back to Jakarta's boom years, while hinting that the Indonesian capital may well get on its financial feet again one day soon.

The 428 rooms are sumptuously decorated, smartly wired and considerately laid out. The inventory Includes 22 suites (some with their own terrace and all with 24-hour butler service) and 15 apartments for long-staying guests, while the club floors enjoy their own lounge with a concierge and a host of other complimentary facilities.

The Hyatt's eateries and drinking holes are excellent both for entertaining clients and colleagues or simply entertaining yourself. The menu at the Grand Cafe – crispy salads, roast station and sashimi bar – changes daily, and the ice cream is home-made. C's Steak and Seafood serves prime US beef while its cellar holds 3,000 labels. There are four private rooms in the Sumire Japanese restaurant, and the poolside Seafood Terrace is transformed into a market-style buffet in the evenings. After dinner, the Burgundy lounge is usually full to the gills with socialites out to listen to one of the international bands and sample the extensive range of wines, spirits and cigars.

When it comes to recreation, the Hyatt surpasses itself. Fans of golf, tennis, squash, basketball and jogging all get their own putting green, courts or track. The lagoon swimming pool is 43 metres long, and the fitness centre fairly bulges with state-of-the-art equipment, jacuzzis, plunge baths and VIP massage rooms. Further off-duty entertainment is available right next door in Plaza Indonesia, a mammoth shopping complex that can be reached directly from the hotel and just goes to emphasise the hotel's top location.

Rates from: **US$ 163**
Star rating: ★ ★ ★ ★ ★
Bellhop rating: ♗ ♗ ♗ ♗ ½

Value:	7.72	Facilities:	8.59
Staff:	8.42	Restaurants:	8.46
Location:	8.81	Families:	7.11
Cleanliness:	8.58		

Hard Rock Hotel Bali

Jalan Pantai, Banjar Pande Mas, Kuta, Bali, Indonesia
T: +62 361 761 869 **F**: +62 361 761 868
http://www.asia-hotels.com/hotelinfo/Hard_Rock_Hotel_Bali/

rigeur. Dining is naturally in the Hard Rock Cafe (there are two other restaurants and three bars), there are endless collectibles in the Mega Store, while the business centre contains a rock 'n' roll library and Centrestage triples as a lobby, bar and live venue. Hard Rock Bali is one of only four such hotels in the world. Oh world.

Wow! Awesome! Cool! This Knickerbocker Glory of a hotel is for the young, families with young(ish) children and the very young-at-heart. Some 418 rooms are mashed into this Technicolor-plus property on Kuta Beach that must be the last word in the science of branding.

Never mind the bright and breezy balconied rooms in six blocks themed blues, reggae etc. you can interact with Radio Wave 87.6 FM DJs, burn your own CD in the Boom Box recording studio or chill out in one of the cabanas by the pool where, of course, piped music is de

Rates from: **US$ 100**
Star rating: ★ ★ ★ ★
Bellhop rating: 🐶 🐶 🐶 🐶 ½

Value:	7.82	Facilities:	8.80
Staff:	8.75	Restaurants:	8.38
Location:	9.01	Families:	8.07
Cleanliness:	8.75		

Holiday Inn Resort Lombok

Jl Raya Mangsit, Lombok, Indonesia
T: +62 370 693 444 **F**: +62 370 693 092
http://www.asia-hotels.com/hotelinfo/Holiday_Inn_Resort_Lombok/

gardens, outdoor bathrooms and direct access to the spotless beach. Families will love the 30 Mangsit apartments with two bedrooms, lounge and dining area and fully fitted kitchen. Staff are active and very helpful, arranging tours, diving and transport with ease. The relative isolation of the resort does not hurt and it is fantastic value for money.

Many people expect rather run-of-the-mill standards of the Holiday Inn chain, and in many cases they are spot on. But its Lombok resort, perched on the shoreline adjacent to Mangsit Village, is excellent. Built in 1995 it still feels new and the design successfully spreads the facilities around the 37 acres in an

appealing way. Located some three kilometres from the low-key shops and bars of Senggigi Beach, the resort is well equipped with a handsome pool, tropical beach and satisfying restaurants. The standard rooms are trim, modern and comfy. But the 14 bungalows are really worth indulging in with their private

Rates from: **US$ 50**
Star rating: ★ ★ ★ ★
Bellhop rating: 🐶 🐶 🐶 🐶 🐶

Value:	8.57	Facilities:	8.48
Staff:	9.09	Restaurants:	8.65
Location:	8.35	Families:	7.61
Cleanliness:	9.30		

Hyatt Regency Yogyakarta

Jl Palagan Tentara Pelajar, Yogyakarta, Java, Indonesia
T: +62 274 869 123 **F**: +62 274 869 588
http://www.asia-hotels.com/hotelinfo/Hyatt_Regency_Yogyakarta/

Yogyakarta is the cultural and intellectual heart of Java and the Hyatt Regency has aptly done its best to reflect this. While its seven storeys are indubitably modern, its design incorporates many of the architectural details and the same axis as the nearby renowned Borobudur temple, just 42 kilometres away. Surrounded by 59 acres of luxuriant gardens, Javanese thatching gives the public areas a village feel, and even the lifts are naturally lit via a glass rooftop stupa. The well-appointed 269 rooms and suites are spread between four wings, looking out over either the 9-hole golf course or Mount Merapati. The health club and free-form swimming pool are both excellent venues in which to relax, children can be safely deposited at Camp Hyatt, and the hotel's facilities are completed by five restaurants and bars.

Rates from: **US$ 75**
Star rating: ★ ★ ★ ★ ★
Bellhop rating: ♪ ♪ ♪ ♪ ½

Value:	8.56	Facilities:	8.73
Staff:	8.81	Restaurants:	8.07
Location:	7.81	Families:	7.32
Cleanliness:	8.95		

Le Meridien Nirwana Golf & Spa Resort

Jl Raya Beraban, Tabanan 82171, Bali, Indonesia
T: +62 361 815 900 **F**: +62 361 815 901
http://www.asia-hotels.com/hotelinfo/Le_Meridien_Nirwana_Golf_and_Spa_Resort/

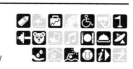

It could almost be called 'The Holy Trinity'. Acres of rice paddy provide the 'rough' alongside a superb Greg Norman-designed 18-hole golf course. The spa proffers a cornucopia of massage and other Balinese treatments. And the island's most photogenic temple, Tanah Lot, stands in full sight of this stunning hotel that is flecked with the spray of the Indian Ocean. While more than adequately catering to guests' sporting, physical and spiritual requirements by day, Le Meridien also provides succour by night, with a combination of rooms, suites and villas. It would be folly not to go for something with an ocean view here, and equally silly to miss out on at least one evening aperitif in the Sunset Lounge overlooking Tanah Lot.

Rates from: **US$ 100**
Star rating: ★ ★ ★ ★ ★
Bellhop rating: ♪ ♪ ♪ ♪ ½

Value:	8.45	Facilities:	8.90
Staff:	8.68	Restaurants:	8.33
Location:	7.94	Families:	7.40
Cleanliness:	8.80		

The Legian Bali

Jl Laksmana, Seminyak Beach 80361, Legian, Bali, Indonesia
T: +62 361 730 622 **F:** +62 361 730 623
http://www.asia-hotels.com/hotelinfo/Legian_The_/

There is a difficult choice for anyone picking The Legian – stay in one of the 67 ocean-front single or 2-bedroom suites, with the regular full-frontal Turneresque sunsets over the beach at Seminyak; or step across the road to the Club with its 11 detached villas (a 3-bedroom and 10 with one bedroom)? Either way you are assured of a secluded retreat in a busy corner of Bali. The suites, each with their own spacious living area, pantry and verandah, look down on the hotel gardens and a deliciously inviting pool that could almost be part of the sea. On the other hand, all the villas have their own 10-metre pool, private butler, outdoor dining bale and gourmet perks like an espresso machine. Whether suite or villa, guests can indulge themselves at the Restaurant, serving Indonesian and international specialties, or at the spa, with its five private suites with individual steam room attached.

Rates from: **US$ 236**
Star rating: ★ ★ ★ ★ ★
Bellhop rating: 🛎 🛎 🛎 🛎 ½

Value:	7.61	Facilities:	8.56
Staff:	8.98	Restaurants:	8.28
Location:	8.94	Families:	6.72
Cleanliness:	9.03		

Mandarin Oriental Jakarta

Jl MH Thamrin, Jakarta 10310, Indonesia
T: +62 21 3983 8888 **F:** +62 21 3983 8891
http://www.asia-hotels.com/hotelinfo/Mandarin_Oriental_Jakarta/

The Mandarin is one of a quartet of established business hotels grouped around the Welcome Statue in downtown Jakarta in the heart of the financial and diplomatic district. Given the Indonesian capital's traffic problems, it certainly has the location right, and the interiors are similarly pertinent. The 404 rooms and suites are a mine of solid comfort backed up with the sort of amenities – high-speed Internet, laptop-friendly safes – that make life simpler for peripatetic executives, and are supported by a business centre that goes the extra mile with services like mobile phone hire and arranging appointments.

The hotel's seven restaurants and bars are highly favoured by local businessmen as venues to wine, dine and parley, and La Casa del Habano is frequently thick with the aroma of Punch or Churchills and fine cognacs. Not quite the same style and calibre as other hotels from this fine group but certainly one of the best in Jakarta.

Rates from: **US$ 99**
Star rating: ★ ★ ★ ★ ★
Bellhop rating: 🛎 🛎 🛎 🛎 ½

Value:	8.18	Facilities:	8.20
Staff:	8.67	Restaurants:	8.42
Location:	8.79	Families:	5.25
Cleanliness:	8.57		

Mandarin Oriental Hotel Majapahit Surabaya

Jl Tunjungan 65, Surabaya 60275, Java, Indonesia
T: +62 31 545 4333 **F:** +62 31 545 4111
http://www.asia-hotels.com/hotelinfo/Majapahit_Mandarin_Oriental_Hotel/

Over the course of the last century, the hotel now known as the Majapahit has witnessed some truly historic events. Opened as the Oranje in 1910 by Lucas Sarkies (from the same family that created Raffles in Singapore and numerous other grand hotels) it has hosted Charlie Chaplin, Joseph Conrad and Prince Leopold of Belgium. The distinguished art deco lobby was added in 1936, and the Japanese used it variously as a prison camp and barracks during World War II. September 1945 witnessed the hotel's greatest red-letter day. Infuriated

by a Dutch flag that had been raised on the roof, a crowd of Indonesians stormed the hotel, ripped the blue part off the colonialists' tricolour and so launched the country's struggle for independence.

Renamed Hotel Merdeka (Liberty) it lapsed into obscurity for some years, until a dazzling renovation and relaunch in 1996 reinstated it as Surabaya's premier address. The Majapahit's graceful low-level design, colonnades, five garden courtyards and creamy white walls from Sarkies' time are still in place, but they have been augmented by the addition of an outdoor pool, tennis court and a comprehensive spa.

The hotel's assortment of accommodation is also highly impressive, with 110 suites and 40 rooms characterised by Asian carpets, polished floors, high ceilings and private balconies or terraces. Nine of the suites have their own theme; the Merdeka was once occupied by the Dutch politicos whose flag caused all the

fuss at the end of the war, and contains many contemporary captioned photos; the Sarkies Brothers commemorates the hotel's founding fathers; and the Wayang pays tribute to Indonesia's folk puppets. Completing the inventory, the Presidential Suite, at 800 square metres, is one of the largest in Asia.

Of the Majapahit's half-dozen restaurants and bars, quite the most intriguing is the Euro-Asian Indigo, with a spectacular show kitchen at one end and wide windows at the other, looking out on to the street where the traders and trishaw drivers dawdle past just as they must have done way back in 1910.

Rates from: US$ 85
Star rating: ★ ★ ★ ★ ★
Bellhop rating: ♗ ♗ ♗ ♗ ♗

Value:	8.80	Facilities:	8.75
Staff:	9.18	Restaurants:	8.60
Location:	8.05	Families:	6.85
Cleanliness:	9.13		

Melia Bali Villas & Spa Resort

Nusa Dua 80363, Bali, Indonesia
T: +62 361 771 510 F: +62 361 771 360
http://www.asia-hotels.com/hotelinfo/Melia_Bali_Villas_and_Spa_Resort/

array of entertainments laid on each day, backed up by eight restaurants and bars, although guests can equally just sit back and relax, with the obvious place to do this – as the hotel's name suggests – in the spa with its bank of both indoor and outdoor treatment rooms.

Unusually for a hotel in Nusa Dua, none of the Melia's 500 rooms and suites has a view over the ocean. Instead, echoing the Balinese ethos of venerating the land rather than the sea, the hotel's prime lookout is over the luxuriant gardens and their free-range population of tame squirrels. This is essentially a family resort, although couples may want to tuck themselves away in one of the 10 villas surrounded by exceptionally large and shady gardens. There is a mind-boggling

Rates from: **US$ 80**
Star rating: ★ ★ ★ ★ ★
Bellhop rating: 🛎 🛎 🛎 🛎 ½

Value:	8.02	Facilities:	8.42
Staff:	8.69	Restaurants:	8.15
Location:	8.26	Families:	6.75
Cleanliness:	8.69		

Hotel Mulia Senayan

Jl Asia Afrika, Senayan, Jakarta 10270, Indonesia
T: +62 21 574 7777 F: +62 21 574 7888
http://www.asia-hotels.com/hotelinfo/Mulia_Senayan/

serves up innovative Indonesian fusion as well as Thai steamboats. What saves the Mulia from being yet another multi-storey bed-and-board monster is its extensive collection of sculptures, paintings, ceramics and glass art pieces, and a exceptionally well-attuned and helpful staff.

If you like your hotels big, bold and well appointed, you will like the Mulia Senayan. Opened in 1997 for the South East Asian Games, it is slightly removed from central Jakarta, and counts an inventory of 1,008 rooms, each at least 48 metres square. The suites come with their own 'mini-spa' – a shower capsule that combines a sauna, water massage and background music. The ballroom can pack in 4,000 people without too much of a push, and there are seven restaurants and bars including the Samudra Suki which

Rates from: **US$ 105**
Star rating: ★ ★ ★ ★ ★
Bellhop rating: 🛎 🛎 🛎 🛎 🛎

Value:	8.55	Facilities:	8.81
Staff:	8.71	Restaurants:	8.80
Location:	8.55	Families:	7.16
Cleanliness:	8.97		

Novotel Coralia Benoa Bali

Jl Pratama, Nusa Dua 80361, Bali, Indonesia
T: +62 361 772 239 **F**: +62 361 772 237
http://www.asia-hotels.com/hotelinfo/Novotel_Coralia_Benoa_Bali/

The name is a bit of a mouthful, but the hotel could not be more straightforward. Towards the end of the Nusa Dua peninsula and bordering the fishing village of Tanjung Benoa, the Novotel has it just right. It is neither too big, nor too small. It is Balinese in decor and style, yet with the necessary international accents. It is a gorgeous hideaway hangout but also fabulously family friendly.

Although the property is split by the main road, this really keeps the hotel to scale and makes it feel as if it is part of the community. The lobby maintains an environmentally amicable theme, being built mainly of wood, but with a bright blue background to the reception desk that makes it look like a fish tank. The complement of 192 rooms – with subtle coconut wood interiors – all have a private balcony or a small garden. Better still, the dozen set back thatched bungalows ranged along the pretty beach comprise lofty ceilings, dual basins and an inspirational outdoor tub that is large enough for a couple to lie side by side. And dozens of quaint fishing boats are drawn up on the sand right alongside jet skis, dinghies and other water sports accessories.

Mediterranean-style lunch or dinner on the beach at Coco's is probably the most idyllic dining location, metres away from the sea or the combined jacuzzi and pool. A second pool – Nirwana – lies on the other side of the road among the 'villages', as the bulk of the Novotel's accommodation is called. Sunbathers are usually out here shortly after breakfast, and Nirwana's attractions continue well into the early hours when it is not unknown for revellers to launch into an impromptu party. As well as offering tennis and other sports, the Novotel also runs a full-day entertainment programme, with indoor alternatives just in case it happens to be raining. Add to this a basic health spa and the Dolfi Kids' Club and it is clear the resort offers something for everyone.

Rates from: **US$ 54**
Star rating: ★ ★ ★ ★ ½
Bellhop rating: 🛎 🛎 🛎 🛎 🛎

Value:	8.67	Facilities:	8.67
Staff:	8.89	Restaurants:	8.21
Location:	8.44	Families:	7.86
Cleanliness:	8.87		

Novotel Coralia Lombok

Mandalika Resort, Pantai Putri Nyale, Pujut, Lombok, Tengah 83111, Indonesia
T: +62 370 653 333 F: +62 370 653 555
http://www.asia-hotels.com/hotelinfo/Novotel_Coralia_Lombok/

Lombok, nestling a few hours boat ride from Bali, is a delightfully secluded and underdeveloped island. But it has to be said it can be a little unstable. The Novotel Coralia Lombok, marooned towards the south of the island, is a good hour from the capital Mataram with virtually nothing in the surrounding areas other than quiet backpacking digs, simple rural villages and the main reason to head so far out – the amazing powdery white sands of Kuta Beach. The resort itself is a superb shoreline collection of bungalows and rooms built in the style of a traditional Sasak village. A cosy rustic feel is brought out by plenty of timber and locally inspired thatched roofs. Huge wooden rooms are great value, especially the cabanas. Facilities are perfectly adequate and include a simple spa, three swimming pools and a host of water sports. The two restaurants are fair, which is just as well given the isolated location. A beautiful setting, but best suited to more adventurous travellers.

Rates from: US$ 52
Star rating: ★ ★ ★ ★
Bellhop rating: ♫ ♫ ♫ ♫ ½

Value:	8.57	Facilities:	8.40
Staff:	8.70	Restaurants:	8.07
Location:	8.57	Families:	6.77
Cleanliness:	8.67		

Nusa Dua Beach Hotel & Spa

Lot North 4, Nusa Dua 80363, Bali, Indonesia
T: +62 361 771 210 F: +62 361 772 617
http://www.asia-hotels.com/hotelinfo/Nusa_Dua_Beach/

As one of the very first hotels to be built in the area, the Nusa Dua went the whole hog when it came to incorporating Balinese architecture. And for months after its opening in 1983 artisans came back to the hotel to show off their handiwork to friends and relations, to the minor bemusement of staff and guests. A great deal of that pride and homespun civility lives on in the 381 rooms, from the 3-bedroomed Residence complete with private pool, through the Palace Club rooms with private club lounge, to the more basic family and superior category. Each room incorporates the rich textures of Bali, from batik textiles to ornate panelled walls. The hotel has been given a thorough makeover in recent years, and to the extensive facilities and nine restaurants and bars, a deluxe spa has been added whose many accoutrements include a 25-metre lap pool that even broadcasts music under water.

Rates from: US$ 120
Star rating: ★ ★ ★ ★ ★
Bellhop rating: ♫ ♫ ♫ ♫ ½

Value:	7.94	Facilities:	8.66
Staff:	8.70	Restaurants:	8.52
Location:	8.39	Families:	7.51
Cleanliness:	8.85		

The Oberoi Bali

Seminyak Beach, Jl Laksmana, Bali, Indonesia
T: +62 361 730 361 **F:** +62 361 730 791
http://www.asia-hotels.com/hotelinfo/Oberoi_Bali/

The spiritual side of Bali comes to the fore at the Oberoi. The resort fronts one of the holiest beaches on the western coast of the island, where every morning local villagers walk on to the sand to lay offerings to placate the gods. Worshippers have flocked to the nearby temple of Pura Petitenget for the past 600 years. The trees in the Oberoi's 15 acres of tropical gardens are believed to have a soothing effect on spiritual well-being. And the lotus pond at the resort's main entrance is dedicated to Dewi Laut, goddess of the sea, who staff pray to before starting work. Little wonder then, that the whole of the Oberoi is infused with an aura of peace and beauty.

Built almost 30 years ago as a private club (and only later converted to a resort), it retains a palpable feeling of exclusivity, from the 15 villas whose coral stone walled courtyard (most with a private swimming pool) ensures absolute privacy to the 60 Lanai cottages – with their teakwood beds, softly toned furnishings and marble floors – which are set in clusters of four around a central lily pond.

Most days spent here are little short of idyllic, but the perfect evening might encompass stepping up out of the beachside pool shortly before dusk, knotting a sarong around your waist and strolling over to the Frangipani Cafe. Peruse the menu for a while – perhaps some of the superb seafood, or one of the Balinese specialities – let the waiter light the candle on the table, and then sit back. The Frangipani overlooks not just the sea and the 200-metre beachfront but the resort's amphitheatre, and here – to the crash of a gamelan orchestra – dancers weave and swirl in an entrancing performance that is entirely magical. This is pure Bali, in one of the most heavenly locations on the whole island.

Rates from: **US$ 230**
Star rating: ★ ★ ★ ★ ★
Bellhop rating: 👍 👍 👍 👍 👍

Value:	8.00	Facilities:	8.85
Staff:	9.22	Restaurants:	8.61
Location:	8.86	Families:	7.00
Cleanliness:	9.11		

The Oberoi Lombok

Medana Beach, Mataram 83001, West Lombok, Indonesia
T: +62 370 638 444 **F:** +62 370 632 496
http://www.asia-hotels.com/hotelinfo/Oberoi_Lombok/

One look at the price will let you know what the Oberoi Lombok aspires to be. It trumpets itself as the best resort on the island, and architecturally that is unquestionably right. It is visually stunning, a beautiful piece of design that has been thoughtfully put together right down to the last detail. There is a peace and tranquillity to this isolated 24-acre property, a wonderful serenity overlooking Medana Beach and its surrounding fishing villages and palm groves.

Even if the resort was absolutely full it would be hard to tell, as most guests staying in this exclusive retreat's 20 superb Luxury Villas have barely any reason to step out. Elegant and very spacious, traditional influences are successfully expressed in a contemporary fashion. Local artefacts such as wooden chests and stone statuettes help set the stylish tone and the villa amenities keep you comfortable and entertained. In most cases their surrounding walls frame a private swimming pool, gardens, dining pavilion, courtyard and pond. The resort's 30 terrace Pavilion Rooms are not quite in the same class of indulgence, but are still highly generous on space with plenty of soothing wood finishes. Each also has a private garden, a rather tempting sunken bath and modern amenities including video, CD player and, for some reason, a dedicated fax machine.

The resort's breezy lobby looks out on to an arcing, cone-shaped swimming pool and reflective ornamental ponds leading to the small beach cove from where you can make out the golden beaches of the Gili Islands, 20 minutes boat ride across the sea. The nearest town of Senggigi is 25 kilometres away and there are few taxis out here, so this means that you are pretty much resort-bound when it comes to meals. Not that this is much of a hardship – with a choice of an informal beachside cafe, fine dining at the Lumbung restaurant or a buffet and cultural performance at the amphitheatre. And in between breakfast, lunch and dinner there is a wealth of diversions, from activities like water sports and tennis to the far less strenuous pastime of indulging in the spa.

Rates from: **US$ 230**
Star rating: ★ ★ ★ ★ ★
Bellhop rating: 🔔🔔🔔🔔 ½

Value:	8.05	Facilities:	8.71
Staff:	9.32	Restaurants:	8.64
Location:	8.64	Families:	5.75
Cleanliness:	9.43		

The Ritz-Carlton Bali Resort & Spa

Jl Karang Mas Sejahtera, Jimbaran 80364, Bali Indonesia
T: +62 361 702 222 **F:** +62 361 701 555
http://www.asia-hotels.com/hotelinfo/Ritz_Carlton_Bali_Resort_Spa_The_/

It may seem odd to start with Kubu Beach, but there is a very good reason for doing so. Several hundred winding steps down a steep cliff lead to rolling breakers and a strip of sand that at first sight appears deserted. But discreetly located next to a placid lagoon at the rear of the beach stands the Ritz-Carlton's tented bar, with loungers, umbrellas and snacks. A few Balinese might be fishing off the rocks, but chances are you will have this place to yourself for much of the day.

Kubu's serendipity is reflected throughout the rest of the resort

perched on a bluff in Jimbaran. From the lobby you look straight down across the infinity pool and out to the Indian Ocean. Beneath the pool, tropical fish swarm in the 42,000-litre saltwater aquarium. And all around the gardens and extensive spa facilities are thick with bougainvillea, monkey pod, banyan, breadfruit and frangipani trees.

The resort's 338 rooms, villas and suites are heavily influenced by their surroundings, with alang alang thatched and tile roofing, limestone carvings and Indonesian art and antiques. Slate, wood and marble floors are used throughout the

public areas, guestrooms and even the 595-square-metre ballroom.

Of the resort's half-dozen wining and dining options, which include the outdoor seating pavilions of Padi that appear to float in a lily pond, and the Langit Theatre with its dinner dance performances, the most impressive is the Kisik Bar and Grill. This sand-floored restaurant and bar has been carved out of the cliff, and serves its signature dish of freshly grilled seafood on banana leaves. Savvy diners book days in advance to get the table closest to the ocean, so they can eat under the stars to the sound of the surf crashing on the rocks below.

Rates from: **US$ 145**
Star rating: ★ ★ ★ ★ ★
Bellhop rating: 🛎 🛎 🛎 🛎 🛎

Value:	8.30	Facilities:	9.15
Staff:	9.37	Restaurants:	8.83
Location:	8.59	Families:	7.37
Cleanliness:	9.35		

Shangri-La Hotel Jakarta

Kota BNI, Jl Jend Sudirman Kav 1, Jakarta 10220, Indonesia
T: +62 21 570 7440 **F:** +62 21 570 3530
http://www.asia-hotels.com/hotelinfo/Shangrila_Hotel_Jakarta/

Jakarta can be a handful for the visitor so it is a relief to find the Shangri-La Jakarta. Although the hotel had its problems in the mid-1990s it is now a fine all-rounder, a true 5-star city hotel setting high standards in every department. Located centrally in the Golden Triangle at Kota BNI, bang in the middle of the business district and minutes from the World Trade Centre on Jalan Sudirman. Its 32 floors hold 668 first-class rooms and suites and the facilities match their refined mood. The restaurants are excellent in both ambience and flavours offering Chinese to quality French cuisine, international to teppanyaki Japanese. And the basement bar BATS is a lively part of Jakarta's nightlife, especially at weekends. With a surprisingly large outdoor pool and fully equipped health spa the Shangri-La attracts business travellers and Jakarta residents alike. Reassuringly, security is taken very seriously in what can be a difficult city.

Rates from: US$ 118
Star rating: ★★★★★
Bellhop rating: ♙♙♙♙ ½

Value:	7.93	Facilities:	8.69
Staff:	8.60	Restaurants:	8.59
Location:	8.21	Families:	6.86
Cleanliness:	8.88		

Shangri-La Hotel Surabaya

Jl May Jend Sungkono 120, Surabaya 60256, Java, Indonesia
T: +62 31 566 1550 **F:** +62 31 566 1570
http://www.asia-hotels.com/hotelinfo/ShangriLa_Hotel_Surabaya/

The Shangri-La Surabaya is one of the best hotels in Indonesia's second city. Its 389 rooms and suites are superbly equipped with every comfort one could reasonably hope for in a bustling metropolis. For business travellers the location is handy, being only 10 minutes from the main business district, close to the harbour and two championship golf courses. A competent business centre is accompanied by a full spread of meeting and banquet rooms, the largest of which holds up to 2,500 people. The hotel's well-appointed interior is smart yet subdued with luxury decor typical for this chain. Rooms follow the theme and have little Javanese touches, and the hotel puts forward a truly international restaurant choice – local, Tex-Mex, Italian, Chinese and Japanese. Good leisure options and a slightly off-centre location help bring a more relaxed mood to this well-packaged hotel.

Rates from: US$ 97
Star rating: ★★★★★
Bellhop rating: ♙♙♙♙ ½

Value:	8.15	Facilities:	8.42
Staff:	8.57	Restaurants:	8.40
Location:	7.83	Families:	6.93
Cleanliness:	8.72		

Sheraton Bandung Hotel & Towers

Jl Ir H Juanda No 390, Bandung 40135, West Java, Indonesia
T: +62 22 250 0303 **F:** +62 22 250 0301
http://www.asia-hotels.com/hotelinfo/Sheraton_Bandung/

Bandung is a picturesque but slightly fading garden city, set about with art deco buildings put up by the colonial Dutch in the 1930s. Their plans to make it the new capital never came to fruition, and today Bandung largely acts as the prime getaway from the turmoil of Jakarta, two-plus hours away. The Sheraton is well placed as a resort – set six kilometres out of the town centre near the 18-hole Dago Endah golf course. It is not overlarge, with only 152 rooms and suites, each with a private balcony or patio, kitchettes, a jacuzzi in the bathroom and masseurs on call or available in the spa. There are two outdoor pools (one for kids), Chinese, Indonesian and Italian restaurants, and the quaintly named SOB fun pub. The Sheraton is an excellent antidote to the hurly burly of Jakarta, as well as a good base for exploring the rest of west Java.

Rates from: **US$ 60**
Star rating: ★ ★ ★ ★ ★
Bellhop rating: ◊ ◊ ◊ ◊ ½

Value:	8.55	Facilities:	8.35
Staff:	8.75	Restaurants:	8.40
Location:	7.85	Families:	8.10
Cleanliness:	8.65		

Sheraton Senggigi Lombok

JL Raya Sengiggi KM 8, Sengiggi, Lombok, Indonesia
T:+62 370 693 333 **F:** +62 370 693 140
http://www.asia-hotels.com/hotelinfo/Sheraton_Senggigi/

In many ways the Sheraton is the star attraction of Lombok's lazy Senggigi Beach. Away from Bali, Indonesia's hotel standards can plunge dramatically but the Sheraton is a true international-class resort. The wings are low-rise with all 154 rooms looking out over the Lombok Straits. Each features a balcony while the ground floor terrace rooms have patios that spill out into tropical gardens. With deep brown teak trimmings, the blinds and shutters contrast with the lighter interior shades and the colourful tropical views outside. The facilities are modern and luxurious including the Laguna Beach Spa and a full selection of water sports. The food from the three restaurants matches the 5-star ambience, but perhaps the option of private dining on one of several beaches would be the highlight for many. The pool must be singled out for special praise – stunningly designed and creative it is exactly what you want when on holiday and is manned by the most courteous of staff.

Rates from: **US$ 80**
Star rating: ★ ★ ★ ★ ★
Bellhop rating: ◊ ◊ ◊ ◊ ½

Value:	8.21	Facilities:	8.44
Staff:	9.03	Restaurants:	8.15
Location:	8.77	Families:	7.79
Cleanliness:	8.77		

Sheraton Laguna Nusa Dua

Nusa Dua, Bali 80363, Indonesia
T: +62 361 771 327 **F:** +62 361 771 326
http://www.asia-hotels.com/hotelinfo/Sheraton_Laguna_/

The Sheraton is very, very Nusa Dua. The area was specifically designed as a tourist resort – a cluster of tailor-made, manicured, spick and span hotels enclosed in their own beachfront compounds. And at the very core is the Sheraton Laguna.

The U-shaped hotel is pointed towards the beach and built around a 5,000-square-metre series of swimmable lagoons. To take full advantage of the aquatic design, go for one of the 48 sea-level rooms. First thing in the morning you can just step on to the balcony and down the steps into the water, and breaststroke your way across to Cafe Lagoon for breakfast.

Naturally, all the Sheraton's 270 rooms and suites are eminently habitable, all the more so as they are distinguished by a butler who escorts you to the door on arrival and remains on call 24 hours a day. A pressing service is also at guests' disposal and the resort's chefs wheel out a complimentary afternoon tea in the lobby lounge as a matter of course. As well as scones and cakes, the Sheraton also does a fine line in fine dining, producing silver service to piano accompaniment at Mayang Seri, which is also in earshot of the resort's lovely waterfall. Beachside meals at the Ocean Terrace are rather more relaxed, and Quinn's hosts its own dance floor and comes with a nautical touch.

The acme of the Sheraton's hospitality lies in the spa, where gym and hydrotherapy treatments are available for a nominal fee, or guests can choose to indulge in something more exotic like a Thalgo body gommage or micronised marine algae body wrap.

The Sheraton is a popular choice for families, but also for executives, who occasionally may be able to tear themselves away from the nearby 18-hole championship Bali Golf & Country Club to explore the delights of the International Convention Centre which stands next to the hotel.

Rates from: **US$ 130**
Star rating: ★★★★★
Bellhop rating: ♙♙♙♙ ½

Value:	8.15	Facilities:	8.74
Staff:	8.78	Restaurants:	8.20
Location:	8.55	Families:	6.96
Cleanliness:	8.82		

The Fullerton, Singapore – Page 211
Singapore's best hotels and resorts – Pages 207-222

JAPAN

CHINA

SOUTH
KOREA

③ TOKYO

Kyoto ①

② Osaka

What is the quintessential Japanese hotel? One of the gargantuan world-class 5-stars that dot Tokyo and other major cities, a traditional ryokan with sliding paper doors, futons and tatami mats, or one of the multi-themed, psychedelic love shacks that get rented out by the hour? Japan's gallimaufry of accommodation provides some clue to the national character. It is a country of extremes and contradictions, one that is as entranced as much by the art of bonsai as by Hello Kitty, as entertained by Disneyland as it is by Noh plays, one that can celebrate the marine beauty of Matsushima Bay (officially dubbed one of the 'Three Great Sights' of Japan) while allowing a power station to be built right next to it.

Japan, formerly known for an economic vigour that spread its cars, stereos and computers around the world, now faces a variety of problems ranging from deflation to bad debt burdens. How it tackles these will greatly shape its role both in Asia – where it remains the

most successful industrial economy – and the rest of the world.

Japan is made up of some 1,000 islands, strung out in a 3,000-kilometre chain from the icy border with Russia to the tropical climes of Okinawa. The Shinkansen, or Bullet Train, system is one of the miracles of Japan, linking much of the country at speeds of up to 300 kilometres per hour and making punctuality a rule rather than an exception. Quite apart from anything else, the Shinkansen means that visitors can take in an enormous amount of Japan in the matter of a few days. Tokyo remains

one of the most vibrant cities in Asia, contrasting starkly with Kyoto, whose temples, shrines and gardens mark the cultural heart of Japan. Many venture no further than these two centres, but further west the drab town of Himeji is crowned by a 5-century-old castle which is one of a handful in the country to have survived in its original (non-concrete) form. Little remained of Hiroshima after the first atomic bomb was detonated in 1945, and its Peace Park stands in mute testament to the horrors of war and the folly of Japanese militarism. From the sublime to the

ridiculous: Huis Ten Bosch, near Nagasaki, is an amusement park incorporating perfect replicas of many of Holland's most scenic buildings, plus windmills, canals and tulips. Away from the cities, there are excellent opportunities for hiking in the mountains, especially in Daisetsuzan National Park on Hokkaido, and the skiing is good even if it is almost as exorbitantly priced as golf. Down south, there are jungle walks, river kayaking and scuba-diving on the remote island of Iriomote Jima. Japan's geological make-up has both a good and a bad side – the ever-present danger of earthquake, but also myriad onsen or hot springs where you can immerse yourself and rejuvenate after a tiring day.

Hotels in Japan tend to be pricier than in the rest of Asia, in some cases with some reason, but many mid-range hotels are run-down with shabby service and facilities. But there is an enormous range of choice, from the infamous 'capsule' hotels to glittering properties like the Park Hyatt Tokyo. In between there is the charm of ryokan and the rather less traditional minshuku, which are more like bed and breakfasts, while the hoteru abec of Love Hotel Hill in Tokyo's Shibuya district are definitely worth a gander, even if you are not in the mood!

Less worldly Japanese sometimes tell visitors at length and with great pride that their country experiences four seasons, and they are indeed quite distinct. Spring (March to May) brings clear skies and cherry blossoms, summer can be sweatily uncomfortable, autumn leaves between September and November turn rural Japan into its most picturesque, while the winter months can be distinctly cold, especially in the northern islands. But 20 degrees south, at the other end of the archipelago, even December is reasonably balmy.

New Year and Golden Week (April 27 to May 6) are best avoided by visitors as much of Japan is on the move at these times, filling hotels, trains and planes to the max. Other festivals – such as Kyoto's Gion Matsuri parade of exotic floats every July, or the slightly later O Bon when lanterns are floated on water and rivers all over the country – are well worth seeing.

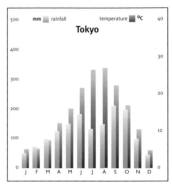

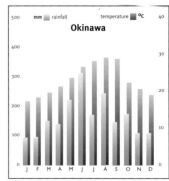

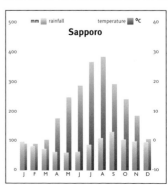

ANA Hotel Tokyo

1-12-33 Akasaka, Minato-Ku, Tokyo 107-0052, Japan
T: +81 3 3505 1111 **F:** +81 3 3505 1155
http://www.asia-hotels.com/hotelinfo/ANA_Hotel_Tokyo/

It is hard to fault the ANA, a highly commendable hotel with excellent service and some 901 rooms spread among its 37 storeys. Convenient for the embassy district, government offices and the manifest joys of Akasaka and Roppongi districts, you can dine extremely well here or simply chill out poolside. In short, it is a very good all-rounder.

All the well-appointed rooms look out on to Tokyo's skyscrapers, the Imperial Palace or Mount Fuji (on a clear day), and are equipped with high-speed Internet, voicemail, satellite TV and some have printers with fax features. Extras like a humidifier, trouser press or VCR are available on loan.

While even the single rooms are perfectly spacious, the best of the bunch have to be the 65-square-metre Corner Suites which make best use of the views of the hotel's surrounds while providing a habitable mini drawing room and double bedroom.

The food and beverage side is well covered with a dozen outlets, ranging from the skilfully prepared traditional Kaiseki meals at Unkai to the flavours, textures and aromas of genuine Cantonese fare in Karin. Live piano music adds to the merry ambience of the top-floor Astral bar, which is next to the Osaka Kyoto Tsuruya restaurant. French, teppanyaki, sushi and Italian cuisine are also available.

Recreational facilities are split firmly between his and hers. The Esthetique Salon lays on fairly heftily priced massages and facials for ladies, while the Sauna (where masseurs are also available) is for men only. Both sexes are free to use the summer-only outdoor pools (one especially for kids) however an admission charge is also levied here – the one real minus point for the hotel. A similar policy exists at

the fitness centre. The hotel also hosts a small shopping arcade, with the boutiques mainly selling fashion items.

Travelling business types should note that the ANA's complement of function rooms is crowned by six 'sky' banquet rooms, each with a celestial name and all with out-of-this-world views.

Rates from: **US$ 183**
Star rating: ★ ★ ★ ★ ★
Bellhop rating: ✿ ✿ ✿ ✿

Value:	7.50	Facilities:	8.20
Staff:	8.63	Restaurants:	8.14
Location:	8.57	Families:	6.13
Cleanliness:	8.81		

Century Hyatt Tokyo

2-7-2 Nishi-Shinjuku, Shinjuku-Ku, Tokyo 160-0023, Japan
T: +81 3 3349 0111 **F:** +81 3 3344 5575
http://www.asia-hotels.com/hotelinfo/Century_Hyatt_Tokyo/

Shinjuku is generally reckoned to be one of the most 'happening' parts of the Japanese capital, a thriving conglomeration of business, shopping, culture and entertainment that is mirrored in the Century Hyatt. It is a substantial hotel, packing 750 rooms and 16 suites, 23 banqueting halls, 10 bars and restaurants, a very stylish top-storey swimming pool and a tea ceremony room into its two solid, box-like towers. Bland from without, inside the hotel is attractively and warmly decorated. The suites are imaginatively laid-out with varying themes, whether Japanese-style with futons, or situated at a corner with

exceptional views over the city. The Rhapsody Bar provides similar vistas, or you can simply ride the elevator to the 28th floor and take a dip in the glass-roofed Sky Pool with its uninterrupted prospect of the heavens.

Rates from: **US$ 222**
Star rating: ★ ★ ★ ★ ★
Bellhop rating: ◖ ◖ ◖ ◖ ½

Value:	7.51	Facilities:	8.56
Staff:	8.97	Restaurants:	8.28
Location:	8.64	Families:	6.57
Cleanliness:	9.14		

Four Seasons Hotel Tokyo at Chinzan-so

10-8 Sekiguchi 2-chome, Bunkyo-Ku, Tokyo 112-8667, Japan
T: +81 3 3943 2222 **F:** +81 3 3943 2300
http://www.asia-hotels.com/hotelinfo/Four_Seasons_Chinzan-So_Tokyo/

One of two Four Seasons' properties in Tokyo, Chinzan-so is set in a 17-acre historic Japanese-style garden which provides a healthy and scenic cordon sanitaire from the surrounding city. The hotel is primarily established as an excellent operations base for the executive traveller. Its 232 rooms and 51 suites

are divided into a slightly complex array of 17 different categories – from the spacious 45-square-metre Superior Rooms through Conservatory Rooms all the way up to the 280-square-metre Imperial Suite. While size and facilities will vary with the room rate, all the way through the hotel guests can

expect the customary peerless Four Seasons service. The staff are especially adept at configuring the hotel's 2,000-plus square metres of meeting space covering 15 function rooms and a 100-seater amphitheatre to guests' conference or other needs – with evening cocktail receptions overlooking the garden a speciality.

Rates from: **US$ 400**
Star rating: ★ ★ ★ ★ ★
Bellhop rating: ◖ ◖ ◖ ◖ ½

Value:	7.51	Facilities:	8.80
Staff:	9.00	Restaurants:	8.30
Location:	7.37	Families:	7.10
Cleanliness:	9.19		

Hilton Tokyo

6-2 Nishi-Shinjuku 6-chome, Shinjuku-Ku, Tokyo 160-0023, Japan
T: +81 3 3344 5111 **F:** +81 3 3342 6094
http://www.asia-hotels.com/hotelinfo/Hilton_Tokyo/

The Hilton has been around in Tokyo for the past four decades, but not always in its present incarnation. This Shinjuku Hilton opened in 1984, with its 38 storeys and 806 rooms enclosed within an unusual S-shaped design. To the outpost of a very American chain are added a number of distinct Japanese touches – so count on digital movies on demand plus shoji screens, voicemail and PC jacks as well as yukata robes and slippers – throughout the hotel. Five floors are dedicated to business travellers, who get a private safe, free high-speed Internet connections and a fax machine as well as their own private – but self-service – lounge. Above them, a further five executive floors get the additional bonus of a concierge in a rather more luxurious lounge.

The amalgam of Asian and international is continued in the Hilton's restaurants. Twenty One is a contemporary dining room with a menu that is essentially French cooked to perfection in the show kitchen; Musashino is deluxe Japanese – sushi and tempura in traditional surroundings; Dynasty is sophisticated Chinese, serving 200 different dishes drawn from all across the country; Checkers is casual, attractive Mediterranean fare; the signature dish at the Teppan Grill is Top Matsuzaka Sirloin Beef; and the Japanese predilection for 'authentic' British pubs is celebrated in St George's with its curry buffets and draft beers.

Even if you are not getting married, or thinking about it, it is worth taking a squint at La Perle, a hi-tech glass and water wedding chapel that is an intriguing mix of kitsch and technology. The adjacent Sakura boardroom leaves out the kitsch bit, and concentrates on top-notch facilities like its 43-inch plasma display screen and comfortable leather seating. The Hilton also features a ballroom that can hold up to 900, and plenty of recreational facilities such as male and female saunas, a pool (indoor) and a brace of tennis courts (outdoor).

Rates from: **US$ 178**
Star rating: ★ ★ ★ ★ ★
Bellhop rating: ♟ ♟ ♟ ♟

Value:	7.42	Facilities:	8.06
Staff:	8.51	Restaurants:	8.11
Location:	8.26	Families:	6.42
Cleanliness:	8.87		

Imperial Hotel

1-1-1 Uchisaiwaicho, Chiyoda-Ku, Tokyo 100-8558, Japan
T: +81 3 3504 1111 **F**: +81 3 3581 9146
http://www.asia-hotels.com/hotelinfo/Imperial_Hotel_Tokyo/

The story of the Imperial – which over the course of a century has set the benchmark for innovation in concert with deluxe hospitality in Tokyo – mirrors the story of modern-day Japan. The first Imperial was founded in 1890 at the behest of the Emperor. A wooden, Victorian-style hotel was raised next to the royal palace on the same site where the modern Imperial stands today. It was a reassuring pied-a-terre for foreigners, equipped with wood-burning fireplaces, Irish linen and English cutlery and was the first hotel in the country to serve beef and pork, which Buddhist precepts had traditionally forbidden. In 1923 a spectacular new building designed by Frank Lloyd Wright opened on the very day of one of Tokyo's worst earthquakes. It suffered minimal damage, but was later bombed during the war and by 1967 had to be dismantled. Parts were incorporated into the new building, which threw open its doors in 1970.

Some three decades later, the Imperial continues to hold sway among the capital's upper-crust accommodation. Divided into a main building and an adjoining tower, it comprises 1,057 rooms including 64 suites. Firmly aimed at the executive market, all the tastefully decorated rooms embrace complimentary high-speed Internet connections, hands-free phones and a very workable desk. An entire wing is given over to the business centre, which as well as the usual secretarial services and conference rooms also includes a soundproof practice chamber for musicians, a relaxation lounge (for early arrivals and late departures) and even showers.

The 13 restaurants include the award-winning French cuisine at Les Saisons, and the subtle flavours of Kyoto – season by season – at Isecho, while the ultra-traditional Imperial Bar continues to serve up the ambience inspired by Frank Lloyd Wright as well as some powerful cocktails. And the hotel provides ample opportunity for relaxation at its fully equipped fitness centre and the heated indoor pool on the 20th floor.

From royal brainchild of the late 19th century to hi-tech hostelry of the new millennium, the Imperial is as pleasing for its historical antecedents as its current offerings and continues to go from strength to strength.

Rates from: **US$ 320**
Star rating: ★ ★ ★ ★ ★
Bellhop rating: 🔔🔔🔔🔔 ½

Value:	7.38	Facilities:	8.29
Staff:	9.02	Restaurants:	8.37
Location:	8.97	Families:	6.55
Cleanliness:	9.16		

Keio Plaza Inter-Continental Tokyo

2-2-1 Nishi-Shinjuku, Shinjuku-Ku, Tokyo 160-8330, Japan
T: +81 3 3344 0111 **F:** +81 3 3345 8269
http://www.asia-hotels.com/hotelinfo/InterContinental_Keio_Plaza_Tokyo/

If they ever remake the classic monster movie *Godzilla*, chances are even it would have a tough job demolishing the Keio Plaza. It is a juggernaut of a hotel, with a nigh-overwhelming line-up of 1,450 rooms, 29 restaurants and bars and 40 function rooms. What saves it from being a maze is the attention that has been paid to giving it a most welcome and hospitable atmosphere. All the artwork (exhibits change every two weeks) in the Lobby Gallery is for sale, but guests are welcome just to sit and talk here. Delicate ikebana flower arrangements dot the public areas. And in contrast to the gritty metropolis outside, the rooms – whether on the executive floor, with tatami mats or a non-smoker – are all pastel hued with extra-spacious windows. Perhaps its major draw though is its prices – a great value property given its very central Shinjuku location in an expensive city.

Rates from: **US$ 190**
Star rating: ★ ★ ★ ★ ★
Bellhop rating: ◗ ◗ ◗ ◗ ½

Value:	7.54	Facilities:	7.98
Staff:	8.71	Restaurants:	8.11
Location:	8.77	Families:	6.87
Cleanliness:	8.86		

Hotel New Otani Tokyo

4-1 Kioi-Cho, Chiyoda-Ku, Tokyo, 102-8578, Japan
T: +81 3 3265 1111 **F:** +81 3 3221 2619
http://www.asia-hotels.com/hotelinfo/New_Otani_Tokyo/

The New Otani is actually nearly 40 years old, having opened just prior to the Olympics in 1964. But it traces its roots back over four centuries, via the exquisitely composed stones, shrubs, ponds, waterfalls and flowers of its celebrated 30,000-square-metre gardens which once belonged to the Samurai warlord Kiyomasa Kato. Juxtaposed with the adjacent hotel's 1,600 rooms and suites (all with high-speed Internet access) and two dozen restaurants, five bars and 28 banquet and conference rooms, the gardens are quite a contrast. Somewhere in this mini-metropolis there is also a post office, dental and health clinics, an art museum, and a chapel, plus indoor and outdoor pools and a gym with ample space for treading the mill or practising yoga. For many, the highlight of the New Otani is the wonderful buffet breakfast with a view at Top of the Tower on the 40th floor, but maybe the best part of the New Otani is still its oldest.

Rates from: **US$ 200**
Star rating: ★ ★ ★ ★ ★
Bellhop rating: ◗ ◗ ◗ ◗ ½

Value:	7.46	Facilities:	8.52
Staff:	8.87	Restaurants:	8.31
Location:	8.53	Families:	6.76
Cleanliness:	9.08		

Hotel Okura

2-10-4 Toranomon, Minato-Ku, Tokyo 105-8416, Japan
T: +81 3 3582 0111 **F:** +81 3 3582 3707
http://www.asia-hotels.com/hotelinfo/Okura_hotel/

The Okura has sat on Embassy Row – one of Tokyo's premier addresses – for the past four decades. No one could call it a beautiful building – or buildings, as it is split into two wings connected by an underground passageway. But beyond its bland, concreted, East-meets-West facade this popular old dog certainly manages to perform a variety of new tricks with the help of some outstandingly professional staff.

The 858 guestrooms may be tinged with the 1960s – some greeny blue upholstery and carpets, gilt and white furniture, and the odd item in shocking pink – but every single one (including the 11 Japanese-style suites) comes armed with broadband and fax machines. Bathrooms are pleasantly marbled with a deep tub and separate shower, while the views from the upper storeys are especially good during the neon-lit twilight hours.

Making a definite choice as to which wing you stay in can help cut down on 'commuting' times, although the walk along the underpass takes no more than a few minutes. Both buildings have shopping arcades, a beauty salon and a pool, but the South Wing also has a poolside restaurant and a health club. Restaurants and bars are split pretty evenly, however the main building hosts primarily Chinese and Japanese eateries – the Sazanka teppanyaki restaurant

enjoys a particularly good reputation – while the South Wing is more Western-oriented with gourmet French dining and art nouveau decor at 12th-floor La Belle Epoque and an a la carte coffee shop. Also featuring strongly here is Bar Highlander, admittedly a mock-up Scotch pub (complete with tartan carpets) but containing more than 200 brands of whisky and other liquors from around the world.

Focussed essentially as a business hotel, the Okura also runs to more than 30 function rooms – again, split between the two wings – with the largest able to hold 2,600 people.

Rates from: **US$ 270**
Star rating: ★ ★ ★ ★ ★
Bellhop rating: 🐟 🐟 🐟 🐟 ½

Value:	7.48	Facilities:	8.56
Staff:	9.16	Restaurants:	8.70
Location:	8.65	Families:	6.42
Cleanliness:	9.31		

Park Hyatt Tokyo

3-7-1 Nishi-Shinjuku, Shinjuku-Ku, Tokyo 163-1055, Japan
T: +81 3 5322 1234 **F:** +81 3 5322 1278
http://www.asia-hotels.com/hotelinfo/Park_Hyatt_Tokyo/

Perched atop the 235-metre 52-storey Shinjuku Park Tower this 14-floor hotel was the first Park Hyatt to open in Asia and remains leader of the pack, besting not only others in the same chain but many kindred properties in the region.

Each of the 178 rooms and suites forms a modernist private residence, tallying hi-tech communications and entertainment accessories with Egyptian cotton sheets, rare water elm from Hokkaido and original artworks by Yoshitaka Echizenya. Also standard are a luxuriously deep bathtub, separate shower and a walk-in wardrobe. The suites are naturally larger and even better appointed, while the Presidential Suite comes with its own sauna, whirlpool and formal dining room and library. In fact, dictionaries are placed in all the rooms as a matter of course, and they are buttressed by a 2,000-volume library (plus several hundred CDs and laser discs)

which is overseen by the concierge.

Similarly impressive is the Hyatt's range of conference and banqueting facilities, which combine sophisticated decor and electronics as both the elegant Ballroom and chandeliered Venetian Room include teleconferencing facilities and video walls.

Four arresting dining outlets at the Hyatt allow guests to put their corporate entertainment allowance to work usefully. The New York Grill

enjoys a dual reputation – for dishes like rotisserie honey-glazed duck and steamed clams dressed with lemongrass, coriander and chilli peppers and also as a venue for gourmet socialites to natter across the tables. At the contemporary Japanese restaurant Kozue, chefs use only the finest and freshest seasonal ingredients, and the hearty, home-style fare is presented on earthenware, porcelain and lacquerware created by noted craftsmen throughout Japan and selected for their warmth and artistry. It is difficult to discern which is more eye-catching at the European-style Girandole – the four massive montages of faces photographed at continental cafes, or the very cosmopolitan menu that ranges through escargots and pastas to mouth-watering deserts. Girandole's

design takes full advantage of abundant natural light, illuminating its elegant interior and rousing its lively atmosphere, while the Ex Libris room in an adjoining alcove displays the hotel's unique collection of bookplates by artists from around the world. Completing the quartet, a sky-lit bamboo garden forms the centrepiece of the Peak Lounge on the 41st floor of the hotel, which is an ideal venue for cocktails or a classic afternoon tea with fresh home-made cakes.

If there is a single part of the Hyatt that defines its ethos and the particular brand of alchemy conjured up by Japanese architect Kenzo Tange and American interior designer John Morford, it is the Club on the Park, the hotel's 2-storey health and fitness sanctuary. Light pours through its 25-metre steel and glass pyramid, 47 floors above the rest of Tokyo, reflecting off the 8 x 20 metre swimming pool. On clear days, a snow-peaked Mount Fuji dominates the horizon like a divinity. Dawn is a particularly popular time to come and put in a few lengths here, while at dusk the glow of metropolitan neon melds with the last rays of the sun. To the side of the pool is an aerobics studio with a unique Bodysonic Floor, providing maximum sound sensation and shock absorption, and a fully equipped gymnasium. An international team of personal fitness specialists is also on hand to tailor fitness programmes to individual needs and there are even classes in aqua exercise and aqua walking. The healthy business of relaxation has never been so pleasurable.

Rates from: **US$ 453**
Star rating: ★ ★ ★ ★
Bellhop rating: 🛎 🛎 🛎 🛎 ½

Value:	7.29	Facilities:	8.68
Staff:	8.95	Restaurants:	8.75
Location:	8.35	Families:	6.70
Cleanliness:	9.22		

Prince Hotel Tokyo (Shinagawa)

10-30 Takanawa 4-chome, Minato-Ku, Tokyo 108-8611, Japan
T: +81 3 3440 1111 **F:** +81 3 3441 7092
http://www.asia-hotels.com/hotelinfo/Shinagawa_Prince_Hotel/

If bonsai had an antonym it would certainly apply to the Prince, as you practically need a map and compass to navigate your way around this overwhelming hotel which sits opposite Shinagawa station. The main tower, containing 1,015 rooms, is backed up by a newer neighbour with 1,736, there are more in the Annex while the Executive Tower brings the total to 3,680. You could eat twice a day for a week without returning to the same restaurant (the 24-hour Yahoo! Cafe with computer terminals is especially popular), while there are also two cinemas (one multiplex, one Imax), a childcare centre, a 104-lane bowling alley, nine indoor tennis courts, 28 karaoke rooms, 14 practice boxes at the golf centre, three pools and billiards and ping-pong in the games centre. It is a little unfair to call this a hotel – it is more like a self-contained community, and a good value one at that.

Rates from: **US$ 90**
Star rating: ★ ★ ★ ★ ★
Bellhop rating: ⬤ ⬤ ⬤ ⬤ ½

Value:	8.12	Facilities:	8.10
Staff:	8.51	Restaurants:	8.12
Location:	8.73	Families:	6.73
Cleanliness:	8.98		

The Ritz-Carlton Osaka

2-5-25 Umeda, Kita-Ku, Osaka 530-0001, Japan
T: +81 6 6343 7000 **F:** +81 6 6343 7001
http://www.asia-hotels.com/hotelinfo/RitzCarlton_Osaka/

Every year the Ritz-Carlton hosts numerous weddings, with couples in tuxedos and silk gowns plighting their troth in the hotel's chapel or Shinto shrine. They are drawn mainly by the Ritz's intriguing European aura – an anomaly in building block Osaka – as its 18th- and 19th-century arts and antiques, Italian marble, silk wall coverings and large-scale fireplaces are reminiscent of a bygone age of elegance. Fast forward to the 21st century and you have 292 luxuriously fitted rooms, all with marble bathrooms; the suites carry extras like CD players while there is even a grand piano in the 233-square-metre Ritz-Carlton Suite. Anyone overindulging at the Japanese, Chinese, French or Mediterranean restaurants can take advantage of the free (a rarity in Japanese hotels) gym, with its state-of-the-art workout studio, saunas and indoor and outdoor whirlpools. Spa services are also available.

Rates from: **US$ 216**
Star rating: ★ ★ ★ ★ ★
Bellhop rating: ⬤ ⬤ ⬤ ⬤ ⬤

Value:	7.60	Facilities:	9.18
Staff:	9.48	Restaurants:	8.80
Location:	8.82	Families:	6.88
Cleanliness:	9.60		

Westin Miyako Kyoto

Keage, Sanjo, Higashiyama-Ku, Kyoto 605-0052, Japan
T: +81 75 771 7111 **F:** +81 75 751 2490
http://www.asia-hotels.com/hotelinfo/Westin_Miyako_Kyoto/

Kyoto, with more than 2,000 temples and shrines, a trio of palaces and scores of gardens and museums, is one of the must-sees of Japan – as its 40 million annual visitors would testify. The more astute of these check into the Westin Miyako, a deluxe 11-storey resort, with a heritage dating back to 1890, on the wooded slopes of Mount Kacho commanding stunning views over the city. It is not exactly boutique, with 516 rooms (including a clutch of Japanese-style rooms in the Sukiya Annex which holds a tea ceremony cottage), a dozen restaurants – Espoir, the French restaurant, is especially good – and 16 banqueting and conference rooms, but it is extremely comfortable. Perhaps the Miyako's greatest asset is its ancient garden, with a design inspired by Kyoto culture and an 800-metre bird-watching trail. Other recreational opportunities include a sauna, jacuzzi, swimming pools (indoor and out) and tennis courts.

Rates from: **US$ 221**
Star rating: ★ ★ ★ ★ ★
Bellhop rating: 🛎🛎🛎🛎🛎

Value:	8.31	Facilities:	8.76
Staff:	9.10	Restaurants:	8.72
Location:	9.10	Families:	7.48
Cleanliness:	9.45		

The Westin Tokyo

1-4-1 Mita, Meguro, Tokyo 153-8580, Japan
T: +81 3 5423 7000 **F:** +81 3 5423 7600
http://www.asia-hotels.com/hotelinfo/Westin_Tokyo_The/

There are not exactly rolling acres of greensward at Yebisu Garden Place, but the self-contained community built on an old Sapporo brewery site does offer a respite from the hectic thoroughfares of Tokyo. Capping its museums, cinemas, shopping and dining facilities (plus a 1,700-seat beer hall) is the 22-storey Westin, a deluxe European-style hotel containing 445 rooms and a host of restaurants and other facilities. The rooms are particularly large by Japanese standards – even standard rooms encompass 42 square metres – and the deluxe bathrooms have a separate tub and shower stall. High-speed Internet access is available in all rooms and guests can choose between 1.8-metre-wide king-sized beds, two double beds or three singles. The fitness centre and pool are located in the Club next door where guests enjoy preferential rates.

Rates from: **US$ 241**
Star rating: ★ ★ ★ ★ ★
Bellhop rating: 🛎🛎🛎🛎 ½

Value:	7.26	Facilities:	8.64
Staff:	9.03	Restaurants:	8.35
Location:	8.59	Families:	6.46
Cleanliness:	9.44		

KOREA (SOUTH)

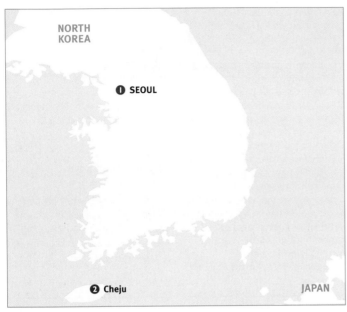

Although it may feel quite complete to the visitor, South Korea is only one half of a nation. Geographically the Korean peninsula was never well placed – sandwiched between China and Japan, it spent centuries being invaded from one side or the other. Things did not get much easier when Russia expanded into the frame and colonial powers came knocking. Looking at the map, Korea sticks out like North Asia's sore thumb. Too tempting to ignore, it has endured a long history of invasions and occupations, and it is of little surprise that Korea became introverted and insular, shunning the outside world. A century ago the West referred to Korea as 'The Hermit Kingdom' but Koreans have learned that the world just will not have it that way.

In the 20th century Korean streets echoed to a variety of military boots – including Japanese, Chinese and American. The Korean War tore through the nation after the surrender of the Japanese at the end of World War II and came to symbolise the world's political struggle of the age. Other nations leapt into the ideological battleground, the devastating war ended in stalemate and the nation broke in two following armistice in 1953. For the past 50 years Korea has been split between North and South.

Today the communist North remains very much the international hermit and is jammed in a political time warp. Strident Stalinist statues boldly salute the continuing cold war. As the world's most heavily fortified and sensitive border, the demilitarised zone (DMZ) separates the two Koreas. Thousands of armed forces are poised either side of the buffer that is roughly four kilometres wide.

South Korea is a total contrast to its northern neighbour, and has diverged into a modern industrialised powerhouse. South of the demarcation line the peninsula liberally sprouts manufacturing plants and heavy industry, yet untouched countryside remains in many parts. South Korea enjoys a temperate climate with four seasons, the best times to go being the autumn and the spring. In autumn the countryside breaks into vivid reds and golds, and spring is popular for the gentle tree blossoms. Sticky summer sees the country pummelled by typhoons and winter is for the most part extremely cold.

The country is by no means overrun by mass tourism. A high proportion of visitors are on short breaks from Japan and China, although the strong US influence sees quite a few Americans shuttling through mainly on business. There is less to see and do when compared with some other countries in Asia, a legacy perhaps of war, pillage and economic boom. The modern capital Seoul is a sprawling – but not unpleasant – metropolis rather bereft of

authentic cultural attractions. It offers some temples and palaces, though mostly reconstructed rather than restored. But one unforgettable highlight for foreigners is the surreal tour to the DMZ. Weird but engaging attractions here include exploring invasion tunnels and peering at mysterious North Korea through the observation point's telescopes.

Seoul's shopping is also extensive with comparatively low prices attracting waves of Japanese shoppers. Restaurants cater mainly for the Asian palate. A visit to Korea is certainly not complete without

munching on some kimchi – salted and spicy cabbage. It does not look exciting but one of the first questions Koreans will ask you is if you have tried it.

In the south, a short way from the port city of Pusan lies the unusual ancient site of Gyeongju, a delightful historic area spanning across the plains and hills. Gyeongju is dotted with tombs and cultural artefacts and was luckily spared destruction during all of the invasions of the past 1,000 years. South Korea also has some beautiful natural scenery – wonderful sweeping mountains for

hikers, good golf courses plus several acceptable ski resorts and to the south the tourist beaches of Cheju Island.

Visitors tend to find hotels to be big and glitzy but well maintained. Some of the newer ones are as good as any in Asia. Koreans are wonderful hosts, being welcoming and friendly, and the vast majority of hotels convey this although English can be a problem away from the top ones. Unfortunately, since Seoul is home to a quarter of the population, property prices have shot up higher than a North Korean missile and hotels are stiffly priced, and this seems to have set the benchmark for the rest of the country.

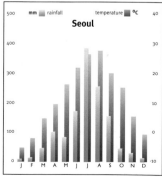

COEX Inter-Continental Seoul

159 Samsung-dong, Kangnam-Ku, Seoul 135976, Korea
T: +82 2 3452 2500 F: +82 2 3430 8000
http://www.asia-hotels.com/hotelinfo/COEX_InterContinental_Hotel_Seoul/

This is frequently touted as South Korea's leading business hotel. The COEX Inter-Continental is bang up to date and has just about everything that could be realistically asked for from a business hotel. There are many good things about the COEX, but the obvious one is the location – set in the most central part of the shiny new business district of Kangnam. The glitzy skyscraper is adjacent to the World Trade Centre and connected to Seoul's leading business facility, the COEX Convention and Exhibition Centre. The complex also has a downtown immigration service and air link for extra convenience, purpose-built for business travellers. Nearly 100 shops and 60-plus restaurants, the Hyundai Department Store, Cineplex with 17 screens, fashion plaza and aquarium complete the picture.

The hotel itself very much mirrors its modern surroundings and is smart, stylish and swanky. The other Inter-Continental, the Grand within the same complex, is more classic and mature, while this one revels in trendy youthful vigour.

The facilities are excellent with regards to upkeep, ambience, practicality and depth. The open kitchen buffet of the Brasserie on the 1st floor is supremely popular and diners can drift from section to section nibbling a broad selection of the world's cuisines. Asian Live on the 2nd floor is equally multinational with fare from Korea, China, Japan, Thailand, India and Indonesia. Other facilities are just as trendy and cosmopolitan – including the aptly named Cosmopolitan Fitness Centre complete with golf room, saunas and massage rooms and a whirlpool spa. The Sky Lounge is worth a look. A sleek, space-age bar 30 floors up, it is a good place to absorb the skyline. Many of the 654 rooms have similar views. Their design is not quite as adventurous as the rest of the hotel, in fact they are pretty indistinguishable from any other luxury hotel room. But they are certainly good enough and are well equipped.

Business facilities are state of the art with no less than 16 meeting rooms with capacities from 15 to 1,500. Some of these are located on the 30th floor and come with excellent views. Eight-language simultaneous translation and teleconferencing are some of the many services available. This is a superb package that should meet the needs of any business traveller, but should this not be the case you can always nip around to the neighbouring Grand Inter-Continental as guests have reciprocal signing rights.

Rates from: **US$ 256**
Star rating: ★★★★★
Bellhop rating: 🛎🛎🛎🛎 ½

Value:	7.53	Facilities:	8.49
Staff:	8.39	Restaurants:	8.27
Location:	8.63	Families:	6.37
Cleanliness:	8.73		

Grand Hyatt Seoul

747-7 Hannam-dong, Yongsan-Ku, Seoul 140738, Korea
T: +82 2 797 1234 **F:** +82 2 798 6953
http://www.asia-hotels.com/hotelinfo/Grand_Hyatt_Seoul/

Certainly among Seoul's top two or three hotels – and arguably the best all-rounder – is this outstanding property from the Hyatt Group. Sat on top of a sparsely wooded hill overlooking a quiet neighbourhood around Namsan Park, the big advantage (and disadvantage) of this sizeable hotel is its location. On the map it looks quite central but it is positioned just off a major slip road and has little within walking distance, lending it a suburban feel. Perched comfortably on its fine vantage point it has plenty of space which it uses well.

The striking granite and marble lobby soothes with the notes of live classical musicians. The subtle lighting, warm woods and greenery all help set a convivial tone. The benefits of the glass exterior then become clear – views from the lobby lounge sweep beyond the greenery and over the capital. The Grand Hyatt's lobby is certainly a triumph. Leading off from it are some very agreeable restaurants indeed, including the Paris Grill brasserie, two Japanese eateries, Akasaka and the more intimate Tenkai, and the Chinese Restaurant complete with open kitchen. Descending from the lobby brings you to one of Asia's most creative outdoor swimming pools. Most of the year it is just an attractive, glassy blue swimming pool complete with sundeck and poolside barbeque facilities. But come Korea's chilly winter months the pool mutates into an ice skating rink. The Hyatt maintains the back-up of an enticing indoor pool and spa all year round, to go with the full complement of other quite excellent business and leisure facilities. Lively JJ Mahoney's, for instance, is one of Seoul's premier bars.

The 602 rooms are also outstanding – cool, crisp and many offering engaging city views. High-speed 'plug and play' Internet access is provided throughout complete with 24-hour technical support. For the privileged, the stylish specialty suites occupy the top three floors while the five floors of club rooms and supporting facilities are truly world-class and well above other hotels' comparable efforts. The hotel is not particularly well positioned but it is certainly not inconvenient, lying just a few minutes from Itaewon Metro by taxi and five kilometres from the central business district.

Rates from: **US$ 202**
Star rating: ★ ★ ★ ★ ★
Bellhop rating: ♙ ♙ ♙ ♙ ½

Value:	7.54	Facilities:	8.46
Staff:	8.35	Restaurants:	8.41
Location:	8.22	Families:	7.05
Cleanliness:	8.65		

Lotte Seoul Hotel

Sogong-dong, Jung-Ku, Seoul 100721, Korea
T: +82 2 771 1000 **F:** +82 2 752 3758
http://www.asia-hotels.com/hotelinfo/Lotte_Seoul_Hotel/

The Lotte claims to be the most prestigious hotel in Seoul, and while this may not be quite true, there is an awful lot going for South Korea's largest hotel. It is not the smartest, but it must be the most convenient for tourists, especially shoppers, being right in the middle of the prime retail areas. It is a few steps from City Hall Metro and has its own attached mega-department store. Towering at 38 storeys the Lotte has a staggering 1,486 rooms and just about all the facilities any hotel can possibly have in a city centre, including an indoor golf driving range. There are, for example, 14 restaurants and bars. Standards are good but maybe not quite internationally 5-star. The rooms are flush with mod cons including wireless Internet. While the hotel's flamboyant decor is less than subtle, with its location and facilities the hugely popular Lotte appeals to a wide audience from families to business executives.

Rates from: US$ 170
Star rating: ★ ★ ★ ★ ★
Bellhop rating: 👍👍👍👍 ½

Value:	7.82	Facilities:	8.38
Staff:	8.29	Restaurants:	8.28
Location:	8.67	Families:	7.59
Cleanliness:	8.62		

Novotel Ambassador Kangnam

603 Yeoksam-dong, Kangnam-Ku, Seoul 135080, Korea
T: +82 2 567 1101 **F:** +82 2 567 7858
http://www.asia-hotels.com/hotelinfo/Novotel_Ambassador_Kangnam/

South Korean hotel prices are pretty steep. Since most 5-star hotels charge stratospheric prices, many visitors either choose or are compelled to drop a star or two when visiting. The 4-star market is not particularly exciting, but there is the salvation of the Novotel in the business and shopping district of Kangnam, 10 minutes walk from the Metro. It is still not that cheap but it does offer a standard of rooms and facilities not far behind the 5-stars for half the price or less. The 336 rooms are well fitted out and include three executive floors, the seven restaurants and bars are reliable and the hotel ambience is comparable to a 5-star – smart, modern, airy and clean – and the service is excellent. There are few distinguishing features about this big block physically, the main point being that it is a good, well-located 4-star for a relatively affordable price – quite a novelty is Seoul.

Rates from: US$ 99
Star rating: ★ ★ ★ ★
Bellhop rating: 👍👍👍👍

Value:	7.50	Facilities:	8.03
Staff:	7.94	Restaurants:	7.69
Location:	8.06	Families:	6.83
Cleanliness:	8.31		

The Ritz-Carlton Seoul

602 Yeoksam-dong, Kangnam-Ku, Seoul 150080, Korea
T: +82 2 3451 8000 **F:** +82 2 3451 8280
http://www.asia-hotels.com/hotelinfo/RitzCarlton_Seoul_The/

mini TVs in the bathrooms. The staff – from the bath butler to the IT assistant – offer very high service standards, and the hotel is fairly well located for business with Kangnam Metro being only 10 minutes walk away. The Ritz-Carlton is a very good hotel with superior standards to many others in the same price bracket.

The jagged exterior may look half-finished but the Ritz-Carlton has perhaps the most stylish and classy interior of any hotel in Korea. Right from the 6-storey atrium, this very chic offering has all the expected facilities, but its refined European feel gives it an edge over other, more modest 5-star properties. Gourmet restaurants are some of the most elegant (and priciest) in Seoul and there is a quite stunning indoor pool and spa. Extra little touches are obvious throughout the 410 luxurious but relaxing rooms, such as VCRs and CD players, and

Rates from: US$ 179
Star rating: ★ ★ ★ ★ ★
Bellhop rating: 👍 👍 👍 👍

Value:	7.13	Facilities:	8.05
Staff:	8.32	Restaurants:	7.99
Location:	7.52	Families:	6.26
Cleanliness:	8.45		

Sheraton Grande Walkerhill

21 Gwangjang-dong, Gwangjin-Ku, Seoul, Kyonggi-Do, Korea
T: +82 2 455 5000 **F:** +82 2 452 6867
http://www.asia-hotels.com/hotelinfo/Sheraton_Walker_Hill/

This Sheraton stands apart from Seoul's rather conformist hotels and has decided to occupy a very different niche. Very leisure oriented, the hotel is set on the green north easterly skirts of the capital, 40 minutes from the town centre. Overlooking Mount A-Cha, this huge 623-roomed hotel has a good spread of sporting facilities, a golf driving range and three pools. Seoul's sole casino is the proud centrepiece, with gambling around the clock and the elaborate Walker Hill Shows – Korean folk dances, bright Latino musicals and raunchy topless extravaganzas – staged in a 720-seat theatre. And with over a dozen fair restaurants, the hotel-cum-resort caters for virtually anyone. The rooms are set in two towers and an annex, and range from the slightly ordinary standard rooms (Main Tower) to the detached villas (Annex). At 40 years old the hotel is beginning to show its age but its popularity shows no sign of waning especially with the Japanese hopping over for weekend gaming breaks.

Rates from: US$ 194
Star rating: ★ ★ ★ ★ ★
Bellhop rating: 👍 👍 👍 👍 ½

Value:	7.61	Facilities:	8.37
Staff:	8.52	Restaurants:	8.33
Location:	7.95	Families:	7.56
Cleanliness:	8.83		

Shilla Hotel Cheju

3039-3 Saekdal-dong, Seogwipo-shi, Cheju-do, Korea
T: +82 64 738 4466 **F:** +82 64 735 5415
http://www.asia-hotels.com/hotelinfo/Shilla_Cheju/

In Korea's subtropical south lies the volcanic island retreat of Cheju, a popular escape for Koreans and Japanese. The Shilla Cheju, part of the Chungmun Resort Complex, is the island's top residence. The hotel optimistically suggests that it has been recognised as one of the four best resorts in the world. This it is not, but it is the best in Korea and a fine respite. Launched in 1990, the resort, with its mock-European styling, spreads out over 21 acres of landscaped cliff-top gardens. Hotel facilities are among the most extensive in the country with extras like a casino, a bowling alley and an unusual indoor/outdoor pool. Each of the 429 guestrooms is spacious and has a private balcony with views of Mount Halla or the ocean. The complex includes a golf course, a beach and some wonderful areas of natural beauty, so it is no surprise the resort bulges with happy families in the summer.

Rates from: **US$ 240**
Star rating: ★ ★ ★ ★ ★
Bellhop rating: 👲👲👲👲👲

Value:	7.77	Facilities:	8.91
Staff:	9.23	Restaurants:	8.73
Location:	9.03	Families:	7.86
Cleanliness:	9.27		

The Shilla Seoul

202 2-Ga, Jangchung-dong, Chung-Ku, Seoul 100856, Korea
T: +82 2 2233 3131 **F**: +82 2 2233 5073
http://www.asia-hotels.com/hotelinfo/Shilla_Seoul_The/

Standing proud on the pedestal of a green hill, the 23-storey Shilla is a significant monument on Seoul's skyline. From a distance it looks dominant and purposeful, almost like a bold, coppery stele. For a relatively central hotel it is huge, somehow managing to have 23 acres of greenery all to itself. It feels much like a university campus in layout when walking up the hill through the gardens and the broad car park. This communal facility feel is maintained inside, the angular lobby with its combination of red-brick, grey columns and pinewood making you wonder if you have stepped into an exhibition or performing arts centre.

The award-winning Shilla has a fine reputation but is visually different to typical top international hotel chains inside. Being a very Korean enterprise it tends to be a very well-packaged and smart product, but also slightly lacking in imagination when it comes to style or flair. That does not mean that it is ugly – it most certainly is not –

but expect everything to blend in rather anonymously in unobtrusive comfort. Luxury is not just defined by artistic impression but by standards and services. And for this the Shilla excels – there are few hotels in the city with broader amenities, and due to the generous space they are simply bigger and tend to be more comprehensive. The jogging track, for example, disappears into a 10-acre sculpture park rather than a miserable lap of a hotel wing. The duty-free shopping centre is literally a packed out plaza. Also expect very Korean service – exemplary. Business facilities are bang up to date technologically (including Bloomberg terminals in the 24-hour business centre), plus there are

more than enough large, capable restaurants including French, Korean, Italian, Chinese and Japanese cuisine. And for a real change in scenery, the adjacent Yeong Bin Gwan, Korea's former state guesthouse has three very Korean-styled banquet halls.

Its 505 light and trim rooms are again generous in size, with traditional Korean fittings and robust and dependable furniture. Internet TV, wireless LAN and multi-lingual voicemail are just some of the standard facilities. A big plus are the views over the city, which given the hotel's raised position are quite superb. With Dongguk station just a 5-minute walk away, the hotel is ideal for those needing a bit of space and fresh air while still being 10 minutes from the main financial districts and within half an hour of just about everything else that counts in Seoul.

Rates from: US$ 122
Star rating: ★★★★★
Bellhop rating: ♜♜♜♜ ½

Value:	7.64	Facilities:	8.49
Staff:	8.79	Restaurants:	8.43
Location:	7.98	Families:	7.23
Cleanliness:	8.83		

The Westin Chosun

87 Sogong-dong, Jung-Ku, Seoul 100070, Korea
T: +82 2 752 1443 **F:** +82 2 756 8848
http://www.asia-hotels.com/hotelinfo/Westin_Chosun/

If one had to pick a hotel for its location, at least for tourists, then it would be the Westin Chosun. It is only a few steps from two Metro stations, and over the road from the buzzing shopping maze of Myong-dong. Also within easy walking distance is Toksu Palace, the famed bargains of Namdaemun Market and the stately City Hall, considered by many as the centre of Seoul. But the Westin Chosun is also set on the edge of Youido, one of Seoul's main business areas, and so sets itself up primarily as a business hotel.

Seoul's oldest hotel has a distinguished past dating back to 1914, which in this modern city makes it an heirloom. The Westin Chosun is not really old or historic, with no elegant colonial airs about it. It is more stately, grandfatherly, perhaps even a tad stuffy. The dim enclosed interior involves lots of deep dark woods with many underground facilities reminiscent of cellars. Three wings stretch out of a central core, to give three concave faces. Each of the 453 rooms is chic but simple and clearly designed with the executive in mind – 10Mbps LAN connections, four lines for telephone, computer, fax and Internet access, and voicemail.

The facilities are in very good shape bearing in mind the hotel's advanced years. Predictably for Seoul the facilities are very expensive, especially the restaurants where the prices are well above those outside. The difference is on the menus, since Korean and Japanese restaurants dominate the district. Apart from junk food joints and the odd pizza bar, the Chosun is one of the only places with anything Western to eat in the area. O'Kim's does not look all that Irish, but the European food is good, as are the offerings from Ninth Gate (continental), Yesterday (Italian) and the Cafe Royale (international). The Asian restaurants offer attractive Chinese, Korean and Japanese dishes and an authentic ambience.

The gym is certainly good and the huge business centre is exemplary with the full range of services laid on. The useful meeting rooms, offices for rent and 24-hour secretarial services make the Westin Chosun one of the preferred business bases north of the river.

Rates from: **US$ 249**
Star rating: ★ ★ ★ ★ ★
Bellhop rating: 🛎 🛎 🛎 🛎 ½

Value:	7.71	Facilities:	8.54
Staff:	8.78	Restaurants:	8.32
Location:	8.99	Families:	6.05
Cleanliness:	9.03		

LAOS

VIETNAM

❶ Luang Prabang

❷ VIENTIANE

THAILAND

CAMBODIA

Hidden away and landlocked into Southeast Asia's inaccessible mountains is one of Asia's forgotten lands. Quiet Laos has very few visitors and refreshingly low-key tourism. Unlike other Asian Third World countries, you will not be hassled by vendors, or feel a financial target. With a population of only six million chiefly involved in agriculture, there is little industry and consequently few hotels, which for the most part are basic and rudimentary.

The restful capital Vientiane, with its population of only 100,000, feels like an escape in its own right. This is about as busy as it gets in dormant Laos, a country where the tallest building is only seven storeys. There can be few capitals with cabbage patches lining the busiest districts. Up country is the magical Luang Prabang, officially designated as the best preserved 'city' in Southeast Asia by UNESCO. The streets are mainly dotted with quaint French colonial houses and the famed temples are ornate and absolutely spectacular. The gentle Mekong winds its way through and the rush hour is an orange tide of monks.

Infrastructure beyond the threads connecting these two is virtually non-existent. The mountains have never really been tamed and are controlled by rebel forces. Even if it was safe, such is the state of the roads that it would take several days to navigate through the northern regions. Flying or boating down the languid Mekong is the only way.

Poor old Laos is the most bombed country in the history of warfare. Around the barren and remote cowboy town of Phonsavan the sad legacy of Agent Orange is visible in the useless soils. Farmers try to make the best of it in the bomb-littered fields. Many deal in scrap metal, with shell casings forming props for huts or troughs for pigs. The main reason to come this far out is to scratch your head over the mysterious Plain Of Jars. Hundreds of ancient stone jars are strewn across the hilltops and no one has quite worked out what they were. In the Vietnam War these drum-sized oddities were used as bomb shelters and many have been raked with gunfire.

The lazy pace, absence of materialism and strong culture is a breath of fresh air. Higher elevations are cool all year round. Laos undergoes a tropical monsoon and is best visited in the dry season, December to April. It is still quite tough to get around, but the challenge is well rewarded for those who take the time.

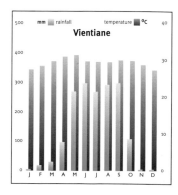

Le Calao Inn

Mekong Road, Luang Prabang, Laos
T: +856 71 212 100 **F:** +856 71 212 085
http://www.asia-hotels.com/hotelinfo/Calao_Inn_Le_/

Le Calao Inn is one of the loveliest hostelries anywhere in Asia. It cannot quite be classed as a hotel even though the price on the tariff puts it in the same bracket. The label 'boutique hotel' may also be a bit vague. Le Calao is best described as a glorious bed and breakfast, low on facilities but absolutely brimming with character. The name is derived from the origins of the owners (Canada and Laos) but for a rather more romantic explanation turn to your French dictionary. Calao is the French/Malay word for the tropical hornbill bird found throughout Asia – it incidentally is also the hotel's emblem.

The building is a lovingly restored 1904 French mansion, a true remnant of the romantic Indochine past. The exterior is lusciously French, with archways, shutters and decorative balconies. The interior is a rare glimpse of a forgotten era. The inn is filled with polished dark wood with depth and soul. Floors creak and give a little underfoot, the small cocktail bar surely belongs to another era. Le Calao is rich in colonial history, but it is not rich in facilities nor luxury. This provides an authentic experience. There are no gyms, TVs or anything else that would feel out of place in the early 20th century.

The inn's simplicity is absolute, being utterly personal it has only six rooms. The rooms are spartan and simple, but in a thoroughly enjoyable way. Beds are solid and sturdy, light switches and wiring exposed and the bathrooms tiled with homely Gallic blue and white tiles. The only traces of the modern world are the air-conditioning units and the rather weak electric showers. From the four upper rooms your every footstep is amplified as you slip along in your socks to the balcony which overlooks the languid

Mekong and provides a perfect spot from which to admire the sunsets. The two lower rooms are much larger and spill into quiet terrace gardens.

Hotel facilities are almost non-existent but the tranquillity here is bliss. The location overlooking the Mekong and within a leisurely stroll of the splendour of Luang Prabang's palaces is pretty much unrivalled, the venerable Wat Xieng Thong is less that 150 metres away. The food at Le Calao is simple and unfussy, but the staff are superbly sweet and helpful. A wonderful, wonderful retreat.

Rates from: **US$ 55**
Star rating: ★
Bellhop rating: **Editor's pick**

Value:	n/a	Facilities:	n/a
Staff:	n/a	Restaurants:	n/a
Location:	n/a	Families:	n/a
Cleanliness:	n/a		

Lao Plaza Hotel Vientiane

63 Samsenthai Road, Vientiane, Laos
T: +856 21 218 800 **F:** +856 21 218 808
http://www.asia-hotels.com/hotelinfo/Lao_Plaza_Hotel/

This is Laos' sole representative of what most of us would consider a 'big hotel'. There are no others in a sleepy land where the capital holds a mere 100,000 residents. In fact, at seven storeys, this is the tallest building in the country and it also has the fullest range of facilities. The formula for a big hotel is only applied at the Lao Plaza. Business facilities quite frankly have no real competition so naturally they get the lion's share of business travellers. A cavernous wood-crafted lobby leads off towards the reassuringly familiar set of amenities including pool, restaurants and a standard fitness offering. The 142 rooms again are a relief – they follow the international mould without ever trying to be characteristic or clever, exactly what many travellers want in this very undeveloped country. And the staff are top class with a real desire to please.

Rates from: **US$ 80**
Star rating: ★ ★ ★ ★
Bellhop rating: ♎ ♎ ♎ ♎

Value:	7.50	Facilities:	7.85
Staff:	8.05	Restaurants:	8.05
Location:	8.70	Families:	7.55
Cleanliness:	8.35		

Novotel Vientiane

Unit 9, Samsen Thai Road, Vientiane, Laos
T: +856 21 213 570 **F:** +856 21 213 572
http://www.asia-hotels.com/hotelinfo/Novotel_Vientiane/

The Novotel Vientiane is the country's sole international hotel chain representative and is the place to go for those playing it safe. Modest, medium and modern, it squashes in all the facilities that qualify it for 4-star status. Some of the facilities are small enough to raise eyebrows but the hotel centrepiece, the lovely pool, is the best in Vientiane. The 168 rooms and suites are mass-produced, claiming French influence, with unusually shaped windows. The business facilities are adequate for individuals, but this is no conference venue. The location is reasonably situated halfway between the airport and the town centre and a short stroll to the Mekong riverside. Happy staff sometimes get their wires crossed but overall you certainly get an international product and, thankfully, not an ugly concrete box.

Rates from: **US$ 51**
Star rating: ★ ★ ★ ★
Bellhop rating: ♎ ♎ ♎ ♎ ½

Value:	8.00	Facilities:	8.05
Staff:	8.52	Restaurants:	8.24
Location:	7.95	Families:	6.71
Cleanliness:	8.43		

Settha Palace Hotel

6 Pang Kham Street, Vientiane, Laos
T: +856 21 217 581 **F:** +856 21 217 583
http://www.asia-hotels.com/hotelinfo/Settha_Palace_Hotel/

A gem of a hotel, the Settha Palace is a beautifully restored piece of French colonial architecture dating from the turn of the 20th century. Of all Vientiane's hotels this is by far the most enjoyable – a recollection of a bygone era in Laos, offering just as much historical grace and depth as other Asian grande dames but at everyday prices.

The colonial French first opened the Settha in 1932. It fell into disrepair in the 1970s, and was only reopened after a painstaking renovation in 1999 by the current owner Billy Theodas – whose parents rather nostalgically were one of the early proprietors.

The authenticity runs deep with an abundance of stately and solid woods, gently creaking floorboards and delightfully spacious rooms with massive hand-carved four-posters and thick Persian rugs. Authentic shutters, period furniture and landscaped gardens all add to the historic charm. The Settha's 29 spacious rooms and suites are simple but enjoyable with generous marbled bathrooms complete with a separate walk-in shower, and all the modern conveniences demanded these days including IDD, laptop ports, satellite TV and in-room safe – by no means common amenities in

Laos. The same can also be said of the well-equipped business centre complete with workstations and secretarial services.

The ever so slightly stiff Belle Epoque dining room, with large French windows and a high wooden-studded ceiling, is very elegant to view but a tad pricey, however the cuisine is more than adequate. Alfresco dining by the pool and jacuzzi is much more casual, together with the open-air Sidewalk Cafe which offers tasty Asian fare.

As the hotel is just a few minutes stroll from the town centre it is well located to take advantage of Vientiane's pleasant little restaurants and cafes as well as the morning market, Presidential Palace, Wat Sisakhet, Thatluang Temple and broad vistas of the Mekong River; alternatively, board the hotel's London Taxi, a charming, anomalous extra to this unique property. Hotels like the Settha are rare indeed.

Rates from: **US$ 88**
Star rating: ★ ★ ★ ★ ★
Bellhop rating: 🔔 🔔 🔔 🔔 ½

Value:	8.76	Facilities:	8.69
Staff:	8.59	Restaurants:	7.69
Location:	8.86	Families:	4.48
Cleanliness:	9.17		

Villa Santi Hotel

Sakkarine Road, Ban Vat Nong Village, Luang Prabang, Laos
T: +856 71 252157 **F:** +856 71 252158
http://www.asia-hotels.com/hotelinfo/Villa_Santi_Hotel_The_/

In many ways, the Villa Santi Hotel sums up the sleepy land of Laos. It is a lovely little boutique hotel that dovetails perfectly with the quaint northern town of Luang Prabang. Right in the heart of a UNESCO-designated World Heritage site, the Villa Santi was once the residence of a Lao princess and is sprinkled with antiques and ethnic handicrafts. A royal history it may have, but this is no sprawling palace – there are just 25 rooms and suites, all elegantly decorated with rosewood furnishings and silk textiles, yet still with discreet modern conveniences such as air-conditioning.

The overall impression is of modest, comfortably upholstered simplicity with gentle French influences. This is especially notable on the first floor where the open restaurant overlooks the quiet street below. Motorised traffic is virtually non-existent in remote Luang Prabang, and you can sit back and enjoy the surreal non-rush hour over your breakfast, while waves of orange-robed monks drift toward their stunningly ornate monasteries. At dinner, the menu features royal Lao cuisine prepared

by a former palace chef, while at any time of day the Elephant Bar is ideal for a snack or a leisurely thirst quencher.

The Santi never really feels like a hotel – it is more a house party of strangers who have been drawn together by a mutual friend who just happens to be absent. Service is exceptionally graceful but a little slow at times and occasionally handicapped by the language barrier; however, the staff's sincere and heart-warming smiles seem to evaporate any frustration this may

cause. It almost goes without saying that the Villa Santi Hotel (not to be confused with the newly opened Villa Santi Resort just down the road) has enormous personality and charm. This is the place to stay for those looking for a genuinely Lao experience and it is one that will leave a lasting and incredibly favourable impression.

Rates from: US$ 80
Star rating: ★ ★ ★ ½
Bellhop rating: 🛎 🛎 🛎 🛎 ½

Value:	7.92	Facilities:	7.44
Staff:	8.88	Restaurants:	8.28
Location:	8.88	Families:	5.68
Cleanliness:	8.48		

MACAU

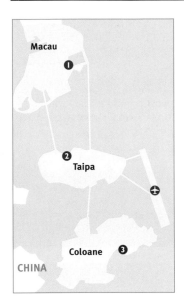

MACAU TOURISM

Macau is a weird place that feels like it should not really exist. This tiny enclave is an unlikely mix of two completely alien cultures – Chinese and Portuguese. After the Portuguese dropped anchor in 1557 and blew away the local pirates, China permitted the Europeans to administer just enough land to park a few galleons. Macau was Europe's first foothold in Asia and the gateway to China until the Opium Wars in the 19th century led to the concession of Hong Kong. It was finally handed back in 1999, but 400 years saw plenty of Latin influence and there are many

interesting historical remnants. Macau is a surreal hybrid, an intriguing canvas of ornate Portuguese flair and Chinese tradition and a unique pocket of Asia. Fine examples of centuries-old colonial architecture include the famous ruined facade of St Paul's Cathedral, the symbol of Macau. Other colonial examples include the Guia Lighthouse, and there are historic Chinese highlights such as incense-filled Ah Ma Temple.

Hong Kong lies just an hour away by jetfoil and the overflow of wealth basically powers the Macau economy. It has evolved from a trade base and port into a Chinese leisure centre with thousands shuttling over for weekend city breaks. Casinos are the big magnet for Chinese visitors with many getting no further than this smoky and murky world. A whopping 50 per cent of Macau's revenue and a quarter of the labour market are tied up in the trade. These are not glitzy Las Vegas razzmatazz showpieces, but more gritty and serious with shady characters and grim expressions. Prostitution is also big business here with scores of girls from over the border (and more recently Eastern Europe) strutting around the casinos. With

all this going on triad gangs are active, although they have kept their heads down since stern China resumed power.

But it is not all about gambling and groping. Macau has an identity of its own and an undeniable charm and warmth. The pace is a welcome step down from Hong Kong and then there is the indulgence of Portuguese food and wine. The combination of Portuguese and Chinese food has resulted in Macanese cuisine. And although it is difficult to get excited about a bread roll, the bread here is some of the best in Asia. Beyond the dining and sightseeing is golf, legitimate bone-cracking massages and the annual Grand Prix – plenty for such a modest pimple of land.

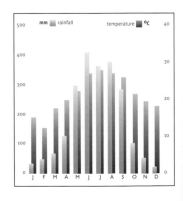

Hyatt Regency Macau

2 Estrada Almirante Marques Esparteiro, Taipa Island, Macau
T: +853 831 234 **F:** +853 830 195
http://www.asia-hotels.com/hotelinfo/Hyatt_Regency_Macau/

The Hyatt Regency sits away from the city lights and on the quieter island of Taipa. Being geographically central this puts almost all of Macau within 10 minutes drive, although there is not much within immediate walking distance. It has been around a while, since 1983, but the Hyatt Regency remains a popular choice for business travellers, the hotel's meeting rooms and conference facilities being some of Macau's most comprehensive. But it is not restricted purely to business. The hotel has a tangible 1980s hangover with big pillars, beams and angles, but is a roomy property with nice Portuguese trimmings and well-maintained if fairly average 5-star rooms. Scenic Flamingos does a Macanese and Portuguese menu sitting out over leafy carp-filled ponds, or if it rains the Greenhouse is a snug shelter. The broad meandering outdoor pool is attractive and worth lazing around, and there are three acres of gardens with plenty of sporting facilities plus a very good kiddies club, Camp Hyatt. The Hyatt Regency is not classy or swanky but works well.

Rates from: **US$ 103**
Star rating: ★ ★ ★ ★ ★
Bellhop rating: 🛎 🛎 🛎 🛎

Value:	7.98	Facilities:	8.22
Staff:	7.94	Restaurants:	8.10
Location:	7.83	Families:	6.99
Cleanliness:	8.10		

Mandarin Oriental Macau

956-1110 Avenida da Amizade, Macau
T: +853 567 888 **F:** +853 594 589
http://www.asia-hotels.com/hotelinfo/Mandarin_Oriental_Macau/

Lining the waterfront this warm and comfortable hotel is so close to the jetfoil terminal you can watch the boats cruise in from your window.

Usefully hugging the Grand Prix track and only a few minutes taxi from Macau's historic centre and the surrounding entertainment areas keeps this hotel active seven days a week rather than just at weekends. Having undergone a major renovation three years ago the Mandarin is Macau's most up to date hotel. Not only are the 435 oriental-style rooms smooth and smart, but the hotel facilities are modern yet invitingly decorated with warm Portuguese flair. The recent addition of the low-rise colonial-style 'Resort' to the rear means they now have Macau's most attractive pool (heated), spa facilities (excellent massage treatments) and kids' entertainment, complimenting the already fine restaurants, bar and casino. Helpful and friendly staff are another big plus. The Mandarin is a great example of how a previously ageing hotel has very successfully reinvented itself – broadly appealing for both business and pleasure.

Rates from: **US$ 128**
Star rating: ★ ★ ★ ★ ★
Bellhop rating: 🛎 🛎 🛎 🛎 ½

Value:	7.73	Facilities:	8.44
Staff:	8.36	Restaurants:	8.08
Location:	8.26	Families:	6.79
Cleanliness:	8.53		

The Westin Resort Macau

1918 Estrada de Hac sa, Coloane, Macau
T: +853 871 111 **F:** +853 871 122
http://www.asia-hotels.com/hotelinfo/Westin_Resort_Macau/

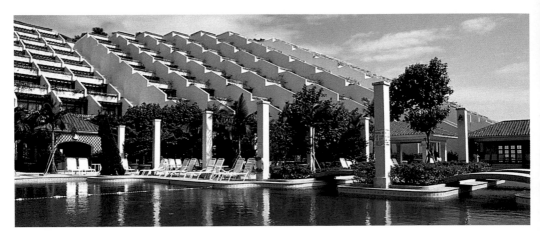

Macau's only true resort is getting a little dated but the Westin remains by far the most popular hotel in the enclave. This large leisure hotel is set in spacious grounds on the lazy east coast of the green island of Coloane. The sloping hotel backs into a hill and is perhaps the embodiment of the perfect Hong Kong getaway. The chief reason to come here is for the facilities. They are not the best by Asian standards, but they are certainly the broadest for Macau and put the Westin in a unique class. The Macau Golf & Country Club, attached to the hotel, is the most memorable and makes the resort especially popular. This good 5,900-metre par 71 championship golf course is accessed from the 9th floor – just take the lift and stroll across to the starter's box and tee off. The Westin makes a concerted effort to appeal to families, offering a childcare centre, kids' club and a games room. The upkeep of these is average, especially in the games room where several game consoles seem constantly out of order. But there is always the choice of enjoyable indoor and outdoor pools plus plenty of sporting facilities such as eight tennis courts. The Wellness Retreat lists a healthy range of soothing massages and body treatments if you fancy a spot of pampering. There is a lot to do come rain or shine and the Westin is lively and boisterous come weekends.

The sloping and staggered design of the hotel is not just a plus for golfers, it is also fully felt in the 208 very large and comfortable rooms. All are sea facing with enormous private terraces that catch plenty of sunshine and give welcome extra space.

Being on relatively remote Coloane means that transport is needed – there is nothing within walking distance other than the pleasant Hac Sa Beach and its famous Fernando's Restaurant. It takes a good 20 minutes for the shuttle to get downtown or to the ferry pier. This remoteness means you finally escape a skyline with a skyscraper on it and find that elusive relaxing holiday mood.

Rates from: **US$ 127**
Star rating: ★★★★★
Bellhop rating: 🔔🔔🔔🔔 ½

Value:	7.79	Facilities:	8.51
Staff:	8.36	Restaurants:	8.10
Location:	7.95	Families:	7.49
Cleanliness:	8.71		

MALAYSIA

Malaysia is one of Southeast Asia's most exotic yet most comfortable countries to visit. In many ways this diverse republic of 23 million people is unique, but also seems to be a composite of surrounding influences. Strongly Islamic since the 13th century, Malaysia grew to its present form under the British who left in 1957. The influx of Chinese and Indian radically altered the ethnic mix, and descendants of these communities now account for almost half of the population.

Malaysia is basically divided into two regions. The busier peninsula dangles from the heels of Thailand, culminating at Johor Bahru next to the city state of Singapore. Malaysia's larger but relatively remoter section – made up of the states of Sarawak and Sabah – occupies roughly the top third of the island Borneo. The two regions

differ substantially, and indeed were only united after World War II. You still need your passport when travelling from the peninsula to Borneo as Sarawak and Sabah still have a high degree of autonomy.

For the tourist, Malaysia is one of the more beautiful and appealing destinations in the region. With rapid economic progress, good infrastructure and English widely spoken it has also become one of the most safe and accessible places to visit. The modern capital Kuala Lumpur has seen heavy investment and is emerging as a world-class city. Its dining and shopping can now compete alongside the likes of Singapore, Bangkok and Hong Kong. Entertainment is picking up too, although it will probably never match the carefree nightlife of other Asian countries. And 'KL', as it is known, has staked a name for itself globally with the completion of the iconic Petronas Towers, at 452 metres the world's tallest buildings.

No other Malaysian city is in the same league as the capital, as most are sleepy and quiet. One thing that might strike the visitor is a relative absence of visible historical

landmarks. Unlike most of Asia, which is bulging with temples and relics, Malaysia seems to be almost entirely new. This is largely due to the fact that the Malays have traditionally constructed with wood and earlier buildings have decayed, but even colonial brick and mortar contributions are few. A glaring exception is in coastal Melaka which lies just a few hours south of the capital and huddles together a collection of Portuguese and Dutch architecture. Further north, approaching the Thai border, the island of Penang is the other main area of historical depth.

The really big pull is Malaysia's natural beauty. The country floats just north of the equator and straddles one of the world's great rainforest belts. The biodiversity is spectacular. Despite the logging mania that has ripped through the forests, some amazing flora survives – such as the world's biggest flower, the Rafflesia. Fauna is truly exotic and includes loveable wonders like the placid orangutans. Sabah's 4,101-metre Mt Kinabalu near the beach resorts of Kota Kinabalu is the highest mountain between the Himalayas and New Guinea, but rises gently and steadily, making it one of the easiest 'big' mountains to climb in the world. Offshore and a little to the north is Sipidan, one of many stunning sites for divers.

With kilometres of tropical coast Malaysia has some great beaches that have developed more slowly than their more popular counterparts in Thailand. Laid-back Langkawi Island has some fantastic white sandy stretches, far superior to those of Penang. The east coast has good ones too; Tioman, Redang and the backpacking Perhentian Islands supply equal beauty though the monsoon rains affect the winter seasons. Peninsular Malaysia's climate is tropical – sunny, hot and humid year-round with short bursts of torrential rain. The monsoon

between October and April hits the east coast harder, while Borneo gets steady rainfall all year. The hill stations of the Cameron Highlands, Fraser Hill and the gambling centre of Genting, with their cool elevated tea plantations, offer a delightful escape from the oppressive heat.

Hotel-wise Malaysia has the lot – from icons of days gone by such as the E&O in Penang to Langkawi's out-of-this-world-class Datai, from the highlands' Tudor replicas right down to quaint beachside lean-tos.

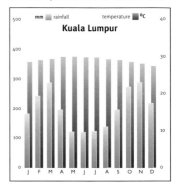

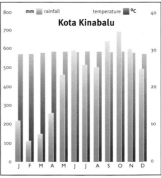

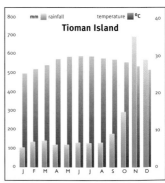

The Andaman Langkawi

Jalan Teluk Datai, 07000 Langkawi, Kedah, Malaysia
T: +60 4 959 1088 **F:** +60 4 959 1168
http://www.asia-hotels.com/hotelinfo/Andaman_Datai_Bay/

At only seven years old the Andaman incorporates some of the most recent advances in resort design. It is clearly one of Langkawi's leaders. The resort has managed to merge all of the features of 5-star luxury with 187 rooms, Malay culture and a rainforest setting. With two 4-storey wings clipped either side of an imposing lobby block, the Andaman is big and bold, but structures are built along traditional Malay lines and contours sit comfortably in the rainforest setting.

The location on the northwest

tip of Langkawi is one of the best for those wanting tropical escapism. Not only is the beach superb (albeit narrow at high tide), it is quiet and peaceful, being shared with only one other hotel. Exploring the surrounding rainforest is a fantastic experience and the Andaman puts on excellent ecotours for the guests. Other facilities are broad with many organised activities, making it a good choice for families with children, and the spectacular Datai Bay golf course lies nearby.

The impressive lobby sets the tone, lots of wood and firm architecture abounds throughout. The rooms are well done and spacious. Ground-floor rooms open out to their own sun decks (lanai) and upper ones have superior balconied views over the delightful Datai Bay.

The Andaman has a history of running at unrealistically high prices, and it has suffered from this. The property has been underused to some extent which means that many of the facilities, although well

designed, feel a little lifeless. Service remains high and the restaurants are excellent, especially the curries at the Gulai House, a gentle stroll down the beach. The free-form pool is huge but surrounding foliage provides plenty of shade. Perhaps the highlight though is the spa – have a massage in one of the open pavilions overlooking the bay – it is quite spectacular. With inflated prices the resort has a ghostly absence about it except at peak season, and this is a real shame. Luckily this is poised to change with a recent management change, and hopefully the Andaman will adjust to occupy its correct niche in the market.

Rates from: **US$ 237**
Star rating: ★ ★ ★ ★ ★
Bellhop rating: 🛎 🛎 🛎 🛎 ½

Value:	7.64	Facilities:	8.54
Staff:	8.71	Restaurants:	8.42
Location:	8.61	Families:	6.93
Cleanliness:	8.86		

Berjaya Langkawi Beach & Spa Resort

Karong Berkunci 200, Burau Bay, 07000 Langkawi, Kedah, Malaysia
T: +60 4 959 1888 **F**: +60 4 959 1886
http://www.asia-hotels.com/hotelinfo/Berjaya_Langkawi_Beach_and_Spa_Resort/

The Berjaya Langkawi Beach & Spa Resort is, as the name suggests, especially proud of two things – its beach and its complete spa. The resort is huge at 400 rooms, one of the largest on the island, and it has a great beachside location staring out over serene Burau Bay. The architecture is much like a local village with the large central structures being attractively surrounded by smaller satellites – some throughout gardens and the trees, and others perched directly over the sea. The accommodation is contained within chalets, elevated on stilts in traditional Malay style. The main body of the resort is nestled at the foot of a hillside but a tail departs and threads along the rocky section of the beach. This line of chalets stands over the lapping water, making relaxing on the balconies especially appealing. The interiors of all the chalets are comfortable enough although they are clearly more rustic than luxuriant. Furnishings are quite standard but with subtle Malay influences throughout, such as polished wooden floors and rugs.

Of the wide and appropriate facilities, the centrepiece is The Spa. The hotel has made a real effort to unite the rainforest with the spa experience, and they have done well to pull it off. The spa is set among the trees with backing vocals supplied by Mother Nature herself. The treatments and packages are extensive – the whole spread of oriental techniques are available as well as acupressure, seaweed wraps and flotation tanks, and prices are reasonable.

The resort has a big and inviting pool with a pool bar. A beach bar is on hand if you prefer, plus several reasonable restaurants. Teppanyaki Corner does a sizzling Japanese grill and Dayang Cafe is open 24 hours with a menu listing local and international options. The resort classes itself 5-star but some areas are showing wear and tear, however it is very competitively priced.

Rates from: **US$ 75**
Star rating: ★★★★★
Bellhop rating: 🛎🛎🛎🛎 ½

Value:	8.17	Facilities:	8.35
Staff:	8.15	Restaurants:	8.16
Location:	8.29	Families:	7.10
Cleanliness:	8.19		

Berjaya Redang Beach Resort

Pulau Redang, Redang, Terengganu, Malaysia
T: +60 9 697 3988 **F**: +60 9 697 3899
http://www.asia-hotels.com/hotelinfo/Berjaya_Redang_Beach_Resort/

Once the word got out about Pulau Redang, it did not take long for the rest of the world to catch on. Backpackers, honeymooners, movie location scouts, divemasters and indeed just about everyone for whom the words 'idyllic tropical island' conjured up a unique magic raced for its shores, 45 kilometres off the east coast of Malaysia. Then the resorts started to spring up, and Redang was well and truly on the map.

Happily, the island is not yet overrun, and the few resorts that are here, like the Berjaya Redang, have kept themselves low-key and well below the palm trees. There are 150 somewhat basic wooden Malay-style chalets and suites here, wedged into a valley that leads down to the breathtaking beach on the north side of the island. Landlubbers can linger in the five restaurants and bars, loll by the pool, venture along Redang's jungle walks or bash tennis and volleyballs around. The adjacent spa resort, owned by the same group, is currently under renovation and expected to reopen in late 2003.

However, the real joy of Redang is its marine park, which is why both island and resort bespeak an underwater Arcadia for the dive fraternity. Redang lies at the centre of the protected Terengganu Marine Park, whose reefs abound with the largest assortment of coral species the peninsula waters have to offer. The resort has a fully equipped PADI centre, ready and waiting to speed your passage to beneath the crystal clear waters. There, splendid underwater gardens are filled with colourful corals both hard and soft, along with a captivating variety of fascinating tropical fish, unspoiled reefs and an array of sea creatures. As a historical footnote, the wrecks of HMS Repulse and HMS Prince of Wales – two British battle ships sunk during the war – lie near Redang, but too deep for casual exploration.

Reaching this paradise is not easy with the once-daily catamaran service currently available but the island is surely worth the effort. With an airstrip under construction (at the expense of the old golf course) getting there will soon be somewhat easier.

Rates from: **US$ 95**
Star rating: ★ ★ ★ ★
Bellhop rating: ♭ ♭ ♭ ♭ ½

Value:	8.15	Facilities:	8.07
Staff:	8.11	Restaurants:	7.95
Location:	8.75	Families:	7.07
Cleanliness:	8.16		

Berjaya Tioman Beach Golf & Spa Resort

Pulau Tioman, Johor, Malaysia
T: +60 9 419 1000 **F:** +60 9 419 1718
http://www.asia-hotels.com/hotelinfo/Berjaya_Tioman_Beach_Resort/

Back in the 1950s Hollywood used Tioman as the location for the all-singin' and dancin' movie *South Pacific*. A half-century on, the island remains firmly anchored in the South China Sea and – although tourism has made some inroads – its scenic beaches and bays still provide some stunning Technicolor backdrops. Tioman is now almost totally geared to tourism, and the Berjaya – on the northwest coast – is a fully fledged, large-scale 4-star resort, counting 400 simple Malay-style chalets and rooms sprawling over 200 acres of beachfront. Perched on the headland, a short buggy ride away, are another 196 more modern one- and two-bedroom suites. The Matahari restaurant is right on the beach, there is a bar by the pool, another restaurant by the 18-hole golf course plus a snooker bar, and a karaoke lounge. Kids get their own playground and a choice of horses, ponies or donkeys to ride plus some wonderful snorkelling.

Rates from: **US$ 80**
Star rating: ★ ★ ★ ★
Bellhop rating: ♗ ♗ ♗ ♗

Value:	7.51	Facilities:	8.03
Staff:	7.95	Restaurants:	7.75
Location:	8.67	Families:	7.17
Cleanliness:	7.87		

Casa del Mar

Jl Pantai Cenang, Mukim Kedawang, 07000 Langkawi, Kedah, Malaysia
T: +60 4 955 2388 **F:** +60 4 955 2228
http://www.asia-hotels.com/hotelinfo/Casa_del_Mar/

On Pantai Cenang Beach on the southwest coast of Langkawi, the Casa del Mar contains just 29 rooms and suites, so this really qualifies as a boutique resort. Ceiling fans spin lazily overhead in the compact terracotta tiled rooms, each with a small balcony overlooking the sea. In the far superior Junior Suites, four-poster beds are swathed in mosquito nets. Small-scale and simple just about sums up the aptly named Casa del Mar. The first-class dining room extends past the swimming pool and into the garden, so you can pick exactly where you want to browse over a thoughtful menu that fuses Japanese cuisine with the Mediterranean, backed up by a cellar that has a strong Californian emphasis. Parts of Langkawi have regrettably been colonised by larger, brasher establishments. Thankfully, Casa del Mar remains a haven of repose with a very personal feel.

Rates from: **US$ 125**
Star rating: ★ ★ ★ ★
Bellhop rating: ♗ ♗ ♗ ♗ ½

Value:	7.77	Facilities:	7.77
Staff:	8.68	Restaurants:	7.64
Location:	8.55	Families:	6.73
Cleanliness:	8.64		

Club Med Cherating

Cherating, 25710 Kuantan, Malaysia
T: +60 9 581 9133 **F:** +60 9 581 9524
http://www.asia-hotels.com/hotelinfo/Club_Med_Cherating/

One of a half-dozen Club Meds in the region, the Malaysian version of the ultimate all-inclusive, all-together-now resort is vastly popular with holidaymakers from all over the peninsula, especially Singapore, and beyond. A conglomeration of traditional Malay stilt houses built along the beach on the edge of the jungle, Club Med is first and foremost family friendly, with three different kids' clubs catering for tots, in-betweens and young teens. There is a huge array of sporting facilities including roller-blading, archery and the high-flying thrills of the beachside trapeze. All this is included in the price of your room, together with three meals a day (plus wine at lunch and dinner) and nightly entertainment. There is also a nearby golf course and an on-site spa, although both attract a modest additional charge. Note that this resort usually shuts down from November to January each year as the monsoon rains stop play.

Rates from: **US$ 85**
Star rating: ★ ★ ★ ½
Bellhop rating: 🐨 🐨 🐨 🐨 🐨

Value:	8.38	Facilities:	9.19
Staff:	9.23	Restaurants:	8.85
Location:	8.15	Families:	9.23
Cleanliness:	8.81		

Concorde Hotel Kuala Lumpur

2 Jl Sultan Ismail, 50250 Kuala Lumpur, Malaysia
T: +60 3 2144 2200 **F:** +60 3 2144 1628
http://www.asia-hotels.com/hotelinfo/Concorde_Hotel_Kuala_Lumpur/

This has got to be one of Kuala Lumpur's most useful and practical hotels, and for those seeking no-nonsense comfort this hits the nail on the head. It is centrally placed in the Golden Triangle, is very close to some of the capital's trendiest nightlife and five minutes or so stroll from the Petronas Towers and the city's best shopping, the Suria KLCC. The Hard Rock Cafe directly adjoins the hotel and the lobby buzzes with activity. As a building it is a bit uninspiring from the exterior, but inside it is rather irregular and spacious with useful facilities including some popular restaurants and the welcoming option of a good sized rectangular outdoor pool. The gym is also surprisingly good. Standard Rooms are fairly ordinary but the Premier Rooms are trendy and spacious and represent tremendous value for money.

Rates from: **US$ 49**
Star rating: ★ ★ ★ ★
Bellhop rating: 🐨 🐨 🐨 🐨 ½

Value:	8.35	Facilities:	8.07
Staff:	8.00	Restaurants:	7.98
Location:	8.62	Families:	6.46
Cleanliness:	8.26		

The Datai Langkawi

Jl Teluk Datai, 07000 Langkawi, Kedah, Malaysia
T: +60 4 959 2500 **F:** +60 4 959 2600
http://www.asia-hotels.com/hotelinfo/Datai_Langkawi/

As timelines go, there is a fair gap between Langkawi's geological genesis 500 million years ago and 1993 AD, when the Datai opened. Bridging these two milestones is resident naturalist, Irshad, whose cheery early morning treks into the rainforest open guests' eyes to the natural wonders around this wonderfully natural resort. Picking his way along the winding trails Irshad unravels the complex eco-system, noting a nesting hornbill here, leaf beetles chomping on their favourite foliage there and pointing out medicinal plants that have been used for eons by indigenous tribes.

Indeed, there is an innate feeling at the Datai that it was not so much built next to the rainforest that covers almost two thirds of the island of Langkawi, but grew up as part of it. The 54 rooms in low-rise wings peaking over the canopy, and 58 villas and suites sprinkled throughout the forest floor are linked by open-air corridors and a series of verdant pathways. Cool Langkawi marble and warm red balau woods provide a gentle contrast within generous interiors. The exterior walls and roofs have a hint of Mayan mixed with Japanese. This unpretentious cosmopolitan aura is augmented by a progression of inducements to relaxation – balconies and daybeds in the rooms, BOSE sound systems in the regular suites and villas (which also have private sun decks), and personal plungeries in the pool suites and villas. The ultimate of all these treats is the Datai Suite, a two-bedroom hideaway with expansive living and dining areas and surrounded by a sandstone balcony with panoramic ocean views.

Throughout its 10 years in operation, the Datai has been overseen by the genial Canadian Jamie Case, whose love of wine and easy-going charm are reflected both in the resort's cellars and its general character. His staff are uniformly courteous, eager to please without being intrusive or arrogant, and are patently proud of their place of employ. You witness this in the tiniest details – the care with

which waiters serve your meals, the spontaneous affection towards children, the delicate manipulations of the therapists' fingers in the Mandara Spa, an isolated haven out of sight of the rest of the resort yet within earshot of a gently meandering stream.

Spread over 1,850 acres on a hillside above a private white sand beach, the Datai never feels crowded. The peaceful main pool (no children under 16 here) is seemingly suspended within the forest canopy, almost in touching distance of the monkeys and flying foxes that leap from branch to branch. Settle into one of the teak chairs in the Lobby Bar, and you might almost be in a tree house. Settle down to dinner at the Pavilion, and the authentic Thai dishes might make you think you have stepped across the border. Malaysian and Gallic cuisines mix and match at the Dining Room, while the Beach Club – next to the resort's second pool – is the most relaxed kid-friendly venue.

Just as the waves lap the Datai's beach and the resort merges into the rainforest, so the adjacent 18-hole championship golf course blends into the

landscape equally naturally. There is a similarly elegant synthesis back at the open-sided spa, where the deep petal-strewn tubs and rich wooden textures are totally at one with nature. The signature treatment – two therapists blending Japanese, Shiatsu, Thai, Hawaiian Lomi-Lomi, Swedish and Balinese massage for a spine-tingling 50 minutes – is one very small step away from outright seduction.

It goes without saying that the Datai is incredibly popular with its guests, a testament both to the

resort which provides a sense of luxury and sophistication while respecting a remote natural environment, and to the extraordinarily dedicated team who run it so smoothly.

Rates from: **US$ 278**
Star rating: ★ ★ ★ ★ ★
Bellhop rating: ♙ ♙ ♙ ♙ ½

Value:	7.60	Facilities:	8.71
Staff:	8.89	Restaurants:	8.56
Location:	8.89	Families:	6.42
Cleanliness:	9.07		

Eastern & Oriental Hotel

10 Lebuh Farquhar, 10200 Penang, Malaysia
T: +60 4 222 2000 **F:** +60 4 261 6333
http://www.asia-hotels.com/hotelinfo/Eastern_and_Oriental_Hotel/

There was no more depressing sight in Penang in the late 1980s than the Eastern & Oriental, a sadly neglected legacy of the pioneering Sarkies brothers. The hotel, fondly referred to as the E&O, first opened in the late 19th century, looked not so much run down as run over and it was not until a RM75 million renovation that it reopened spick and span again, just before the new millennium.

The newly refurbished E&O falls somewhere between the glitz of Raffles in Singapore and the authenticity of the Galle Face in Colombo. The exterior and many of the original fixtures and furniture have been preserved, but the hotel is not packaged with an unduly commercial slant. And rather than being dwarfed by skyscrapers, it sits securely in the historic part of Georgetown, within walking distance of landmarks like Fort Cornwallis and the Penang State Museum.

The general verdict is that the E&O has emerged looking pretty good, as much a pleasure to stay in as it is to drop by for afternoon tea or a sundowner. All 101 butler-serviced suites have been thoughtfully appointed to provide a blend of history with modern amenities, and you can elect to stay in one of the Writers Suites (Kipling, Coward, Hesse et al) or go the whole hog in the E&O Suite which, apart from anything else, has a dining room that can seat 22.

On the subject of food, the hotel has seven different wining and dining venues, each especially appropriate to the meal in question. Palm Court is set beneath the E&O's hallmark dome, and is ripe for afternoon tea with scones and cakes. A sunrise breakfast outside on the Verandah is a must, and a long colonial-style dinner is almost obligatory at 1885. And after a session at the gym or in the sea-facing pool, stretch out with some fresh juice on the Deck.

Rates from: **US$ 105**
Star rating: ★★★★★
Bellhop rating: ◖◖◖◖ ½

Value:	8.06	Facilities:	8.06
Staff:	8.75	Restaurants:	8.08
Location:	8.77	Families:	6.37
Cleanliness:	9.00		

Hotel Equatorial Kuala Lumpur

Jl Sultan Ismail, 50250 Kuala Lumpur, Malaysia
T: +60 3 2161 7777 **F:** +60 3 2161 9020
http://www.asia-hotels.com/hotelinfo/Equatorial_Kuala_Lumpur_Hotel/

For the practical or the unfussy, this hotel is ideal. The Equatorial Kuala Lumpur is not the most stylish of properties but it does offer a great central location in the Golden Triangle and very attractive rates. This modest block is a tad aged now with a distinct 1980s hangover, however the hotel facilities are quite varied and very fair overall with a decent selection of restaurants doing well – the Chalet Swiss and Golden Phoenix are particularly popular with local residents. The outdoor pool and gymnasium lag behind somewhat but the 300 tidy, beige rooms are functional and very presentable with all the necessary mod cons. The price is highly competitive indeed, with or without the top location. Be warned though that the Equatorial does charge for extras that usually are taken for granted, such as access to the gym. But if you steer clear of these, this otherwise standard mid-range hotel offers unbeatable value for money and very friendly staff.

Rates from: **US$ 57**
Star rating: ★ ★ ★ ★
Bellhop rating: 🐻🐻🐻🐻 ½

Value:	8.17	Facilities:	7.71
Staff:	8.25	Restaurants:	8.05
Location:	8.40	Families:	6.96
Cleanliness:	8.32		

Hotel Equatorial Melaka

Bandar Hilir, 75000 Melaka, Malaysia
T: +60 6 282 8333 **F:** +60 6 282 9333
http://www.asia-hotels.com/hotelinfo/Equatorial_Melaka_Hotel/

All in all the Equatorial is the newest and among the best hotels in the historic town of Melaka. It boasts a great location, standing tall and proud over the town centre. Although near a busy roundabout the noise is kept at bay, and it is within easy walking distance of the prime tourist attractions and restaurants of Jalan Merdeka. This good 4-star hotel is all about straightforward comfort and space. The Equatorial's facilities are inviting, with a selection of six food and beverage outlets and a superb outdoor swimming pool. The 496 rooms are bright, spacious and modern, and represent excellent value. For business, the club floor is well done and the Equatorial has meeting and conference facilities capable of holding up to 1800. Staff are generally good but some find that more demanding guests stretch them beyond their capabilities. For the price, a dependable hotel indeed.

Rates from: **US$ 50**
Star rating: ★ ★ ★ ★
Bellhop rating: 🐻🐻🐻🐻

Value:	7.91	Facilities:	7.82
Staff:	7.88	Restaurants:	7.62
Location:	8.45	Families:	6.98
Cleanliness:	8.22		

Hilton Batang Ai Longhouse Resort

C/o Hilton Kuching, 93100 Kuching, Malaysia
T: +60 83 584 388 **F:** +60 83 584 399
http://www.asia-hotels.com/hotelinfo/Hilton_Batang_Ai_Longhouse_Resort/

Batang Ai is an interesting resort on three counts. Built on the shore of a lake, it cannot be reached directly by road, rather a 15-minute boat ride (after a 4-hour drive from Kuching). It is laid out in longhouse style with accommodation grouped among 11 blocks. And it is as 'green' as the surrounding jungles; local timber was used throughout, and only indigenous plants grow in the gardens; leave your room and the lights go out; open the window, and the air-con switches itself off; everything possible is recycled and nothing is allowed to pollute the pristine waters of the lake.

The resort contains 100 rooms including 12 duplex suites, rustically decorated but still including home comforts like IDD phones and private showers. Each of the blocks, like the longhouses in nearby villages, has an open gallery called a ruai where, traditionally, men and women would work during the day.

Integral to the resort is resident naturalist and jungle expert Winston Marshall, who leads guests on forest treks (either at ground level or via a treetop walkway) identifying edible and medicinal plants and relating anecdotes of

local Iban lore. Other excursions take in fishing expeditions and trips into the depths of Batang Ai National Park, or you can fossick around the river trading settlements of Lubok Antu or Sri Aman for local arts and crafts. One of the most adventurous trips leads upriver to the most remote reaches of the region, and shoots the rapids at breakneck speed on return.

Dining is fairly simple at the Nanga Mepi restaurant, which specialises in fish freshly caught from the lake, while the Wong Irup bar is a cool place to nurse a drink for an hour or two. There is a pool, a tennis court and table tennis, as well as various board games to pass the hours. However, the main attraction of Batang Ai, which is especially popular with local residents, is the wall-to-wall nature that lies around the resort.

Rates from: **US$ 38**
Star rating: ★★★★ ½
Bellhop rating: 🛎🛎🛎🛎 ½

Value:	8.91	Facilities:	8.57
Staff:	8.87	Restaurants:	7.87
Location:	8.78	Families:	7.48
Cleanliness:	8.91		

Hilton Kuching

Jl Tunku Abdul Rahman, 93748 Kuching, Sarawak, Malaysia
T: +60 82 248 200 **F:** +60 82 428 984
http://www.asia-hotels.com/hotelinfo/Hilton_Kuching/

Facing each other on opposite sides of the Sungai Sarawak River, the Hilton and Fort Margarita make for a sharp contrast; the fort was built in 1879 to repel pirates, the hotel rather more recently to extend a cordial welcome to all-comers. And it makes a very successful job of it, with 315 comfortably appointed rooms and suites set back slightly from the city's picturesque waterfront promenade. Kuching's cosmopolitan population is reflected in the Hilton's eateries, with Chinese, international and local dishes on offer, as well as a sushi and oyster bar. For recreation, there is a tennis court, pool (and pool table) and a playground for children. Business travellers are similarly well catered to here, with Internet connections and fax machines available, and private check-in on the executive floors whose 12th-floor clubroom and library provide commanding views over the city.

Rates from: **US$ 48**
Star rating: ★ ★ ★ ★ ★
Bellhop rating: 🛎 🛎 🛎 🛎 ½

Value:	7.91	Facilities:	8.12
Staff:	8.25	Restaurants:	7.98
Location:	8.33	Families:	6.91
Cleanliness:	8.44		

Hilton Petaling Jaya

No 2 Jl Barat, Petaling Jaya, 46200 Kuala Lumpur, Malaysia
T: +60 3 7955 9122 **F:** +60 3 7955 3909
http://www.asia-hotels.com/hotelinfo/Hilton_Petaling_Jaya/

The Hilton sits in the industrial and commercial satellite city of Petaling Jaya, only half an hour or so from Kuala Lumpur's city centre if the traffic is light, or 45 minutes from the airport. A rather ageing property built in 1984, it seems to have had its day as a building. But it remains efficiently run and hugely popular, especially with businesses in the area. Facilities are predictable, although the practical conference rooms are extensive – no surprise here given the clientele. Leisure facilities equally are dated but popular – the decent gym barely has a piece of equipment spare during peak hours and the four restaurants buzz with a steady stream of visitors. Uncle Chilli's pub is the best in the area and wonderfully grungy with plenty of soul. The 553 rooms are fair, although nothing special, visually at least. But staff are proactive and polite, and despite a little age and road noise, this is the best hotel in the suburb of 'PJ'.

Rates from: **US$ 72**
Star rating: ★ ★ ★ ★ ½
Bellhop rating: 🛎 🛎 🛎 🛎 ½

Value:	8.07	Facilities:	8.09
Staff:	8.27	Restaurants:	8.31
Location:	8.31	Families:	7.23
Cleanliness:	8.42		

Holiday Inn Resort Damai Beach

Teluk Bandung, Santubong, 93756 Kuching, Sarawak, Malaysia
T: +60 82 846 999 **F:** +60 82 846 777
http://www.asia-hotels.com/hotelinfo/Holiday_Inn_Resort_Damai_Beach/

The Holiday Inn sprawls over 90 acres behind Damai Beach, so much so that it is almost like two hotels rather than one. It is all connected in a couple of minutes by shuttle bus, but choice of accommodation is key here as each wing has a very different character. Down in the intimate beach chalets – the slightly older section – you might hardly be aware of the more modern, two-storey longhouse-style buildings up on the hill which have the better views over the sea and surrounding tree-covered hills. The hotel has just been completely renovated and although there is a total of 227 guestrooms here, the resort never feels crowded. Water sports, snooker, squash and a wealth of other entertainment are all on offer, and daily – free – organised games and competitions help children work up an appetite between meals.

There are a half-dozen spots for eating and drinking at the resort, but pride of place must go to the cleverly conceived Treez Pub. Built into and on top of the forest, its planked floors, rainforest decor and open sides have a very Tarzan feel. Hawker specialties like satay add to the jungly ambience, and the whole pub starts to shake ever so gently when the band gets going. At weekends, even Kuching residents make the 35-kilometre drive out here to let rip, which must rank as a pretty good recommendation.

The Holiday Inn's other real plus is the state-run Sarawak Cultural Village just past the hotel's 242 room sister property (Holiday Inn Resort Damai Lagoon) across the road; spread over 17 acres it comprises seven different ethnic houses with appropriately garbed inhabitants and some enthusiastic dancing expos, to say nothing of photo opportunities. Spend a morning here and you feel like you have toured the whole of Sarawak. Non-culture vultures can enjoy a different excursion just outside the front gate in the shape of the 18-hole, par 72 Arnold Palmer-designed golf course.

Rates from: **US$ 52**
Star rating: ★★★★
Bellhop rating: 🛎🛎🛎🛎

Value:	8.52	Facilities:	8.19
Staff:	8.39	Restaurants:	7.52
Location:	8.52	Families:	7.16
Cleanliness:	8.42		

Hyatt Regency Kuantan

Telok Chempedak, 25050 Kuantan, Pahang, Malaysia
T: +60 9 566 1234 **F:** +60 9 567 4677
http://www.asia-hotels.com/hotelinfo/Hyatt_Regency_Kuantan/

sufficient, with a well-equipped gym, tennis and squash courts, kids' club, plus beach activities. Three popular restaurants cover Malay, Italian and Szechuan cuisine, and the Hyatt Regency fulfils its obligation as one of the leading hotels in the state capital by laying on a full compliment of business amenities and function rooms.

The east coast city of Kuantan does not draw a large number of international visitors despite the great local beach Telok Chempedak or the leafy jungle nearby. Neither the city nor the beach area has a large choice of hotels so the Hyatt Regency Kuantan easily emerges as the area's place to stay. An attractive and airy hotel complex divided into four blocks, it is thoughtfully designed with local Malay architectural lines. Within are 336 bright rooms, all enjoying balconies with garden or sea views. The resort has two beguiling azure pools literally a stone's throw from the sea. The leisure facilities are happily

Rates from: **US$ 56**
Star rating: ★ ★ ★ ★ ½
Bellhop rating: 🐾 🐾 🐾 🐾 ½

Value:	8.31	Facilities:	8.33
Staff:	8.30	Restaurants:	8.22
Location:	8.72	Families:	7.37
Cleanliness:	8.25		

Hyatt Regency Saujana

2 Km off Sultan Abdul Aziz Airport Highway, 47200 Subang, Kuala Lumpur, Malaysia
T: +60 3 7846 1234 **F:** +60 3 7846 2789
http://www.asia-hotels.com/hotelinfo/Hyatt_Regency_Saujana/

Sitting in extensive lush tropical gardens and surrounded by two 18-hole golf courses, the Hyatt Regency Saujana is located in Malaysia's cyber corridor. Subang Jaya, Petaling Jaya and Shah Alam are all within 10 to 15 minutes drive. The Formula One track and Sunway Lagoon Theme Park are also not far away and, importantly, it has easy access to either the capital (just 28 kilometres away) or the international airport (40 minutes by car). The hotel is housed in four low-rise square blocks and enjoys a lot of interior light due to the generous use of glass. The facilities cover both suburban relaxation and business. Five restaurants offer a good selection of dining, two being within the calm golf and country club. The Hyatt Regency's 386 rooms and suites reflect the well-used but well-maintained feel of the hotel.

Rates from: **US$ 55**
Star rating: ★ ★ ★ ★ ½
Bellhop rating: 🐾 🐾 🐾 🐾

Value:	7.95	Facilities:	8.10
Staff:	8.17	Restaurants:	7.75
Location:	7.62	Families:	6.67
Cleanliness:	8.42		

Istana Hotel

73 Jl Raja Chulan, 50200 Kuala Lumpur, Malaysia
T: +60 3 2141 9988 **F**: +60 3 2144 0111
http://www.asia-hotels.com/hotelinfo/Istana_Hotel/

Kuala Lumpur is one of the world's most progressive Islamic cities and there are echoes of the faith in some of its architecture. This can be said of the Istana, the Malay word for palace, which has incorporated Islamic elements into its design and decor. The 23-storey exterior seems modestly veiled and within is a characteristic large lobby with tiles, marble, trickling water and thick pillars. The corridors and rooms continue the Middle Eastern theme, although they are a bit jaded in areas and could do with updating. Nonetheless, the 516 rooms are spacious, comfy and well equipped, and the hotel facilities are excellent. A good fitness centre lurks unusually next to an underground car park and the neon-clad entertainment centre, Musictheque Club 73, gets loud and lively late on. An otherwise reasonable hotel is elevated by a fine location on the junction of Jalan Sultan Ismail and Jalan Raja Chulan, near the shops and restaurants of Lot 10 and Jalan Bukit Bintan.

Rates from: **US$ 61**
Star rating: ★ ★ ★ ★ ★
Bellhop rating: ♙ ♙ ♙ ♙ ½

Value:	8.19	Facilities:	8.42
Staff:	8.36	Restaurants:	8.22
Location:	8.77	Families:	7.14
Cleanliness:	8.58		

JW Marriott Hotel Kuala Lumpur

183 Jl Bukit Bintang, 55100 Kuala Lumpur, Malaysia
T: +60 3 2715 9000 **F**: +60 3 2715 7000
http://www.asia-hotels.com/hotelinfo/JW_Marriott_Hotel_Kuala_Lumpur/

Built in 1997 the JW Marriott is one of Kuala Lumpur's newer properties and as such benefits a modern interior design. The style is somewhat European, even regal, with plenty of pale creamy-beige tone in the polished pillars and marble. The 561 richly elegant rooms with generous floor area, voicemail, call waiting, desk-level electrical outlets, ergonomic chairs and adjustable desk lighting, together with a spacious club floor, are primarily aimed at the corporate market. However, given that a number of the guests are en route to one of the two stunning resorts under the same ownership (Pangkor Laut and Tanjong Jara), and the top location of the hotel, it serves the leisure market just as well. By location read: right in the middle of the Golden Triangle at the end of the Bintang Walk connecting Lot 10 with the 7-storey Starhill Shopping complex directly adjacent. These, again under the same ownership, house numerous dining options which make up for the hotel's rather limited but popular selection.

Rates from: **US$ 77**
Star rating: ★ ★ ★ ★ ★
Bellhop rating: ♙ ♙ ♙ ♙ ½

Value:	8.14	Facilities:	8.43
Staff:	8.26	Restaurants:	8.15
Location:	9.12	Families:	7.11
Cleanliness:	8.73		

The Lakehouse Cameron Highlands

30th Mile Ringlet, 39200 Cameron Highlands, Pahang, Malaysia
T: +60 5 495 6152 **F:** +60 5 495 6213
http://www.asia-hotels.com/hotelinfo/Lakehouse_Cameron_Highlands_The/

The Lakehouse is an unusual discovery and a bit of an oddity. The Cameron Highlands were a respite for the colonial British and the Lakehouse clings closely to this identity. The hotel overlooks Sultan Abu Bakar Lake just off the main road to Tanah Rata, 10 kilometres further up the hill and 2 kilometres from the Boh Tea Plantation. The building is mock-Tudor and very appealing. With the cooler altitude, well-attended gardens and ivy climbing up the walls, it would be easy to forget which continent you are in. Inside, it feels very much like an old English country pub – heavy furniture, a crackling fireplace and low ceilings with exposed wooden beams. The rooms are of the same ilk, more inn-like than hotel-like and sparsely furnished but snug. Facilities throughout are scarce with just one restaurant and bar, with a broadly European menu. The service is again along the lines of an inn – friendly but clearly finite, although the Lakehouse does wash guest's cars and arrange walking tours.

Rates from: **US$ 73**
Star rating: ★ ★ ★ ½
Bellhop rating: ♗ ♗ ♗ ♗ ½

Value:	8.06	Facilities:	7.44
Staff:	8.75	Restaurants:	8.19
Location:	8.75	Families:	6.38
Cleanliness:	8.56		

Langkawi Village Resort

Jl Teluk Baru, Pantai Tengah, 07000 Langkawi, Kedah, Malaysia
T: +60 4 955 1511 **F:** +60 4 955 1531
http://www.asia-hotels.com/hotelinfo/Langkawi_Village_Resort/

Langkawi has many big format 4- and 5-star hotels, so it is nice to have an alternative. Rather than featuring blocks and wings, the 3-star Langkawi Village Resort is made of 100 basic one- and two-storey bungalows together with two suites, all dotted among the coconut palms facing the sea. The small rooms have an appealing simplicity and are sparsely furnished with struggling air-conditioners, but all provide that essential bubble of personal space. Quiet and private, each has its own balcony. As well as the intimacy, advantages include the superb value for money and direct access to a truly fabulous beach. Service is 3-star and facilities are also modest – there is a compact but good pool and a manageable restaurant. However, there is a variety of good dining options close by. The minuses for this resort are heavily outweighed by the pluses – an attractive resort both to the eye and especially to the wallet.

Rates from: **US$ 39**
Star rating: ★ ★ ★
Bellhop rating: ♗ ♗ ♗ ♗ ½

Value:	8.59	Facilities:	7.69
Staff:	8.16	Restaurants:	7.86
Location:	8.14	Families:	7.04
Cleanliness:	8.14		

Mandarin Oriental Kuala Lumpur

Kuala Lumpur City Centre, 50088 Kuala Lumpur, Malaysia
T: +60 3 2380 8888 **F**: +60 3 2380 8833
http://www.asia-hotels.com/hotelinfo/Mandarin_Oriental_Kuala_Lumpur/

What was once the Malaysian capital's racecourse has been transformed into the city's new centre, KLCC. It fuses a 50-acre park and shopping and performing arts centres with the totemic Petronas Towers which, at 452 metres, remain (for the moment) the world's tallest buildings. At the nucleus of this metropolitan hub, the Mandarin has successfully incorporated local aesthetics with an international appeal and a residential feel.

The hotel complements rather than competes with its monolithic, pewter-clad neighbour, even to the extent of camouflaging rooftop fittings to make itself look attractive from above. Custom-made copper lanterns and Malay lattice grills for external louvres add a practical touch of local colour, one that is reinforced inside with custom-carved Kris door handles, antique Nonya screens in gold leaf and sword reliefs on the handrails.

Perfectly suited to its environment, the Mandarin also provides a sympathetic, nigh perfect environment for its guests. Some 300 original artworks – including Malay dancing scenes and symbolic Islamic pieces – decorate the public areas and 643 guestrooms (including 51 serviced apartments), all characterised by warm, invitingly soft furnishings and set against earthy Malaccan wood tones.

The executive side of life is catered for by two-line IDD telephones, voicemail and dataports, while thickly upholstered furniture and marbled bathrooms with separate tub and shower induce a definitive air of luxurious relaxation. The top seven storeys of the Mandarin are given over to its club, where breakfast, snacks and cocktails are served in the private lounge that also includes a very civilised billiards room. But the lounge's forte undoubtedly lies beyond its windows, for it is impossible to glance outside and not be stopped short – perhaps for the third or fourth time – by the Brobdinagian Petronas, whether bathed in

glistening sunshine or flashing black and silver at the height of a thunderstorm.

In keeping with the spacious and inviting effect of all its public areas, the Mandarin's restaurants were designed to make the best use of natural light and maximum visibility. The all-day dining Biba's Cafe is divided into three levels that make it informal yet intimate. In contrast, the Pacifica Grill & Bar mixes its design textures and flavours in its Asian open kitchen, so you dine surrounded by a dazzling, contemporary melange of mosaic tiles, wood, iron, glass, fabric and murals. Lai Po Heen is an entirely different scene again – an architectural shell reminiscent of Shanghai's heyday, with a wok cooking area and private dining areas furnished with Malaccan antiques. And the Wasabi Bistro is a modern take on intricate, traditional Japanese fare in the quiet elegance of an intimate setting.

Despite being in the heart of the city, the Mandarin's extensive recreational facilities ensure it doubles as a resort. From the infinity outdoor pool you can gaze

down on the joggers, strollers and tai chi-ers in the park below. You can work off surplus energy at the tennis or squash courts, and surplus frustrations with a bout of kick-boxing in the aerobics studio. Cardiovascular and other state-of-the-art exercise machines throng the gymnasium, while specialists at the Thalgo Marine Spa can personally guide you through a customised, far-ranging menu of beauty and wellness treatments. For more leisurely exercise, shop 'til you drop at the adjacent Suria

KLCC Shopping Centre, with its extensive range of top retail outlets.

Rates from: **US$ 100**
Star rating: ★★★★★
Bellhop rating: 🛎🛎🛎🛎 ½

Value:	8.16	Facilities:	8.64
Staff:	8.49	Restaurants:	8.42
Location:	9.13	Families:	7.11
Cleanliness:	8.91		

Mutiara Beach Resort Penang

1 Jl Teluk Bahang, 11050 Penang, Malaysia
T: +60 4 886 8888 **F:** +60 4 885 2829
http://www.asia-hotels.com/hotelinfo/Mutiara_Beach_Resort_Penang/

Certainly one of the better hotels in the slightly faded holiday destination of Penang, the Mutiara is a surprisingly good resort that lives up to each of its five stars. The 16-storey resort sits on 18 acres of palm-studded land, wrapped in hills on one side and lined by a beach cove on the other. Quiet and secluded there is little within walking distance, but five minutes drive away lies the tourist strip of Batu Feringgi. The facilities of the resort are ideal for a short sunny break, the handsome exterior gardens pointing proudly towards the large swirling pool and an excellent kids' pool. These provide the essential alternative to the shallow beach, unfortunately a minefield of jellyfish. Its 438 large rooms (over 50 square metres) are another highlight – cheerful with rattan furniture and roomy balconies overlooking the sea. Cuisine is good if a tad pricey, with Italian favourite La Farfalla winning numerous local awards.

Rates from: **US$ 104**
Star rating: ★ ★ ★ ★ ★
Bellhop rating: 🛎 🛎 🛎 🛎 ½

Value:	7.93	Facilities:	8.60
Staff:	8.51	Restaurants:	8.34
Location:	8.12	Families:	7.64
Cleanliness:	8.69		

Mutiara Burau Bay Beach Resort Langkawi

Teluk Burau, 07000 Langkawi, Kedah, Malaysia
T: +60 4 959 1061 **F:** +60 4 959 1172
http://www.asia-hotels.com/hotelinfo/Mutiara_Burau_Bay_Resort/

The location and architecture helps set this simple resort apart – instead of the usual apartment block, the 3-star Mutiara consists of 150 simple cabana chalets. Set among pretty gardens and trees, each is stand-alone with its own private balcony. The cabanas are not luxurious but basic; externally they look somewhat prefabricated while inside they are compact with low beds and walk-in showers. However, they are great value. Facilities and services are modest, but the resort does manage to offer a fair choice of food and a good free-form pool. The big bonus is the splendid remote beach front – set in front of sprawling gardens complete with sleepy monitor lizards – one of the nicest on Langkawi. It is 20 minutes ride from town and therefore more peaceful than some other more expensive alternatives on this peaceful island.

Rates from: **US$ 61**
Star rating: ★ ★ ★
Bellhop rating: 🛎 🛎 🛎 🛎 🛎

Value:	9.12	Facilities:	7.96
Staff:	8.69	Restaurants:	8.27
Location:	9.12	Families:	7.58
Cleanliness:	8.96		

Palace of the Golden Horses

Jl Kuda Emas, Mines Resort City, 43300 Kuala Lumpur, Malaysia
T: +60 3 8943 2333 **F:** +60 3 8943 2666
http://www.asia-hotels.com/hotelinfo/Palace_of_The_Golden_Horses/

Part of the mega 1000-acre landscaped Mines Resort City complex and billed, presumably without any intended irony, as 'Asia's Most Extraordinary Hotel', the Palace of the Golden Horses was built on top of a disused tin mine. Indeed, 'over the top' is the phrase that comes to mind on a tour of the hotel, with its 480 rooms and suites (18 of the latter are categorised Head of State), seven restaurants and multiple function rooms, all presented in a blend of Malay Moorish architecture. On the assumption that you are not one of the many delegates attending the international conference centre, the Palace is within trotting distance of a man-made beach resort and spa, a shopping plaza, an amusement park and an 18-hole golf course, so it is well placed for a one-stop family vacation – and a popular one at that, especially with local residents.

Rates from: US$ 83
Star rating: ★ ★ ★ ★ ★
Bellhop rating: ♘ ♘ ♘ ♘ ½

Value:	8.02	Facilities:	8.65
Staff:	8.44	Restaurants:	8.32
Location:	7.66	Families:	7.75
Cleanliness:	8.81		

Pan Pacific Hotel KLIA

Jl CTA 4B, 64000 KLIA, Sepang, Selangor, Malaysia
T: +60 3 8787 3333 **F:** +60 3 8787 5555
http://www.asia-hotels.com/hotelinfo/Pan_Pacific_Hotel/

Although there is only one reason to stay here (two if you are a Formula One buff as it is close to the Grand Prix circuit) – to catch a plane from Kuala Lumpur's isolated international airport – this is an excellent property and it would succeed if placed elsewhere. Unlike other airport hotels that specialise in disappointing a captured market, the Pan Pacific has been well thought out and maintains high standards. The roomy lobby displays flight information and adjoins the airport via an immeasurably convenient walkway. But the hotel is more imaginative than just an airport extension and is well appointed with cosy rooms, the Pacific Floor being especially good. Facilities are capable and useful, with late-closing restaurants and a 24-hour spa. There is a small and pleasant tropical pool to soak in, sitting rather memorably in the shadow of the looming air traffic-control tower. The Pan Pacific has some superb staff and it is run very smoothly. Definitely one of the best airport hotels anywhere.

Rates from: US$ 87
Star rating: ★ ★ ★ ★ ★
Bellhop rating: ♘ ♘ ♘ ♘ ½

Value:	8.16	Facilities:	8.26
Staff:	8.20	Restaurants:	7.98
Location:	8.24	Families:	6.64
Cleanliness:	8.55		

Pangkor Laut Resort

Pangkor Laut Island, 32200 Lumut, Perak, Malaysia
T: +60 5 699 1100 **F**: +60 5 699 1200
http://www.asia-hotels.com/hotelinfo/Pangkor_Laut_Resort/

Take, in approximate chronological order, a two-million-year-old rainforest, a 120-hectare island off the west coast of Malaysia and some seven score villas and suites. Garnish with food, drink and recreational diversions and the result is the resort of Pangkor Laut, which has the island of the same name all to itself.

'Exclusive' and 'idyllic' are words easily associated with Pangkor Laut, which opened in 1995, but last year the resort edged even further upmarket with the opening of its own spa. No mere massage joint, this is an entire village spread over four acres between the sea and the rainforest. Interspersed with open courtyards, lotus ponds, a herb garden and a reflexology path, it also mirrors the country's ethnic make-up, providing Ayurvedic and Chinese herbal treatments in surroundings that are Malaysia at its most ravishing. And forget any idea of hurried, in-out-spa-it-all-about modus operandi. Visits here start with a well-defined ritual that lasts three quarters of an hour: a Chinese footbath and mini

massage, a Malay river bath, a Japanese goshi-goshi cloth scrub, an exfoliating Shanghai scrub, a cup of tea and then – and only then – does the real treatment begin.

As might be expected, the 22 new villas built out over the sea next to the spa village are Pangkor Laut's paramount accommodation. But all of the resort's 148 villas are superbly appointed, with spacious interiors and cushioned deckchairs on generous private balconies, so the main question is to decide whether you want to stay overhanging the sea, up the hill overlooking the bay, on the beach or in one of the garden villas. There are CD players in each villa and a wide selection of discs in the library, however anyone looking for a TV is going to have to search

long and hard for the single lounge. The message is clear – never mind Discovery or National Geographic channels, you can find reality TV right on the doorstep.

This being Pangkor Laut, you do not simply wander off on a jungle trek, but venture forth accompanied by resident naturalist Uncle Yip, who is on first-name terms with the yellow-pied hornbills, monitor lizards and troupes of macaques. Excursions usually end up at Emerald Bay, a stunning crescent-shaped bay often cited as one of the most beautiful beaches in the world. Further afield, you can swim, snorkel and island-hop around the Pulau Seribu, while back at the resort there is a quintet of tennis and squash courts, two swimming pools, a jet pool and a cold dip.

Pangkor Laut's six restaurants round off its almost hypnotic offerings, for this is somewhere most guests feel they need to hang around and savour for far longer than the bounds of a brief holiday. Chef Uncle Lim – one of the resort's characters who has been here from

the beginning – runs his eponymous eatery on a rocky outcrop overlooking the sea, serving delicious Nyonya and Hockchew delicacies. The open kitchen at Fisherman's Cove rustles up a mixture of Western, Italian, Chinese and pure, fresh seafood. Or you can hire the resort's teakwood tongkang junk and spend an evening at sea over a 4-course dinner.

One of Pangkor Laut's biggest – large pun intended – fans is tenor Luciano Pavarotti, a regular visitor all too happy to sing the resort's praises by rendering the not

exactly unpredictable aria: *O Paradiso*. Cue standing ovation from just about everyone who has ever stayed here.

Rates from: US$ 176
Star rating: ★ ★ ★ ★ ★
Bellhop rating: ♙♙♙♙ ½

Value:	7.75	Facilities:	8.48
Staff:	8.83	Restaurants:	8.33
Location:	8.73	Families:	6.83
Cleanliness:	8.83		

Pelangi Beach Resort Langkawi

Pantai Cenang, 07000 Langkawi, Kedah, Malaysia
T: +60 4 952 8888 **F:** +60 4 952 8899
http://www.asia-hotels.com/hotelinfo/Pelangi_Beach_Resort/

It is not often that you stumble across a beach resort with 350 rooms that is almost entirely made of wood. The Pelangi Beach Resort is one of Langkawi's largest but is cleverly spread out – and sensitively designed – to avoid the mass-produced atmosphere often found in hotels this big. Its 30 acres are plenty to liberally sprinkle low-rise buildings among beautifully tended lawns and gardens, quiet lakes and two very large free-form pools.

The impressive timber lobby reveals the principle theme throughout the resort. Everywhere you look there is local kempas and kapor timber. Shunning practical concrete materials and high-rise profiles, the Pelangi's wooden design is inspired by the local Malay kampungs or villages. A total of 51 double-storey chalets or bungalows house the guests below sweeping roofs. Chalets are supported by stilts with naked beams and broad verandahs very much in evidence. Inside, the rooms

are rustic, trim and cosy. The wooden construction has a few drawbacks though. Windows are small and the deep colours absorb a lot of light, resulting in dark interiors. More problematic are the acoustic properties – noise transfers from room to room, footsteps and vibrations carry easily. The hotel has taken effective measures to dampen and muffle the noise, but the problem still exists albeit to a much more limited extent. Also note that the resort is

conveniently close to the airport so the occasional plane passes overhead, but they are few and do little to dent the peace.

Colourful resort facilities are inviting with the fullest range of tours, water sports and activities for all the family. If you are knocking around the tennis or squash courts, the good kids' club can take care of the little ones. The restaurants are pretty good although they tend to offer rather safe menus. Some look out to the golden stretch of Langkawi's main beach lining the resort. And if it is the ocean you love then it might be worth opting for the Marina Club rooms – they have the best sea views and the added benefit of free cocktails in the club lounge.

Rates from: **US$ 112**
Star rating: ★ ★ ★ ★
Bellhop rating: 🐾🐾🐾🐾 ½

Value:	8.21	Facilities:	8.41
Staff:	8.51	Restaurants:	8.22
Location:	8.63	Families:	7.74
Cleanliness:	8.55		

The Regent Kuala Lumpur

160 Jl Bukit Bintang, 55100 Kuala Lumpur, Malaysia
T: +60 3 2141 8000 **F**: +60 3 2142 1441
http://www.asia-hotels.com/hotelinfo/Regent_KL/

As an all-rounder, The Regent excels. This well-established and respected property is parked happily opposite the Starhill Shopping Centre on Jalan Bukit Bintan with its mass of retailing outlets. Such is its appeal that the hotel draws people in from the buzzing streets rather than being anonymous or overlooked – the sweeping lobby is alive with constant activity. All the restaurants from Lai Ching Yuen (Cantonese) to the Terrace with its high tea at weekends, from the ground floor Brasserie to the ever-so-chic modern Italian menu of Oggi are popular both with guests and shoppers seeking to rest their weary legs. The pleasant service definitely helps. The 468 rooms are perfectly comfy and surprisingly peaceful given the location. And the recreational and business facilities are complete and well above average. Accessible, both geographically and financially, this is everyone's 5-star hotel.

Rates from: **US$ 92**
Star rating: ★ ★ ★ ★ ★
Bellhop rating: 🏨 🏨 🏨 🏨 ½

Value:	8.09	Facilities:	8.38
Staff:	8.72	Restaurants:	8.29
Location:	8.99	Families:	6.65
Cleanliness:	8.80		

Renaissance Kuala Lumpur Hotel

Corner of Jl Ampang & Jl Sultan Ismail, 50450 Kuala Lumpur, Malaysia
T: +60 3 2162 2233 **F**: +60 3 2163 1122
http://www.asia-hotels.com/hotelinfo/Renaissance_Kuala_Lumpur_Hotel/

One of Kuala Lumpur's giants, with almost 1000 rooms, the Renaissance offers the works if you want a list of facilities as long as your arm. It is all here in terms of leisure and recreation, with five excellent restaurants offering Chinese, Japanese, Mediterranean and Asian cuisine and a fabulous free-form outdoor pool to relax beside. For business, the hotel certainly rises above others with its impressive Convention Centre and banquet facilities, big enough to host major events. The hotel is split into two vast wings, the superior Renaissance wing with its black marble and elegant chandeliers and the rather more simple New World wing. Each has its own entrance, lobby and check-in, which can get quite confusing if you are new to the hotel. The New World rooms are straightforward while the Renaissance rooms follow the more regal decor that the hotel embraces in general. With a good central location and many rooms that gaze out over the Petronas Towers, it is a popular choice.

Rates from: **US$ 51**
Star rating: ★ ★ ★ ★ ★
Bellhop rating: 🏨 🏨 🏨 🏨 ½

Value:	8.19	Facilities:	8.38
Staff:	8.09	Restaurants:	8.08
Location:	8.38	Families:	6.71
Cleanliness:	8.50		

Renaissance Melaka Hotel

Jl Bendahara, 75100 Melaka, Malaysia
T: +60 6 284 8888 **F**: +60 6 284 9269
http://www.asia-hotels.com/hotelinfo/Renaissance_Melaka_Hotel/

Melaka does not offer a lot in terms of hotel quality but one of the better ones is clearly the Renaissance. The property does not stand out – it is simply good and dependable which in Melaka is rare. Architecturally, the 24-storey tower block is not going to win any prizes but the 300 rooms are well furnished offering generous space and good views, especially from the Renaissance Club rooms on the top three floors. The range of facilities is generally good – two glass-backed squash courts, fully fitted gym including sauna and swimming pool. Of the four restaurants, Capers show kitchen serves an excellent fusion of Western and Asian cuisine. Hotel service is functional but overall the Renaissance is reliable, fairly priced and with an unbeatable location in the heart of historic Melaka.

Rates from: **US$ 53**
Star rating: ★★★★
Bellhop rating: 🔔🔔🔔

Value:	7.87	Facilities:	8.04
Staff:	7.94	Restaurants:	7.11
Location:	8.05	Families:	5.87
Cleanliness:	8.24		

Rihga Royal Hotel Miri

Jl Temenggong Datuk Oyong Lawai, 98008 Miri, Sarawak, Malaysia
T: +60 85 421 121 **F**: +60 85 425 057
http://www.asia-hotels.com/hotelinfo/Rihga_Royal_Hotel_Miri/

The first oilmen arrived in the 1900s when Miri was a mere smattering of houses. Since the first rig – the Grand Old Lady – was first spudded in 1910, the small cowboy town on Borneo Malaysia has mushroomed to 200,000 inhabitants. Still dominated by the oil industry (now mainly offshore) and a crossing point to Brunei, Miri is one of Sarawak's major revenue earners. Even so, it does not have much when it comes to hotels. No doubt one of the best is the Rihga Royal but the generous 5-star rating is more in keeping with local expectations. The hotel does boast Sarawak's largest outdoor pool sitting on the edge of Brighton Beach and the South China Sea, three restaurants and five bars including RIGS – named after the local oil rigs – a popular nightspot. The 225 comfortable but simple rooms include 172 chalet-style housed near the beach and pool.

Rates from: **US$ 37**
Star rating: ★★★★★
Bellhop rating: 🔔🔔🔔🔔

Value:	8.61	Facilities:	8.73
Staff:	8.82	Restaurants:	8.21
Location:	8.30	Families:	8.52
Cleanliness:	8.88		

The Ritz-Carlton Kuala Lumpur

168 Jl Imbi, 55100 Kuala Lumpur, Malaysia
T: +60 3 2142 8000 **F**: +60 3 2143 8080
http://www.asia-hotels.com/hotelinfo/RitzCarlton_The/

The inevitable boast from hotels everywhere is that their service is the best. But of all the hotels in Kuala Lumpur, it must be said that some of the most professional, thorough and sincere staff are found at the Ritz-Carlton. Their genuine effort to put the guest first – whether waiting in the lobby, getting into an elevator or strolling the corridors – makes your stay here a real pleasure. In keeping with the staff, the hotel itself is intimate and personal. The building is small and snug with a refreshing calm once inside – you could never get lost in a crowd here. The interior design is classical European with touches of Asian. Gentle colours are balanced with dark woods and subtle lighting in both the 248 rooms and corridors.

The European-Asian blend permeates the restaurants. From the Mediterranean, Rossini's serves authentic Italian cuisine in elegant surroundings, from the Far East, Li Yen specialises in Cantonese and dim sum. And for a combination of Western and Malaysian food try César's Bistro, a satellite restaurant just away from the hotel on Bintang Walk. A rather civilised bar adjoins the lobby while the club rooms on floors 17 through 20 have the rather plush Club Lounge with its dedicated concierge, 24-hour beverages and five daily food servings.

The soothing and lavishly furnished rooms, at a minimum of 46 square metres, are some of the largest in Kuala Lumpur and refreshingly wide with a T-shaped floor plan. The personal feel is maintained with the attentive services of a 24-hour dedicated butler, and repeat guests enjoy added touches such as having the room laid out to their previous preferences, and their names embroidered on their pillow cases.

Full business facilities, the magnetic pull of the top-end spa, and a handsome outdoor pool (albeit slightly noisy) complete the picture. All are maintained and run with the same style and warmth. The Ritz-Carlton tends to appeal to corporate clients, but there is no reason why its appeal should not be broader, especially as it is located conveniently near the shops of lively Jalan Bukit Bintan, and the service would be appreciated by anyone far away from home.

Rates from: **US$ 113**
Star rating: ★ ★ ★ ★ ★
Bellhop rating: 🛎 🛎 🛎 🛎 ½

Value:	**8.38**	Facilities:	**8.37**
Staff:	**9.06**	Restaurants:	**8.10**
Location:	**8.64**	Families:	**7.02**
Cleanliness:	**9.17**		

Shangri-La Golden Sands Resort

Batu Feringgi Beach, Batu Feringgi, 11100 Penang, Malaysia
T: +60 4 881 1911 **F:** +60 4 881 1880
http://www.asia-hotels.com/hotelinfo/ShangriLa_Golden_Sands_Resort/

Start the day with a guided 2-hour jungle walk through one of the nearby rainforests, ease down a gear with a stretching tai chi lesson at the Pavillion Terrace – now for a hard-earned breakfast at the Garden Cafe. The boat for Monkey Beach leaves from the Watersports Centre at 10 am or maybe today just lounge by the beachside pool and have that tension-breaking foot massage. Snack lunch at the Kuda Laut poolside bar before the satay cooking class at 3 pm followed by an archery tournament and evening tennis competition. Sigi's by the Sea for bistro dinner before enjoying the live band over an evening cocktail at the Sunset Lounge. Retire to your 7th-floor Deluxe Room and admire the sea view from the balcony before collapsing into bed – totally exhausted.

To say Golden Sands has activities would be a gross understatement. Every waking hour, seven days a week, there is something going on, from juggling lessons to table tennis competitions, from aquarobics to palmistry, from trapeze demonstrations to napkin folding. The focus for the activities is Starfy's, an activity centre-cum-team building village, nestled between the resort and its sister property the Rasa Sayang. And the fun is not restricted to adults – children have their own Star Kids' Club broken into the Betty Club (4 to 7 years) and the Kids' Club (8 to 12 years). Circus school, origami, face painting, trampolining and treasure hunts all ensure the younger ones return at the end of the day equally worn out. And for those difficult in-between teenagers, the Teen Club is the cool hangout. Oh, and if it rains there is a full menu of indoor to-dos.

The sands and sea of Penang's Batu Feringgi Beach are sub-standard for Asia but the 395-room Golden Sands, with its extensive selection of entertainment and two large free-form pools, more than makes up for this. The old adage says that change is as good as a rest – Shangri-La Golden Sands certainly is a change, whether you return rested is another issue.

Rates from: **US$ 59**
Star rating: ★ ★ ★ ★
Bellhop rating: 🛎 🛎 🛎 🛎 ½

Value:	8.11	Facilities:	8.45
Staff:	8.38	Restaurants:	8.18
Location:	8.62	Families:	7.87
Cleanliness:	8.42		

Shangri-La Hotel Kuala Lumpur

11 Jl Sultan Ismail, 50250 Kuala Lumpur, Malaysia
T: +60 3 2032 2388 **F:** +60 3 2070 1514
http://www.asia-hotels.com/hotelinfo/Shangri-La_Hotel_Kuala_Lumpur/

Since its recent refurbishment the centrally located Shangri-La is now back in line with the high standards of other properties in the group and returns to being one of the top hotels in Kuala Lumpur. The modern and chic lobby sets the tone for the whole hotel but is nicely offset by the lush leafy gardens. Perhaps it is the eight restaurants and bars which stand out most with some excellent and varied choices. Chefs of the Lemon Garden Cafe prepare a-la-minute dishes for the 'live' buffet in their multi-Asian show kitchens, and the aromas from Cinnamon's oven-fresh pastries are salivating. The floor-to-ceiling wine displays, designer lights and central water cascade continue the stylish design at Lafite. Wine and sake is displayed in similar fashion at Zipangu, the contemporary Tokyo-style brasserie. Slightly more traditional is the 1st-floor English-style pub with pool table and live entertainment. The 701 well kitted out rooms and top-class service mean the Shangri-La Kuala Lumpur is definitely back to its best.

Rates from: US$ 114
Star rating: ★ ★ ★ ★ ★
Bellhop rating: 🛎 🛎 🛎 🛎 ½

Value: 8.21   Facilities: 8.49
Staff: 8.54   Restaurants: 8.40
Location: 8.57   Families: 6.67
Cleanliness: 8.72

Shangri-La Rasa Ria Resort

Pantai Dalit, 89208 Tuaran, Sabah, Malaysia
T: +60 88 792 888 **F:** +60 88 792 777
http://www.asia-hotels.com/hotelinfo/Shangri-La_Rasa_Ria_Resort/

The defining aspect of the Rasa Ria is its location, some 45 minutes drive north of Kota Kinabalu. This remoteness lends some of the escape factor that many visitors seek when heading for Borneo, and the resort sits contentedly between a trio of appealing environments – leafy rainforest, a splendid 18-hole championship golf course and a scenic stretch of white sand beach. It is also well placed for forays into Sabah's country parks, while Mount Kinabalu and the Poring hot springs are within easy day tripping reach.

The 330-room Rasa Ria is similar to its sister property, the Shangri-La Tanjung Aru, in both design and layout. Big and broad wings span out from the spacious open lobby. The ground-floor rooms have private lanais accessible through the verdant,

landscaped gardens, while the other accommodation is split-level with private balconies. All rooms are equipped with numerous modern amenities, from air-conditioning to in-house movies.

The resort's recreational facilities are extensive for both adults and kids, with everything from tennis to mountain bikes outside and a professional spa, compact gym and very reasonable games room and kids' club inside. However, when the sun shines the resort comes into its own – the pool and beach are perfect places to pass your time and there is the immaculate Dalit Bay Golf & Country Club next door.

The most memorable feature of the Rasa Ria is its proximity to nature. The resort's 400 acres include a dedicated nature reserve complete with walking trails, bird

watching and the magic of resident orangutans swinging down from the branches for feeding time. Diners at either the Pool Bar or poolside Tepi Laut, two of the seven restaurants and bars, are in danger of losing their snacks to an enormous, colourful hornbill which sometimes swoops down to scoff French fries. Despite the Rasa Ria's 'walk on the wild side' there is no compromise on comfort – this is one of the better resorts in Asia for eco-tourists.

Rates from: **US$ 85**
Star rating: ★★★★★
Bellhop rating: ԁԁԁԁԁ

Value:	8.43	Facilities:	8.68
Staff:	8.95	Restaurants:	8.33
Location:	8.14	Families:	7.90
Cleanliness:	8.74		

Shangri-La Rasa Sayang Resort

Batu Feringgi Beach, 11100 Penang, Malaysia
T: +60 4 881 1811 **F:** +60 4 881 1984-2739
http://www.asia-hotels.com/hotelinfo/Shangri-La_Rasa_Sayang_Resort/

The beach scene on Penang is far from the best. However, the fascinating colonial history of this early trading post and the culinary blend resulting from the cosmopolitan mix of immigrants makes for a diverse and interesting destination for those looking for more than just the seaside. The Shangri-La Rasa Sayang is very much the same – an excellent all-round resort with something for everyone.

For those looking to relax, there is Feringgi Beach (the best Penang has to offer), two free-form pools set in 15 acres of lush gardens and a health club with soothing massages and cleansing saunas. For those looking for action, there is Starfy's – an entertainment and team-building village – and the Star Kids' Club shared with the resort's neighbouring sister property, the Golden Sands, and providing packed days of adult and child entertainment. For culture vultures, Georgetown with Fort Cornwallis, a fine selection of museums and traditional architecture of a bygone period is only 20 minutes drive. And for food lovers, there are the nine restaurants and bars serving Chinese, Japanese, European and

local foods, a further five at Golden Sands (where guests have signing rights) and, if that is not enough, Feringgi's strip of restaurants is a few minutes walk away.

The Rasa Sayang is huge, split into the Rasa and Garden Wings, but makes an effort to appeal to the eye, topping each wing with sweeping traditional-styled roofs. The biggest hotel on the island, it has 514 comfortable rooms, all fully equipped, with sliding glass doors leading out to good balconies, many with lovely sea views. Suites

are very generous with bright colours and hints of traditional Malay culture.

Although the vast majority of guests are here for leisure, this 'Jack' of many trades has an impressive array of business and corporate facilities. Banquet and conference capacities can reach 800 and Starfy's arranges inventive team building courses and activities. Few resorts of this size offer this degree of choice without losing a little edge in ambience or service, but the Shangri-La Rasa Sayang manages to pull it off with a certain amount of style.

Rates from: **US$ 72**
Star rating: ★★★★★
Bellhop rating: ◊◊◊◊ ½

Value:	8.04	Facilities:	8.65
Staff:	8.52	Restaurants:	8.46
Location:	8.56	Families:	7.78
Cleanliness:	8.59		

Shangri-La Tanjung Aru Resort

20 Jl Aru, Tanjung Aru, 88100 Kota Kinabalu, Sabah, Malaysia
T: +60 88 225 800 **F:** +60 88 244 871
http://www.asia-hotels.com/hotelinfo/ShangriLas_Tanjung_Aru_Resort/

The Tanjung Aru turns its substantial back on nearby downtown Kota Kinabalu to look out over the South China Sea and, in particular, the five uninhabited islands which lie a short boat trip offshore. For a morning or even an entire day, you can voyage out here and while away the hours beachcombing, sunbathing and snorkelling, often with no one else in sight. Talk about a resort with added extras. The basics are not far short of excellent either. The Tanjung Aru's 500 spacious rooms and suites are split between the Kinabalu and Tanjung wings, furnished in local timber, rattan and bamboo to give them an appropriately tropical slant. The blinds are split bamboo, ceiling fans join forces with the sea breezes, the furniture on the verandahs is

comfortably cushioned and the views extend out to sea or up to the majestic craggy peaks of the 4,101-metre Mount Kinabalu.

Even if the idea of exploring isolated islands palls, no one can really complain about getting bored here. Two free-form pools, four tennis courts, and a 9-hole pitch and putt complement a full range of water sports and the resort's leisure and health clubs. Landscape luminary Nining, aka 'Mr Greenfingers', leads guests around the 25 acres surrounding the hotel, pointing out the more exotic plants. And if the prospect of jollifications like mah-jong challenges and family egg tossing competitions lack a certain je ne sais quoi, you can always hive off to the spa, poolside or your own room for a massage or reflexology

session. Pre-teen youngsters will be kept fully occupied at the Sunshine Club, with crab catching, shell collecting, flower arranging and a host of other activities. If that is not enough: golf, rock climbing, horse riding, jungle trekking (treetop or earthbound) and a bird sanctuary are all nearby and, of course, Mount Kinabalu is there to be climbed.

On the food front, the six restaurants and bars serve up the best of Malay, Chinese, Indian and Western dishes, with Peppino's – the Italian restaurant – being especially popular, and the Borneo Lounge catering to late-night snackers and drinkers. The Sunset Bar is the place to watch the sun disappear behind those magical islands and plan the next day's fun-filled agenda.

Rates from: US$ 95
Star rating: ★ ★ ★ ★ ★
Bellhop rating: ◖◖◖◖ ½

Value:	8.32	Facilities:	8.71
Staff:	8.80	Restaurants:	8.41
Location:	8.56	Families:	7.43
Cleanliness:	8.75		

Sheraton Langkawi Beach Resort

Telok Nibong, 07000 Langkawi, Kedah, Malaysia
T: +60 4 955 1901 **F:** +60 4 955 1968
http://www.asia-hotels.com/hotelinfo/Sheraton_Langkawi_Beach_Resort/

This enjoyable 231-roomed resort is in many ways typical of Langkawi and of the standards and service one expects from a high-end Malay resort. Sitting just metres from the Andaman sea, the resort is a pleasantly sprawling mass of low-rise kampong-style cabins. Wood dominates both the setting and the decor. The 38 acres of rainforest is home to a wide variety of wildlife, from the rather cute dusky leaf monkey often spotted in the trees around the lobby to the rather less endearing groups of long-tailed macaque commonly found near the tennis courts. Giant squirrels, flying lemurs and tree shrews can be seen throughout the resort along with clouded monitor lizards which grow up to 1.5 metres long.

The rooms, at 51 square metres, are very spacious and have a wonderful but ageing rustic charm. Finished in natural hardwoods and local fabrics, each has full-length French-style windows opening on to generous terraces from which to enjoy the forest canopy above or the wonderful sea views. It is a pleasant walk from the rooms through the grounds to the numerous facilities, but a little bus does scoot around every 15 minutes to transport guests between pick-up points.

On the fringes of the shore lies a pretty little beach with a large decked pool and adjacent well-shaded kids' pool. From here a raised wooden walkway, from which it is not uncommon to spot dolphins, winds along the shore to Captain's seafood grill, one of six restaurants and bars. Spice Trader, perched looking over the sea, offers Asian cuisine with an emphasis on Indian while Karma Jaya is a more international mix. Black Henry, a rather lively nightspot, features some good bands. Given, the wonderful natural environment and extensive activities including tennis, fishing, a full spa, eagle feeding, jungle trekking and a daily recreational program for both adults and children, it is no surprise that this resort is adored by families. This is all helped by the staff who are warm, accommodating and attentive and are the resort's chief asset beside its pretty setting.

Rates from: **US$ 105**
Star rating: ★ ★ ★ ★ ½
Bellhop rating: ◗ ◗ ◗ ◗ ½

Value:	8.26	Facilities:	8.40
Staff:	8.48	Restaurants:	8.18
Location:	8.32	Families:	7.19
Cleanliness:	8.57		

The Smokehouse Hotel

By the golf course, 39000 Cameron Highlands, Pahang, Malaysia
T: +60 5 491 1215 **F:** +60 5 491 1214
http://www.asia-hotels.com/hotelinfo/Smokehouse_Hotel/

It used to be called Ye Olde Smokehouse Inn and, in a way, that name best suits this vaguely twee yet prepossessing anachronism. The mock-Tudor beams and latticed windows, creaky corridors and chintzy sofas, lovingly tended lawns and shrubs, unconventional menus and conventional seen-and-not-heard attitude to children all belong to the 1930s in what was then called Malaya. All this makes sense when you know that the Smokehouse opened for Christmas in 1937 and was firmly intended for homesick expatriates, who only got home leave every eight years. The cooler climes of the Cameron Highlands allowed them to pull on woolly jerseys, toast themselves in front of a real fire and turn their backs on the tropics for a weekend or longer.

A succession of Englishmen and a solitary Scot (with a brief interregnum by the Imperial Japanese Army) ran the place with varying degrees of success until 1975, when it was taken over by the Lee family who oversee the hotel to this day.

Recognising that Smokehouse's attractions lie in being the antithesis of just about every other hotel in the country, they have sensibly altered and enhanced only a little. The 10 suites are named after the houses at English boarding schools where the Lee progeny studied, and are variously furnished with four-poster beds and antiques. The kitchen is perfectly at home with staple meals like full English breakfast, steak and kidney pudding, and roast beef with Yorkshire pudding, while afternoon tea in the garden (scones, Devonshire cream, a selection of home-made jams) is practically de rigeur.

The hotel is right next to the golf course, and easily spotted by the traditional red telephone and post boxes outside. Anglophobes, nouvelle cuisine gourmands, modernists and – in all fairness – families with toddlers in tow should seek out diggings more suited to their particular needs. Just about everybody else with any sense of history is going to love it here.

Rates from: **US$ 105**
Star rating: ★ ★ ★
Bellhop rating: 🛎 🛎 🛎 🛎

Value:	6.54	Facilities:	7.46
Staff:	8.92	Restaurants:	8.85
Location:	9.00	Families:	7.15
Cleanliness:	8.39		

Sunway Lagoon Resort Hotel

Pesiaran Lagoon, Bandar Sunway, 46150 Selangor, Malaysia
T: +60 3 7492 8000 **F**: +60 3 7492 8001
http://www.asia-hotels.com/hotelinfo/Sunway_Lagoon_Resort_Hotel/

The Sunway Lagoon Resort is Malaysian Disneyland complete with monorail. Think big, think total excess, think fun. The approach to the huge, vivid lobby lets you know what you are in for – giant tusked elephants outside are outdone by what look like mounted flying saucers. Over the top decor jumps out throughout. That said, the facilities are absolutely endless. The resort connects with a sprawling theme park and one of the world's largest surf wave pools, an Egyptian 'pyramid' shopping and entertainment mall with multiplex cinemas, an ice-skating rink and a 48-lane bowling centre, and more than 10,000 square metres of meeting, convention and exhibition space. The staff are surprisingly welcoming given the huge stream of boisterous visitors and the rooms are spacious and well equipped, though some of the themed suites will raise a smile. The capital and the airport are easily reached in 30 minutes making this versatile resort useful for business purposes as well as highly appealing to families.

Rates from: **US$ 89**
Star rating: ★★★★ ½
Bellhop rating: ♘♘♘♘ ½

Value:	7.66	Facilities:	8.51
Staff:	8.11	Restaurants:	8.01
Location:	7.90	Families:	7.89
Cleanliness:	8.43		

Sutera Harbour Resort & Spa

1 Sutera Harbour Boulevard, 88100 Kota Kinabalu, Sabah, Malaysia
T: +60 88 318 888 **F**: +60 88 317 777
http://www.asia-hotels.com/hotelinfo/Pacific_Sutera_The/

The biggest of all of Kota Kinabalu's hotels is set in the sweeping 384-acre grounds of the ambitious redeveloped area of Sutera Harbour, just minutes from town. This massive resort makes no effort to be subtle, in fact it could be called slightly garish. The colossal lobby is almost like an aircraft hangar and the vast Magellen and Pacific hotel wings house some 956 good sized rooms. The modern decor is bright and colourful but in keeping with local tastes. Needless to say the facilities are extensive and include a 27-hole golf course, 41-bay two-storey driving range, 17 bars, restaurants and nightclubs, 100-plus berth marina, tennis, badminton and squash courts, 12-lane bowling centre, two kids' clubs, numerous pools, a spa and even a movie theatre. Active, popular and supported by some excellent and attentive staff – it is hardly surprising that families love this place.

Rates from: **US$ 63**
Star rating: ★★★★
Bellhop rating: ♘♘♘♘♘

Value:	8.42	Facilities:	8.86
Staff:	8.75	Restaurants:	8.42
Location:	8.92	Families:	7.06
Cleanliness:	8.81		

Tanjong Jara Resort

Batu 8 off Jl Dungun, 23000 Dungun, Terengganu, Malaysia
T: +60 9 845 1100 **F:** +60 9 845 6014
http://www.asia-hotels.com/hotelinfo/Tanjung_Jara_Resort/

Tanjong Jara – halfway between Kuala Terengganu and Kuantan, an hour from the local airport or a 6-hour drive from Kuala Lumpur – is inconveniently situated for the international traveller. This does however save it from mass tourism and the resort maintains a wonderful aura of a hidden beachside escape. Its traditional architecture, derived from the elegantly crafted wooden palaces of Malay sultans, is set in scenic tropical gardens offering panoramic views over the South China Sea

First impressions suggest the resort is new, so it comes as a surprise that it is some 25 years old and has had an eventful history. This part of the east coast was earmarked for tourism and the Tanjong Jara was built to help precipitate it. Opened by the government's Tourist Development Corporation, the resort won widespread praise and scooped up many accolades including the coveted Aga Khan Award for Architecture. But tourism never flourished on this side of the peninsula, and Tanjong Jara deteriorated before being salvaged by a private company (coincidentally, the owner of the lovely Pangkor Laut Resort) which embarked on a glorious renovation programme. The

new design preserved the traditionally constructed buildings while incorporating an elegant modern theme and maintaining a fundamentally Malay experience.

The accommodation is rich, creative and dominated by a mix of belian wood and teak. Small 2-storey buildings contain the Serambi and Bumbung Rooms, both well fitted and catching the tropical mood. The lower Serambis have terraces for sunbathing – the upper Bumbungs are identical but terrace-less, though with better views as compensation. The third category, Anjung, lines the shore – a series of stunningly designed 88-square-metre cottages with sunken baths and canopied terraces.

Comprehensive resort facilities are in the same league – two beautiful pools, a top gym and relaxing spa pavilions. Authentic Malay cuisine is served at Di Atas Sungei overlooking the Marang River while Nelayan specialises in seafood caught by the resort's own fishermen. Visiting the local prince (second cousin to the reigning Sultan of Terengganu), turtle watching at a WWF-affiliated sanctuary, jungle trekking along Jara Hill, touring local villages, learning to cook Kari Ayam (chicken curry), and diving off Tenggol Island are just some of the pursuits available at this wonderful backwater.

Rates from: **US$ 176**
Star rating: ★ ★ ★ ★ ★
Bellhop rating: ♘ ♘ ♘ ♘

Value:	7.36	Facilities:	8.02
Staff:	8.31	Restaurants:	7.48
Location:	7.81	Families:	6.95
Cleanliness:	8.29		

Tanjung Rhu Resort

Mukim Ayer Hangat, 07000 Langkawi, Kedah, Malaysia
T: +60 4 959 1033 **F:** +60 4 959 1899
http://www.asia-hotels.com/hotelinfo/Tanjung_Rhu_Resort/

Tanjung Rhu is one of Langkawi's best, if you have faith in what you often hear on the grapevine. But first impressions may have you scratching your head. The approach is not the most flattering angle – the resort resembles an isolated horseshoe-shaped apartment block and the lobby is virtually non-existent. But once you breach the ugly tenement stairwells it indeed transforms into a superb resort, clearly built to be appreciated from within.

The 135 rooms capture the resort essence and possess in abundance that most elusive luxury – space. They are bountifully spacious, among the biggest rooms and best value in Asia. The Damai Rooms are the lowest category but at 50 square metres compare with a typical suite in other establishments. Large bathrooms have shutters that open into the lounge to give that extra length and breadth. Fittings include rosy timber flooring, with full-length windows and balconies overlooking the garden courtyard. The ever expanding higher-room categories are almost small flats and enjoy beguiling pool or sea views. Each room is equipped like home with TV, CD player and VCR,

and an ample selection of videos and discs for all the family is available from the library.

Spread over 30 acres with ample lawns and foliage, the Tanjung Rhu faces the Andaman Sea with an impressive 2.5 kilometres of private golden sands. A pleasing 60-metre sunset pool stretches off towards the sundeck and horizon. Alternatively, the lagoon pool is shaded by greenery and wrapped within the ring of the building, broken only to allow access to the sea – and kids just love it.

No doubt the Tanjung Rhu is remote – a good half an hour by car from town or airport – and with virtually nothing in the surrounding area other than 1,100 acres of deserted mangrove-lined coast and forest. The resort benefits from the seclusion and puts on some

wonderful nature tours, including the most spectacular eagle feeding. The isolation essentially limits wining and dining to the three resort restaurants that meander between the rather average Sands and the truly excellent fine dining of Rhu, but there is nothing more relaxing or romantic than a sundowner on the deck of the 1st-floor reading room with live piano music drifting through the evening air.

Rates from: **US$ 198**
Star rating: ★ ★ ★ ★ ★
Bellhop rating: 🛎 🛎 🛎 🛎 ½

Value:	7.86	Facilities:	8.66
Staff:	8.93	Restaurants:	8.47
Location:	8.84	Families:	6.63
Cleanliness:	8.99		

MALDIVES

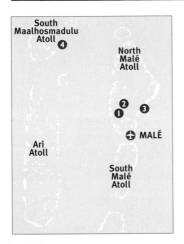

Hotel	Page
1 Angsana Resort & Spa Maldives Ihuru	173
2 Banyan Tree Maldives Vabbinfaru	174
3 Four Seasons Resort Maldives at Kuda Huraa	175
4 Soneva Fushi	176

The prototypical Maldives tourists would be a pair of newly-wed underwater enthusiasts. Well, make that a flush couple of honeymooning scuba-divers, for this is a potentially pricey destination. But as the old adage runs, you get what you pay for, and the Maldives' 1,190 islands grouped on 26 atolls in the azure waters of the Indian Ocean are without doubt one of the most exclusive destinations in the region.

Only around 200 of the islands are inhabited, and some 80 of them are home to resorts fully geared to the whims of 'paradise-seekers' and divers. Many of these grace the upper echelons of 5-star accommodation, designed with flair and sympathy for their surrounds and dispensing cuisine and service more readily associated with major

cities rather than far-flung sandy islets. Expect full-board packages, as there are few dining options off site, and be aware that your hotel is the only place you will find alcohol, the Maldives is very Muslim in this respect.

The vast majority of visitors fly into the international airport near Malé, the capital city, if that is the right term for a huddle of mosques, markets and a neat maze of streets. In its favour, Malé does offer some inexpensive accommodation, as well as granting a window into local culture.

The Maldives are warm and sunny year round, however the dry season (December – April) is most favoured by visitors. Rain is more likely between May and November. Divers usually agree that the best underwater visibility is during the months of seasonal change in April and November. And it is diving (with the peripheral attraction of other water sports) that acts as the Maldives' chief allure, although El Nino has had a damaging impact in recent years. There are hundreds of easily accessible sites, while more can be reached on diving safari trips. Once below the surface there are veritable academies of fish, magnificent coral gardens, prowling turtles,

manta ray, whales and sharks as well as what experts agree is one of the world's most exciting wreck dives, the Maldive Victory, off Hulule Airport. Above the waves, parasailing, waterskiing and windsurfing are on offer, and there are some excellent if slightly remote surf breaks. Big game fishing is also popular, although a strict 'tag and release' policy is in force.

As for other recreation, this is a definitely a couples venue rather than singles' vacationland, and there is little in the way of nightlife. However, a blissful tropical island and the seclusion of a four-poster swathed in a mosquito net should be inspiration enough for most couples, whether they have just got married or not.

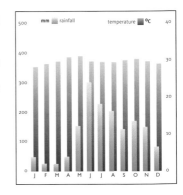

Angsana Resort & Spa Maldives Ihuru

Ihuru, North Malé Atoll, Maldives
T: +960 443 502 **F:** +960 445 933
http://www.asia-hotels.com/hotelinfo/Angsana_Resort_Spa/

Ihuru means old palm trees in the Maldivian language. Angsana is a tree found in tropical rainforests and noted for its crown of flowers that burst into a fragrant shower of golden-yellow blooms. So it almost goes without saying that the Angsana Resort and the tiny islet of Ihuru are a flawless marriage of location and concept.

With such inspirational surroundings, it is hardly surprising that many couples elect to hold their nuptials here, surrounded by the natural beauty of the Maldive archipelago. Forget that conventional walk down the aisle – here you can plight your troth on the beach by a crystal clear lagoon, on a sandbank way out in the ocean, or – assuming you're correctly PADI'd – exchange your vows underwater. And come back here for your anniversary and you get a free night stay.

Even if you are not considering tying the knot, Angsana reeks of romance. Its 45 beachfront villas are set around the island's circumference, thatched with palm, surrounded by a private garden, with outdoor showers and a swing to laze the days away upon. Decorated in fresh, summery colours, all have a queen-size bed and 10 come with an open-air jacuzzi.

Assuming you can shake yourself out of a rather pleasing inertia, there is plenty of recreation to fill the hours between buffet breakfasts at the Riveli Restaurant and cocktails at the Velaavani Bar, a vantage point over the reef where turtles and dolphins swim.

The spa's signature therapy is specially designed to relieve tension and aid blood circulation, and there is also a variety of wraps, scrubs and facials. You can also get your circulation going and let off steam canoeing, island hopping, wakeboarding or windsurfing, all of which can be organised at the resort. And of course the surrounding reefs and dive sites are superb. Just ask anyone who has bubbled 'I do'.

Rates from: **US$ 416**
Star rating: ★ ★ ★ ★ ★
Bellhop rating: ◙ ◙ ◙ ◙ ◙

Value:	8.58	Facilities:	8.77
Staff:	8.73	Restaurants:	8.62
Location:	9.15	Families:	7.00
Cleanliness:	8.96		

Banyan Tree Maldives Vabbinfaru

Vabbinfaru Island, North Malé Atoll, Maldives
T: +960 443 147 F: +960 443 843
http://www.asia-hotels.com/hotelinfo/Banyan_Tree_Maldives_Vabbinfaru/

While many resorts in the Maldives are eco-friendly, the Banyan Tree has gone that extra nautical mile to ensure that its gorgeous undersea surroundings remain exactly that.

The Banyan Tree rests on Vabbinfaru, which means round island encircled by a coral reef. Arriving here, making an almost regal progress atop the lengthy jetty, there is a tingling sense of excitement as you pass above the aquamarine waters swarming with marine life.

The resort is unarguably lovely, with its rondavel-style villas on the fringes of the white sand beach, their furnishings crafted in polished black granite, and glass doors open to Indian Ocean breezes that will stir the canopy enveloping the four-poster beds. There is a Zen-like calm here, a palpable sense of indulgence, and an overriding feeling of untrammelled luxury. You can get spa'd in one of the open-air pavilions, fly off sightseeing from a seaplane, or dine a deux at the end of a jetty or on a secluded beach where you are greeted with chilled champagne and poems hand-written in the sand. More conventionally, there is a smorgasbord of Maldivian, Mediterranean and Asian cuisine at the newly refurbished Ilafaathi restaurant, and barbeques in the Sangu Garden.

All this is as nothing compared to the sub-aqua delights of Vabbinfaru. Quite apart from the reef ringing the island, 10 spectacular, top-of-the-world dive sites lie within an hours boat ride, home to whale sharks, manta rays, moray eels, white tip sharks and myriad other species. Rather than simply admiring the treasures on display, Banyan Tree guests are encouraged to play a part in preserving the marine ecology. One of the most popular activities is helping to build artificial coral gardens, which enjoy a 70 per cent success rate and are particularly rewarding for guests when they return in years to come. Alternatively, the Napwatch project logs sightings of the endangered Napoleon Wrasse, and divers are urged to photograph any that they come across to add to a database tracking the fish's habits and migration. Naturally, the Banyan Tree's PADI centre is fully equipped and instructors are on hand to advise and teach both qualified divers as well as those making their first tentative strokes underwater.

Rates from: US$ 500
Star rating: ★★★★★
Bellhop rating: ♗♗♗♗ ½

Value:	7.68	Facilities:	8.24
Staff:	8.69	Restaurants:	8.31
Location:	8.79	Families:	6.54
Cleanliness:	8.69		

Four Seasons Resort Maldives at Kuda Huraa

Kuda Huraa, North Malé Atoll, Maldives
T: +960 444 888 **F**: +960 443 388
http://www.asia-hotels.com/hotelinfo/Four_Seasons_Resort_Maldives_Kuda_Huraa/

By launching its 11-stateroom dive catamaran in 2002, the Four Seasons pulled off something no other hotel in the Maldives had quite yet achieved. The 39-metre Island Explorer is a mini resort in itself, ranging the length and breadth of the archipelago in the lap of luxury, to all intents and purposes a floating Four Seasons. Naturally, this is no common or garden cruiser. The 20-strong crew includes a marine biologist to escort divers and snorkellers, and a therapist to massage them once they are back on board. All the staterooms contain a king-size bed and sound and entertainment systems, you can dine inside or on deck, and the Explorer drops anchor at deserted coves and beaches for kayaking or exploring.

Back at Kuda Huraa, the 106 bungalows and villas of the resort proper await. All are beautifully decorated and furnished, however the Water Bungalows each have a private sun deck and steps leading straight down into the turquoise lagoon, while the villas encompass a larger area and have a private outdoor shower.

On the recreation side, it is difficult to conjecture how anyone could even think about visiting a gym here, but there are treadmills aplenty in the Activity Centre. Rather more sybaritically, the infinity pool has a swim-up bar and is one of the largest in the Maldives. Even less strenuous is the spa, a short trip by wooden dhoni across the lagoon, where Oceanic, Maldivian and Javanese Lulur body elixirs and other treatments are dispensed in thatched pavilions with Arabic, Moroccan and Indian design influences.

Three restaurants more or less complete the picture at Kuda Huraa, with Indian and Maldivian cuisine at Baraabaru, Mediterranean specialties in the Reef Club and all-day dining at Cafe Huraa. Plus of course it would be sheer folly to miss out on a sunset drink at the Nautilus Lounge when the Indian Ocean goes Technicolor ballistic.

Rates from: **US$ 350**
Star rating: ★ ★ ★ ★ ★
Bellhop rating: 🛎 🛎 🛎 🛎 ½

Value:	7.84	Facilities:	8.70
Staff:	9.04	Restaurants:	8.42
Location:	8.97	Families:	6.82
Cleanliness:	9.13		

Soneva Fushi

Kunfunadhoo Island, North Baa Atoll, Maldives
T: +960 230 304 **F:** +960 230 374
http://www.asia-hotels.com/hotelinfo/Soneva_Fushi_Maldives/

If you accept the adage that many of Asia's best hotels are extensions of their owners' personalities, then Soneva Fushi is its prime example. Tycoon Sonu met top Swedish model Eva aboard a yacht in Monaco, and the ensuing Mr and Mrs Shivdasani spent their honeymoon jetting around the world. When they came upon

Kunfunadhoo, an abandoned resort on a 99-acre atoll in the Maldives, they knew at once that this was the place to build their dream. The result, opened in 1995, was Soneva Fushi, an amalgam of their names, vision and inherent taste for good living, together with the Maldivian word for island.

Largely designed by Eva, Soneva Fushi combines simplicity with sophistication, luxury with 'back to nature', while emphasising a strong commitment to the environment. The villas are supported by recycled telegraph poles; if guests need wheels to get about they come in the shape of non-polluting sit-up-and-beg bicycles; faxes are distributed in hand-woven reed tubes and if you

call for a television it is delivered in a water hyacinth basket.

With a sturdy, eco-friendly philosophy, the resort – not to put too fine a point on it – is bliss itself.

A seaplane bridges the 60 nautical miles between the international airport at Malé and the island, and on arrival guests are invited to shed their shoes – with the inference of getting rid of cares and inhibitions as well. Kunfunadhoo is just 1,400 metres long and no more than 400 wide, and scattered along the beaches and among the island's unusually rich vegetation are some threescore rooms and villas. The interiors, whether in one of the two Presidential Villas or a rather more compact Rehendi Room make much of the bathrooms, keep furnishings plain yet attractively simple, and discreetly tuck the CD players away behind rattan screening.

Soneva Fushi is nothing if not seductive, and enthusiastic couples could easily be lured into doing nothing here apart from alternating between bed and beach and bathroom with the occasional stop for sustenance. There are some diversions that, while not compulsory, are pretty unique, such as a private sunrise breakfast on the Sandbank, which lies right out in the ocean 10 minutes away from the resort. The management also throws a weekly cocktail party here – champagne and canapés but otherwise pure Crusoe. Rather than a one-size-fits-all menu, the spa goes for tailor-made, one-on-one treatments, which vault beyond the routine massages, facials and scrubs with some wacky specials like the chocolate and milk bath (which you sit in), accompanied by a glass of iced mocha (which you drink).

The spa should certainly whet your appetite, and the resort's restaurants are fully equipped to assuage it. Two formal dining rooms are backed up by a 500-strong wine list, and there are also informal buffets on the beach, island picnics and moonlit barbeques. The general feeling is not simply that the food and service should be impeccable, but the setting has to be perfect too. In between meals, there is boules, tennis, badminton, a small gym and a large range of water sports including deep-sea fishing by

dhoni, waterskiing and windsurfing.

Finally, if you do not dive, this is good place to take your first strokes underwater. If you are already qualified – what are you waiting for?

Rates from: US$ 250
Star rating: ★ ★ ★ ★ ★
Bellhop rating: 🐶 🐶 🐶 🐶 🐶

Value:	8.64	Facilities:	8.86
Staff:	9.57	Restaurants:	8.89
Location:	9.39	Families:	7.43
Cleanliness:	9.50		

MYANMAR

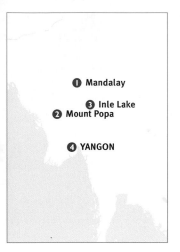

Since independence from Britain after World War II, Myanmar has been torn by ethnic divisions and internal strife and today finds itself a fractured pariah state run by corrupt generals. It is a great shame because this is one of the most beautiful and interesting countries in Asia. It has a stunningly rich and deep culture, fertile land and wonderful people. As a tourist destination Myanmar has bags of potential but is haunted by the political situation. Many, although not all, democracy activists have implored tourists to keep away.

Myanmar has always had its problems but since the military junta seized control and stamped out the democracy movement it has been shunned by the international community. There is zero investment and minimal interaction with outsiders. The unintentional result is unspoiled land that has fallen well behind the progress of the world. Awash with colour and charm, the nation certainly has its issues. Much of this country is shut off to foreigners and is lawless. There are rebel insurgencies, vast poppy fields and a huge smuggling network that the government would rather tourists did not stumble upon.

Infrastructure has not had any major investment for generations. With ground transport erratic and cumbersome, most visitors are realistically limited to four destinations separated by little more than an hours flight – the capital Yangon, second city Mandalay, beautiful remote Inle Lake and Bagan. Dusty Bagan is by far Myanmar's most spectacular site with thousands of ancient red-brick temples strewn across the arid plains. Trotting around with a pony and cart is a great way to soak it up, and the sunsets are quite magnificent.

Yangon is the only place that can be considered international. Hotels are of a high standard with good service levels but everything starts to disintegrate very quickly further out. Most of the country is sleepy and agricultural with simple cottage industries; this lifestyle is reflected in the hotels. Banking is a major problem and credit cards are also almost totally impractical outside the capital.

Myanmar is a difficult country to sum up in terms of weather since it has a varied terrain with tropical beaches, lowland plateaus and the shoulders of the Himalayas. Monsoons sweep up the coast from May to October so a generally better time to visit is during the dry season from November to April. Visiting Myanmar does pose moral questions – those who decide to visit will witness one of the last exotic outposts of a rapidly changing world.

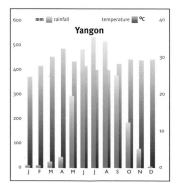

Grand Plaza Parkroyal Yangon

33 Alan Pya Phaya Road, Dagon Township, Yangon, Myanmar
T: +95 1 250 388 F: +95 1 252 478
http://www.asia-hotels.com/hotelinfo/Sofitel_Plaza_Yangon_Hotel

Centrally located in bustling downtown Yangon, the Grand Plaza Parkroyal (formerly Sofitel Plaza) is convenience all round. And for the bargain price they charge, you get an absolutely superb product. The modern property is warm, relaxing and luxurious with contemporary Burmese flashes. Facilities are all top class and are very popular with the local community. Restaurants brim, especially Yangon's best Japanese outlet, Shiki-Tei. The nightclub, the Music Club, is one of Yangon's premier dance spots and the spa gets rave reviews. Service throughout is also excellent, and staff show a little more initiative here than most hotels. The 359 soothing rooms are well polished in every sense, the teak floors in particular, and some of the upper floors have enviable views of the striking golden Schwedagon pagoda. A highly competitive hotel with no obvious drawbacks.

Rates from: **US$ 65**
Star rating: ★ ★ ★ ★ ★
Bellhop rating: ♨ ♨ ♨ ♨ ½

Value:	8.69	Facilities:	8.28
Staff:	8.63	Restaurants:	8.47
Location:	8.69	Families:	7.19
Cleanliness:	8.69		

Inle Princess Resort

Magyizin Village, Inle Lake, Shan State, Myanmar
T: +95 1 211 226 F: +95 1 211 226
http://www.asia-hotels.com/hotelinfo/Inle_Princess_Resort/

The isolated Princess Resort is one of the top properties on the breathtakingly scenic Inle Lake. Partly built on stilts out on the lake it is best accessed by boat, lending it true tranquillity among the emerald paddies and the sapphire waters. Roomy cabins are connected by walkways beside the gently lapping lake. These great little escapes are well constructed, secure and cosy. Big comfy sofas and reliable hot water give the chalets a welcome homely feel. Room facilities are sparse with little technology other than mosquito nets. Hand-cranked telephones link only to reception (shore is reached through the hotel's CB radio). Balconies offer intoxicating views of the lake, the paddies or the distant mountains and hotel facilities are refreshingly absent. Forget the typical set up – the mood can only be helped by the lack of mod cons. In fact all they have is a quiet but finely crafted restaurant bar which puts on ethnic shows and fair Shan food. Room rates are reasonable but extras can be overpriced.

Rates from: **US$ 70**
Star rating: ★ ★
Bellhop rating: **Editor's pick**

Value:	n/a	Facilities:	n/a
Staff:	n/a	Restaurants:	n/a
Location:	n/a	Families:	n/a
Cleanliness:	n/a		

Pansea Yangon

35 Taw Win Road, Dagon Township, Yangon, Myanmar
T: +95 1 229 860 **F:** +95 1 228 260
http://www.asia-hotels.com/hotelinfo/Pansea_Hotel_Yangon/

This is what most people are looking for when they hunt for a boutique hotel. The Pansea's appeal lies in that it is a fabulous piece of architecture and very easy on the eye. It was formerly a colonial mansion and has recently been restored to its former impressive self. The structure is almost entirely teak and ornately crafted, and set quite perfectly in a peaceful and leafy tropical garden. Lily-padded ponds croak, and satisfying squawks and chirps emanate from the thick surrounding undergrowth. Being set in the quiet diplomatic area it really does not feel in the slightest like a city hotel. The cocoon of greenery and virtual absence of local traffic easily conjures up an imaginary location somewhere much more remote than a mere kilometre or two from downtown Yangon.

The Pansea is quite perfectly proportioned and thoughtfully laid out in graceful European style. Being rather small it is very personal and does not have a hotel ambience as such, but more that of a glorious bed and breakfast. The facilities are far superior of course, even if not much more extensive. The serene lagoon pool jumps out at you as you stride along the garden boardwalk – it is very tempting to just leap in. The Mandalay verandah restaurant is also worth investigating, the authentic French cuisine being highly praised. A pool table and bar on the breezy open 1st floor is a fine place to bide your time. And that is just about all there is to do.

The Pansea continues to impress in the rooms – equally uplifting and beautiful and arguably the best rooms in all Myanmar. Again they are all teak, the polished floors emitting a contagious rosy warmth. The 49 rooms are superbly designed and presented, with a homely cabin feel and plenty of angles and corners. Bathrooms are also adventurous – each has a splendid big granite bath.

This boutique hotel is a slow and quiet corner of the world, and hits just about every nail on the head. It is wisely hidden away and one of the few places that lives up to its brochure.

Rates from: **US$ 85**
Star rating: ★ ★ ★ ★
Bellhop rating: 👍👍👍👍👍

Value:	8.65	Facilities:	8.44
Staff:	9.18	Restaurants:	8.88
Location:	8.65	Families:	5.94
Cleanliness:	9.18		

Popa Mountain Resort

Mt. Popa, Kyaukpadaung Township, Mandalay Division, Myanmar
T: +95 2 69168 **F:** +95 2 69169
http://www.asia-hotels.com/hotelinfo/Popa_Mountain_Resort/

This resort has one of the most incredible locations in Asia. An hour from Bagan the remote Popa Mountain Resort stands alone, halfway up a forest-clad dormant volcano. The volcano, Mount Popa, is sacred and inhabited by the spiritual guardians, the Nats. The fact that the surrounding plains are semi-arid and Mount Popa is contrastingly lush and green adds to the significance of this site. Surrounded by fertile undergrowth, the resort is an oasis of thriving nature and a favourite with ecologists and nature buffs. But the layman can also appreciate the pristine mountain's wealth of wildflowers, butterflies and birdlife. Professional guided walks and tours are offered by the hotel.

Popa Mountain Resort enjoys an absolutely stunning view out over Popa Taungkalat monastery perched atop a crumpled cylinder of rock – a volcanic plug blasted from Mount Popa millennia ago. The resort is comprised of a collection of 55 unobtrusive chalets and cabins set on stilts, some with generous balconies looking out towards the monastery. Morning views, when the clouds swirl around it, are mesmerising. Clouds also cloak the resort at night and, when tiptoeing along the boardwalks draped in mist at night, there is an eerie sense of those guardian spirits.

The entire resort is built from teak and sensitively constructed so as to make the least impact on the environment. Walkways steer around trees or in some places allow them to grow right through it. Polished chalets are simple yet comfortable with a few surprising features like in-room safes. They do get a bit damp though, and the odd lizard or bug does venture in. But bearing in mind the isolation, they are a triumph. Other facilities are limited but fair – the pool is handsome and enjoys those fantastic views. The Sagawa restaurant menu is limited and the service sweet and sincere, but sometimes forgivably erratic. The Popa Mountain Resort is admittedly not in a luxury class but is one of the most endearing places to stay in Myanmar.

Rates from: **US$ 55**
Star rating: ★ ★ ★ ★
Bellhop rating: **Editor's pick**

Value:	n/a	Facilities:	n/a
Staff:	n/a	Restaurants:	n/a
Location:	n/a	Families:	n/a
Cleanliness:	n/a		

Sedona Hotel Mandalay

No. 1, Junction of 26th & 66th Street, Chanayetharzan Township, Mandalay, Myanmar
T: +95 2 36488 **F**: +95 2 36499
http://www.asia-hotels.com/hotelinfo/Sedona_Hotel_Mandalay/

This is Mandalay's best hotel by a mile. It is the only 5-star hotel in Third World Mandalay and unquestionably offers the city's best range of facilities, best rooms and best service. The large, bright and smart lobby sets the tone with its modern and reassuringly familiar 5-star ambience against a subtle backdrop of Burmese decor.

The Sedona successfully competes for the luxury tourist market and is accordingly well positioned directly opposite the moats of Mandalay Fort and facing sacred Mandalay Hill. The 247 rooms are large, but cosy and equipped as well as the price would suggest. The restaurants are indeed international and considering the lack of competition are surely the best in town. Uno is the city's only luxury restaurant, with its Mediterranean fare. There is a gym, which closes rather inconveniently early, and a pool which offers a welcome relief after sightseeing. Hotel standards really slip outside Yangon, but not here.

Rates from: **US$ 75**
Star rating: ★ ★ ★ ★ ★
Bellhop rating: 👍👍👍👍 ½

Value:	8.76	Facilities:	8.06
Staff:	7.89	Restaurants:	7.83
Location:	8.17	Families:	6.56
Cleanliness:	8.22		

Sedona Hotel Yangon

No. 1 Kaba Aye Pagoda Road, Yankin Township, Yangon, Myanmar
T: +95 1 666 900 **F**: +95 1 666 356
http://www.asia-hotels.com/hotelinfo/Sedona_Hotel_Yangon/

Every hotel likes to brag that they have the best service, especially 5-stars. Let's face it – smiles sometimes come through gritted teeth if they come at all – but not here. The Sedona Yangon offers some of the best service in Asia and knocks the spots off many more expensive hotels across the region. It should by all rights be rather impersonal – it is vast, almost a cruise liner of a hotel. But the staff are fantastic throughout, genuinely putting the guest first, and are a role model for the industry. The 366 homely, spacious rooms are a touch predictable but perfectly decent and the extensive and roomy facilities, including five restaurants and bars, capture a hint of resort given the slightly inconvenient location three kilometres both from downtown and the airport. None of these facilities are the best of the best, but put together and run by exemplary staff the Sedona is all one could hope for in a big hotel.

Rates from: **US$ 50**
Star rating: ★ ★ ★ ★ ★
Bellhop rating: 👍👍👍👍👍

Value:	8.51	Facilities:	8.59
Staff:	8.79	Restaurants:	8.41
Location:	8.61	Families:	7.69
Cleanliness:	8.77		

The Strand

92 Strand Road, Yangon, Myanmar
T: +95 1 243 377 **F:** + 95 1 289 880
http://www.asia-hotels.com/hotelinfo/Strand_Hotel_The/

If you are looking for a bit of colonial Rangoon rather than present day Yangon, the grand old Strand is where you will find it. This classy throwback is steeped in history, with some ridiculously colourful events since its opening in 1901. The hotel took a direct hit from a World War II bomb, which nestled rather untidily in the GM's

office, and changed hands in the various struggles that have featured in Burma's turbulent history. It also faded into disrepair, even being used to stable horses before being restored to its former glory. The British, Japanese, the bombs and the decay have all been swept aside but somehow the Strand remains. Today it feels

almost like it has always been, capturing the sophistication and class of the good old days, with a few modern day distractions for convenience.

It is in the magnificent chambers of the wood-panelled Strand Bar, or the elegant Strand Grill with its vaulted ceiling and chandeliers, or the oh-so-civilised Strand Cafe with its huge teak-framed windows staring out on the Strand Road that perhaps you can get rather carried away to a bygone age. The rarefied air has been preserved particularly well, as scruffy riff-raff will indeed find. But if you go along with it, it is a friendly and intimate place. Intimate due to its modest size (and that is all that is modest about the Strand) and the mere 32 enjoyable suites.

Rather than being cocooned in an exclusive area, the Strand is conveniently set downtown, opposite the river, and not surprisingly it rather sticks out on the cluttered and noisy main road. The view from the quiet, soothing and irregularly shaped River View Suites will not hold your attention for long, but this is far better than the other rather drab views from the Superior Suites, where you may feel the need to pull the curtains. Ignoring the outside world you will enjoy polished wood floors, high ceilings, free-standing baths, enormous beds and the satisfaction that you are staying in a room with personality – something absent from the mainstream and mass-produced 5-star luxury properties.

There are a few minuses, the big one perhaps being the whopping price tag. The rate for one night here is rather perversely equivalent to nearly a years wages for many Burmese. Little things that go wrong in other top hotels go wrong here, but more so – this is Myanmar after all, and you are getting ambience for your money rather than the endless list of hotel facilities you would usually get for top dollar in any other city hotel. Perhaps that is its charm. Still, it is the premier address in Myanmar and an absolute jewel of a hotel.

Rates from: **US$ 380**
Star rating: ★★★★★
Bellhop rating: ۝۝۝۝

Value:	7.21	Facilities:	7.56
Staff:	8.82	Restaurants:	8.13
Location:	8.31	Families:	6.07
Cleanliness:	8.74		

NEPAL

CHINA

INDIA

 **KATHMANDU**

HOTEL	PAGE
① **Kathmandu**	
Dwarika's Hotel	187
Kathmandu Guest House	188
Yak & Yeti Hotel	188

This fabled Himalayan kingdom has seen its unfair share of trouble in recent years, from the massacre of many of the leading members of its royal family in June 2001 to continuing problems with Maoist insurgents. Many of the more remote areas of Nepal are now off-limits to foreigners, and visitors should pay special attention to government travel advisories. Yet while the country is no longer automatically synonymous with Shangri-La, its natural beauty, historical wonders and generally hospitable inhabitants are little changed.

While usually viewed as a destination for hearty trekkers, river rafters, and mountain climbers or bikers, Nepal exercises equal appeal for anyone content to shop, visit the myriad of temples and palaces and take in the Himalayas from the comfort of a specially chartered mountain flight. Much of the country is drenched by a monsoon from June to September, so it is best to visit during the rest of the year. While it can be sunny by day during the winter months, it can be bitterly cold at nights, especially at altitude.

Most visitors fly into the capital, Kathmandu, a city that traces its history to medieval times and beyond, although old brick buildings are gradually being replaced with concrete, and pollution from an increasing number of motor vehicles is rearing its ugly head. It would be perfectly possible to spend a fortnight or more exploring the valley, venturing out to the towns of Patan and Bhaktapur, taking in the vast panorama of the Himalayas from the ridgetop at Nagarkot, and wandering the bazaars and backstreets of Kathmandu itself. Pokhara is one of the main jumping off points for trekking, as it sits on the old trade route linking Tibet and India. Further south, Nepal's character changes completely in the Terai, a totally flat area where jungles are still roamed by tiger and rhino. One of the best vacations here combines sightseeing in Kathmandu, trekking around Pokhara and concludes with a wildlife safari.

Accommodation has moved on from the 1960s, when Nepal was besieged by hippies in search of their own personal Nirvana. While there are still plenty of low-budget guesthouses around, international standards of comfort and service are becoming the norm, whether in the old established hotels or newly built ones. The Banyan Tree is planning to open in Nepal's second city, Pokhara, next year, and other mainstream brands are already up and operating in Kathmandu.

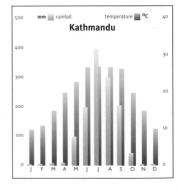

Dwarika's Hotel

Battisputali, Kathmandu, Nepal
T: +977 1 479 488 **F:** +977 1 471 379
http://www.asia-hotels.com/hotelinfo/Dwarika/

Dwarika's is so much more than a hotel, and delightfully so. Part museum, part cultural centre, its most remarkable genesis was due to the vision of Dwarika Das Shrestha, who determined to build a hotel that would preserve Kathmandu's heritage. Mr Shrestha had been salvaging the intricately carved windows, doors and pillars – some dating back centuries – that are characteristic of the Nepalese capital for some time but he concluded that they needed to be put to their original use. After employing masons and carpenters using traditional building methods, Dwarika's opened in 1978 – a cluster of courtyards and red-brick (handmade) cottages that would

act as an architectural showcase as well as generate income for future preservation projects.

Since Mr Shrestha's death in 1992, the hotel has been run by his wife and daughter, and has gone from strength to strength. It now houses some 74 rooms and suites, many with windows that were carved in the 16th century, some with private courtyards, and all furnished with hand-printed fabrics decorated with Buddhist symbols. Dwarika's is infused with a gentle, peaceful ambience; it is somewhere to wander and explore and absorb. The shrine to the elephant-headed god Ganesh is bedecked with offertory flowers; you can browse through the library; cool off from the summer heat by the

aquamarine pool, which is fed by gushing stone water spouts; dine on Nepalese specialties at Krishnarpan; or blend with the rhythm of an Ayurvedic massage in your own room.

While the essence of Dwarika's is tradition and history, it has also imported some modern pleasantries – live jazz hums through the Fusion Bar most evenings, and the Internet lurks discreetly in the business centre. As part of its contribution to the community, Dwarika's also runs a workshop where artisans and their young apprentices restore carvings similar to the ones that are already part of the hotel. This may be a property anchored in the past, but it has a firm stake in the future.

Rates from: **US$ 110**
Star rating: ★ ★ ★ ★ ½
Bellhop rating: **Editor's pick**

Value:	n/a	Facilities:	n/a
Staff:	n/a	Restaurants:	n/a
Location:	n/a	Families:	n/a
Cleanliness:	n/a		

Kathmandu Guest House

Thamel, Kathmandu, Nepal
T: +977 1 413 632 **F:** +977 1 418 733
http://www.asia-hotels.com/hotelinfo/Kathmandu_Guest_House/

It does not matter which of the Kathmandu Guest House's 115 rooms you are in or what rate you are paying – top whack is a mere US$60 – it is a bargain. Smack in the heart of backpacker Thamel, it is not in the least downmarket, and a stone's throw from a good number of eateries, travel agents, souvenir shops and bookshops. The clean, comfortable rooms may only rate three stars, but the service deserves five. Kathmandu Guest House also acts as a magnet for mountaineers, pop stars, actors, troubadours and eccentric characters, while more than a few couples have met and later honeymooned here. Both garden and roof terrace are welcome lungs in what is a pretty grubby surrounding city – and the entire hotel is an extremely sociable place where you can find a trekking partner, swap travel tips or simply shoot the breeze.

Rates from: US$ 17
Star rating: ★ ★ ★
Bellhop rating: ♙♙♙♙ ½

Value:	8.80	Facilities:	7.92
Staff:	9.32	Restaurants:	7.28
Location:	9.68	Families:	7.20
Cleanliness:	8.72		

Yak & Yeti Hotel

Durbar Marg, Kathmandu, Nepal
T: +977 1 248999 **F:** +977 1 227781
http://www.asia-hotels.com/hotelinfo/Yak_and_Yeti_Hotel/

The name alone should be enough to sell this intriguing, unique hotel, set back from Durbar Marg and comprising Lal Durbar – a century-old former Rana family palace – as well as more modern accommodations. Balancing out the plethora of history – the Chimney restaurant pays tribute to Russian renaissance man Boris Lissanevitch who started Nepal's modern tourism movement – are the 270 rooms and suites, the more superior of which come with computers and laser printers. Kathmandu is starting to see its first international chain hotels, but the Yak & Yeti remains fiercely independent, blending first-class facilities with charm and a great deal of character, not to mention personal service from the staff who tend to welcome guests as if they were personal friends. Tea in the garden (weather permitting) is essential for anyone not actually staying. Indoors, traditional cultural shows are performed at Naachghar, the Nepalese theatre restaurant.

Rates from: US$ 98
Star rating: ★ ★ ★ ★ ★
Bellhop rating: ♙♙♙♙

Value:	7.65	Facilities:	7.80
Staff:	8.15	Restaurants:	7.98
Location:	8.58	Families:	6.28
Cleanliness:	8.10		

NEW ZEALAND

Auckland

HOTEL	PAGE
Auckland	
Carlton Hotel Auckland	190
Sheraton Auckland Hotel & Towers	190

Pristine New Zealand is characterised by its isolation. One look at an atlas will tell you that this boot-shaped double island is one of the most remote countries in the world. A decision to go to New Zealand is therefore entirely deliberate, no one is just passing through unless they happen to be en route to the South Pole.

New Zealand has a population of less than four million people, nearly all of whom live in and around Auckland and Wellington. These cities suffer little from pollution, and while some of the country's indigenous forests have been chopped down to make room for New Zealand's countless sheep, it remains one of the greenest and cleanest places in the world. With an acute environmental awareness, New Zealand has a proud reputation for championing the green cause.

Nowhere else can quite match New Zealand for the great outdoors. This is the world centre for adventure sports, and zany activities like bungee jumping were invented here. The sporty Kiwis are into exploring their engaging landscape in the most adrenaline-inducing fashions – tramping, rock climbing, snowboarding, kayaking, and just about any other land, sea or air activity; as a bonus most are easily accessible and safe for novices.

The country is split into North and South Islands which, as they are separated from the major continents, are both filled with unusual wildlife and rare species. The more temperate North Island is the more densely populated and home to the largest city, Auckland. This is the main gateway to the country as well as the centre of New Zealand's business, and it outstrips the mellow yet urbane capital Wellington for pace and sights. Instead, Wellington is the political and geographical lynchpin of the country, functioning as a balancing transit point between the two islands. North Island's attractions include its native woodlands, barren volcanoes and spouting geysers, plus the strong

Maori culture. The South Island is sleepier and greener, and many visitors find it more distinctive than the North. Gentle hills roll for kilometres before bursting into the dramatic Southern Alps, with stunning snow-capped peaks and glaciers. Apart from the higher elevations which receive snow all year round, New Zealand's mild weather is comparable to Britain but with the seasons in reverse due to the southerly latitude.

Hotel wise, New Zealand does not shine. It is fair to say that the country has a bed and breakfast culture. These small, mainly family-run establishments are generally clean, friendly and good value but are unlikely to win many international awards.

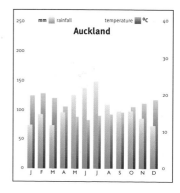

Carlton Hotel Auckland

Corner of Mayoral Drive and Vincent Street, Auckland 1036, New Zealand
T: +64 9 366 3000 **F:** +64 9 366 0121
http://www.asia-hotels.com/hotelinfo/Carlton_Hotel_Auckland/

The Carlton's exterior is modern and angular, almost like an office building. On entry the atrium opens 12 floors above you, the glass and marble reinforcing the smart, corporate theme. The decor is professional and suitable, for this bright and efficient property is Auckland's top business hotel. It is located centrally for business, and opposite 'The Edge', the city's arts and entertainment complex. A few minutes walk away is Queen Street, New Zealand's best shopping district. Facilities are tailor-made for the business traveller, with a top business centre and meeting facilities, including one of the city's biggest ballrooms. Restaurants offer broadly Western food although Katsura serves authentic Japanese cuisine. The heated indoor lap pool, trim gymnasium and steamy sauna give guests the opportunity to unwind. The Carlton's 455 rooms are large, crisp and good value with great city views through the floor-to-ceiling windows.

Rates from: **US$ 87**
Star rating: ★ ★ ★ ★ ★
Bellhop rating: 🛎🛎🛎🛎 ½

Value:	8.27	Facilities:	8.50
Staff:	8.81	Restaurants:	8.46
Location:	8.54	Families:	6.73
Cleanliness:	9.27		

Sheraton Auckland Hotel & Towers

83 Symonds Street, Auckland, New Zealand
T: +64 9 379 5132 **F:** +64 9 377 9367
http://www.asia-hotels.com/hotelinfo/Sheraton_Auckland_Hotel/

The Sheraton Auckland is modern and professional with perhaps the most pleasing environment of any city hotel in New Zealand. It is well-located just metres from Queen Street, the backbone of Auckland's best entertainment and shopping. The city centre and the waterfront can be reached on foot, but it is best to hop on the complimentary shuttle that can get you down there in minutes. The 410 handsome rooms are lively and fully equipped with handy extras like dataports. Glowing facilities are excellent in scope and design, with a choice of outdoor pool and some good upscale restaurants and bars, and you can order a meal at SBF Brasserie & Oyster Bar 24 hours a day. Meeting and events facilities are also up to date, with the ballroom holding up to 900 people. A very capable and complete city hotel.

Rates from: **US$ 80**
Star rating: ★ ★ ★ ★ ★
Bellhop rating: 🛎🛎🛎🛎 ½

Value:	8.40	Facilities:	8.49
Staff:	8.83	Restaurants:	8.20
Location:	8.57	Families:	6.14
Cleanliness:	9.14		

PHILIPPINES

① Angeles
② MANILA

③ Boracay

⑤ Cebu

④ Palawan

⑥ Davao

INDONESIA

The Philippines represent a series of the scattered islands along the fringes of the Pacific Rim stretching from Malaysia's Sabar in the south to Taiwan in the north. The nation cobbles together some 7000 islands or more, and it is this geological disintegration that characterises the Philippines. The infrastructure and development is as broken as the contours of the land, and each province or island has traditionally been somewhat separate from the rule of the capital. Endemic corruption and conflicting religious backgrounds means the country grapples with overwhelming social, economic and political problems. Also, rather unluckily, its location means it suffers a catalogue of natural disasters – typhoons, hurricanes, earthquakes and volcanic eruptions. In fact, the unfortunate Philippines was recently cited as the most disaster-prone country in the world! So quite why would you come? Could it be the fascinating rice terraces of north Luzon, or Borocay's White Beach oft cited as the best beach in the world, or the steep limestone cliffs and spectacular diving around the secluded islands of Palawan or the chocolate hills of Bohol or could it be just that infectious Filipino smile which welcomes all comers to these stunningly beautiful shores? No doubt for delicate travellers the Philippines might prove intimidating, but for the majority the diversity and sheer beauty make the effort worthwhile.

Being the only Asian country colonised by the Spanish, the Philippines is quite apart from any other land of the East. It exudes a Latin flair and pulse and has more in common with South American countries than near neighbours Taiwan, Malaysia, Hong Kong or Japan. The culture is heavily rooted in religion and spirituality, with the vast majority of Filipinos following Catholicism. Most pay more heed to their church leaders than their traditionally weak governments (periodically turfed out by incredible surges of 'People Power').

The country can broadly be split into three regions – the northerly fertile island Luzon, the central island band of the Visayas and Palawan, and the large island of Mindanao furthest south. Metro Manila is found on Luzon and is a sprawling and chaotic city. It is not

fantastic, with crystal waters and abundant marine life drawing underwater enthusiasts from all over the world.

Distant Mindanao is closer to Malaysia and Indonesia than Manila and culturally separate from the rest of the country. By the time you get down there the capital's influence has all but dissipated. It has a predominantly Moslem population with a strong separatist movement characterised by some guerilla activity. Mindanao has real security issues and it is strongly advisable to give the island a wide berth.

Filipino hotels are not the best by Asian standards but this is more down to shaky infrastructure than anything else. Within the mediocrity are some real gems of resorts and some world-class business hotels. The staff are almost always a total delight. Smiles are a constant in the Philippines, no matter what life conjures up, so it is almost impossible not to be drawn to them, and the level of English spoken is remarkably high, among the best in Asia.

a pretty city and for visitors it is more famed for its raunchy nightlife, Manila and Bangkok being considered international leaders in the ambiguous massage field. The commercial centre Makati is orderly and smooth except for the traffic, but the poverty elsewhere is quite obvious and some areas are best avoided.

As soon as you leave the city behind the pace drops. The Visayas and Palawan feel much more remote than they look on the map. Cebu City is a major commercial hub but not far away are the developed beaches of Mactan and countless quieter forgotten ones. The dive sites around this region are absolutely

Typhoons can bring the Philippines to a standstill so it is best to visit it away from the wet season during the humid and sticky summer months around July to September. Outside this period you can expect beaming sunshine to match the smiles of this happy people.

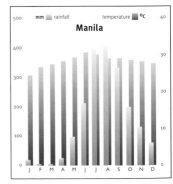

Amanpulo

Pamalican Island, Cuyo Islands, Palawan, Philippines
T: +63 2 759 4040 **F:** +63 2 759 4044
http://www.asia-hotels.com/hotelinfo/Amanpulo/

The Amanpulo experience starts long before you touch down at the airstrip on the remote Philippine island of Pamalican. Cruising south for 80 minutes from Manila over extinct volcanoes, thick jungles and deserted archipelagos in a private 19-seat, twin-engine turboprop, you know you are headed for somewhere distinctly exotic.

It is said that it is better to travel than to arrive, but that well-worn aphorism is utterly disproved here. There is nothing on the island but Amanpulo and its 40 casitas (65-square-metre beachside and hillside bungalows loosely modelled on Philippine village homes) and two villas. Cruise ships do not drop anchor in the bay, vendors do not come hawking along the silky white sand beaches. As you explore, the realisation steals over you that this 5-kilometre-long island (just 500 metres wide) is pretty much all yours, and it is hard to extinguish a spontaneous jiggle of utter pleasure.

Free and easy is the credo here. Nearly half of the casitas' interior is given over to a Cebu marble

bathroom, and the romance of the king-sized bed is augmented by details like pebble-washed walls and coconut-shell tables. Outside, the deck and his-and-her divans are hidden behind lush foliage. So let your imagination run wild, and simply wander free around the island and its surrounding seas. Kingfishers, sea eagles and black-napped orioles inhabit the forest, Hawksbill turtles, parrotfish and manta ray colour the waters of the reefs. There are canoes, sailing boats and windsurfers, a 30-metre aqua tiled pool and numerous dive sites for water lovers. And a library, tennis, massages, nature walks and mountain bikes for those preferring dry land. The main restaurant spills out on to a terrace for alfresco dining, and after dinner there is no better entertainment than the Milky Way, brought a little closer by an astronomical refractor telescope.

Amanpulo has become a popular remedy for 'too much reality', and its name, by the way, means 'peaceful island'. As if you needed telling.

Rates from: **US$ 625**
Star rating: ★★★★★
Bellhop rating: 🐚🐚🐚🐚🐚

Value:	7.74	Facilities:	9.06
Staff:	9.25	Restaurants:	8.69
Location:	8.93	Families:	7.83
Cleanliness:	9.33		

The Barcelo Pearl Farm Island

Kaputian Samal Island, Davao, Philippines
T: +63 82 221 9970 **F**: +63 82 221 9979
http://www.asia-hotels.com/hotelinfo/Barcelo_Pearl_Farm_Beach_Resort/

Caveat vacationer. Pearl Farm is one of the most picturesque resorts in the Philippines, but its location off Mindanao makes it a so-so no-go area until the current troubles simmer down. While a sizeable number of visitors still choose to take the 90-minute flight from Manila and putter across the Gulf of Davao to Samal Island, for others it has to be a case of wait and see.

The resort opened just over 10 years ago, after a 44-acre former pearl farm was skilfully transformed by architect Francisco Manoza. It has grown over the years, and now offers a diverse collection of 73 rooms, villas, stilt houses and 2-storey suites. Some are built out over the sea, others atop the hill, there is a distinct cluster on their own mini island (Isla Malipano) and yet others on the beach. All of them owe their design and ambience to local influences, with rattan, bamboo and various hardwoods strongly in evidence and fabrics woven from abaca and banana fibres.

Life at the hotel revolves around the central infinity pool, overlooked by the triple-decker thatched Parola Bar. It would be perfectly possible to spend a day or more here, moving no further than the Ylang Ylang soothing lounge for a touch of variety and the Maranao Restaurant (which does a neat line in Spanish cuisine) for sustenance.

Tempting as the resort is, there is a lot to explore in the vicinity. Eight other islands complete the Samal archipelago, and there are five marine sanctuaries nearby with two wrecks from World War II and a terrific array of corals and fish. Pearl Farm has several kayaks and Hobie Cats at its disposal, while back on Samal itself there is a network of 100 different caves to explore.

In happier days Pearl Farm hosted numerous society wedding receptions and international beauty pageants. It is a natural choice for such events, and hopefully should be so again in the not too distant future.

Rates from: US$ 73
Star rating: ★ ★ ★ ★
Bellhop rating: 🛎 🛎 🛎 🛎 ½

Value:	8.04	Facilities:	8.62
Staff:	8.96	Restaurants:	8.31
Location:	8.73	Families:	7.96
Cleanliness:	8.89		

Discovery Suites

25 ADB Avenue, Ortigas Centre, Pasig City 1600, Manila, Philippines
T: +63 2 635 2222 **F**: +63 2 683 8111
http://www.asia-hotels.com/hotelinfo/Discovery_Suites/

The old cliché 'a home away from home' has popped up on many a flowery brochure, but the Discovery Suites is probably one of the few properties here to have truly captured that essence. Why? Because it is not a hotel. The residence presents serviced apartments for the long- and short-stay guest and therefore is designed to act as a true home. Cosy yet spacious one-, two- and three-bedroom suites are decked out in a warm and personal fashion. Each has a great kitchen and all the household appliances one usually tries to escape from. Crucially, the suites are very habitable – touches include pillows that flump, sofas you can snuggle into and fluffy toys in the kids' bedrooms. The communal facilities are accessed via the atrium and have no real sense of luxury, more of comfortable functionality. The affordable restaurant closes conveniently late, there is a small but good gym, a lively kids' room and a decent pool. Although the restaurant features a point-blank view of a monstrous abandoned construction project, the location near the shopping and office space of the Ortigas Centre is excellent.

Rates from: **US$ 85**
Star rating: ★ ★ ★ ★
Bellhop rating: 🐾 🐾 🐾 🐾 🐾

Value:	8.89	Facilities:	8.77
Staff:	8.75	Restaurants:	7.96
Location:	8.92	Families:	8.27
Cleanliness:	8.98		

Edsa Shangri-La Manila

1 Garden Way, Ortigas Centre, Mandaluyong City 1650, Manila, Philippines
T: +63 2 633 8888 **F**: +63 2 631 1067
http://www.asia-hotels.com/hotelinfo/Edsa_Shangri-La_Hotel/

The Edsa is a large 5-star hotel by Manila standards. If big is beautiful, then the Edsa is a corker, with some pretty tempting vital statistics. The hotel is set in mature gardens giving it a resort feel that makes it a frequent weekend retreat for locals. It is split into two wings (Garden and Tower) joined at the base, sometimes leading to a bit of confusion in navigation for the uninitiated. The 658 bright and well-appointed rooms follow a typical Shangri-La formula, so there are no surprises here. The seven restaurants and bars (Italian Paparazzi is a favourite with locals), lagoon-style pool, first-class gym, banqueting and business amenities are fully rounded, and the service is surprisingly warm and attentive for such a large and bustling property. The location in the business district near Ortigas, next to several mega malls and within strolling distance of MRT links, makes Edsa a convenient and very popular choice.

Rates from: **US$ 144**
Star rating: ★ ★ ★ ★ ★
Bellhop rating: 🐾 🐾 🐾 🐾 🐾

Value:	8.36	Facilities:	8.77
Staff:	8.72	Restaurants:	8.75
Location:	8.84	Families:	8.10
Cleanliness:	8.95		

Friday's Resort Boracay

Boracay Island, Malay, 5608 Aklan, Philippines
T: +63 36 288 6200 **F**: +63 36 288 6222
http://www.asia-hotels.com/hotelinfo/Fridays_Beach_Resort_Boracay/

Getting to Boracay is no easy task which may explain why the island has kept its laid-back lifestyle. The vistas during descent after a 55-minute hop from Manila, followed by a 15-minute banca ride the length of the island, provide a fabulous introduction to White Beach, unquestionably one of the best beaches in the world. Wet feet are unavoidable when disembarking but as your toes sink into the soft sand a garland of flowers drops over your head and fresh fruit punch appears to hand, making all the effort of the trip worthwhile.

Friday's is no doubt one of the most visually appealing beach retreats you will find anywhere in Asia. It certainly is not the epitome of luxury, but for rustic charm it does not come more authentic. The simple construction of weathered wood and wind-raked thatch makes this a perfect place to kick back.

At the far end of White Beach the resort enjoys one of the best stretches of beach in this part of the world. The sand has an almost unbearable, dazzling glare and its talcum powder texture is so fine it squeaks underfoot. Friday's location means that Boracay's gyrating, groovy beach parties are kept well at arm's length and the resort maintains an addictive low-key calm. However the 'main town' area and its amenable ragbag of restaurants and souvenir galleries is a lazy walk away.

Friday's single restaurant spreads out casually on the sands, with a cool beach bar at its heart. At night the gentle breeze and ambient lighting create an atmosphere as alluring as by day. Food served here, in particular the buffets, is by far the best on the island although it should be said that Boracay is no culinary centre. Behind the restaurant rests a small shaded pool offering cooling respite from the intense beachside sun, that is if the huge thatched sunshades do not suffice.

The 34 rooms, made from local materials, are set in one- and two-storey bungalows that in all honesty are very simple but are more than adequate. Sparse but spacious, the rooms fitted with air-conditioning and mosquito nets are comfy enough but could do with sprucing up. Staff though are smart and well drilled, and make a big effort, keeping Friday's well ahead of the competition and a family favourite on this lovely tropical island.

Rates from: **US$ 105**
Star rating: ★★★ ½
Bellhop rating: ♦♦♦♦ ½

Value:	8.32	Facilities:	8.06
Staff:	8.88	Restaurants:	8.27
Location:	9.44	Families:	6.71
Cleanliness:	8.71		

Holiday Inn Resort Clark Field

Mimosa Drive, Mimosa Leisure Estate, Clark Field, Pampanga, Philippines
T: +63 2 845 1888 **F:** +63 2 843 1363
http://www.asia-hotels.com/hotelinfo/Holiday_Inn_Resort_Clark_Field/

The American military occupied Clark Field, 90 kilometres north of Manila, for the best part of a century, but when GI Johnny went marching home in 1991, Holiday Inn came marching in. Clark was turned into a special economic zone, and what had been the officers' quarters was neatly transformed into a hotel. The eruption of Mount Pinatubo had hastened the Americans' departure, and clearing up took some time, but underneath the acres of ash was an embryo resort with assets to spare. To start with, there was an airport on the doorstep, and the US Air Force had done everything possible to make sure its personnel were not short of home comforts. The 36-hole golf course formed the centrepiece of a carefully landscaped estate covered with 7,000 trees, including 100-year-old mimosa rain trees and magnificent yellow flame trees. A casino was quickly added, nearby Angeles offered a certain residual appeal after hours and Pinatubo had a one-of-a-kind natural attraction on flight-seeing trips.

As for the hotel, the main building – once home to the bachelor officers – provided 273 spacious guestrooms; and the former family quarters were easily adapted to become 34 private villas, each with two bedrooms, kitchen, living room and a servants' annex, as well as a terrace and garden.

Naturally there was a free-form pool, which only needed the addition of a tennis court and a gym to round out the fitness and leisure facilities. Doubtless the pilots dined well here, but the Holiday Inn chefs have gone one better, serving international and the delicately seasoned Pampanga cuisine in the Mequeni Cafe and more exotic fare at the Mongolian Barbeque. There are videos and other entertainments in the Clarky Kids' Club, video conferencing and other facilities for meeters, conventioneers and similar types in the hotel function rooms. So thank you Uncle Sam, especially from the Manila weekenders escaping the big city: swords have never been so readily converted into ploughshares.

Rates from: **US$ 60**
Star rating: ★ ★ ★ ★ ½
Bellhop rating: 🛎🛎🛎🛎🛎

Value:	8.55	Facilities:	8.47
Staff:	8.54	Restaurants:	8.44
Location:	8.28	Families:	8.45
Cleanliness:	8.69		

Lagen Island (El Nido)

Lagen Island, El Nido, Northern Palawan, Philippines
T: +63 2 894 5644 **F:** +63 2 810 3620
http://www.asia-hotels.com/hotelinfo/Lagen_Island_Resort/

Lagen Island is Palawan personified and personalised – all the natural beauty of one of the Philippines' most beautiful regions delivered to the doorstep of a 5-

star resort. A hop, skip and a banca ride from Manila, Lagen is one of the largest islands in the El Nido Protected Area and host to a single resort. Guarded by sheer

cliffs that rise 300 metres out of the sea, its numerous natural coves are perfectly attuned to the needs of snorkellers and other marine sports lovers, while the forest that covers the island is inhabited by 70 species of birds. Arriving guests are given an eco-checklist to give them an idea of what to watch out for, as Lagen is also home to mammals such as the scaly anteater and the Palawan porcupine, and the surrounding seas host hundreds of different kinds of fish and coral.

The resort itself is horseshoed round a sunset-facing bay; the best of its 51 cottages are built out over the water, others sit on the beach and there are also rooms and suites set in the forest. All the rooms are decorated with indigenous Filipino materials, and have their own video and CD players, while a private verandah fronts each of the cottages. Guests are also provided with biodegradable soap, shampoo, conditioner and bath gel to help preserve the environment. As if anyone needed encouraging!

A 30-minute hike from the resort leads past the wild flowers and orchids in the forest to a picturesque cove where you can snorkel or simply sunbathe. Further afield in Bacuit Bay, there are around 20 islands to visit, many with untouched beaches that you can make your own for a day. Pinasil Island has a cathedral-like cavern best reached by kayak or dinghy, low tide at Vigan Island reveals a natural S-shaped sandbar that snakes its way into the water, while the pocket white sand Secret Beach on Matinloc Island (where Lagen has a sister resort) can only be reached by snorkelling through a sinkhole.

The main island of Palawan is favoured by birdwatchers for the hundreds of egrets that roost in the mangroves at the mouth of the Aberawan River. There is also a score of dive sites in the immediate area, with a choice of reefs, drop-offs and tunnel dives. Visibility rises to around 30 metres in the spring, and hovers between 10 and 15 metres at other times of year.

When it comes to food, the best possible dish of the day is a DIY fishing expedition, leaving early in the morning or late in the afternoon. The squid are running between March and May, and back at the resort the kitchen staff are only too happy to prepare your catch to your liking. Otherwise, buffet meals – a blend of Asian and Western with some Filipino specialties – are served in the clubhouse overlooking the beach and bay, although an a la carte menu is available.

It is a natural conclusion that Lagen is a sylvan seaside holiday spot for children. A 25-metre swimming pool is situated right in front of the clubhouse, and there are board games and table tennis inside. Learning how to weave a coconut leaf hat will absorb busy little fingers and minds for enough time to give parents a respite, and the resort's staff have a natural affinity for children that is reflected in affectionate testimonials from many guests.

Rates from: US$ 180
Star rating: ★ ★ ★ ★ ★
Bellhop rating: 🛎 🛎 🛎 🛎 🛎

Value:	8.00	Facilities:	8.40
Staff:	9.17	Restaurants:	8.20
Location:	9.17	Families:	7.63
Cleanliness:	9.17		

Makati Shangri-La Manila

Corner of Ayala Avenue and Makati Avenue, Makati City 1200, Manila, Philippines
T: +63 2 813 8888 **F:** +63 2 813 5499
http://www.asia-hotels.com/hotelinfo/Makati_ShangriLa_Manila/

The Makati Shangri-La is probably the best and most complete hotel in the Philippines. There are no obvious weaknesses in this upmarket property which maintains its top position through a constant renovation programme, irrespective of the roller coaster Manila economy. The Makati Shangri-La is superior to competitors in just about every area and its imposing smooth exterior towers over the junction of Ayala and Makati Avenues, making it ideal for business travellers.

The lobby is adorned with a huge chandelier and twin-sweeping staircases that say a lot about the hotel in general – smart, spacious, stylish and immaculate. The top feature of the Shangri-La is the standard of the unique rooms – hip, trendy and very hi-tech. Irregularly shaped, they include sweeping curves rather than right angles that somehow, although sacrificing space, result in the rooms actually feeling larger. Bright colours and arty flashes here and there are a triumph of interior design, at least as far as hotels go. The ceilings also demonstrate imagination, a domed light source being sunk into a trim circular pit. Bedside lighting is again sleek yet very functional. Extra thought shines through everywhere, such as the dataport located on the desk to avoid having to scramble around at ankle level to plug in your laptop. These are well-designed, well-equipped and well-maintained rooms.

Rather than the usual long vacant spaces, the corridors too have been remodelled with eye-catching designs and curves, and as ridiculous as it may sound, they are pleasant and warm. Superior hotel business facilities are truly international and include a 24-hour business centre, hence the high proportion of corporate guests who are particularly well catered for at the chic Horizon Club. Leisure facilities are a slight notch down but still very competitive. The outdoor pool for example is a tad small but catches every sunray, and the gym is tidy if not comprehensive. A series of excellent restaurants including the Shang Palace Chinese, the immensely popular Japanese Inagiku, and the fine French Cheval Blanc complete the picture for this outstanding hotel. If you were being fussy you could say the professional and genuine service can be a little stretched at times, such is the popularity of this top-rate Shangri-La.

Rates from: **US$ 144**
Star rating: ★★★★★
Bellhop rating: 🛎🛎🛎🛎🛎

Value:	8.21	Facilities:	8.88
Staff:	8.77	Restaurants:	8.83
Location:	9.23	Families:	8.11
Cleanliness:	9.06		

Mandarin Oriental Manila

Makati Avenue, Makati City 1226, Metro Manila, Philippines
T: +63 2 750 8888 **F**: +63 2 817 2472
http://www.asia-hotels.com/hotelinfo/Mandarin_Oriental_Manila/

This refined old-timer has much going for it, although it is tired in places. The Mandarin clings tightly to its roots and has more than a hint of the 1970s about it. A traditional oriental theme is very prominent – dark combinations of deep woods, black marble, brassy trimmings and Chinese flair in the form of vases and fans, while female staff slink along in elegant cheongsams. The architecture barely allows for any natural light, and on entry your eyes need to adjust. The Standard Rooms are in need of renovation, whereas the upper categories are more than adequate. A popular haunt for the local business community is the buzzing Captain's Bar, leading from the hotel's diminutive lobby, as is the Clipper Lounge on the second floor. Other facilities are well above average and service is consistently courteous and professional. The overall product may slightly disappoint Mandarin fans but the price is very competitive and some renovations are currently underway.

Rates from: **US$ 72**
Star rating: ★ ★ ★ ★ ★
Bellhop rating: 🛎 🛎 🛎 🛎 ½

Value:	8.36	Facilities:	8.40
Staff:	8.65	Restaurants:	8.67
Location:	8.76	Families:	7.79
Cleanliness:	8.76		

The Marco Polo Davao

C.M. Recto Street, Davao City 8000, Philippines
T: +63 82 221 0888 **F**: +63 82 225 0111
http://www.asia-hotels.com/hotelinfo/Marco_Polo_Davao_The/

Davao is not the swishest of Asian cities so visiting executives – and the Marco Polo is primarily a business hotel – normally make this convenient retreat their working headquarters. It is efficiently run and only a short hop from the commercial district and airport. While all the hotel's 245 rooms are perfectly acceptable, the two club floors at the top of the 18-storey building make the most sense, with a mini business centre in its lounge, fax machines in every room, clued-up butlers and a roomy boardroom. Foodwise, if the international buffet at Cafe Marco does not appeal there is the Lotus Court's Cantonese cuisine, or snacks are available from the pool terrace (next to a well-equipped fitness centre) with good views both up to Mount Apo and down to the sea. Potential guests might want to take note of prevailing security issues on Mindanao.

Rates from: **US$ 65**
Star rating: ★ ★ ★ ★ ½
Bellhop rating: 🛎 🛎 🛎 🛎 🛎

Value:	8.85	Facilities:	8.66
Staff:	8.86	Restaurants:	8.71
Location:	8.87	Families:	8.19
Cleanliness:	9.03		

New World Renaissance Hotel

Esperanza Street, Corner of Makati Avenue, Makati City, Manila, Philippines
T: +63 2 811 6888 **F**: +63 2 811 6777
http://www.asia-hotels.com/hotelinfo/New_World_Renaissance_Hotel/

The New World's prime selling point is its location – just off the EDSA highway, the Greenbelt shopping centre is just across the street and top Makati business addresses, art galleries and a range of dining options are all a stone's throw away. Essentially a business traveller's hotel, the 600 pastel-toned rooms are functional rather than luxurious, with the cream of the crop laid out on the triple-decker club level. As well as enjoying free access to the gym, sauna and steam room, club guests get reasonable discounts at the hotel restaurants, which include the Cantonese Emperor Court and the fusion menus of Bocarinos – both of which incidentally enjoy a top reputation in Manila. The hotel's ballroom and other meeting facilities are unusually capped by the Cats Celebration Centre, a multi-level function area embracing a private music lounge, karaoke rooms and a disco.

Rates from: US$ 94
Star rating: ★ ★ ★ ★ ★
Bellhop rating: 🐚🐚🐚🐚🐚

Value:	8.44	Facilities:	8.46
Staff:	8.58	Restaurants:	8.53
Location:	8.92	Families:	7.92
Cleanliness:	8.77		

Oakwood Premier Ayala Centre

6/F Gloriette 4, Ayala Centre, Makati City, Manila, Philippines
T: +63 2 729 8888 **F**: +63 2 728 0000
http://www.asia-hotels.com/hotelinfo/Oakwood_Premier_Ayala_Centre/

The Oakwood is right on top of the Ayala Centre, one of Makati's main shopping malls, and metres from the business district. Successfully cut off from the vibrancy below, it is accessed via a discreet 6th-floor lobby. From a business traveller's perspective, the Oakwood has everything, with smart serviced apartments, extensive meeting facilities and serviced offices all under the same roof. The 306 one-, two- and three-bedroom apartments are spacious and stylish. Elegant furnishings, fully equipped kitchens and even washing machines make it ideal for long-stay guests, although daily stays are welcome. The styling actually does not feature any traditional oak, opting for lighter and crisper tangile. The professional ambience though is not just cosmetic as the Oakwood offers state-of-the-art business amenities including video conferencing. One restaurant, a health club with two tennis courts and 25-metre pool, a kids' playroom and a few leisure distractions complete a very successful and popular package.

Rates from: US$ 136
Star rating: ★ ★ ★ ★ ★
Bellhop rating: 🐚🐚🐚🐚 ½

Value:	8.38	Facilities:	8.73
Staff:	8.52	Restaurants:	7.69
Location:	9.12	Families:	7.93
Cleanliness:	8.85		

The Peninsula Manila

Corner of Ayala and Makati Avenues, Makati City 1226, Manila, Philippines
T: +63 2 887 2888 **F**: +63 2 815 4825
http://www.asia-hotels.com/hotelinfo/Peninsula_Manila_The/

There are not many historical remnants in Manila beyond the churches and the old quarter of Intramuros. Certainly no original grand dames exist in the hotel sector, with the possible exception of the Peninsula, which has been welcoming guests for the last three decades.

It is a graceful hotel that feels like a classic and looks it, at least from the inside. The concrete exterior does nothing to prepare you for one of the most splendid lobbies in Asia. The elegant marble, cavernous ceilings and overall air of extravagance pull in many a movie star, politician and visiting dignitary, with the flashier ones making their grand entrance via the helipad.

Shared between the Ayala and Makati Tower wings, the Peninsula's 498 smooth creamy rooms are slightly irregularly shaped, a welcome touch, and are reassuringly subtler than the extrovert lobby. Bathrooms are thoroughly versatile and the multi-jets of the brass-trimmed surround shower save you from the usual swivelling and rotating that most of us never realised was such a chore.

The Peninsula's food and beverage choices are immaculately presented and the food is rarely short of excellent. The signature restaurant, Old Manila, is decorated with stunning artwork by contemporary Filipino artists and blends Eastern and Western cuisines with a strong French influence. The Lobby is the place to meet for Manila's captains of industry and chattering socialites, with its afternoon tea set and supporting jazz ensemble. Some of the best local soul and blues bands regularly perform at the Conservatory overlooking Ayala Avenue. Mi Piace is rustically Italian, while from Spices you can gaze over the inviting leaf-fringed pool. The kids' pool is one of the few efforts to cater for children as this is very much a hotel for the refined adult. This is nowhere better emphasised than in the spa, a luxurious amalgam of fitness and pampering in cool and crisp surrounds.

Throughout the Peninsula, professional and well-trained staff pride themselves on their service, providing the icing on the cake that makes it far and away one of the most exclusive hotels in the city.

Rates from: US$ 120
Star rating: ★ ★ ★ ★ ★
Bellhop rating: 🛎 🛎 🛎 🛎 🛎

Value:	8.35	Facilities:	8.67
Staff:	8.75	Restaurants:	8.74
Location:	9.09	Families:	7.99
Cleanliness:	8.91		

Plantation Bay Resort & Spa

Marigondon, Mactan Island, Cebu 6015, Philippines
T: +63 32 340 5900 **F:** +63 32 340 5988
http://www.asia-hotels.com/hotelinfo/Plantation_Bay_Mactan/

Plantation Bay stretches over 17 acres of tropical grounds and the emphasis here is on having the space to spread your wings. The most striking feature is the vast inland saltwater lagoon, ringed by the hotel buildings. The man-made lagoon is fine for swimming, being waist-deep for the most part, but deeper in other areas for scuba diving lessons. And for those who want their waters to be a little more interactive, there is a waterfall, diving rock and two giant slides, and the serene lagoon itself rings the country's largest freshwater pool, equipped with eight whirlpools. Night bathers may (or may not) be pleased to see the pool is beautifully lit. The hotel also opens out on to a short and slightly ordinary stretch of beach, but few swimmers make it this far unless to dive on coral walls and caves just offshore.

Back on land, the location is a mix of convenient and isolated. Centrally located on Mactan Island and only 20 minutes from the international airport, there is little outside the resort and few taxis passing by so transport needs to be arranged.

The architecture echoes the theme of a colonial plantation with white wood and deep grey roofs. The 188 rooms are set in lodges and houses around the pools and feature Waterside Rooms from which you can slip into the lagoon, Clubrooms which are a combination of bunks and queen beds for up to eight people, and a selection of one- and two-bedroom suites. Within they are basic but trim and bright, with wood or rattan furnishings.

Facilities lean towards sports and recreation. Extensive water sport activities take full advantage of the location, with fish feeding and reel fishing among the more relaxed choices. Wall climbing (when open) and a games room are on site, and golf or even pistol shooting are available nearby.

Children can indulge in various supervised activities from mini car racing to origami. The recently opened Mogambo Springs spa offers a range of massages, body scrubs and facial treatments in its canyon-like setting. Overall the service is usually good but can be erratic. The food at the three restaurants is similar – mostly good, sometimes excellent, but occasionally below par.

Rates from: **US$ 145**
Star rating: ★ ★ ★ ★ ★
Bellhop rating: ♗ ♗ ♗ ♗ ♗

Value:	8.35	Facilities:	8.85
Staff:	9.05	Restaurants:	8.48
Location:	8.31	Families:	8.20
Cleanliness:	8.96		

Shangri-La Mactan Island Resort

Punta Engano Road, Lapu-Lapu City 6015, Cebu, Philippines
T: +63 32 231 0288 **F:** +63 32 231 1688
http://www.asia-hotels.com/hotelinfo/ShangriLas_Mactan_Island_Resort/

Traditionally the most internationally accessible of the Philippines' holiday spots, Cebu's eastern coast is a quiet and unexpected oasis. The relatively remote northeast tip of Mactan Island points decidedly away from the sprawling metropolis of the country's second city. Little other than resorts dot its blue coastline, and little traffic has a need to come this way. So when staying at the Shangri-La you know that the city is nearby without necessarily feeling it.

It may look functional rather than exotic from a distance, but this resort is very popular indeed and not just with the local residents. It feels like a typical late 1980s resort – large, spread-out (31 acres), chunky and high-rise (9-storey) – but with 547 rooms it would be very difficult to be anything else. Close up it is much more appealing – bright, lively and brimming with fun facilities. The airy lobby is big and tropical. Huge floral displays and a flamboyant chandelier encompass the cheerful Filipino exuberance you will find in the staff.

The Shangri-La has a good reputation, mainly for its consistent treatment and high standards since it opened in 1993. Its second pull is a dazzling length of picture postcard white beach whose sand is carefully combed daily. Excellent leisure facilities fully utilise the tropical shoreline and the hotel provides a good programme of things to do. With the free-form pools, a complete menu of water sports and other recreation on offer it would be difficult for any member of the family to get bored. Scuba diving, jet-skiing, fishing, windsurfing, parasailing or simple banca rides to outlying islands are all on offer. And if you need to escape the kids, then toddlers to teenagers have a range of supervised activities.

Nine restaurants and bars are on site which is just as well bearing in mind it usually takes 45 minutes to get into town on the free shuttle. Food is generally excellent, especially by Philippines standards. The rooms are well furnished and light but offer few surprises other than perhaps the balconies complete with seating areas. All in all – a fun place for a straightforward holiday escape.

Rates from: **US$ 130**
Star rating: ★ ★ ★ ★ ★
Bellhop rating: 👍 👍 👍 👍 👍

Value:	8.41	Facilities:	9.11
Staff:	9.00	Restaurants:	8.74
Location:	8.81	Families:	8.43
Cleanliness:	9.09		

SINGAPORE

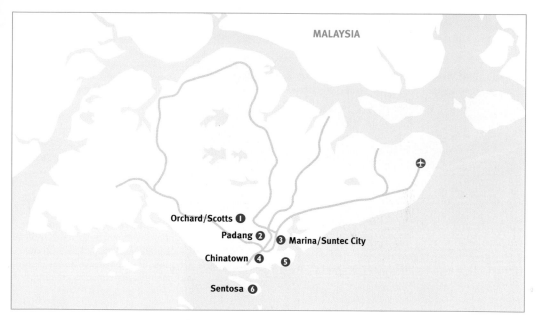

A clean, green, hyper-efficient machine, Singapore is the most user-friendly city in Asia. The four-lane freeway from Changi International Airport is bordered with flowering trees and shrubs. The Mass Rapid Transit whisks its way round the island with barely a hint of a rumble or rattle. Taxi drivers help passengers load their luggage into the boot. Glitzy shopping malls rub shoulders with 5-star hotels and gourmet restaurants. It is as if the entire republic is wired on broadband to EasyLife.com.

Yet despite the modernity, what makes Singapore so pleasurable is its very traditional Asian identity. Eddies of smoke from smoldering joss sticks waft the streets of Chinatown, the air has a gentle aroma of spices in Little India and the muezzin's call rings out over Arab Street. Conversations

overheard in a lift or a bar might include the sing-song of Mandarin, a lilt of Bahasa, the quickfire jabber of Hindi or the Lion City's own brand of 'Singlish', whose quirky expressions often carry the idiosyncratic tag 'lah'. All in all, the island is like one vast and very cosmopolitan buffet.

When the British colonialist Sir Stamford Raffles landed in

Singapore in 1819, it was little more than a fishing village. But he realised that the island's position – just off the equator in the Straits of Malacca – could be exploited to make it the mercantile crossroads of the Far East. Advocating free trade and laying out a town plan that is still followed today, he only spent four years on the island, but it was long enough for him to be

Singapore, is still a relatively undeveloped 'kampong'.

Shopping is another major Singapore attraction, and while the days of it being a bargain basement are largely gone, there is certainly a wealth of choice, from the smart boutiques of Orchard Road to the nerds' paradise of computer mazes like the Funan Centre.

What Singapore does best however is food, largely thanks to its multinational inhabitants who were eating their own brand of fusion cuisine long before anyone thought to put a name to it. The menu ranges from dead cheap and cheerful in the hawker centres, which sell a range of Chinese, Indian and Malay dishes in a no-frills atmosphere, to cutting-edge designer fare in smartly themed restaurants, to absolute gourmet dining with prices to match. Add as garnish African, Middle Eastern, organic and herbal eateries, not to mention Peranakan, a creation derived from early Chinese immigrants and Malay women who married their cuisines.

Singapore's hotels also rank among the finest in Asia. Everyone knows of Raffles, which has been endlessly mythologised, but there are numerous other top-class properties, as well as delightful little boutique hotels nestling in the back streets of Chinatown, providing a dose of the Singapore of yesteryear before it became quite so squeaky clean.

commemorated as the founder of Singapore. Following the war and later independence, Singapore – guided by the helmsmanship of elder statesman Lee Kuan Yew – carved a niche for itself in financial and service industries. Today it is one of the most prosperous states in the region, a remarkable achievement considering the lack of natural resources on its 646 square kilometres.

The year-round tropical Singapore attracts two sorts of weather – hot and wet. The temperature rarely falls below 23°C and it rains most between November and January. Storms tend to be heavy and sudden but blow over fairly quickly. The only antidote for the heat and humidity is the city's ubiquitous use of air-conditioning.

As a city attuned to trade, many visitors come here on business, however it also makes for a pleasant family vacation, as well as a jumping off point to the Malaysian peninsular and Indonesian archipelago. The island of Sentosa has been specifically organised as the city's playground, complete with beaches, attractions and a connecting cable car – although you can get there just as easily by bus. The Singapore Zoo is recognised as one of the best in the world, not simply for its innovative breeding techniques but also for the way in which animals are displayed both by night and in the daytime. Boat Quay and neighbouring Clarke Quay are a melange of high-rolling bars and restaurants, while Pulau Ubin, one of 58 smaller islands surrounding

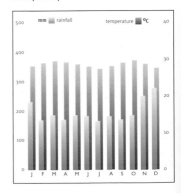

The Beaufort Singapore

2 Bukit Manis Road, Sentosa, Singapore 099891
T: +65 6275 0331 **F**: +65 6275 0228
http://www.asia-hotels.com/hotelinfo/Beaufort_Sentosa_Hotel/

Singapore is sometimes accused of lacking in zest and vitality – 'Asia Lite' say the cynics. Step forward the Beaufort, preening itself in the wake of a S$15m renovation. All the hotel's 210 rooms and suites (plus its four villas) have been redecorated in soft browns and greens. They all have high-speed Internet access, flat-screen televisions and whistle-and-bell sound systems too. However, this is primarily a vacation rather than a business spot, so it is fairly certain that most guests will be firmly shutting their room doors and scampering towards the new 6,000-square-metre Spa Botanica shortly after check-in. A first for Singapore, this garden spa has 14 indoor rooms and six outdoor pavilions as well as mud pools, floatation tanks, and Turkish-styled steam baths, although the last seems to come with a touch of irony given Singapore's equatorial climate. The overall impression is of a complete escape from the city, and even from the surrounding island with its plethora of amusements.

Capping the Beaufort's renaissance is the Cliff, designed by Japanese architect Yasuhiro Koichi, with its glittering open kitchen specialising in contemporary cuisine, water features and a new split-level platform built over lush jungle as well as extended outdoor seating. Alternatively, the Terrace provides a lovely venue for enjoying international fare, whether alfresco overlooking the pool or inside air-conditioned comfort. And the vistas from the Pavilion bar are a ready inducement for a midday aperitif, the first one after the sun is over the yardarm, a nightcap or indeed any excuse you need for a couple of cocktails. Sentosa has always been touted as the groovy getaway on Singapore's doorstep, and indeed there is a beach and two 18-hole golf courses right outside the resort. The new-look Beaufort at least grants some license to the hyperbole.

Rates from: **US$ 144**
Star rating: ★ ★ ★ ★ ★
Bellhop rating: ♗ ♗ ♗ ♗ ½

Value:	7.72	Facilities:	8.29
Staff:	8.38	Restaurants:	8.02
Location:	8.05	Families:	7.08
Cleanliness:	8.78		

Conrad Centennial Singapore

2 Temasek Boulevard, Singapore 038982
T: +65 6334 8888 **F**: +65 6333 9166
http://www.asia-hotels.com/hotelinfo/Conrad_Centennial_Singapore/

Clumps of bamboo. Swirling sculptured lights. Glistening polished marble. Soft pastel furnishings. It is not just the food that is fusion at the Conrad, whose 509 deluxe rooms and suites provide a very East-meets-West welcome. Even the smallest rooms cover some 40 square metres, including a bathroom with a separate shower stall, and suites are half as big again.

While being well tailored for the executive (tick off broadband access, audio and video conferencing, and a desk that you can happily spread your sheets on) the Conrad should also hold special appeal for leisure travellers. In addition to the pool/spa/restaurant/cocktail bar within the hotel, immediately outside are some 1,300 plus shops and eateries in the adjoining malls, which provide an illuminating undercover walkway to the MRT station and nearby exhibition centre at Suntec City.

Rates from: **US$ 102**
Star rating: ★ ★ ★ ★ ★
Bellhop rating: ◉ ◉ ◉ ◉ ½

Value:	7.92	Facilities:	8.30
Staff:	8.58	Restaurants:	8.13
Location:	8.45	Families:	7.24
Cleanliness:	8.92		

Four Seasons Hotel Singapore

190 Orchard Boulevard, Singapore 248646
T: +65 6734 1110 **F**: +65 6733 0682
http://www.asia-hotels.com/hotelinfo/Four_Seasons_Hotel_Singapore/

Subtlety is the leitmotif for the Four Seasons, an ultra-discreet retreat just off Orchard Road. High-rise it

may be, but the interiors are all rich seclusion. The lobby is more like a drawing room than a public area, and the restaurants – the One-Ninety cafe or the Jiang-Nan Chun – could be the private dining rooms of the sort of club that features a rather long waiting list. Up above, the 254 rooms and suites are sumptuously furnished, with multi-disc CD/LD players as a standard fixture and all requisite electronic business accoutrements to hand. Valets transfer the contents of suitcases into wardrobes. Shoes are burnished to a gleaming shine while you sleep. The underlying message here would seem to be if you are not a CEO already, you are on the way up.

Rates from: **US$ 155**
Star rating: ★ ★ ★ ★ ★
Bellhop rating: ◉ ◉ ◉ ◉ ½

Value:	7.78	Facilities:	8.55
Staff:	8.95	Restaurants:	8.28
Location:	8.69	Families:	7.04
Cleanliness:	9.17		

The Fullerton Singapore

1 Fullerton Square, Singapore 049178
T: +65 6733 8388 **F:** +65 6735 8388
http://www.asia-hotels.com/hotelinfo/Fullerton_The/

Magnificent in both concept and execution, the Fullerton ranks as one of the most imaginative new hotels to open its doors in Asia in quite some time. The original building was commissioned as part of Singapore's centennial celebration in 1919, and opened its doors in 1928 when it was the city's largest building. After functioning as the General Post Office for many years, it closed in 1998 prior to its conversion to a luxury, 400-room, 5-star hotel. The resulting transformation has been handled with both style and sympathy. The neo-Palladian exterior – marked by towering granite Doric columns that bespeak colonial puissance – is practically unchanged, while within the elegant rooms and public areas are a perfect blend being both hi-tech and highly attractive.

The Fullerton is in the very hub of the city, and within walking distance of Boat and Clarke quays. With its central atrium beaming a cone of light on to the smartly dressed guests nattering over coffee at the Courtyard, and a broad double circular staircase leading down to the ballroom and function rooms, first impressions of the Fullerton are that this is a hotel at the centre of things. Other restaurants include the contemporary Cantonese Jade, and Town, a bistro cafe and bar serving Mediterranean and Asian fare.

The rooms themselves are sensibly laid out, wired and decorated with a distinctive panache. The gym is stacked with a fair range of glistening perspiration inducers, however the outside swimming pool – with an invigorating infinity view over the river and up to the skyscrapers which now dwarf the Fullerton – is the hotel's sporting piece-de-resistance. Not that it is imperative to exercise here, as you can easily loll in the loungers for an afternoon or more, backed by what imagination could easily prompt to be your very own colonial mansion. Indeed, Sir Stamford Raffles,

Singapore's visionary founding father, would surely have approved of this innovative property that incorporates an inspirational original building and adapts it to modern needs.

Rates from: US$ 124
Star rating: ★★★★★
Bellhop rating: 🛎🛎🛎🛎 ½

Value:	7.70	Facilities:	8.46
Staff:	8.54	Restaurants:	8.46
Location:	8.74	Families:	7.03
Cleanliness:	9.04		

Goodwood Park Hotel

22 Scotts Road, Singapore 228221
T: +65 6737 7411 **F:** +65 6732 8558
http://www.asia-hotels.com/hotelinfo/Goodwood_Park/

Built in 1900, this is Singapore's second oldest hotel. It started life more than a century ago as the Teutonia Club and its two storeys and 235 rooms sit on a hillock overlooking Scotts and Orchard Roads in a measure of refined, semi-colonial splendour. However, its interior decor is a bit of a mish-mash – a slightly glitzy rather than gracious lobby gives way to the central courtyard which houses the main pool. The rooms are decorated neutrally, nodding more to the late 1980s than the 1880s, although there are some monochrome photographs on the walls that add much character.

Where the Goodwood Park notches up points is in its quaint

raggle-taggle layout. The best option is to go for one of the rooms opening out on to the second pool – the Mayfair – which is altogether more intimate and charming. Other alternatives include the Parklane Suites, which come with their own kitchenettes and balconies in a separate wing and are more suitable for long-staying guests. Top of the range is the Brunei Suite, described by the hotel as

'one of the most beautiful rooms east of Suez'.

Surprisingly for a relatively small hotel, the Goodwood Park fits an octet of restaurants and bars within its perimeters, as well as a franchised spa operation. There is a certain expat effect in the Highland Bar and Gordon Grill, while Asian influences predominate in the Japanese Shima restaurant and the brace of Chinese restaurants which specialise in Shanghainese and Sichuan cuisines. It should be said that there is no other hotel like the Goodwood Park in Singapore, and if it does not quite fit its assumed template of Asian masterpiece, it is still very habitable.

Rates from: **US$ 166**
Star rating: ★ ★ ★ ★ ★
Bellhop rating: 🛎 🛎 🛎 🛎 ½

Value:	7.97	Facilities:	8.17
Staff:	8.53	Restaurants:	8.53
Location:	8.82	Families:	7.16
Cleanliness:	8.73		

Grand Hyatt Singapore

10 Scotts Road, Singapore 228211
T: +65 6738 1234 **F**: +65 6732 1696
http://www.asia-hotels.com/hotelinfo/Grand_Hyatt_Singapore/

The 'Grand' in the Hyatt's name may well refer to its two separate and very smart wings containing 683 rooms and suites, which but for Singapore's firm anti-littering laws could be described as a stone's throw from the retail hubs of Orchard and Scotts roads. 'Grand' could equally indicate the chance to indulge not only in deluxe accommodation but also in the hotel's half-dozen restaurants and bars. Pete's Place is an especially atmospheric Italian restaurant, while mezza9's show kitchen serves up Western, Chinese and Japanese alongside a cigar room and a martini bar. Breakfast is served up at the Cafe, lunch goes down a treat at the

alfresco poolside Oasis, and Scotts Lounge overlooking a 4-storey waterfall is the place for afternoon tea at weekends. After hours, the basement BRIX offers a drinking and dancing double act with the self-explanatory Wine and Whisky Bar and its adjacent Music Bar.

Rates from: **US$ 153**
Star rating: ★ ★ ★ ★ ★
Bellhop rating: ◊ ◊ ◊ ◊ ½

Value:	7.72	Facilities:	8.41
Staff:	8.34	Restaurants:	8.44
Location:	9.01	Families:	7.17
Cleanliness:	8.77		

Holiday Inn Park View Singapore

11 Cavenagh/Orchard Road, Singapore 229616
T: +65 6733 8333 **F**: +65 6734 4593
http://www.asia-hotels.com/hotelinfo/Holiday_Inn_Park_View_Singapore/

A frisbee-like throw would land your credit card in the retail adventure playground of Orchard Road; the Presidential Park is just across the street – eminently viewable from the all-day Window on the Park restaurant; and the rates for this 312-room 4-star are reasonable by any standards. So

there should be no complaints vis-à-vis location, dining, price or indeed much else about this extremely workable hotel.

Prime accommodation here for those on a work trip is one of the three business suites, which come with their own computer, cordless phone and dedicated fax line,

while the double queen configuration rooms are ideal for families. But whether guests are schlepping between meetings or simply sightseeing and shopping, the Holiday Inn's crowning glory is its recently refurbished rooftop half-Olympic pool, a guaranteed stress-buster together with steam room, gym and jacuzzi.

Rates from: **US$ 87**
Star rating: ★ ★ ★ ★
Bellhop rating: ◊ ◊ ◊ ◊ ½

Value:	7.90	Facilities:	8.00
Staff:	8.13	Restaurants:	7.74
Location:	8.59	Families:	6.83
Cleanliness:	8.44		

Inter-Continental Singapore

80 Middle Road, Singapore 188966
T: +65 6338 7600 **F**: +65 6338 7366
http://www.asia-hotels.com/hotelinfo/InterContinental_Singapore/

The grand entrance to the Inter-Continental Singapore is via a set of what could almost be French windows. Marbled floors and an elegant hush distinguish the lobby. Can this really be the way into a 403-room, internationally branded 5-star? The reassuring answer is that yes it is, and this gentle, unassuming theme is continued right the way through the hotel.

The all-day-dining Olive Tree is lit via its skylights, rather as the central areas of Singapore's traditional Peranakan houses were left open to the elements. And the rooftop swimming pool is encompassed by palms and shrubs where you can relax with ease. This is a garden hotel in a garden city, pleasantly influenced by Singaporean heritage.

While the Inter-Continental is well suited to the leisure market (especially its signature 'shophouse' rooms), executives will fit well into its seamless business atmosphere. Designated room desk outlets are surge-protected to safeguard laptops, and are within arm's reach of a state-of-the-art printer/fax/copier/scanner. There is a line each for voice and e-mail, ergonomically designed chairs and enhanced lamps to work by. A cyber-relations desk provides any necessary back-up, and complements the hotel's ballroom and avant-garde Bugis Vault meeting rooms.

Spouses tagging along on business trips might care to amuse themselves with Singapore's answer to 'Yan Can Cook' – head chef Lee Hoong Wan – who runs master classes in how to prepare a banquet, which participants end up eating. For informal corporate entertaining, or indeed a simple drink after the laptop is shut for the day, the Victoria Bar has gained a reputation as the place to wind down, with live international and local bands. As a bonus, a side exit from the Inter-Continental leads straight into the covered streets of the Parco Bugis shopping mall, while an escalator ride downstairs leads to the MRT station.

Rates from: **US$ 110**
Star rating: ★ ★ ★ ★ ★
Bellhop rating: 🐾 🐾 🐾 🐾 ½

Value:	7.96	Facilities:	8.30
Staff:	8.44	Restaurants:	8.23
Location:	8.65	Families:	6.72
Cleanliness:	8.79		

The Keong Saik Hotel

69 Keong Saik Road, Singapore 089165
T: +65 6223 0660 **F:** +65 6225 0660
http://www.asia-hotels.com/hotelinfo/Keong_Saik_Hotel/

At the upper end of the guesthouse scale, the Keong Saik is not quite a boutique – so perhaps 'bootique' would be a more appropriate term. But for ready charm, rates that are more than reasonable, an exotic and authentic location and staff who go out of their way to sort out the most trivial request, this 25-room hotel is a gem. Slap in the heart of Chinatown, right next to a gaudy temple, this is the sort of Singapore that mainstream hotels can never deliver. The most basic rooms do not even have a window, but are spotless even if they are a bit of a squeeze. Breakfast (included in the rate) is a matey, DIY affair, and an excellent way to kick off a day of touring the sights.

Rates from: **US$ 34**
Star rating: ★ ★
Bellhop rating: 🛎🛎🛎🛎

Value:	8.16	Facilities:	6.66
Staff:	8.28	Restaurants:	4.74
Location:	8.31	Families:	5.68
Cleanliness:	8.28		

The Oriental Singapore

5 Raffles Avenue, Marina Square, Singapore 039797
T: +65 6338 0066 **F:** +65 6339 9537
http://www.asia-hotels.com/hotelinfo/Oriental_Singapore/

Fan-shaped like its group logo, the Oriental's 527 rooms are built around an 18-storey atrium, granting the entire hotel a refreshing and open feel. Peer over the balcony from one of the upper storeys and you have a bird's eye view of Morton's of Chicago, the Wasabi Bistro and the fringes of the buffet in Cafe des Artiste. The rooms are immaculately set out, however pride of place goes to the newly renovated club floor with an eclectic lounge that reflects contemporary and oriental design accents. Right on top of the Millenia Walk and Suntec City malls, the Oriental is also just across the road from Singapore's newest arts venue, Esplanade, whose curved roofs have led it to be nicknamed The Durians. In short, top notch, top location and top of the range.

Rates from: **US$ 101**
Star rating: ★ ★ ★ ★ ★
Bellhop rating: 🛎🛎🛎🛎 ½

Value:	7.98	Facilities:	8.30
Staff:	8.46	Restaurants:	8.14
Location:	8.41	Families:	6.73
Cleanliness:	8.69		

Raffles Hotel

1 Beach Road, Singapore 189673
T: +65 6337 1886 **F**: +65 6339 7650
http://www.asia-hotels.com/hotelinfo/Raffles_Hotel/

Raffles is a noun, an adjective, a verb – and a much-honoured institution. The hotel itself is the one most readily identified with deluxe Asian accommodation, and being 'Raffle'd' has come to mean giving a stately Asian hotel a much-needed makeover.

Opened in 1887 by the pioneering Sarkies brothers, and eulogised over the years by all the usual Asian literary types ('feed at Raffles' is the most-aired Rudyard Kipling quote), there is no question that by the late 1970s the hotel was looking worn at the edges.

After being declared a national monument in 1987, Raffles was given a substantial, spruce wash-and-brush-up and reopened amid much fanfare in 1991. Today guests might feel not so much that they are staying at one of the world's top hotels, but instead invited to take on a part in a long-running costume drama, as the heritage

aspect is subject to a fair bit of theatre. The building provides an apposite backdrop, with its stark white columns and colonnades standing out from the lush Singaporean surroundings. Ten of the 103 suites have their own 'personality', named and decorated after such long-departed guests as Noel Coward, Joseph Conrad, Charlie Chaplin and the world-famous-in-Chile poet Pablo Neruda.

There are numerous opportunities to feed at Raffles nowadays, from curries in the Tiffin Room to continental at the Grill, and it is de rigueur to knock back a

couple of the hotel's signature cocktails, the Singapore Sling, in the 2-storey Long Bar. The renovation saw the addition of a number of shops that while not completely authentic, do provide some very upmarket retail opportunities.

Despite its heavily marketed 'lifestyle', and top-dollar room rates, Raffles is a welcome change from yet more concrete and glass structures. The suites are especially luxurious, with parlour and dining area leading into bedroom, dressing room and bathroom all beneath 4.3-metre ceilings. The Raffles legend continues unabated, and viewed objectively it is really very enjoyable.

Rates from: **US$ 365**
Star rating: ★ ★ ★ ★ ★
Bellhop rating: ◔ ◔ ◔ ◔ ½

Value:	7.62	Facilities:	8.58
Staff:	8.89	Restaurants:	8.77
Location:	8.99	Families:	7.14
Cleanliness:	9.14		

Raffles The Plaza

2 Stamford Road, Singapore 178882
T: +65 6339 7777 **F**: +65 6337 1554
http://www.asia-hotels.com/hotelinfo/Westin_Plaza/

Not to be confused with Raffles per se, although it is part of the same group, the Plaza sits foursquare in Raffles City, sharing a number of facilities with its sister Swissotel. The whole property is very much 'modern Singapore' – confident, efficient, and with all the essential goods and services delivered with a hint of pizzazz. Even in the smartly decorated Premier Deluxe rooms – the lowest in the 769-strong pecking order – luxury 'raindrop' showers and broadband access are standard; while at the top of the chain the theme suites and penthouses have their own jacuzzi and sauna. A string of 17 restaurants, two outdoor pools, a hyper-efficient business centre – not to mention the considerable adjacent shopping arcades – round out the picture of this new millennium Raffles.

Rates from: US$ 121
Star rating: ★ ★ ★ ★ ★
Bellhop rating: ♬ ♬ ♬ ♬ ½

Value:	7.52	Facilities:	8.44
Staff:	8.39	Restaurants:	8.40
Location:	9.12	Families:	7.35
Cleanliness:	8.75		

The Regent Singapore

1 Cuscaden Road, Singapore 249715
T: +65 6733 8888 **F**: +65 6732 8838
http://www.asia-hotels.com/hotelinfo/Regent_Hotel/

The Regent basks in a quiet backwater off Tanglin Road, metres from Orchard Road and is practically faultless. The waiters glide across the floor of the Summer Palace, bearing succulent Cantonese dishes prepared by a team of master chefs. Each of the 441 rooms and suites is decorated to reflect a rich Asian heritage, with complementary executive mod cons. The reference library in the 24-hour business centre really is just that, rather than a motley collection of outdated books. In need of a swim, sauna or Shiatsu massage? The spa awaits. And from the doorman to the general manager to the cleaners, staff demonstrate a palpable air of pride in the hotel. As one guest memorably recorded: 'Nothing in this world is perfect, but the Regent Singapore comes close.'

Rates from: US$ 119
Star rating: ★ ★ ★ ★ ★
Bellhop rating: ♬ ♬ ♬ ♬ ½

Value:	8.05	Facilities:	8.26
Staff:	8.83	Restaurants:	8.30
Location:	8.45	Families:	7.13
Cleanliness:	9.04		

The Ritz-Carlton Millenia Singapore

7 Raffles Avenue, Singapore 039799
T: +65 6337 8888 **F:** +65 6338 0001
http://www.asia-hotels.com/hotelinfo/RitzCarlton_Millenia_Singapore/

Over the past couple of years, the Ritz-Carlton has garnered a string of accolades and awards from international organisations. 'Best this' and 'Best that'; 'Hotel of the Year'; 'World's favourite'. You do not need to be on the panel of judges to work out why. A leisurely glance around the 32-storey, 610-room property anchored in seven lush acres on the waterfront sums it all up. It is not simply the design or the facilities. The staff move around their statuesque surroundings with the ease and confidence that comes from knowing that they work in one of Asia's best.

There is no single reason for the Ritz-Carlton's pre-eminence, but there are a lot of contributing factors – and the guestrooms are an obvious help. The mammoth plate glass windows that let natural light stream into the corridors and lift lobbies are continued in the rooms, where they make up almost the entirety of one wall in both bed and bathroom. A single phone call galvanises the butler into drawing one of the hotel's specialty baths – filled with essences of sandalwood and musk for chaps (accompanied by a Cohiba cigar and a Cognac), or a creamy Cleopatra mix for ladies, or an encouraging flower and fruit honeymoon melange for couples, with champagne, strawberries and roses on the side. Sit back, up to your neck with bubbles and bubbly, contemplate the view through the octagonal pane, and it is hard to restrain a triumphant grin. Walk-in showers and closets add to the sense of space – even the standard guestrooms are 51 square metres – and there is nothing in the way of clutter like occasional tables or hat stands. This leaves the main room, with its warm parquet flooring, dominated by a high king-sized bed.

Laptop carriers can log on via broadband, but Internet access is also possible courtesy of the television and 'Guestnet' with a wireless keyboard. Further up the accommodation chain, the 23 suites provide more space. Inhabitants of the upper-storeyed club floors can make free with an unusually generous five meals and snacks laid out in the course of a day in their private lounge, starting with breakfast and ending with evening cocktails and snacks.

Most Ritz-Carlton guests commence their day with breakfast in the Greenhouse, a vibrant hub with glass and greenery predominating as the design aspects in a fresh and airy ambience. At other times of the day, dim sum morsels like deep-fried prawn dumplings with diced water chestnuts and yellow chives in homemade XO chili sauce are typical of the outstanding fare in the Summer Pavilion, while Snappers specialises in seafood. And afternoon tea – think freshly baked scones and Devonshire clotted cream to the accompaniment of a string quartet – is a classic event in the Chihuly Lounge, illuminated by glass artist Dale Chihuly's arresting wall sculpture 'Sunrise'.

The elegance and sophistication of the Ritz-Carlton's dining and accommodation options is reflected below ground, with a 1,115-square-metre ballroom and 10 meeting and function rooms. Just outside, the serenity of the swimming pool is enhanced by threads of water cascading down in a mini cataract at its entrance. On the same level, the fitness centre features a host of free weights, a spa, sauna and massage facilities. Within walking distance of shops, MRT, International Convention and Exhibition Centre (Suntec City) and cultural centres, the Ritz-Carlton is pretty close to faultless and is worthy of all its awards.

Rates from: **US$ 154**
Star rating: ★ ★ ★ ★ ★
Bellhop rating: 🛎 🛎 🛎 🛎 ½

Value:	7.77	Facilities:	8.77
Staff:	8.86	Restaurants:	8.45
Location:	8.43	Families:	7.20
Cleanliness:	9.14		

The Royal Peacock Hotel

55 Keong Saik Road, Singapore 089158
T: +65 6223 3522 **F:** +65 6221 1770
http://www.asia-hotels.com/hotelinfo/Royal_Peacock/

Keong Saik Road – once infamous for 'short-time' hotels which did not need loyalty programmes to attract repeat guests – is now home to a new breed of boutique hostelries. The Royal Peacock is a lovely row of former shophouses, with muted pastel walls, solid staircases and Straits antique furniture. It could almost be the home of a well-to-do merchant who lets out rooms. There are just 78 rooms and suites at the Peacock, packing the sort of facilities and comfort that you might expect of a far more mainstream hotel. While some are windowless, there is no sense of being hemmed in, rather that this is your own cocoon to wallow in. The ground-level bar-cum-cafe dispenses breakfast in a relaxed atmosphere where it is not unusual to strike up a conversation with fellow diners. This is a hotel for anyone who wants to sidestep the dichotomy of international chain hospitality and revel in a smartened-up but budget version of one of the few remaining pockets of genuine old Singapore.

Rates from: **US$ 53**
Star rating: ★ ★ ★
Bellhop rating: ♗ ♗ ♗ ♗

Value:	8.45	Facilities:	6.10
Staff:	8.05	Restaurants:	5.40
Location:	8.70	Families:	4.80
Cleanliness:	8.25		

Shangri-La Hotel Singapore

Orange Grove Road, Singapore 258350
T: +65 6737 3644 **F:** +65 6737 3257
http://www.asia-hotels.com/hotelinfo/ShangriLa_Hotel_Singapore/

One of the Lion City's largest hotels, the 760-room Shangri-La Singapore is divided into three wings – Tower, Garden and Valley – set in a 15-acre botanical garden housing more than 110 varieties of 133,000 plants, flowers and trees off the top end of Orchard Road. The Tower features contemporary design, and is most suited to business travellers, the bougainvillea-hung Garden has more of a vacation feel to it, while Valley guests can enjoy their own private dining and reception rooms.

Although it markets itself as a business 5-star, the Shangri-La's all-pervading jungle ambience could well entice even the most rabidly driven executives to lounge by the free-form pool, scrabble up the electronic rock climbing simulator, play the 3-hole pitch and putt course and linger over high tea in the Rose Veranda or dabble in the Californian ease and cuisine of BLU.

Rates from: **US$ 145**
Star rating: ★ ★ ★ ★ ★
Bellhop rating: ♗ ♗ ♗ ♗ ½

Value:	7.72	Facilities:	8.61
Staff:	8.56	Restaurants:	8.42
Location:	8.13	Families:	7.26
Cleanliness:	8.83		

Shangri-La Rasa Sentosa Resort

101 Siloso Road, Sentosa, Singapore 098970
T: +65 6275 0100 **F:** +65 6275 0355
http://www.asia-hotels.com/hotelinfo/ShangriLa_Rasa_Sentosa_Resort/

Ask any of Singapore's most exacting hotel guest niche market segment about their favourite weekend getaway, and the best place to stay therein, and the answer comes back in a flash: 'The cabanas at the Shangri-La Rasa Sentosa Resort' usually followed by the exact room number. Needless to say, the average age of the members of this select band is about eight and three quarters, for Singapore's only beachfront resort is like a boundless Toys 'R' Us with rooms and restaurants attached.

Sunny, airy, with natural colours and materials predominating, all the Shangri-La Rasa Sentosa's 459 rooms and suites have a balcony or patio. Not that anyone will be spending much time within except to snatch a few hours sleep. Step out of the room to whizz about on a beach buggy, a mountain bike or a set of rollerblades. Dig into the beach, the buffet in the Silver Shell Cafe or some seafood at Sharkey's down by the water. Surf some video games or splash into the outdoor pool. There is a rock wall to climb, scooters to scoot, petanque and paddle skiing. Head off on a nature walk or make up a team for volleyball. And this, remember, is before you have even ventured off to the rest of Sentosa.

Singapore's somewhat ersatz playground island is not quite Disneyland but it does encompass a full complement of fun activities all within a short hike of the Shangri-La. The trip by cable car is a thrilling way to arrive, and Sentosa's 1,235 acres cover child-friendly aquariums, butterfly parks, mini-golf et al, the only catch being that many attract an admission fee.

With their all-pervading air of good clean wholesome family fun, the Shangri-La and Sentosa have a lot to offer. Adults can tee off on the island's golf courses, then finish off in the resort's spa. And teenagers will be relieved to hear that Siloso Beach also hosts the odd rave. Now for Singapore, that is really cool.

Rates from: US$ 111
Star rating: ★ ★ ★ ★ ★
Bellhop rating: 🔔🔔🔔🔔 ½

Value:	7.82	Facilities:	8.43
Staff:	8.38	Restaurants:	8.04
Location:	8.12	Families:	7.88
Cleanliness:	8.60		

Sheraton Towers Singapore

39 Scotts Road, Singapore 228230
T: +65 6737 6888 **F:** +65 6737 1072
http://www.asia-hotels.com/hotelinfo/Sheraton_Towers_Singapore/

Just off Newton Circus, the Sheraton is a solidly reliable hotel with the emphasis on comfort. Collapse into any of the beds in the 413 bay-windowed rooms and suites and you find yourself nestling between Egyptian cotton sheets, your head pillowed on goose down with the whole atop a Simmons Beautyrest System. And naturally the rooms are fully fitted for the modern executive, while there is a phalanx of ball, function and conference rooms to cope with meetings and similar events. With the essentials more than adequately covered, a browse round the rest of the hotel embraces an outdoor pool with attached bar, a gym, one Cantonese restaurant, one Italian and the fully fledged all-American Dining Room. The Sheraton's a very straightforward business hotel, well run and well up to the city's high standards.

Rates from: **US$ 126**
Star rating: ★ ★ ★ ★ ★
Bellhop rating: ♗ ♗ ♗ ♗ ½

Value:	8.06	Facilities:	8.31
Staff:	8.66	Restaurants:	8.33
Location:	8.23	Families:	7.00
Cleanliness:	8.84		

Swissotel The Stamford

2 Stamford Road, Singapore 178882
T: +65 6338 8585 **F:** +65 6338 2862
http://www.asia-hotels.com/hotelinfo/Westin_Stamford/

Designed by I. M. Pei, the high-rise Swissotel is a behemoth of a hotel, suspended above an equally outsized shopping and entertainment complex that it shares with its sister Raffles The Plaza. Soaring 72 storeys, counting more than 1,200 tasteful rooms and suites, with a host of restaurants (Kopi Tiam, like an upmarket hawker centre, specialises in Singaporean fare) and 8,361 square metres of meeting space, Swissotel is a multi-functional accommodation umbrella. Just about everything guests might desire is available here, from high-speed Internet access to low-key relaxation in the Amrita Spa, with its 40 private treatment rooms, two free-form swimming pools and a cardio theatre. Plus the gym is open 24 hours a day – a cunning way to combat jet lag if it strikes in the wee hours. If that is not enough, try the stylish collection of restaurants and clubs which make up the Equinox Complex, perched on the 70th to 72nd floors with stunning views over the city.

Rates from: **US$ 112**
Star rating: ★ ★ ★ ★ ★
Bellhop rating: ♗ ♗ ♗ ♗ ½

Value:	7.79	Facilities:	8.44
Staff:	8.34	Restaurants:	8.33
Location:	8.95	Families:	7.02
Cleanliness:	8.74		

SRI LANKA

INDIA

③ Dambulla

❶ COLOMBO

❷ Galle

The prospect of peace in Sri Lanka is quite the best news to come out of Asia for a long time. Ravaged by factional violence for the best part of two decades, the island has suffered numerous terrorist attacks and enormous loss of life. Negotiations between Tamil separatists from the north and the Sinhalese majority, who live largely in the south, drew to a successful conclusion in 2002, finally granting this beautiful island nation certain hope for the future.

Sri Lanka has had a chequered history. Known to Arab traders as 'Serendip', it fell first under Portuguese then later Dutch and British rule. It was the British who imported Tamil labourers from India to work on tea and coffee plantations, and after Sri Lanka achieved independence in 1948 relations between the two main

ethnic groups gradually went downhill.

In the past, visitors to Sri Lanka have tended to keep to the south, mainly due to the terrorist problems but also because most of the island's attractions are concentrated there. The chief delight of Sri Lanka is its variety –

from the beaches along the coast to the rolling hill country around Kandy, whose main temple is home to a sacred tooth venerated by Buddhists (who make up 70 per cent of the country's inhabitants) and the focus of a spectacular procession of drummers, dancers and elephants every July. Galle, centred around the beautifully preserved 17th-century Dutch fort, resonates with history, as does Nuwara Eliya, a hill station highly favoured since British colonial times. Ratnapura forms the heart of the country's gem industry, Arugam Bay on the east coast enjoys a top ranking among the world's surfing community and Kataragama hosts an annual fire-walking ceremony. Wild elephant roam around Uda Walawe and the

the northern winter. Incidentally, every full moon in Sri Lanka is marked by a public holiday ('poya'), when alcohol is not supposed to be sold in hotels, restaurants or shops, though some establishments have been known to oblige with 'special' pots of tea.

Both the island's geography and its multi-ethnic community are reflected in the national cuisine. Spices, in particular cinnamon, initially drew traders from overseas, and they feature strongly in curries, which tend to be rather hotter than their Indian equivalents. 'Hoppers', a delicious sort of pancake, make a welcome appearance at breakfast buffets, and a cornucopia of locally grown fruit – mangosteen, rambutan, mango and a host of others – can be turned into juice or eaten at any time of day.

Marco Polo waxed lyrical about Ceylon, as Sri Lanka was then known, and its even more ancient name – Serendip – has come to imply making fortunate discoveries by accident. After a chapter of accidents over the past 20 years, Sri Lanka is in the fortunate position of being at relative peace once more, meaning that the island that Marco Polo described as 'the finest in the world' is fully open for business – and even more importantly pleasure – once again.

rainforest is practically untouched in the Sinharaja National Heritage Wilderness Area. Further north, culture vultures can hop between the millennia-old ruins of Polonnaruwa and Anuradhapura and climb the famed rock fortress at Sigiriya. The 2002 ceasefire should see other parts of Sri Lanka opening up again, in particular the untouched beaches of Nilaveli on the northeast coast. The special joy of Sri Lanka is that its relatively small size allows visitors to take in the best of its attractions within a couple of weeks, perhaps starting in the capital, Colombo, venturing into the interior to explore tea country and the historical sights, and then ending with a couple of days kicking back at a beach resort.

Sri Lankan hotels are a mixed bag, starting with the hospitable likes of Mrs Chitrangi de Fonseka's Paying Guesthouse, all the way up to grand colonial dames like the Mount Lavinia and Galle Face hotels. International chains are

few, and the bulk of the country's accommodation is locally owned and – patience, patience – locally run. Service priorities can see smiles put before speed, and facilities can be a touch makeshift, however rates are generally reasonable, especially in the low season when the monsoon strikes from April to November. Sri Lanka is at its most climatically hospitable between December and March, which is when it sees the majority of visitors, especially Europeans on packages, escaping

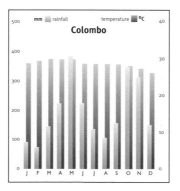

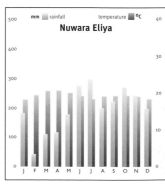

Colombo Hilton

2 Sir Chittampalam A Gardiner Mawatha, Colombo 2, Sri Lanka
T: +94 1 544 644 **F:** +94 1 554 657
http://www.asia-hotels.com/hotelinfo/Hilton_Colombo/

Smack in the heart of Colombo's business district, next to the World Trade Centre, the high-rise, 384-room Hilton may not have the charm of some the city's older hotels, but it is certainly the place for executives to stay. Set on a 7-acre site next to Beira Lake, with views to the Indian Ocean from the upper storeys, it is a highly efficient property yet with a slightly quaint appeal. The Frangipani Floor is specially dedicated to female customers, with women attendants and extra security arrangements, while the Sakura Floor has been adapted to meet the needs of Japanese guests. Whatever their nationality or sex, everyone can enjoy the hotel's seven restaurants and bars (the Blue Elephant discotheque is one of the Colombo's most popular nightspots) plus the pool, gym, tennis and air-conditioned squash courts.

Rates from: **US$ 65**
Star rating: ★ ★ ★ ★ ★
Bellhop rating: ◔ ◔ ◔ ◔ ½

Value:	7.97	Facilities:	8.40
Staff:	8.16	Restaurants:	8.52
Location:	8.16	Families:	6.79
Cleanliness:	8.42		

Galle Face Hotel

No 2 Galle Road, Colombo 3, Sri Lanka
T: +94 1 541 010 **F:** +94 1 541 072
http://www.asia-hotels.com/hotelinfo/Galle_Face_hotel/

The Galle Face is an eccentric pile, trading largely off its century and a half of heritage with only an eyebrow cocked to modernity, although a renovation programme is currently under way. As such, it is well worth staying here for the utterly unique atmosphere. Many of the staff have worked in the hotel for a generation or more. A marble plaque in the lobby commemorates comments from previous guests such as the Aga Khan's 'Happiness is the Galle Face Hotel' and function rooms are named after HRH Prince Philip and Cyril Gardiner, the former highly charismatic owner.

Built right on the ocean, overlooking Galle Face Green, the 84 rooms and suites were designed when ample space was a given, not an indulgence, a munificence which sums up the whole hotel.

Rates from: **US$ 50**
Star rating: ★ ★ ★ ½
Bellhop rating: ◔ ◔ ◔ ◔

Value:	7.94	Facilities:	6.71
Staff:	8.00	Restaurants:	7.47
Location:	8.06	Families:	5.77
Cleanliness:	7.41		

Kandalama Hotel

Dambulla, Sri Lanka
T: +94 66 84100 **F:** +94 66 84109
http://www.asia-hotels.com/hotelinfo/Kandalama_Hotel/

The Kandalama is one of the most amazing hotels in Asia, let alone Sri Lanka, a masterful blend of hospitality and eco-engineering that looks wonderful and feels even better. Much more than just rooms, restaurants and rest and recuperation, it combines history with an unparalleled natural location in the heart of the island.

For a start, as the hotel is built into a cliff and festooned with greenery, it is barely visible from a distance and up close practically merges into its surroundings. Set near the foot of two mountains – Ereulagala and Dikkandahena – on the border of Sri Lanka's intermediate and dry zones, the Kandalama's environs enjoy an especially rich bio-diversity. The hotel looks down on the Dambulla tank, a two-millennia-old reservoir that still supplies water to farms in the area, and is right in the middle of a 54-acre forest that encompasses trees, medicinal plants and 165 species of arboreal, terrestrial and aquatic birds including the dusky blue flycatcher, yellow fronted barbett and grey hornbill.

Containing 158 rooms and four suites, the Kandalama was designed on strict eco-friendly lines, unobtrusively strung out along the hillside for a full kilometre. Through its architecture, the hotel ingeniously grants nature centre stage: rocks, caves and cascades of rainwater add drama and charm to the corridors. Forest trees brush against galleries and the windows of public rooms, while flowering woodland creepers

curtain balconies and the roofs are terraces of wild grass. The rooms are sparingly yet comfortably decorated, providing 21st-century amenities like satellite TV and IDD phones while still retaining something of the placid aura of a cliffside monkish cell.

The slightly confusingly named trio of restaurants – Kasyapa, Kanchana and Kaludiya – and brace of bars – Kachchan and Katakatha – belong more to the surrounding acres than the hotel itself, with vistas stretching out to the tank, mountains and jungles. Using fresh farm produce and locally grown fruit whenever possible, the kitchens serve up a variety of delicious local and international cuisines.

One of the Kandalama's top draws is its Eco Park, where guests can see at first hand sewage being dried by the sun and composted, water being recycled for the rooftop gardens and garbage being sorted and dispatched for approprlate disposal. It is not by any means the sort of excursion that normally confronts 5-star habitués, but one that expresses the entire ethos of the hotel. Guests can also tour the plant nursery and beehives, and delve into the extensive eco-library.

More conventional entertainments include tennis,

ping-pong, a fully equipped gym, billiards and the board game Carrom. And beyond the Kandalama – whose site was chosen only after an extensive search by helicopter – sits the heartland of the 'cultural triangle'. The 5th-century rock fortress of Sigirya is in sight of the hotel's infinity swimming pool (one of three pools), and the ancient cities of Anuradhapura and Polonnaruwa are both within driving distance. You can venture to the surrounding areas by horse, elephant and bicycle, or board a dugout canoe for a safari on nearby irrigation tanks like the Sea of Parakrama. On foot, an hours hike leads to the pond named

Kaludiya Pokuna, an ancient archaeological site where the ebony trees reach more than five metres in circumference. Returning mentally invigorated but possibly physically lacking, there is a whole range of treatment at the Ayurvedic spa – the most natural form of therapeutics in a hotel inspired by, and devoted to, nature.

Rates from: **US$ 71**
Star rating: ★★★★
Bellhop rating: 🛎🛎🛎🛎🛎

Value:	9.12	Facilities:	8.46
Staff:	8.91	Restaurants:	8.91
Location:	9.27	Families:	7.52
Cleanliness:	9.06		

Lighthouse Hotel

Dadella, Galle, Sri Lanka
T: +94 9 23744 **F**: +94 9 24021
http://www.asia-hotels.com/hotelinfo/Lighthouse_Hotel/

With a style that might be called 'Robinson Le Corbusier', the Lighthouse is a constant surprise, dominating a headland near the historic city of Galle. Designed by Sri Lankan architect Geoffrey Bawa, who was inspired by the nearby three-century-old Dutch fort, the hotel is a delirious expanse of cinnamon-coloured buildings topped with red tiled roofs, linked by airy open corridors looking down on to the ocean and a beach that stretches away to the horizon.

Only opened in 1997, the Lighthouse comprises just 60 rooms and three suites. The rooms are floored with teak, with large en-suite granite and wood bathrooms and a separate shower, and give out on to a private balcony or terrace. Each of the suites, which come with a jacuzzi, pantry and separate sitting room, enjoys a playful individual theme that draws on Galle's long-time global trading associations. The Ibn Batuta echoes a Moroccan souk, Fa Hsien provides a taste of China, while the Spielbergen is solidly Dutch.

Dining at the Lighthouse is similarly inspired and likewise international. The Cardamom Cafe is open round the clock, while the Cinnamon Room – noted for its fondues – opens only at dinner. The Anchor Bar occupies a convenient spot near both the main and children's pools while the Coat of Arms Bar must have a deal going with whoever organises the dazzling sunsets that manifest themselves almost without fail on a daily basis. Alfresco fans can also request an evening barbeque down on the beach, with fresh seafood cooked over crackling open fires and the waves crashing on the rocks as a symphonic backdrop.

By day, there is an enormous amount to occupy guests – billiards, squash, ping-pong and tennis for anyone who likes knocking balls about, and of course a fully equipped gym. An array of excursions are available or just stay on the beach which is ideal for fishing – and pretty good for toasting in a few UVs as well.

Rates from: **US$ 200**
Star rating: ★ ★ ★ ★ ★
Bellhop rating: ♗ ♗ ♗ ♗ ½

Value:	8.54	Facilities:	8.08
Staff:	8.69	Restaurants:	8.00
Location:	8.46	Families:	7.92
Cleanliness:	8.92		

Mount Lavinia Hotel

100 Hotel Road, Mount Lavinia, Sri Lanka
T: +94 1 715 221 **F:** +94 1 738 228
http://www.asia-hotels.com/hotelinfo/Mount_Lavinia_Hotel/

From a British governor's secret love nest, to a holiday home, to a wartime hospital, Mount Lavinia has gradually metamorphosed from its genesis in the 19th century to its incarnation as a luxury hotel. The hotel's present form neatly reflects its antecedents, as this 275-room (private) beachside property is as well placed for honeymooners as it is for guests who simply need to relax and recuperate.

The Mount Lavinia's nucleus is the marbled Governor's Wing, one-time residence of Sir Thomas Maitland, who built the house so he could rendezvous with a dancing girl – one Lovina

Aponsuwa – who had unduly excited his passions. It now contains 40 rooms – with wooden floors and windows that open wide to the sea breezes, accentuating its colonial charm – as well as the duplex Governor's Suite. Other accommodation is split between the Bay Wing and Sea & Garden Wing, more recently built but all with the requisite sea view, as well as more current amenities like satellite TV and IDD phones.

The Lavinia's main dining room also takes its name from the Governor, with bay windows and lofty pillars and palms providing the backdrop to the Western and oriental menu. Lobster and prawns are the prime fare at Seafood Cove and sunset cocktails slip down easily at the thatched Tropical Bar on the beach. Dancing at the hotel nightclub – Little Hut – encouraged by the live band, usually lasts until the wee hours.

Above all, Mount Lavinia is an especially stylish hotel, with a talent for organising unusual events. This might be a wedding, complete with Kandyan drummers and dancers, elephants and a chorus of local girls, or simply the regular Saturday film night, when classic movies are shown on the terrace with nothing to cover the audience but the stars and moon above.

Rates from: **US$ 73**
Star rating: ★ ★ ★ ★ ½
Bellhop rating: ✿ ✿ ✿ ✿ ½

Value:	8.44	Facilities:	7.61
Staff:	8.00	Restaurants:	8.11
Location:	8.50	Families:	6.67
Cleanliness:	8.06		

TAIWAN

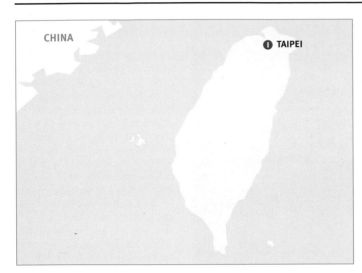

The emerald island lying just 160 kilometres off the Chinese mainland is a feisty character. It lives an uneasy existence, precariously overshadowed by its vast and uncompromising neighbour. Taiwan is a land at peace, but embroiled in one of the thorniest dilemmas of the East.

Originally populated by seafaring peoples from the Pacific islands and groups from the archipelago that today forms the Philippines, Malaysia and Indonesia, Taiwan remained a backwater for millennia. By the time the Portuguese dropped anchor in 1517 and christened it Ilha Formosa – Beautiful Island – it was being steadily settled by Fujianese from across the Strait, and displaying a predominantly Chinese population. In subsequent centuries, the Chinese, Spanish and Japanese were to play a game of musical chairs with the island until after World War II, when the newly formed United Nations decreed that Taiwan would be

returned to China. But before that could happen, the communists won the bloody civil war on the mainland, the nationalists fled to the province of Taiwan and each side settled down to plot the other's downfall.

The dispute simmered for decades and the two governments were to diverge along very separate paths. Both sides have evolved into different entities, and much to China's indignation Taiwan did very well for itself. The economy boomed, leaving the sluggish mainland in its wake. Since taking control of its own affairs in the 1950s Taiwan has enjoyed an average GDP growth of 9 per cent a year, ensuring it emerged as one of the four 'tiger economies' alongside Hong Kong, Singapore and South Korea. Despite recent wobbles in the Asian financial arena, Taiwan remains financially robust and a major manufacturing base. Finally China is blossoming economically and, ironically, the greatest threat

from across the Strait now looks to be cheap and inexhaustible labour rather than menacing missile launchers.

Currently Taiwan's international status is a grey area so its awkward position means it falls into a category all of its own. It exists in diplomatic no-man's-land. For the apolitical it is best described as an unofficial country. Taiwan never declared independence, and Beijing's non-negotiable stance is that Taiwan is a renegade province – and that reunification is inevitable. Chinese foreign policy is almost defined by the issue and takes a very dim

view of anyone in the international community daring to treat Taiwan as a country. No country may maintain official diplomatic relations with both Taipei and Beijing and for the Taiwanese it has been a long diplomatic march into oblivion. Faced with the choice, only 27 nations now recognise Taiwan, most of which are Third World recipients of economic aid. Taiwan, incidentally, held the Chinese seat at the United Nations until 1971 when it was replaced by the PRC.

Despite the diplomatic slide, Taiwan booms and the capital Taipei encapsulates a boundless entrepreneurial energy. A sprawling, gritty metropolis, it is home to three million and known for its tide of zipping mopeds and – to be brutally honest – ugly architecture. Most visitors are here for business, but you do not need to look too hard to find pockets of tradition, impressive monuments, good food and uncommonly friendly inhabitants. Taipei also hosts the National Palace Museum, one of the best

collections of Chinese artefacts in the world. Away from the big city are traditional temples and some prime hiking country. Majestic scenery exists along the east coast, across the dramatic mountainous interior and within national parks such as Taroko Gorge and Hsiukuluan River. Across the Strait are more islands dotted like stepping stones to China. From one, Kinmen, you can actually see the mainland.

Taiwan's hotels mirror its persona – functional business hotels with below-average architecture. First-class friendly service is a major plus even if English is not widespread. The best hotels are in the capital and the standards deteriorate pretty quickly outside, although there are some pockets of excellence.

Being comparatively small Taiwan shares a fairly uniform climate, with slight variations due to latitude and altitude. Generally speaking, the north and the mountainous regions are colder and wetter than the south. Despite its northerly latitude, the island

experiences a tropical monsoon climate, seemingly drawing the leftovers of the various typhoons that have battered Southeast Asia. Most are dissipating by the time they get there but occasionally it is buffeted by vicious storms. Intermittent typhoons and torrential rains wash over Taiwan during the otherwise humid summer – roughly June to September – while the winter is mostly cold, blustery and cloudy. Taipei can be visited all year round, but, like the rest of the country, is at its best around spring or autumn.

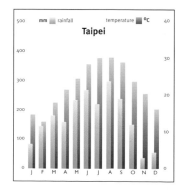

Far Eastern Plaza Hotel

201 Tun Hwa South Road, Section 2, Taipei, Taiwan
T: +886 2 2378 8888 **F:** +886 2 2377 7777
http://www.asia-hotels.com/hotelinfo/Far_Eastern_Plaza_Hotel/

Well-established and reliable, this shiny 422-roomed tower managed by the Shangri-La Group is well up to international 5-star service and standards, even if the somewhat dark interior is now starting to show its age. Considerate staff do a splendid job and the Far Eastern is well located in the busy eastern sector of the city, only a few hundred metres from the metro station and five minutes from the World Trade Centre, with an array of shops, restaurants and bars close by. The competitive facilities ensure this hotel's appeal is broader than just business, even though this is where it principally excels. It has fine views from the small heated rooftop pool (one of two pools) and since there is only a select number of rooms on each of its 43 floors, there is a pleasant impression of privacy. Add to this eight restaurants, the 40th-floor spa and well-equipped health club and it is not difficult to see why the Far Eastern Plaza consistently ranks as one of Taipei's, and therefore Taiwan's, most popular hotels.

Rates from: **US$ 155**
Star rating: ★★★★★
Bellhop rating: ◊◊◊◊

Value:	7.62	Facilities:	8.26
Staff:	8.22	Restaurants:	8.03
Location:	8.09	Families:	6.45
Cleanliness:	8.51		

Grand Formosa Regent Taipei

41 Chung Shan North Road, Section 2, Taipei, Taiwan
T: +886 2 2523 8000 **F:** +886 2 2523 2828
http://www.asia-hotels.com/hotelinfo/Grand_Formosa_Regent_Taipei/

Sitting on Taipei's main boulevard the Grand Formosa Regent is well placed, appealing especially to business guests but also to tourists. Its 21 storeys firmly encompass 538 traditionally styled, spacious rooms and 60 suites, all with floor-to-ceiling bay windows and separate bath and shower. Even the lowest category Superior Rooms measure a generous 45 square metres. Regular visitors to Taiwan will appreciate the relative novelty of the non-smoking and women's floors, so single female guests can rest assured of extra security. The hotel interior opens up with a bright atrium and is smart and professional, while its dedicated Executive and Formosa Club floors and conference facilities are well run. The pool is small but good restaurants offer diverse cuisine choices for the varied guests – Chinese, European and Japanese. The Formosa may not be the cheapest option, but it is complete and very practical.

Rates from: **US$ 142**
Star rating: ★★★★★
Bellhop rating: ◊◊◊◊ ½

Value:	7.98	Facilities:	8.50
Staff:	8.40	Restaurants:	8.40
Location:	8.45	Families:	7.15
Cleanliness:	8.76		

Grand Hyatt Taipei

No 2 Sung Shou Road, Taipei, Taiwan
T: +886 2 2720 1234 **F:** +886 2 2720 1111
http://www.asia-hotels.com/hotelinfo/Grand_Hyatt_Taipei/

The Grand Hyatt is Taipei's shiniest 5-star hotel with absolutely everything, plus a familiar name for those who do not wish to stray outside their comfort zones. It is massive with 856 rooms, making it one of the biggest in Taiwan. The prime advantage of staying here is the Hyatt's spectrum of facilities, but of equal importance is its strategic location. The hotel lies right next to the landmark World Trade Centre with direct access to the Exhibition Hall and Convention Centre, in Taipei's emerging business and entertainment district. Opened in 1990, this is one of Asia's newer breed of hotels and is broadly considered Taipei's best.

The interior design is especially smart and classy. Contemporary fittings, deep colours and subdued lighting makes for a refined yet relaxed appearance throughout. The lobby enjoys a classical mood and feels a little like a giant conservatory, with grand pillars and arcing balconies sealed beneath a modern glass-paned roof that allows natural light to flood in. Six excellent restaurants cater for cosmopolitan palettes; Ziga Zaga mutates at 9.30pm from an Italian dining outlet into a chic dance hang-out with live music; Shanghai Court captures the 1930s with its haute cuisine; the Irodori features modern Japanese buffet style; and the show kitchens of Cafe serve up fresh Western and Asian fare. The Oasis Fitness Centre includes an excellent temperature-controlled outdoor pool (complete with underwater stereo sound system!), a sharp, spacious gym and full spa treatments. Appealing rooms and suites are smooth and trim, generously fitted including three phone lines and broadband Internet access.

The business centre runs conveniently from dawn till late evening and the club floors have several plush conference rooms. Such is the overall appeal of the Grand Hyatt that it can occasionally fall victim to its own success. The lobby is busy to the point of noisy and if the adjacent World Trade Centre is hosting an exhibition then the hotel seems to function as an overflow and is swamped by hundreds of visitors. The hotel is hugely popular, and rightfully so, but be prepared for the crowds.

Rates from: **US$ 152**
Star rating: ★ ★ ★ ★ ★
Bellhop rating: 🖐 🖐 🖐 🖐

Value:	7.41	Facilities:	8.34
Staff:	8.30	Restaurants:	8.33
Location:	8.12	Families:	6.34
Cleanliness:	8.71		

Le Petit Sherwood Taipei

370 Tun Hwa South Road, Section 1, Taipei, Taiwan
T: +886 2 2754 1166 **F**: +886 2 2754 3399
http://www.asia-hotels.com/hotelinfo/Le_Petit_Sherwood_Taipei/

Taipei has no shortage of big, impersonal hotels that were put up in a hurry, so it is nice to stumble across luxury boutiques like Le Petit Sherwood. With a manageable 62 rooms Le Petit Sherwood is intimate and snug, and importantly it is able to provide a more attentive and personal service to its limited number of guests. The service ranks very highly – friendly, yet sophisticated and efficient. The polite staff's good level of English is especially welcome in Taipei, and check-in and checkout is a breeze. In a way, the whole hotel feels like a club floor.

The understated European elegance of Le Petit Sherwood is another influential strength. The interior is modestly proportioned but never claustrophobic with its high ceilings and warm lighting. Furnishings are contemporary with a hint of the classic. The combination of pastel shades, subtle gold trimmings and shiny marble create a luxuriant and classy environment. But the abundant use of smooth fabrics, such as flowing curtains and comfy chairs with squashy cushions

helps soften the interior. Ample pot plants and greenery contribute further to the affectionate mood and set a truly relaxing and homely ambience.

Le Petit Sherwood tends to attract weary business travellers looking to unwind. Petite it is and the facilities are finite. The function room holds up to 60 people and is fitted with full conference facilities. Carrara Restaurant is smart and

cosy and it serves some excellent Mediterranean cuisine. They have an Italian wood-burning stove and all of the pizzas are baked from handmade dough, and a good selection of wines are on offer too. As for the rooms, they are of equal merit. Although they are modestly sized, they are bright with long windows, optimistic colours and chic bathrooms. And with a convenient location just a few blocks from the World Trade Centre and the Sun Yat Sen Memorial Centre, Le Petit Sherwood seems to have no obvious weaknesses.

Rates from: **US$ 122**
Star rating: ★ ★ ★ ★ ★
Bellhop rating: 🎩🎩🎩🎩 ½

Value:	7.87	Facilities:	8.02
Staff:	8.80	Restaurants:	8.14
Location:	8.46	Families:	5.82
Cleanliness:	8.98		

The Landis Taipei Hotel

41 Min Chuan East Road, Section 2, Taipei, Taiwan
T: +886 2 2597 1234 **F:** +886 2 2596 9223
http://www.asia-hotels.com/hotelinfo/Ritz_Landis_Hotel_Taipei/

The Landis is sat reasonably conveniently downtown and is a 5-minute taxi ride from just about all the major landmarks and communications hubs. The hotel is not far from the main business districts to which it lays on free shuttle services. This is a warm and enjoyable boutique hotel – small, cosy, yet complete. The hotel has an appealing and intimate interior decor, a blend of arty modernism with a hint of the 1930s. The 200 rooms are bright and smart, even perhaps a tad groovy despite their age. It is the staff however that are the prize asset. Helpful, cheerful and courteous, the personal Landis is one hotel where the staff make an effort to remember your name. The facilities are compact and sensibly limited, but they are enough. The restaurants are reasonable and 1930 Paris gets regular thumbs up for food and ambience.

Rates from: US$ 122
Star rating: ★ ★ ★ ★ ★
Bellhop rating: 🛎 🛎 🛎 🛎 ½

Value:	7.86	Facilities:	8.14
Staff:	8.96	Restaurants:	8.53
Location:	8.02	Families:	5.80
Cleanliness:	8.92		

The Westin Taipei

133 Nanking East Road, Section 3, Taipei, Taiwan
T: +886 2 8770 6565 **F:** +886 2 8770 6555
http://www.asia-hotels.com/hotelinfo/Westin_Taipei_The/

Virtually brand new (built in 1999), the Westin Taipei is spotlessly clean, shiny and fresh. Do not let the rather sober hospital-like exterior put you off – a step inside reveals much more imagination. This is a warm and homely hotel with a chic European ambience. The Westin is especially well put together for business travellers, with sharp and well-appointed facilities including Internet and fax hook-up in the 288 rooms, and a 184-person auditorium conference hall. The excellent restaurants (four Chinese, Japanese, Italian, international and a New York-style Deli) have creative menus, and the basement pub, Sean's, is a popular watering hole. Other welcome facilities include a fair gym, spa and sauna, and a sleek indoor swimming pool. The central location on Nanking East Road is great for Taipei's business and financial districts and near to the metro station. The Westin Taipei is well staffed by competent and friendly professionals and very smoothly run indeed.

Rates from: US$ 135
Star rating: ★ ★ ★ ★ ★
Bellhop rating: 🛎 🛎 🛎 🛎 ½

Value:	7.93	Facilities:	8.37
Staff:	8.59	Restaurants:	8.40
Location:	8.45	Families:	6.30
Cleanliness:	9.01		

THAILAND

Thailand is one vast holiday buffet, where visitors can gorge to their hearts' content on culture, shopping, sun, sand and several other sybaritic recreations. Better still, the kingdom is refreshingly affordable by any standards, making it a favourite for everyone from parents with children in tow to honeymooning couples to individuals with backpacks.

Travelling executives will usually find themselves in Bangkok, where the great majority of hotels blend the Thai tradition of gracious hospitality (served up with the smile that is a national marketing tool) with ultra-modern facilities. Indeed, with properties like the Sukhothai, Amanpuri and the Regent Chiang Mai to conjure with, Thailand can lay claim to hosting some of the world's most stunning hotels.

Shaped roughly like an elephant's head and trunk, the country's diverse offerings begin in the north with opportunities to trek in the jungles around Chiang Mai and Chiang Rai and take a first-hand look at the ethnic tribes who live in the region. Bangkok, known locally as Krung Thep, has been greatly liberated by the introduction of the Skytrain, which when combined with the ferry system is a superb way to get around the awesome temples, palaces, retail areas and restaurants – to say nothing of the nightlife. Pattaya, the resort closest to the capital, remains more attuned to the single male

than anyone else. To the south, laid-back Hua Hin has a wealth of golf courses, while the more remote Krabi entices both those who want to scale its picturesque limestone karsts or simply admire them while basking on sugar sand beaches. The less-developed islands of Koh Samui and Koh Phangan draw the younger party crowd, and Phuket exercises a universal appeal with beaches, nightlife, sports and shopping. Families will welcome the news that children are always accorded special treatment by Thais, who happily drop whatever they are doing to coo over babies and natter to youngsters.

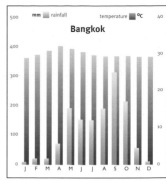

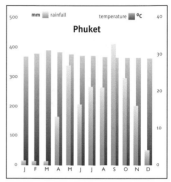

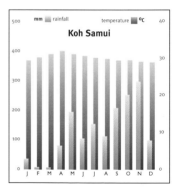

Wherever visitors end up, there will be no shortage of recreations and diversions on offer. The worldwide popularity of Thai cuisine has led many hotels to open their kitchens as cooking schools, taking guests into the markets in the morning, showing them how to prepare the food, and finishing off with a gourmet lunch or dinner. Water sports are a given at beach resorts, and mountain biking and horse riding provide a new way of exploring the countryside. Massage is an ancient Thai art and most major hotels now sport a spa offering a variety of body scrubs, facials and other similarly rejuvenating treatments. It needs to be said that some independent establishments use 'massage' as a cover for more adult-oriented activities and, while official efforts have been made to curb the more outrageous side of red-light areas in Bangkok, Pattaya, Phuket and elsewhere, the sex industry continues to flourish. Personal indulgence remains a matter of choice, but AIDS is an acronym no one can afford to ignore.

Thailand's variable geography is mirrored by its three-season climate. The rainy season (June – October) hits Phuket and Krabi especially hard, but not Koh Samui, which faces its own monsoon between October and January. The cool season (November – February) is one of the best times to visit. And between March and May expect the temperature to rise to around 40°C. Peak visitor periods (with corresponding accommodation prices) are Christmas and Lunar New Year.

The chance to take in one of Thailand's major festivals is a real bonus; a free-for-all public water fight celebrates Songkran or Thai New Year in mid-April, an event that attracts particular fervour in Chiang Mai. December 31st is also a signal for a wild party, and Loy Kratong in November is especially picturesque as couples and children launch candle-lit floats into waterways at night.

Two Thai words – 'sanuk' and 'sabai' – sum up the main reasons why so many foreigners return to Thailand time and again. Sanuk means having a good time and, whether on a beach holiday or trekking through malls or mountains, it is difficult not to have fun here. Similarly, Thailand emanates a very happy-go-lucky atmosphere. Whether you are lying prone beneath a masseur's fingertips, downing a beer in a plush bar or just watching the sun go down on a deserted beach 'sabai', or taking it easy, is the watchword.

The Allamanda Laguna Phuket

29 Moo 4, Srisoonthorn Road, Cherngtalay, Amphur Talang, Phuket 83110, Thailand
T: +66 76 324 359 **F:** +66 76 324 360
http://www.asia-hotels.com/hotelinfo/Allamanda_Laguna_Phuket/

The Allamanda's star attraction is without doubt its family-friendly rooms, or rather its suites which come in five different flavours. Top of the range are the 22 triplex Allamanda Suites, each containing a double and twin bedroom with ensuite bathrooms, and capped with a rooftop deck that is tailor-made for sunbathing or evening drinks. The 87 duplex 2-bedroom suites are not quite so accessoried, but are still eminently comfortable, while the 84 one-bedroom suites are ideal for couples and the 42 Junior Suites just lack a dining area. Each suite contains a kitchenette and separate living area together with tidy little balconies with views of the golf course fairways, the lagoon or one

of the three pools, So far, so predictable. But this resort really comes into its own with the two exclusive Kids' Suites – each adjoining an adult bedroom and specially equipped with bunk beds, games, videos and even Gameboys. Even the bathroom is brightly decorated, right down to a duck suspended from the shower head.

Suite deals apart, the Allamanda is a full-on, hands-on, on and on activity centre for anyone who cares to dabble in canoe tours round the lagoons (which camouflage old mine shafts beneath the entire Laguna complex), sailing lessons, Thai language lessons, aquaball and basketball, darts tournaments, water polo, croquet competitions,

garland making, paddle boat races, frisbee tourneys, fruit carving, coconut bowling, bike tours, egg tossing, snorkelling lessons and a whole load more. Phew. Most of these are free or attract only a minimal charge, and there is also a fully functioning Camp Laguna Kids' Club to get the little tykes off your hands for a few hours.

Food gets served up here in a similarly fun, outdoorsy fashion – guests can choose from the Lagoon Grill or the Courtyard Cafe, or hop on a shuttle to any of the other restaurants in Laguna's four other hotels. The Allamanda is ultra-ideal for families with children in tow, and remains the most inexpensive deal in the whole of the Laguna complex.

Rates from: **US$ 75**
Star rating: ★ ★ ★ ★
Bellhop rating: 👍 👍 👍 👍 ½

Value:	8.49	Facilities:	8.24
Staff:	8.77	Restaurants:	7.74
Location:	8.51	Families:	7.80
Cleanliness:	8.57		

Amanpuri

Pansea Beach, Phuket 83000, Thailand
T: +66 76 324 333 **F:** +66 76 324 100
http://www.asia-hotels.com/hotelinfo/Amanpuri/

Sail past Amanpuri, and you could easily miss it among the coconut groves. There is not even a sign at the entrance from the road. And flying over it you might think it was a temple or a palace. The first of the legendary Amanresorts, Amanpuri is now well past its 12th birthday, but its distinctive unassuming style has only improved with age. Some 40 private pavilions (go for numbers 103 or 105 for the most awesome sea views) are complemented by

an additional 30 villas set a little apart from the main hotel. Amanpuri means Place of Peace, and as far as names go, this could hardly be more apt. Set on its own headland, looking down on what is practically a private beach, this is a place to utterly relax, totally detox and completely wind down. Naturally, the food and beverage arrangements are everything that you would expect of an Aman – ditto the rates – but here nearly everything is perfect, from the

folded towel laid just so on your lounger by the pool to the librarian's omniscient acquaintance with the 1,000-plus books and CDs under her care.

The Amanpuri idyll was completed in 2001 with the addition of a purpose-built spa – with a half-dozen treatment salas spread across the hillside and room for everything from massage to meditation to tai chi. Spa treatments can be as simple as hand and foot massages – using reflexology to cleanse, exfoliate and invigorate. Or it might be something a little more intricate, like a lymphatic draining massage which is recommended for stimulating the circulation. And after a long day out in the sun, a full body treatment using yoghurt and aloe vera is the perfect skin conditioner before heading for the hushed bliss of your sea-facing villa.

Rates from: **US$ 600**
Star rating: ★ ★ ★ ★ ★
Bellhop rating: 🛎 🛎 🛎 🛎 ½

Value:	7.70	Facilities:	8.88
Staff:	9.20	Restaurants:	8.66
Location:	9.11	Families:	6.38
Cleanliness:	9.21		

Amari Palm Reef Resort

Chaweng Beach, Koh Samui 84320, Thailand
T: +66 77 422 015 **F:** +66 77 422 394
http://www.asia-hotels.com/hotelinfo/Amari_Palm_Reef_Resort/

Chaweng Beach is Koh Samui's premier playground – a lengthy, sandy stretch of seaside restaurants and hotels backed by assorted shops and cafes – and the Amari stands at its heart. This is a resort tailor-made for parents with kids in tow, on the small side with just 102 rooms and bungalows, but with just about everything the nuclear family might write on its vacation wish list.

The ideal accommodation lies within the bungalows, with a 2-floor mezzanine design which sleeps four with room to spare, although the regular rooms all have a balcony or terrace and wide windows that seem to allow a touch of Koh Samui inside.

Once unpacked, there is the entire resort to romp around, with two free-form pools for swimmers and a splash pool for kids, a jacuzzi and tennis and air-conditioned squash courts. The beach swarms with water sports merchants, from jet skis to windsurfers to banana boats, and there is also a fleet of mountain bikes for hire for a little 2-wheeled exploration along the Chaweng strip and beyond into the coconut plantations that were once the island's main source of income. Divers, whether fully qualified or taking their first steps underwater, can head for the nearby dive centre, whose instructors are well briefed on Koh Samui's best sites.

With the whole host of Chaweng's eateries to choose from, gourmets are spoiled for choice when it comes to meal times or just a snack during the day. However, the Amari's seaside restaurant – the Merante – does provide a fair measure of peace and quiet away from the town's hustle and bustle as well as delightful views over the sea, not to mention some delicious Thai and international specialities whipped up by its team of dedicated chefs.

Rates from: **US$ 80**
Star rating: ★ ★ ★ ★
Bellhop rating: 🔔🔔🔔🔔 ½

Value:	8.18	Facilities:	8.29
Staff:	8.65	Restaurants:	7.94
Location:	8.74	Families:	7.02
Cleanliness:	8.79		

Amari Watergate Hotel

847 Petchburi Road, Bangkok 10400, Thailand
T: +66 2 653 9000 **F**: +66 2 653 9045
http://www.asia-hotels.com/hotelinfo/Amari_Watergate_Hotel/

Location, location, location are supposed to be the three cardinal rules for a hotel's success. It is a dictum the Amari Watergate has followed to the letter, with 569 rooms slap bang next to the World Trade Centre in one of Bangkok's mainstream commercial and retail areas and in walking distance of the Skytrain. This is a thoroughly business-friendly hotel, the three uppermost floors are specifically dedicated to executives, and in addition to the standard 40 square metres, rooms come with 24-hour butler service and their own cocktail lounge. Continuing the corporate theme, both Grappino, the Italian restaurant, and Heichinrou, serving Chinese fare, are well set up for business dinners or lunches, while the Henry J. Bean Bar and Grill offers a more relaxed atmosphere.

Rates from: **US$ 82**
Star rating: ★ ★ ★ ★
Bellhop rating: 👍 👍 👍 👍 ½

Value:	8.32	Facilities:	8.44
Staff:	8.51	Restaurants:	8.24
Location:	8.54	Families:	7.00
Cleanliness:	8.66		

Baiyoke Sky Hotel

222 Rajprarop Road, Rajthevee, Bangkok 10400, Thailand
T: +66 2 656 3000 **F**: +66 2 656 3666
http://www.asia-hotels.com/hotelinfo/Baiyoke_Sky_Hotel/

At 309 metres and 88 storeys, the Baiyoke Sky is Thailand's tallest hotel – but does it really rise above all the others? Its main selling points are the view and the rates – even by Bangkok standards – are very reasonable. Just off Petchburi Road, the hotel's 673 suites are spread between the 22nd and 74th floors with a decor best described as multi-hued, and basic facilities which do not go much beyond phone, TV and fridge. Where the Baiyoke does score is in its meeting rooms – the Rainbow Hall can accommodate 1,200, while the two panoramic view function rooms can hold up to 90. There is a fairly predictable revolving restaurant on the 84th floor and similar vistas, without the food, on the 77th-floor observation deck.

Rates from: **US$ 42**
Star rating: ★ ★ ★ ★
Bellhop rating: 👍 👍 👍 👍

Value:	8.40	Facilities:	7.84
Staff:	7.92	Restaurants:	7.79
Location:	8.29	Families:	6.60
Cleanliness:	8.20		

Bangkok Marriott Resort & Spa

257 Charoennakorn Road, Bangkok 10600, Thailand
T: +66 2 476 0022 **F:** +66 2 476 1120
http://www.asia-hotels.com/hotelinfo/Bangkok_Marriott_Resort_Spa/

The Bangkok Marriott Resort & Spa was one of the first of the city's riverside hotels to come up with the idea of getting hold of a restored, 100-year-old teak rice barge fitted out with cabins and galley, and sending guests off on a cruise for cocktails, dinner or even an overnight onboard stay at the old Thai capital Ayutthaya.

Suffice to say the Manohra Song cruise is a glorious way to take in the sights and sounds of Bangkok, almost as if a part of the hotel itself had been floated away on the water. And the innovation and style behind the Manohra Song are characteristic of its parent resort and spa.

Made up of some 413 rooms and suites on an 11-acre site beside the Krung Thep bridge, its only disadvantage is the slightly remote location, 15 minutes from the heart of Bangkok. Rather than yet another tower block, this particular Marriott is a low-rise, quasi-colonial-style pile, spread between three buildings with the outdoor swimming pool as its centrepiece. Every room gives way to a balcony – a rarity to be

treasured here in Bangkok. Within, guests may count on a gentle Thai-themed decor and all the mod cons that make life so much easier.

No one is going to starve here either. The Marriott's healthy complement of 10 restaurants and bars embraces a fair amount of theatre; there is a Thai cultural show to spice up meals at the Riverside Terrace, while the acrobatic Japanese chefs at Benihana dispense teppanyaki with a showmanship that goes hand in hand with their culinary skills, making a real feast for the eyes.

Topping off the Marriott menu is the Mandara Spa – purpose-built as

a mini city escape with a half-dozen treatment suites overlooking the hotel gardens dispensing therapeutic pampering by the hour or even longer.

Rates from: **US$ 105**
Star rating: ★ ★ ★ ★ ★
Bellhop rating: 🛎 🛎 🛎 🛎 ½

Value:	8.40	Facilities:	8.78
Staff:	8.69	Restaurants:	8.62
Location:	8.19	Families:	6.45
Cleanliness:	8.88		

Banyan Tree Bangkok

21/100 South Sathon Road, Bangkok 10120, Thailand
T: +66 2 679 1200 **F:** +66 2 679 1053
http://www.asia-hotels.com/hotelinfo/Westin_Banyan_Tree/

There is a vast gulf between Banyan Tree city hotels and their resorts. Although this is not a tropical paradise grafted into the middle of a sprawling capital, it is at least a drop in gear. The exterior of the tall and slim building is a little out of the ordinary, but thankfully it is set back away from the main road, drastically cutting down the noise. The interior is surprisingly dark for a building with so many windows, but the trickling waters and leafiness create that spa-like ambience for which the chain is so famed, and throughout the property are those little Banyan Tree touches such as scented joss sticks. The

quiet rooms echo nature's colour scheme with brown tweed-like wallpaper, and the bathrooms are stocked with the superior accessories one comes to expect from this upmarket group.

The Banyan Tree Bangkok excels in the spa area, and boasts one of the capital's largest spa gardens. The white pebbled walls in the 23 spa rooms have soothing water cascades and wall-to-ceiling windows with some fine views over the city. Three exclusive spa suites are available – Lavender, Champaka and Sandalwood – each with their dedicated ensuite treatment room. In addition to the numerous

massage and body scrubs, meditation, aerobics or aqua-aerobics classes are offered. To complete the picture the 6-storey spa has jacuzzi, sauna, steam bath, dip and current pools.

The hotel has some additional bonuses like the architecturally stunning Bai Yun restaurant and the open air panoramic 59th-floor champagne and grill bar aptly named Vertigo. For those wanting action, the hotel is just 10 minutes walk from Silom Road shopping district and the Skytrain. The Banyan Tree Bangkok is no doubt a small oasis of calm amid the crazy pace of Bangkok, and provides an unusual opportunity to be totally pampered and rejuvenated right in the centre of town.

Rates from: **US$ 139**
Star rating: ★ ★ ★ ★ ★
Bellhop rating: 🛎 🛎 🛎 🛎 ½

Value:	8.14	Facilities:	8.58
Staff:	8.83	Restaurants:	8.16
Location:	8.13	Families:	6.66
Cleanliness:	9.10		

Banyan Tree Phuket

33 Moo 4, Srisoonthorn Road, Cherngtalay, Amphur Talang, Phuket 83110, Thailand
T: +66 76 324 374 **F:** +66 76 324 356
http://www.asia-hotels.com/hotelinfo/Banyan_Tree_Phuket/

It might be your honeymoon, your second honeymoon, or simply some practice for one or the other. Whether your stay is spread over a couple of weeks or a couple of nights, there is no gainsaying the overwhelming sexiness of this dazzling resort's 121 villas. Throw off the duvet and throw open the villa's doors to the pool, which is concealed from without by a high wall and verdant foliage. Plunge in together, then turn your gaze upwards. Whether the sky is a vast palette of cobalt and azure or lit by a galaxy of silver asterisks, that delirious, aqueous sensation of luxury and privacy is all utterly Banyan Tree Phuket.

Although it is part of the Laguna Phuket hotel and resort complex, you cannot really call this a hotel, nor a resort. Banyan Tree was designed to reflect the most harmonious elements of an Asian village. The buildings are set in clusters, while the bathrooms are open to the elements, granting a luscious 'back to nature' effect. The deeply pitched roofs and open-air pavilions (salas) here characterise traditional Thai architecture which evolved in

response to the country's climate. The overall effect is one of total tranquillity, while the interiors' warm colours, rich textures, smooth surfaces and subtle fragrances create sensuous aesthetics that are simultaneously restrained yet exuberant.

Tempting though it may be to linger endlessly chez villa, with its dictator-sized bed and au naturel bathroom, there are other temptations outside. The first tee of the 18-hole, par 71 Max Wexler-designed championship golf course is more or less opposite the hotel lobby. Its undulating fairways are dotted with coconut groves and scenic lagoons while the signature hole – the 16th – enjoys glorious views of the Andaman Sea: assuming you can tear your eyes away from the 12 surrounding bunkers.

Guests who find golf a bit active can while away the days by the 40-metre pool or take classes in tai chi, batik painting or yoga. But the quintessence of Banyan Tree Phuket lies in its spa, which is

the perfect mirror for its philosophy. It is an experience that can only be described as wholly holistic. Guests are bidden to recline on massage beds draped in green and gold silk brocade. The loudest noise comes from the therapists' fingers, unknotting muscles and smoothing sinews as if they were deftly unwrapping a birthday present. At the end of their spa session, guests are gently directed to a wooden sofa or dang where they are given a refreshing herbal drink and – much more importantly – time to reflect on all that they see and feel. The spa menu is nothing if not comprehensive; to a full range of massages add body treatments – perhaps a mud or a seaweed wrap – as well as a panoply of facials, waxing and hair care. Not signing up for a 7-hour programme, which includes lunch at the Tamarind Spa Restaurant, takes a lot of will power.

The Tamarind's cuisine places due emphasis on healthy eating and carefully balanced dishes, but

if you need to mildly offset the effects of being cleansed inside and out at the spa, there are six other restaurants and bars featuring international and Thai food as well as numerous other options at the other four Laguna sister resorts. Best option of all is to order up a fully fledged barbecue – or even a simple sandwich – back in that haven, your villa.

Rates from: **US$ 300**
Star rating: ★ ★ ★ ★ ★
Bellhop rating: 🛎 🛎 🛎 🛎 ½

Value:	7.58	Facilities:	8.89
Staff:	9.00	Restaurants:	8.36
Location:	8.48	Families:	7.06
Cleanliness:	9.05		

The Boathouse (Mom Tri's)

182 Koktanod Road, Kata Beach, Karon District, Phuket 83100, Thailand
T: +66 76 330 015 **F:** +66 76 330 561
http://www.asia-hotels.com/hotelinfo/Boathouse_Phuket/

The Standard Rooms are looking a little past their best; so the savvy (but pricey) alternative is to take one of the six new suites at the hotel's Villa Royale on the adjacent hillside, which are furnished with antiques and curios and enjoy their own private pool.

The Boathouse, shaded by towering Potalay trees at the northern end of Kata Beach, has a curious history. Started as a restaurant in 1989, its unconventional owner, Mom Tri Devakul, later added 36 rooms. But it is for food and wine that the hotel should be celebrated, for both the cellar and the restaurants are stupendous. The former contains 420 different labels including such prestigious names as Muga and Pingus, while the zest of the European and Thai menu is augmented by the views out over the turquoise sea.

Rates from: **US$ 80**
Star rating: ★ ★ ★ ½
Bellhop rating: 🛎🛎🛎🛎 ½

Value:	8.45	Facilities:	7.31
Staff:	9.17	Restaurants:	9.00
Location:	9.03	Families:	5.72
Cleanliness:	8.86		

Cape Panwa Hotel

27 Moo 8, Sakdidej Road, Cape Panwa, Phuket 83000, Thailand
T: +66 76 391 123 **F:** +66 76 391 177
http://www.asia-hotels.com/hotelinfo/Cape_Panwa_Hotel/

away from the hustle and bustle of more mainstream resort areas. Star-struck guests should note that Leonardo Di Caprio hid out from the papparazzi here while filming *The Beach*. As an added bonus, one of the island's cheapest and most interesting attractions, the Phuket Aquarium, is just around the corner.

Where is Cape Panwa? It is a good question, and one that the hotel's fans would rather not have answered too explicitly. Secure above almost the only habitable beach on the east coast of Phuket, the Cape Panwa delivers what a lot of rivals only promise. A choice of sunny, comfortable rooms, suites and bungalows, water sports for the active, petanque for those seeking a more sedentary challenge, a selection of restaurants specialising in French, Italian and Thai with an emphasis on local seafood, and all of it well

Rates from: **US$ 61**
Star rating: ★ ★ ★ ★
Bellhop rating: 🛎🛎🛎 ½

Value:	8.20	Facilities:	8.45
Staff:	8.65	Restaurants:	8.30
Location:	9.00	Families:	7.00
Cleanliness:	8.85		

Central Samui Beach Resort

38/2 Moo 3, Borpud Chewang Beach, Koh Samui, Suratthani 84320, Thailand
T: +66 77 230 500 **F**: +66 77 422 385
http://www.asia-hotels.com/hotelinfo/Central_Samui_Beach_Resort/

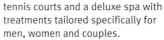

Looking at the Central Samui Beach Resort from the sea, you might be led astray by the exterior – an unusual melange of lofty, stark white columns and glass capped by brick-red roof tiles. A coconut expo centre? A museum dedicated to hedonism? Well, partly right. Central is not unacquainted with the pursuit of pleasure, and the island's signature fruit crops up regularly in both the resort's cocktails and cuisine – and of course there are a fair few palm trees dotted around the grounds.

Central is big and bursting with energy. Its four storeys contain 208 rooms and suites, all facing the ocean and all tastefully and freshly decorated in a style that is both island and international. The pool forms the resort's focus – a huge stretch of water that is big enough for an Olympic-style water polo match yet with semi-concealed channels and jacuzzis where couples can snuggle up together. It also features the Dip & Sip, a swim-up bar where guests can stop for a drink and a snack with their feet still dangling in the water.

Elsewhere, there are playrooms and special pools for children, two tennis courts and a deluxe spa with treatments tailored specifically for men, women and couples.

Despite the sporting and recreational facilities on offer, and the chance to swim in or walk by the ocean, anyone arriving at Central and planning to lose a bit of weight by the end of the holiday should think again. Of the resort's eight restaurants and bars, Hagi's Japanese is utterly authentic, Spice Island serves up traditional Thai, the Seabreeze terrace offers great beach views and Surfers provides a heady mix of drinks, Internet access and a widescreen TV for international sporting events.

Rates from: **US$ 101**
Star rating: ★ ★ ★ ★ ★
Bellhop rating: 🛎 🛎 🛎 🛎 🛎

Value:	8.42	Facilities:	8.99
Staff:	9.00	Restaurants:	8.55
Location:	9.17	Families:	7.89
Cleanliness:	8.94		

Chaweng Regent Beach Resort

115/4 Chaweng Beach Road, Koh Samui, Suratthani 84320, Thailand
T: +66 77 422 008 **F:** +66 77 422 222
http://www.asia-hotels.com/hotelinfo/Chaweng_Regent_Beach_Resort_The/

Arriving at the Chaweng Regent is like being bungee jumped on to Koh Samui. This is the centre of all the action, with the bars and eateries at one end of the resort and the myriad pleasures of the beach at the other. In between, the Regent supplies a host of diversions and luxurious accommodation, a haven from the rigours of an in-yer-face party island. And haven it really is. Unlike some hotels which have gone for the 'big is better' design solution, the Regent is all 2-storey buildings and bungalows, with a total of just 145 rooms, all of which are fully kitted out right down to bathrobes, umbrellas and sandals.

A stroll around the Regent's grounds would lead past the two freshwater swimming pools, the gym and spa, the indoor games room, the kids' play area and finally down to the water where free sun loungers and umbrellas are attended by the resort's beach boys. Two traditional local experiences are also on offer here – kick-boxing lessons with a personal coach and the rather more sedentary option of submitting to a classic Thai massage, which focuses on stretching the muscles while applying a certain amount of pressure. Alternative treatments include hot poultice massage, Swedish aromatherapy, foot reflexology and even a special 'after sun' rub for anyone who has overdosed on ultraviolets. The Regent also runs free introductory lessons to scuba diving in the pool, an easy way to get acquainted with one of Samui's top outdoor recreations.

The resort, while providing a complete range of Thai and international menus in its restaurants and bars, also goes to town with regular theme night buffets, complete with music and dancing under the stars. There is a fair bit of that beyond the front gate too.

Rates from: **US$ 105**
Star rating: ★★★★½
Bellhop rating: ½

Value:	7.97	Facilities:	8.26
Staff:	8.45	Restaurants:	8.24
Location:	8.90	Families:	7.00
Cleanliness:	8.63		

The Chedi Hotel

Pansea Phuket Bay, 118 Moo 3, Cheong Talay, Thalang, Phuket 83110, Thailand
T: +66 76 324 017 **F:** +66 76 324 252
http://www.asia-hotels.com/hotelinfo/Chedi_The/

Sometimes known as the poor man's Aman, the Chedi is in fact the smart man's Aman – the reason being it is right next door to Amanpuri, enjoys similar if not quite such highfalutin facilities and is substantially more credit card friendly. It is also a touch more down to earth, with a less rarefied atmosphere. Rather than design-diva villas, the Chedi puts its guests up in thatched cottages, the sort of place you might hope to borrow from a well-placed friend or distant relation. The accommodation is carefully spaced up the steep hillside which rises from Pansea Beach – the 89 one-bedroom cottages are fine for a couple even with a child in tow, and there are 19 with double bedrooms which can happily take in your average mum, dad and 2.4 children. Each cottage has its own sundeck, and the interior design – panels of woven palm fronds and earthen-coloured fabrics – brings the outdoors inside. All in all, this is a resort that is at one with nature.

With a swimming pool dramatically tiled in black, a brace of tennis courts and a full fleet of water sports facilities, the Chedi's corporate side is easy to overlook. The floor-to-ceiling windows of the 50-square-metre conference room provide a sensational backdrop and there is a phalanx of audio-visual equipment on hand as well. That five international-standard golf courses – where, after all, most deals are clinched anyway – lie within 30 minutes drive of the Chedi's front door can only be an additional incentive.

A word of warning – not many guests leave the Chedi weighing less than when they arrived. This is largely due to the Thai and Asian specialities served beneath the soaring rafters of the Lomtalay restaurant which overlooks the Andaman Sea, and remains one of the best locations to dine on the island.

Rates from: **US$ 157**
Star rating: ★ ★ ★ ★ ½
Bellhop rating: 🛎 🛎 🛎 🛎 ½

Value:	7.94	Facilities:	8.11
Staff:	9.11	Restaurants:	8.10
Location:	9.02	Families:	6.79
Cleanliness:	9.10		

Chiva-Som International Health Resort

73/4 Petchkasem Road, Hua Hin, Prachuab Kirikhan 77110, Thailand
T: +66 32 536 536 **F:** +66 32 511 154
http://www.asia-hotels.com/hotelinfo/ChivaSom_International_Health_Resort/

Most hotels start with rooms, restaurants and the rest, and then tack on a spa as a small afterthought. Breaking the mould, Chiva-Som did things the other way round, taking the spa and its maze of treatment rooms as its centrepiece and raison d'etre and locating its 57 clustered pavilions – a refreshing blend of Thai-tinged elegance and simplicity – around about. As the first purpose-built health resort in Asia, it has enjoyed a distinct measure of success. Many of Chiva-Som's treatments and facilities are unrivalled anywhere else in the region, so guests are free to therapy themselves as healthily as imaginable, but they can also simply sit back and enjoy being surrounded by seven acres of lush gardens right on the beach at Hua Hin. It is not by any means a 'fat farm' – the dishes at the buffet

(steak – yes, chips – no) are discreetly labelled for calorie content and avoid oily cooking fats, but no one is weighing up how many times you go back and forth. There are some house rules though – children under 16 and mobile phones are forbidden, as is smoking except in designated areas, coffee is frowned upon and a limited alcohol selection is available in the evenings.

Visits to Chiva-Som start with an informal check-up, a mild holistic assessment of your fitness chiefly to advise on the best treatments to go for, whether deep tissue massage or an eyelash tint. As in the restaurant, no one is flourishing a list of rules and regulations, and you are free to pick and choose whether your stay is ultra active or downright idle. With 80-plus treatments and activities from lifestyle coaching to

traditional Chinese acupuncture the choice is extensive. Lying suspended in salt water in the flotation suite, it is very difficult to avoid drifting off to sleep – surely one of the most relaxing therapies available anywhere. Slightly higher on the vigor-ometer, you can indulge in tai chi, yoga lessons, Pilates sessions, a bit of sea kayaking or take out all your pent-up frustrations with a bout of Thai boxing. Programmes are typically one on one and tailored to the individual, although some sessions offer group therapy.

Rates from: **US$ 322**
Star rating: ★ ★ ★ ★ ★
Bellhop rating: ◊ ◊ ◊ ◊ ½

Value:	8.10	Facilities:	9.22
Staff:	9.22	Restaurants:	8.49
Location:	7.68	Families:	3.63
Cleanliness:	9.29		

Dusit Laguna Resort Hotel

390 Srisoontorn Road, Cherngtalay, Amphur Talang, Phuket 83110, Thailand
T: +66 76 324 324 **F:** +66 76 324 174
http://www.asia-hotels.com/hotelinfo/Dusit_Laguna_Resort_Hotel/

In the beginning, the lagoons of Laguna merely camouflaged abandoned tin mines that had ravaged the local environment. One eco-triumphant, multi-million dollar restoration project later, a 5-hotel resort complex rose like a phoenix from the ashes, and the first of these was Dusit.

Despite having opened its doors in 1987 the Dusit is far from showing its age. Its 226 balconied rooms and suites have a fresh, clean feel to them, and the resort is so laid out that it is only a short walk to the half-dozen restaurants, the multi-taskable recreation

centre including the Busy Bee Kids' Klub or the glories of Bang Tao Beach, which runs for kilometres in either direction. Plus there is the added merit of being able to hop aboard the shuttle boat which putters around the rest of 1,000-acre Laguna site.

Set right next to the sea, the Dusit is unique among the Laguna properties in having a wide and shady lawn between its pool and the beach. With a calm, restful air, this is somewhere to chill, submit to an outdoor massage, drink fresh coconut juice straight from the husk, or laze for a while out of

range of the ultraviolets. It may seem bizarre to think of anything but rest and recreation here. However, the Dusit also holds three large meeting halls and a slightly smaller function room, all adaptable to various business needs and is popular with conventioneers and incentivees.

Whether here on business or pleasure, guests can be sure of eating exceptionally well. There is a choice of royal Thai cuisine – once the exclusive preserve of the upper crust but now available to all and sundry – at Ruen Thai, or traditional Italian at La Trattoria. But quite the most 'Dusit' of the resort's eateries is the Casuarina Hut, a lovely alfresco location dishing up the freshest seafood and barbecues.

Rates from: **US$ 93**
Star rating: ★★★★★
Bellhop rating: ◊◊◊◊ ½

Value:	8.00	Facilities:	8.43
Staff:	8.59	Restaurants:	8.28
Location:	8.44	Families:	7.62
Cleanliness:	8.61		

Dusit Resort and Polo Club

1349 Pethkasem Road, Cha-Am, Petchaburi 76120, Thailand
T: +66 32 442 100 **F:** +66 32 520 296
http://www.asia-hotels.com/hotelinfo/Dusit_Resort_and_Polo_Club/

It is an open secret that there is actually no polo club at the Dusit in Cha-Am, so put aside any thought of getting in a few chukkas on the coast. It is a great name anyway and the resort does have its own stables, but the old polo pitch is sadly set aside for more sedate cricket matches. There are few more exhilarating ways to greet a new day than to saddle up and go for a leisurely canter along the beach, with the sounds of rolling surf and the measured thud of hooves mixing with the fresh dawn breeze. You do not have to be an accomplished equestrian either – both the Dusit's grooms and the horses they care for are used to novice riders, and will set the pace accordingly.

And you can set your own pace in the rest of this very well tended resort nestling outside Cha-Am, some 15 minutes from Hua Hin town. The equine theme runs throughout the hotel, with polo sticks for door handles, bellboys in jodhpurs and the horsebox-style corridors. Doubtless you could bed down on straw if you asked, but in fact the 300 rooms and suites are supremely comfortable, and all equipped with their own balcony.

Grab a sea-facer if you can, as the views down over the pools – each with a palm tree'd mini island in the centre – and out to sea is worth a 24-channel TV any day.

No real surprises that the resort's main drinking hole is called the Polo Bar, but there is a live band here playing 'the sound of surprise' with a good mixture of blues every night. On the food side, the royal Thai cuisine at Ban Benjarong by the lagoon is indeed fit for a king while San Marco serves up pizza and pasta in a casual terrace setting and fine continental cuisine is served at the Ascot – no hats required. And as something to look forward to, the resort's Devarana Spa opens in 2004.

Rates from: **US$ 101**
Star rating: ★ ★ ★ ★ ★
Bellhop rating: 🛎 🛎 🛎 🛎 🛎

Value:	8.43	Facilities:	9.00
Staff:	8.98	Restaurants:	8.77
Location:	8.67	Families:	7.55
Cleanliness:	8.93		

Dusit Resort Pattaya

240/2 Pattaya Beach Road, Pattaya City, Chonburi 20150, Thailand
T: +66 38 425 611 **F**: +66 38 428 239
http://www.asia-hotels.com/hotelinfo/Dusit_Resort_Pattaya/

Pattaya started its touristic life as a sun-n-sand, R&R for American troops from Vietnam, and it is similar diversions that keep hotels like the Dusit doing a thriving trade. What you get for your dollar is a smart, 462-roomer, set away (but not too far away) from the whirligig entertainments of the city centre at the northern end of the beach. Two swimming pools, a sports club, a fitness centre containing gym, sauna and steam rooms, one Chinese restaurant and two serving international fare make it all very user-friendly. The hotel is of modern design, so expect concrete and glass rather than anything too traditionally Thai. There again, as Pattaya almost rhymes with party, it is not as if anyone stays here to get away from it all.

Rates from: **US$ 83**
Star rating: ★ ★ ★ ★ ★
Bellhop rating: ◔ ◔ ◔ ◔ ½

Value:	8.25	Facilities:	8.65
Staff:	8.77	Restaurants:	8.18
Location:	8.50	Families:	7.15
Cleanliness:	8.87		

Dusit Thani Hotel

946 Rama IV Road, Silom, Bangkok 10500, Thailand
T: +66 2 236 0450 **F**: +66 2 236 6400
http://www.asia-hotels.com/hotelinfo/Dusit_Thani_Hotel/

The Dusit Thani Bangkok is a classic Thai city 5-star. Sandwiched between Rama IV and Sathorn Roads, its 500-plus sumptuous rooms and suites – decorated with silks and teak – dozen bars and restaurants, Devarana Spa (meaning 'garden in heaven'), outdoor swimming pool and golf driving range (plus resident professional) make it an ideal pied-à-terre. Certain facets deserve to be singled out. Deluxe Rooms rarely come larger than those here – 56 square metres, and with a 24-hour buttler service. The cocktail lounge Library 1918, overlooking the hotel gardens, evokes the elegance and ease of a bygone era. And the hexagonal outdoor swimming pool provides a sunny counterpoint to the state-of-the-art fitness club. In short, this is a hotel that is hard to fault.

Rates from: **US$ 101**
Star rating: ★ ★ ★ ★ ★
Bellhop rating: ◔ ◔ ◔ ◔ ½

Value:	8.23	Facilities:	8.43
Staff:	8.78	Restaurants:	8.51
Location:	8.61	Families:	6.90
Cleanliness:	8.72		

Grand Hyatt Erawan Bangkok

494 Rajdamri Road, Bangkok 10330, Thailand
T: +66 2 254 1234 **F:** +66 2 254 6308
http://www.asia-hotels.com/hotelinfo/Grand_Hyatt_Erawan_Bangkok/

The Grand Hyatt Erawan takes its cue from the street-level shrine at its northwestern corner, which was installed to ward off ill fortune during the original hotel's (Erawan Hotel) construction in the 1950s. Every day, thousands of supplicants pray that the deity Than Tao Mahaprom will grant their wishes, draping his golden image in garlands of marigolds and jasmine or paying the resident troupe of classical dancers to perform as a mark of gratitude. Right next to one of the city's most hectic intersections, the shrine is a picturesque haven of serenity. The same might also be said of the Grand Hyatt, which has adopted the Brahma god's personal vehicle, the three-headed Erawan elephant, as its logo.

Preening itself in the wake of an extensive renovation, the Hyatt's 387 rooms go the extra mile that executives on a marathon trip should appreciate. The glass-topped desk is right next to the window, and backed by a full-length mirror that not only makes the room look bigger but also reflects natural light. The decor is subtle, subdued and thoroughly functional with a convenient bedside control panel set against the lacquered coconut shell headboard.

Essentially spiritual, decidedly comfortable, eminently practical, the Grand Hyatt also offers up a rooftop heliport for high-flyers, three club floors, a smart fitness spa plus outdoor swimming pool and walkways to adjacent shopping centres and the mass transit system. Of the nine restaurants and bars, You & Mee is a refreshingly unusual concept, serving noodles and congee as an alternative to a full meal. But pride of place must go to Spasso, which masquerades as an Italian restaurant by day but come late evening transmogrifies into a high-decibel live music joint with more than a little boy-meets-girl thrown into the mix.

Rates from: **US$ 185**
Star rating: ★ ★ ★ ★ ★
Bellhop rating: 🛎 🛎 🛎 🛎 ½

Value:	7.98	Facilities:	8.53
Staff:	8.69	Restaurants:	8.52
Location:	8.77	Families:	6.95
Cleanliness:	8.82		

Holiday Inn Resort Phuket

52 Thaweewong Road, Patong Beach, Phuket 83150, Thailand
T: +66 76 340 608 **F**: +66 76 340 435
http://www.asia-hotels.com/hotelinfo/Holiday_Inn_Resort_Phuket/

Holiday Inn may seem an unusual choice as one of Asia's best hotels, but this Patong property is one of those rare beings – a resort that is all things to all people. To start with, it is not really one hotel but three. To the main building's 265 rooms add the new Busakorn Wing, with 104 studios, and then pile on 36 villa-style rooms. Given that the Holiday Inn is at the southern end of Patong Beach (somewhere you 'get into' rather than 'get away from' it all), that the resort is something of an oasis is a cause for celebration.

Executives might be tempted by the Holiday Inn's modest yet adequate business facilities – two conference rooms and a fully equipped business centre. Libertines will be happy to know it is only a short stagger to the adult playground called Soi Bangla. But this is primarily a resort that families can fit into seamlessly. So popular are the specially designed Kids' Suites (room within a room featuring bunkbeds, TV and Playstation) and Family Suites (connecting themed rooms) that they are difficult to book. The Busakorn Wing, with its own swimming pool, is preserved for those wishing to escape the din of children while the villa rooms have their own private swimming facilities, making an ideal retreat for couples. Guests can enjoy the two free-form pools with swim-up bars and shallow pools for kids. Even the most furiously sulky teenagers might deign to admit that Club 12+ – with Internet, movie lounge, MTV, games and books – is 'all right', while their younger siblings can be safely occupied in the Kids' Club. Which leaves parents as carefree as in pre-progeny days to kick back, partake of Sam's Steakhouse or the Pizzeria, dip into the 13-room (six specially for couples) Aspara Spa, or even make the trek to the beach just a minute walk away.

Rates from: US$ 62
Star rating: ★★★★
Bellhop rating: 👍👍👍👍 ½

Value:	8.42	Facilities:	8.37
Staff:	8.60	Restaurants:	8.28
Location:	8.85	Families:	7.84
Cleanliness:	8.48		

Hua Hin Marriott Resort & Spa

107/1 Phetkasem Beach Road, Hua Hin, Prachuabkirikhan 77110, Thailand
T: +66 32 511 881 **F:** +66 32 512 422
http://www.asia-hotels.com/hotelinfo/Hua_Hin_Marriott_Resort_And_Spa/

Some of the very best aspects of Thailand are packed into the Hua Hin Marriott. Backing up the 216 rooms and suites on seven storeys are a perfectly gorgeous swimming pool, with its low hanging thatched roof bar, a luxurious spa and the chance to pick up some Thai cooking tips on the hotel's specially run courses. Invigorating both spiritually and physically, the Marriott also lays out some gourmet surprises at its half-dozen restaurants and bars including the Steakhouse, serving grain-fed cuts from the United States and Australia. Equally attractive is the Garden Cafe – a show kitchen restaurant featuring live demonstration cooking where the dishes are whipped up before your very eyes. Theme nights are the most popular time to dine here, when Mongolian, Hawaiian or European cuisine is dished out by suitably garbed staff. Located on a spacious, airy verandah, the cafe is surrounded by beautiful landscaped gardens, making it a wonderful setting in which to eat any time.

All the Marriott's rooms are well appointed, with views of the gardens, pool or ocean, however the jacuzzi and roof garden of the Penthouse Suite – making all the usual assumptions about 'money' and 'no object' – should provide a really memorable stay.

This beachside haven also benefits from an excellent location; apart from the white and sandy, albeit narrow, beach, six championship golf courses are within driving range, including the Royal Hua Hin – Thailand's oldest golf course which teed off in 1924. The Marriott's Sand Trap bar – with nightly live entertainment – is the 19th hole of choice.

Younger guests can take advantage of the Chang Noi Kids' Club, with its playground, toys and puppet theatre. Kids should also enjoy excursions to the night market in Hua Hin – 15 minutes walk away – a blaze of lights, sounds and smells with some pretty neat shopping bargains too. All in all, this is a delightful escape for all the family.

Rates from: **US$ 88**
Star rating: ★ ★ ★ ★
Bellhop rating: ♎ ♎ ♎ ♎ ♎

Value:	8.32	Facilities:	8.94
Staff:	8.98	Restaurants:	8.66
Location:	8.81	Families:	7.51
Cleanliness:	9.06		

JW Marriott Hotel Bangkok

4 Sukhumvit Road, Soi 2, Bangkok 10110, Thailand
T: +66 2 656 7700 **F:** +66 2 656 7711
http://www.asia-hotels.com/hotelinfo/JW_Marriott_Hotel_Bangkok/

Over the years, the JW Marriott has garnered a select bunch of fans. Some guests rave about its 435 'exec-slick' rooms, specially designed for business travellers living out of a suitcase and off their laptops. Others refer to it as 'Sukhumvit Central' in praise of its convenient location. Still others wax lyrical about its outdoor pool and 6th-floor indoor spa. But a lot make little comment at all, the reason being they are fully occupied with the hotel's food and beverage operations, which they cite as the prime reason for staying here. Speaking of prime, the New York Steakhouse delivers quite outstanding cuts of beef, while the White Elephant is something of a misnomer, serving Thai food that is as delicious as it is authentic. And for an all-round, all-day, all-you-can-eat breakfast, lunch or dinner, call in at the Marriott Cafe buffet, winner of many local dining awards.

Rates from: **US$ 120**
Star rating: ★ ★ ★ ★ ★
Bellhop rating: 🛎 🛎 🛎 🛎 ½

Value:	8.15	Facilities:	8.33
Staff:	8.64	Restaurants:	8.32
Location:	8.34	Families:	6.89
Cleanliness:	8.74		

Kata Thani Hotel & Resort

14 Kata Noi Road, Karon, Phuket 83100, Thailand
T: +66 76 330 124 **F:** +66 76 330 127
http://www.asia-hotels.com/hotelinfo/Kata_Thani_Hotel_and_Beach_Resort/

It is huge. And it is old. And so what? Kata Thani – occupying almost all of a quiet cul-de-sac on pretty Kata Noi Beach – keeps pulling them in and with very good reason. One of the first large purpose-built resorts in Phuket, Kata Thani has kept itself up to the mark by regularly refurbishing its 530 rooms and public areas. Management has ensured that the beach is kept clear of the sort of cheapo snack shacks that tend to spring up around hotels. And the broad shady lawn that fronts the hotel and its four swimming pools, acting as a universal locale for sunbathing, massages and general games-playing, needs little in the way of maintenance. This is by no means a luxury deluxe resort, but it can be immensely enjoyable.

Rates from: **US$ 63**
Star rating: ★ ★ ★ ★
Bellhop rating: 🛎 🛎 🛎 🛎 🛎

Value:	8.81	Facilities:	8.81
Staff:	9.06	Restaurants:	8.59
Location:	8.72	Families:	7.66
Cleanliness:	9.16		

Laguna Beach Resort

323 Srisoonthorn Road, Bangtao Bay, Phuket 83110, Thailand
T: +66 76 324 352 **F:** +66 76 324 353
http://www.asia-hotels.com/hotelinfo/Laguna_Beach_Resort_/

Three cheers for this cheerful resort and its 252 generous balconied rooms and suites. The herd of elephants etched in stone around the swimming pool, the colourfully designed children's playground, the breezy informality of the Andaman Pool Bistro (one of six bars and restaurants), the proximity of the Angsana Spa with its 28 exclusive treatments – all contribute to one of the most relaxed and fun of the five Laguna Complex properties. There is a wealth of different recreational activities, including a 4-acre water park feature incorporating a 50-metre waterslide, three outdoor and one indoor tennis courts, golf driving range, squash, sailing, windsurfing or snorkelling lessons, and even a scuba session in the dive pool – all at no extra cost. Even the kids (4 to 12 year olds) have a full daily programme of outings and activities. It is no wonder everyone smiles here.

Rates from: **US$ 127**
Star rating: ★ ★ ★ ★ ★
Bellhop rating: ♙ ♙ ♙ ♙ ½

Value:	7.85	Facilities:	8.61
Staff:	8.46	Restaurants:	7.95
Location:	8.22	Families:	8.24
Cleanliness:	8.40		

Le Royal Meridien Bangkok

973 Ploenchit Road, Bangkok 10330, Thailand
T: +66 2 656 0444 **F:** +66 2 656 0555
http://www.asia-hotels.com/hotelinfo/Le_Royal_Meridien_Bangkok/

One of the city's newer 5-stars, Le Royal Meridien has seized the opportunity to cram its 37 floors with the latest and best. A Spiderman-style swoop from its uppermost storey would lead from its 360 degree rooftop panorama pool and spa down past 381 rooms and suites (including the club floors and lounge), restaurants serving Chinese, Japanese and Western cuisine and land up in the statuesque lobby with its massive Mother of Pearl inlaid columns and host of oil paintings depicting rural Thai scenes. Swish? Certainly. Business-friendly? More so. Even bottom-of-the-rack Deluxe Rooms encompass 45 square metres, blackout curtains for the jet-lagged, dataports, voicemail and everything else scurrying executives should need. And as it is right on Ploenchit within a block of the Chidiom Skytrain station, it could hardly be better located.

Rates from: **US$ 128**
Star rating: ★ ★ ★ ★ ★
Bellhop rating: ♙ ♙ ♙ ♙ ½

Value:	8.12	Facilities:	8.36
Staff:	8.64	Restaurants:	8.05
Location:	8.87	Families:	6.86
Cleanliness:	8.76		

Le Royal Meridien Baan Taling Ngam

295 Moo 3, Taling Ngam Beach, Koh Samui, Suratthani 84140, Thailand
T: +66 77 423 019 **F:** +66 76 423 220
http://www.asia-hotels.com/hotelinfo/Le_Royal_Meridien_Baan_Taling_Ngam/

With only a hint of imagination, it might seem as if Baan Taling Ngam is suspended in mid-air rather than built on a hillside overlooking the Gulf of Thailand and on out toward the aquatic splendours of Ang Thong Marine Park. And gravity disappears altogether in the infinity pool, its lip gazing down on to the surrounding coconut groves and village huts. Very much removed from the frenetic party atmosphere on the east of Koh Samui, Baan Taling Ngam is surely one of the most lovely resorts on the whole of the island. Electric buggies swoop and wheel around the resort's vertiginous slopes like circling kites, from the uppermost of its 72 rooms, suites and villas – elegant yet simple with exotic Thai tinges – down past the main building to the secluded sandy shore, seaside restaurant and beach villas.

The happy result of the extreme topography is to divide the resort into secluded sections. The villas – with outsize sliding glass doors and magnificent balconies – are clustered together around their own swimming pool,

perfect for a private early-morning or late-night dip. The beach is shaded by the arching trunks of postcard-perfect coconut palms, where you can launch into soccer or volleyball games, venture out to the coral reef for a bit of snorkelling, or simply put in some serious work on a tan. And the

ideal chill-out hang-out has to be the cushioned, open-sided sala that stands slightly away from the pool.

Come evening, guests tend to congregate in the Verandah Bar, just by the lobby where a Thai lady will be sitting cross-legged patiently carving soap or tropical fruit into intricate, beautiful shapes. Transforming the mundane is something of an art form here, and it only takes a short while before you begin to appreciate that.

Rates from: **US$ 185**
Star rating: ★ ★ ★ ★ ★
Bellhop rating: 🛎 🛎 🛎 🛎 🛎

Value:	8.48	Facilities:	9.17
Staff:	9.33	Restaurants:	8.95
Location:	8.77	Families:	7.29
Cleanliness:	9.41		

Le Meridien Phuket Beach Resort

8/5 Moo 1, Tambon Karon, Amphur Muang, Phuket 83100, Thailand
T: +66 76 340 480 **F**: +66 76 340 479
http://www.asia-hotels.com/hotelinfo/Le_Meridien_Phuket_Beach_Resort/

The Meridien got lucky. With a whole private cove to itself, midway along but well below the road running between Karon and Patong, it is neatly secluded. This cosmopolitan resort's 470 rooms are popular with European families, and the comparison that most readily suggests itself is a Mediterranean cruise liner beached on a tropical shore.

While all beaches in Thailand are open to the public, the strand here is not really accessible except via the hotel. So you can hunker down on your lounger knowing that you will not be bothered by hawkers or similar types constantly badgering you to take out a jet ski. Steeply wooded hills flank the beach so there are no ramshackle cafes, and you are left to enjoy sun and sea in peace.

The beach is backed by an extensive swimming pool that stretches practically across the width of the entire hotel. There is also a host of other sporting and recreational facilities on daily offer, and the cruise leitmotif is emphasised by regular themed buffet dinner nights – Treasure Island plus piratical high jinks or maybe a Salsa Carnival with music to match. Sporting types can indulge themselves on two hard and two grass tennis courts, two squash courts, a rock climbing wall, a golf practice range or the putting green, and archery is a further option. Instructors are available, as well as what are termed 'hitting partners'. No question about it, this is primarily a resort for vacationers who want to join in the fun rather than take a quiet break.

Of course, it is not all 100 per cent non-stop action here. The Massage Centre provides a range of massage, facials and body treatments, and you can also indulge at the hotel's 10 restaurants and bars. Le Phuket's offers Mediterranean dishes and fresh seafood from the Andaman Sea, while Ariake, a casual Japanese restaurant, features a sushi bar and teppanyaki table. Portofino, the Italian restaurant, offers traditional cuisine with home-made pizza, fresh pasta and ice cream. Le Cafe Fleuri – with its hand-painted murals in soft pastel shades, exotic cane chairs and views of the hotel lagoon – serves a large selection of Asian and European dishes.

Rates from: **US$ 140**
Star rating: ★ ★ ★ ★ ★
Bellhop rating: 🛎🛎🛎🛎 ½

Value:	8.00	Facilities:	8.81
Staff:	8.92	Restaurants:	8.68
Location:	8.84	Families:	7.03
Cleanliness:	8.94		

Majestic Suites Hotel

110-110/1 (Between Soi 4-6) Sukhumvit Road, Klongtoey, Bangkok 10110, Thailand
T: +66 2 656 8220 **F**: +66 2 656 8201
http://www.asia-hotels.com/hotelinfo/Majestic_Suites_/

Small but perfectly formed sums up the Majestic Suites. You do not come here for vast rooms with panoramic vistas, extensive dining options or a wealth of recreational pursuits. Instead, what you get for an incredibly reasonable rate is perfectly functional bed and board, but without the slightly faded aura that sometimes attaches itself to lower-end hotels. The 55 rooms are spick and span, you may not be able to swing a cat in the bathrooms but you can shave and shower etc in perfect comfort. At the bachelor end of the scale, the Single Studios are not much more than a room with a bed, however the Deluxe Rooms are a tad more spacious and definitely couple-friendly. Whatever the size of the room, you can count on a safe, fridge, satellite TV, alarm clock and all secured behind a door with a microchip transponder locking system. Even the corridors, narrow though they may be, are hung with framed prints. Especially worthy of mention are the staff, from the front office team who meet and greet, to the housekeepers who will appear at the drop of a hat in the unlikely event of problems needing to be fixed – something that hotels with more stars and more zeroes on their prices would do well to emulate.

The one drawback worth mentioning is that the lift can be a trifle slow, so book a room on the lower floors if possible.

There are few complaints about the lobby bar and coffee shop, and the whole of Sukhumvit plus the Nana Skytrain station lies right outside the main door.

Single gentlemen may be interested to know that the triple-decker den of propinquity, Nana Plaza, lies right at the back of the hotel. Note that the single room and breakfast package means one breakfast only.

Rates from: **US$ 23**
Star rating: ★ ★
Bellhop rating: 👍👍👍👍

Value:	8.71	Facilities:	7.43
Staff:	8.48	Restaurants:	6.86
Location:	8.81	Families:	3.67
Cleanliness:	8.95		

Marina Phuket

47 Karon Road, Karon Beach, Phuket 83100, Thailand
T: +66 76 330 493 **F:** +66 76 330 516
http://www.asia-hotels.com/hotelinfo/Marina_Phuket/

Formerly known as Marina Cottage, it is a relief to record that the only thing that has changed about this lovely cliff-top resort is the name. The bougainvillea and frangipani strewn grounds could well be a formal botanical gardens, the accommodation is delightful, welcoming wooden cabins each with their own verandah, and the trip to the signature seaside restaurant On The Rock along raised walkways through the jungle is an adventure in itself. Equally attractive, the open-air Thai restaurant, Sala Thai, stands next to the resort's small swimming pool, surrounded by trees and more of the lush greenery that is Marina's hallmark. The beach is about five minutes walk out of the resort, and the commercial 'delights' of Kata Town a similar stretch in the opposite direction. Marina Phuket does raise a single pertinent question – why are there not more hotels like this?

Rates from: **US$ 83**
Star rating: ★ ★ ★
Bellhop rating: 🖑🖑🖑🖑🖑

Value:	8.64	Facilities:	8.14
Staff:	9.04	Restaurants:	8.54
Location:	9.14	Families:	6.75
Cleanliness:	9.07		

Novotel Coralia Resort Phuket

282 Pra-Baramee Road, Talung Patong, Amphur Muang, Phuket 83150, Thailand
T: +66 76 342 777 **F:** +66 76 342 168
http://www.asia-hotels.com/hotelinfo/Novotel_Coralia_Phuket_Resort/

Of Patong, but not in it, the Novotel stands apart from Phuket's most high-density, high-activity tourist centre. Set on a hill at the very northern end of the beach, it presents guests with a unique twin opportunity. Plunge down the hill for shopping, R&R or to join the ranks of cerise, bikini'd sardines that carpet the sands from dawn till dusk; or simply gaze down on the town from the sanctuary of the Novotel's triple-decker swimming pool, the social hub of this thoroughly amenable and smart property. Designed Thai style and sensitively landscaped, the Novotel hosts 215 guestrooms, each with its own balcony – a mini private retreat within a retreat. Of the five restaurants and bars to graze, cognoscenti pick Le Mirage poolside bar for an aptly named sundowner looking out over the Andaman Sea.

Rates from: **US$ 63**
Star rating: ★ ★ ★ ★
Bellhop rating: 🖑🖑🖑🖑 ½

Value:	8.37	Facilities:	8.54
Staff:	8.80	Restaurants:	7.99
Location:	8.43	Families:	6.85
Cleanliness:	8.83		

The Oriental Bangkok

48 Oriental Avenue, Bangkok 10500, Thailand
T: +66 2 659 9000 **F:** +66 2 659 0000
http://www.asia-hotels.com/hotelinfo/Oriental_The/

The Oriental is not so much a hotel as a very well-appointed museum. More than a century and a quarter old, presided over by the legendary Kurt Wachtveitl for the past 34 years, it is the Far Eastern must-stay for numerous Who's Who entries, venerated for its double-plus plush spa and riverine purlieus. Cock your ear in the lobby near the sign proscribing backpackers (it might as well say riff-raff) and you can practically hear the sacred cows mooing. Let it be said that there are other, newer, less snooty places along the River of Kings where you can sleep and eat just as well as at the Oriental. But this one-time seamen's hostel turned jewel in the crown of accommodation has charisma in spades.

The bulk of the hotel's 393 rooms and suites are in the recently renovated River Wing; the Garden Wing's split-level suites are rather more attractive, however cream of the crop is the Authors' Wing, with four rooms named for former guests Conrad, Maugham, Michener and Coward. Afternoon tea in the ground-floor Authors' Lounge, which is open to the public, is something of an event.

Indeed, there is no such thing as mundane eating and/or drinking anywhere in the Oriental. Weather permitting – and it usually is –

breakfast should be taken at the Riverside Terrace, with a characteristic cavalcade of traffic steaming back and forth along the Chao Praya. Alternatively, the Verandah has both indoor and outdoor seating and a slightly more secluded feel. Just outside the hotel, but still a part of it, the China House is a beautifully restored and decorated colonial-style residence offering classic Cantonese cuisine and other regional food from China prepared by leading Chinese chefs, with the highlight being the dim sum lunches. As well as the main restaurant, there are also six private dining rooms here for a more intimate meal. Or you can spend a long lunch picking your way around the magnificent seafood buffet in Lord Jim's.

Come cocktail hour, the sound of surprise emanates from the Bamboo Bar when the jazz band strikes up – an excellent precursor to dinner. Very much top of the bill is Le Normandie, with splendid French cuisine, impeccable service and superb wines from an exceptional cellar.

Rather less formal, Ciao's pizzas and other Italian dishes go down well on the marble terrace beside the lush tropical gardens. Or you can sail away on a veritable slice of the Oriental, dining on northern Thai-style food aboard the hotel's own golden teakwood rice barge 'Maeyanang' – an evening that is as memorable for the night-time river sights as it is for dinner.

But without doubt the

Oriental's ace in the hole is its spa, situated across the river next to the Sala Rim Naam Thai restaurant and the hotel's sporting facilities. Its splendid antique style, with 14 private treatment suites, contrasts gently with ultra-modern treatments like hydrotherapy, yet also blends with the traditional curative Thai massage. Catch the shuttle boat across and submit to the tender ministrations of the therapists for an hour, or rather longer, and you return to the hotel almost as if you had been reborn.

The Oriental itself has undergone a number of reincarnations, consistently winning awards and high praise. If nothing else, it deserves a visit from everyone at least once – but no riff-raff please.

Rates from: **US$ 189**

Star rating: ★ ★ ★ ★ ★

Bellhop rating: 👍 👍 👍 👍 👍

Value:	8.04	Facilities:	8.81
Staff:	9.13	Restaurants:	8.88
Location:	8.56	Families:	6.95
Cleanliness:	9.14		

Pan Pacific Bangkok

952 Rama IV Road, Suriyawongse, Bangrak, Bangkok 10500, Thailand
T: +66 2 632 9000 **F:** +66 2 632 9001
http://www.asia-hotels.com/hotelinfo/Pan_Pacific_Bangkok_The/

It is not difficult to like the Pan Pacific. Halfway between Mr Thompson's silk emporium and the green pleasures of Lumphini Park, with a rooftop swimming pool that looks like the setting for a Roman orgy and its 235 rooms spread over the uppermost tiers of the Ramaland Building, this is somewhere you can check into – and spend considerable time in – with consummate ease. Eminently suitable for road warriors (close to Rama IV business district) or simply those dallying among frenetic Bangkok's multifarious pleasures (metres from the Skytrain and Silom Road), the Pan Pacific doubles as an ideal base for sallying outside or as a haven to relax and recuperate within. Especially noteworthy is the number of Japanese guests tucking in among the five distinctive sections (sushi, robatayki, teppanyaki, a la carte and the traditional tatami rooms) of the Keyaki restaurant, one of five food and beverage outlets.

Rates from: US$ 110
Star rating: ★ ★ ★ ★ ★
Bellhop rating: 👍 👍 👍 👍 ½

Value:	8.01	Facilities:	8.49
Staff:	8.67	Restaurants:	8.33
Location:	8.72	Families:	6.21
Cleanliness:	8.88		

Pathumwan Princess Hotel

444 Phayathai Road, Wang Mai, Pathumwan, Bangkok 10330, Thailand
T: +66 2 216 3700 **F:** +66 2 216 3730
http://www.asia-hotels.com/hotelinfo/Pathumwan_Princess/

Take the side exit from the Pathumwan's reception area and you are plunged into that retail Valhalla, Mahboonkrong. Walk across the footbridge and Siam Square is at your feet. Cross the road via the Skytrain station and you are surrounded by the Siam Centre. Jim Thompson's House is just around the corner. If the message is not clear yet, the Dusit Group's Pathumwan Princess should appeal primarily to leisure travellers, and to their primal instincts for shopping. The 462 rooms are comfortable, adequately sized, and many look out over Chulalongkorn campus. European, Thai, Japanese and Korean tastes are individually catered for in the hotel's restaurants. But the hotel's trump card is the string quartet playing a soft welcome in the lobby as you shoulder open the doors with an armful of bags after a hard day flattening the credit card.

Rates from: US$ 68
Star rating: ★ ★ ★ ★
Bellhop rating: 👍 👍 👍 👍 ½

Value:	8.20	Facilities:	8.28
Staff:	8.27	Restaurants:	7.96
Location:	9.16	Families:	6.93
Cleanliness:	8.49		

The Peninsula Bangkok

333 Charoennakorn Road, Klongsan, Bangkok 10600, Thailand
T: +66 2 861 2888 **F:** +66 2 861 1112
http://www.asia-hotels.com/hotelinfo/Peninsula_Bangkok/

Search in vain for the club floor at the Peninsula on the west bank of the Chao Praya. There is not one. But it is safe to say that all 39 storeys and 370 rooms of this exceptional, W-shaped building that is blended hi-tech with high art are like a club floor to themselves, standards of service and accommodation that other properties can only think of emulating and all with river views and a very affordable price tag.

First-time guests should try out the following regimen on their first day, about half an hour before dusk, and repeat it as often as necessary. Broach your duty free, or call room service for a suitable whistle wetter. Illuminate the 'Do Not Disturb' sign. For the sheer hell of it, close the curtains using the electronic control system, then open them again. Fiddle with the mood lighting until it suits. Reach for the CD player and make sure it is playing something that suits both your and the lighting's mood. Add salts or foam to the marble bathtub, and fill to the brim,

ignoring for the present the multi-channelled TV set into the wall. Of course, there is a valet to do all this for you if you are feeling especially pamper-deficient. Should you be lucky (or pecunious) enough to be staying in one of the themed suites, you can look down on the famed regal river and angelic city with the suds up to your neck. The room's outdoor temperature and humidity indicator will show you what the benighted millions below are having to put up with. Sit back, enjoy and just try not to look overly smug.

When the Peninsula opened in 1998, the wiseacres said it was 'on the wrong side' and prophesied an early demise. They have since been proved wrong by legions of guests who have been all too happy to catch the shuttle boat across the Chao Praya and make free with the hotel's infinite capacity to surprise. Part of one of Asia's most respected and venerable hotel chains, it is not in the least bit staid or stuffy. Take

Jesters, whose Technicolor funk decor and Pacific Rim cuisine are served up in a split-level locale that is off-limits to under-12s. Or the outdoor swimming pool, which is no rectangular watering hole, but rather a 60-metre, triple-tiered channel that is reminiscent of a (clean!) Bangkok klong flanked by sundeck areas and salas.

In the face of such cutting-edge opulence, the Peninsula might not seem to automatically suggest itself to the executive guest, however its rooms come pre-loaded with discreetly placed fax machines with personal numbers, dataports, dual-voltage sockets and double-lined telephones. More than 400 guests can be fitted into the pillarless Sakuntala Ballroom, and there are four breakout rooms right next to it. Deep-pocketed CEOs and their ilk, if they do not fancy the trip to the airport in a Rolls-Royce Silver Spur or a Mercedes-Benz S-class 280, can hop into a helicopter via the classic aviation lounge, the Paribatra Lounge, on the 37th floor.

Nit-pickers might say that the Peninsula lacks a proper, full monty spa (although herbal massages and aromatherapy are currently both available) and a dedicated Thai restaurant – both staples of the country's hospitality, and therefore frowning if not actually glaring omissions. Rest assured, quibblers, plans are in hand to introduce both within the next year or so.

Rates from: US$ 140
Star rating: ★ ★ ★ ★ ★
Bellhop rating: 🔔 🔔 🔔 🔔 🔔

Value:	8.68	Facilities:	8.90
Staff:	8.92	Restaurants:	8.44
Location:	8.09	Families:	6.38
Cleanliness:	9.19		

Poppies Samui

28/1 Moo 3, Chaweng-Suratthani, Koh Samui 84320, Thailand
T: +66 77 422 419 **F:** +66 77 422 420
http://www.asia-hotels.com/hotelinfo/Poppies_Samui/

Following the rash of guesthouses that sprang up to cater to the backpack rat pack who 'discovered' Koh Samui in the 1970s, what the island really needed was a boutique hotel. It got it in the shape of Poppies, a sister property to its fine namesake in Bali.

Two dozen small but pretty Thai-style cottages have been woven into the scenery at the end of Chaweng Beach, surrounded by colourful and exotic gardens, with meandering paths, bubbling streams, fishponds, teak bridges and waterfalls. The layout ensures that each cottage enjoys privacy from the others, and the open bathrooms – with shower, sunken marble tub and a mini garden – act as a private sanctum. Teak and the finest Thai cotton and silk lend an intimate feel to the interiors, which are in effect small suites with separate sleeping and living areas as well as an outside terrace. Once ensconced here, it is easy to fall into the highly pleasurable trap of not venturing out again.

Poppies has its own spa, the free-form swimming pool is surrounded by natural rocks and the jacuzzi overlooks the sea. And between the pool and the beach, Poppies' restaurant offers fresh Californian and Thai cuisine, either alfresco or in the shade of an Ayuthya-style teak pavilion. Dining here on the nights when the moon is full – and some months it takes on the proportions of Halley's Comet – is an unforgettably beautiful experience.

Poppies has been run for the past four years by hotel veteran Michael Holehouse and his wife, Susan, who – together with their 'family' of 87 long-serving staff – treat the place like an extension of their own home and their guests accordingly. If there is a better recipe for a really good hotel, it has yet to be invented.

Rates from: **US$ 147**
Star rating: ★★★★
Bellhop rating: 🛎🛎🛎🛎 ½

Value:	7.88	Facilities:	7.67
Staff:	8.46	Restaurants:	8.38
Location:	8.63	Families:	6.25
Cleanliness:	8.71		

Rayavadee

214 Moo 2, Tambol Ao-Nang, Amphur Muang, Krabi 81000, Thailand
T: 66 75 620 740 **F:** +66 75 620 630
http://www.asia-hotels.com/hotelinfo/Rayavadee_Premier_Resort/

A mythical princess inhabits the cave at the base of the soaring limestone cliff at the end of Phra Nang Beach. But it would not exactly be lèse majesté to wonder if sometimes she does not cast an envious eye from her slightly damp grotto – furnished only with an altar and piles of fisherfolks' offerings – at the Rayavadee next door.

Not that the resort is in any way conspicuous. So designed that not a single palm tree was cut down during construction, the Rayavadee is barely visible from the sea.

Surely the best way to arrive here would be to pitch up on the white and super-soft sand of Railey Beach by long tail and make your way across the strand into the delirious haven of the resort itself. In fact, there is no road here, so a seaborne arrival at the resort's jetty is the most usual way in.

The Rayavadee is not exactly cheap, but you do get top of the range for top dollar. Some 100 recently renovated pavilions and villas are scattered about the resort's 26 acres. Each is hexagonal

in shape, and the glass walls of the living room create a flowing space to the garden outside; upstairs the high domed ceiling allows the bedroom more breathing space, and there is an ensuite and very romantic bathroom with 2-person bathtub. The more luxurious accommodation comes with jacuzzis or hydropools attached, while the 2-bedroomed Rayavadee Villa occupies its own private compound.

The place to eat at Rayavadee is the beachside Krua Pharanang which specialises in Thai and seafood. Jet skis are banned in Krabi, so there is no noise to interrupt the lingering repasts that the location almost demands. And at low tide, you can walk straight out of the restaurant and wade across to a couple of uninhabited islands in the bay. This is Mother Nature at her best.

Rates from: **US$ 476**
Star rating: ★ ★ ★ ★ ★
Bellhop rating: 👍 👍 👍 👍 👍

Value:	8.12	Facilities:	9.23
Staff:	9.40	Restaurants:	9.23
Location:	9.69	Families:	7.25
Cleanliness:	9.44		

The Regent Bangkok

155 Rajadamri Road, Lumpinee Patunwan, Bangkok 10330, Thailand
T: +66 2 251 6127 **F**: +66 2 253 9195
http://www.asia-hotels.com/hotelinfo/Regent_Bangkok_The/

wealth of unusual ideas that it does not hesitate to share with its guests. Next to the Skytrain and opposite a 9-hole golf course, the Regent's 356 rooms (including 37 suites) each feature hand-painted silk murals and digital telephones, blending the best of Thai art with modern technology.

Kick back over a drink at Aqua, the semi-outdoor bar in the Regent's shopping arcade, and before long a brace of Mandarin ducks will be wandering along from the nearby pond to cadge a few peanuts. Stroll over to the concierge and pick his brains for a tailor-made shopping itinerary. Or smack your lips over the celadon pots of sauces from the Spice Market restaurant that are on sale at the Regent Shop. Natural, original, inspirational, this hotel has a

Rates from: **US$ 185**
Star rating: ★ ★ ★ ★ ★
Bellhop rating: 🐠🐠🐠🐠 ½

Value:	8.08	Facilities:	8.49
Staff:	8.82	Restaurants:	8.71
Location:	8.78	Families:	6.91
Cleanliness:	8.94		

The Regent Cha-Am Beach Resort

849/21 Petchkasem Road, Cha-Am, Petchburi 76120, Thailand
T: +66 32 451 240 **F**: +66 32 471 491
http://www.asia-hotels.com/hotelinfo/Am_Beach_Resort/

with both European package travellers and Bangkok weekenders, as might be expected from a resort of this size, there is a wealth of recreation on offer, from the quartet of plexi-paved tennis courts to the trio of swimming pools, two squash courts as well as the numerous golf courses on the doorstep.

Back in the 1920s, the King of Thailand built himself a seaside palace along the beach here, naming it Klai Kangwon, or 'Far From Worries'. Hotels and condominiums are the most prominent structures here nowadays, but Cha-Am – quieter, more gentle even than its neighbour Hua Hin – is still pretty hassle free. This huge resort is in fact made up of three hotels – the Regent Main Wing, the Regency Wing and the Regent Chalet – totalling 700-plus rooms. Popular

Rates from: **US$ 57**
Star rating: ★ ★ ★ ★
Bellhop rating: 🐠🐠🐠🐠🐠

Value:	8.46	Facilities:	8.82
Staff:	9.18	Restaurants:	8.57
Location:	8.61	Families:	7.61
Cleanliness:	8.96		

The Regent Chiang Mai Resort & Spa

Mae Rim-Samoeng Old Road, Mae Rim, Chiang Mai 50180, Thailand
T: +66 53 298 181 **F**: +66 53 298 189
http://www.asia-hotels.com/hotelinfo/Regent_Resort_Chiang_Mai/

The north of Thailand conjures up visions of hill tribes in ethnic dress, elephant treks through dense jungle, antiques, art and culture. All of these come together in an ethos brilliantly celebrated by the Regent, where 80 Lanna-style pavilions merge into the paddy fields and groves of trees in a picturesque river valley outside the kingdom's second city.

The pavilions are more like mini

palaces than anything else. The regular suites are some 70 metres square, filled with locally made furniture and textiles, and with a luxurious bathroom and private verandah-style sala that simply invite lazing in. The largest of the Residence Suites covers nearly 350 square metres, encompassing three bedrooms, lounge, dining room, kitchen and a live-in Mae Baan or housekeeper, who is on 24-hour call. The air is soft and fresh here, and there is little noise to disturb the idyllic panoramas that lie outside every pavilion.

The main restaurant, Sala Mae Rim, provides similar vistas. With its high gabled ceiling and exposed beams, rich tapestries, crafted teak tables and cane-backed colonial dining chairs, the room exudes a sophisticated but rustic atmosphere. This then is the place to dine on northern Thai cuisine, and signature dishes such as Yum Hua Plee (banana blossom salad), Kaow Soi Kai – Chiang Mai's own version of curry noodle soup with chicken – or Thom Som, a robustly flavoured sea bass cooked in young tamarind leaves and coriander root.

For a more casual snack, afternoon tea or a couple of drinks in the evening, the open pavilion-style Elephant Bar is the perfect place to relax after an active day of sightseeing and elephant trekking.

Rest and recuperation being the predominant theme here, guests can pick up a few tips from the resident tennis professional, work out on the strength and cardiovascular equipment in the fitness centre, shoot a few holes in one of the quartet of world-class golf courses nearby or join the newly opened Cooking School for a course on the art of Thai cuisine. And if that seems overly active, the Lanna Spa provides everything from couples' tropical rain shower massage tables to its own beauty salon. No mere adjunct to the hotel's leisure facilities, the Regent has really gone to town on making the spa one of the resort's major attractions. It is housed in a magnificent 3-storey building, covering some 900 square metres and practically camouflaged by the surrounding lush tropical vegetation. Its seven treatment suites are elegant and exceedingly spacious, offering total privacy for individuals or couples. You can shower outdoors in a secluded garden, or gently poach yourself with a variety of herbs inside a steam room, while there are also romantic tubs quite big enough for two where you can soak alfresco. The individual changing areas, showers and bathroom facilities in all the treatment suites grant extra privacy.

The Spa offers an eclectic range of treatments that make extensive use of Thai herbs and aromatic oils, sourced from their traditional rural origins. Most indulgent of all are the 'Spa Rituals', lasting three or four hours, which combine herbal steam with massage, body scrubs, wraps, facial treatments, and hair care – total pampering packages for the body, mind and spirit.

And as a souvenir both of your time in the spa and at the Regent you can always purchase any of the range of aromatic oils, essential oils, soaps, candles, incense – or even the spa robes and slippers.

Rates from: **US$ 431**
Star rating: ★★★★★
Bellhop rating: ♭♭♭♭♭

Value:	7.95	Facilities:	9.08
Staff:	9.47	Restaurants:	8.69
Location:	8.84	Families:	6.52
Cleanliness:	9.47		

Royal Cliff Beach Resort

353 Phra Tamnuk Road, Pattaya, Cholburi 20150, Thailand
T: +66 38 250 421 **F:** +66 38 250 511
http://www.asia-hotels.com/hotelinfo/Royal_Cliff_Beach_Resort/

One of the first major hotels to open in Thailand's first proper beach resort, the Royal Cliff has expanded considerably over the years. Pattaya markets itself as 'a city by the sea' and if that is so then the Royal Cliff is a city within a city. The original Royal Cliff Terrace started operation in 1973 with 88 suites; it was joined a year later by the Beach Hotel's 527 rooms; 85 more suites were added with the inauguration of the Royal Wing & Spa in 1986 and – with the incentive and conference market in mind – the 372-room Grand welcomed its first guests six years later. With the emphasis very much

on quantity, this is by no means a classic Thai hideaway, rather a full-on, full of fun resort city spread over 64 acres. Just visiting the private beach, three ballrooms, four bars, five swimming pools, six tennis courts, 10 restaurants, 15 meeting rooms and giving the Cliff Spa a try could take up the best part of several days.

A huge swathe of different guests come to enjoy this mini metropolis, from conventioneers congregating in the adjacent PEACH (Pattaya Exhibition and Convention Hall) to families who are happy to lap up the water sports. Picking where you stay here

is fairly crucial. There are a dozen different room types, from the Beach Hotel's themed suites decorated in different styles, such as Japanese Bonsai or Indian Maharajah, to the Terrace's mini suites with a step-up lounge area and 2-bedroom Family Suites. The Grand's Executive Rooms all have a sea-facing balcony with loungers and walk-in shower, while the Royal's Presidential Suites contain three bedrooms with ensuite bath, a private butler and a beach sala. Mounted on its own headland with views over the beach and the city, this hotel is pretty much a microcosm of Pattaya.

Rates from: **US$ 66**
Star rating: ★ ★ ★ ★ ★
Bellhop rating: 🛎 🛎 🛎 🛎 ½

Value:	7.88	Facilities:	8.39
Staff:	8.32	Restaurants:	8.25
Location:	8.13	Families:	7.28
Cleanliness:	8.47		

Royal Orchid Sheraton Hotel & Towers

2 Captain Bush Lane, New Road, Siphya, Bangkok 10500, Thailand
T: +66 2 266 0123 **F:** +66 2 236 8320
http://www.asia-hotels.com/hotelinfo/Royal_Orchid_Sheraton_Hotel_and_Towers/

There is a lot to say about the 28-storey, dual lobbied 740-room Royal Orchid Sheraton. Note its brace of ballrooms and pair of swimming pools; remark the dedicated conference area on the second floor with 16 tech-happy function rooms; technophobes will heave a sigh of relief over the specialised staff who are pre-programmed to sort out laptop problems and even to buy IT accessories from nearby malls; and no one has any quarrel with the delicious temptations served up in the 8-room Mandara Spa or the six restaurants and bars.

But where this hotel really scores is in its design. Opened two decades ago, the architects had the forethought and sheer common sense to make the building Y-shaped, so each chic room looks out over the Chao Praya River. Recent renovations have brought the hotel up to date, making it a most charming place to stay in Bangkok.

Rates from: **US$ 136**
Star rating: ★ ★ ★ ★ ★
Bellhop rating: 🛎 🛎 🛎 🛎 ½

Value:	8.02	Facilities:	8.48
Staff:	8.63	Restaurants:	8.33
Location:	8.48	Families:	6.37
Cleanliness:	8.76		

Santiburi Dusit Resort & Spa

12/12 Moo 1, Tambol Mae Nam, Amphur Koh Samui, Suratthani 84330, Thailand
T: +66 77 425 031 **F:** +66 77 425 040
http://www.asia-hotels.com/hotelinfo/Santiburi_Dusit_Resort/

The 23 rolling acres around the Santiburi's 14 suites and 57 deluxe villas are not merely for show, for they include spice, vegetable and herb gardens whose produce goes into the resort's home-made Thai cuisine, teas and even ice cream. It is not just the food that receives such total attention to detail here. Bordered by Mae Nam Beach (15 kilometres from the main strip at Chewang), the Santiburi has been painstakingly designed using Thai architecture as its inspiration. The rooms – which also hold modern state-of-the-art amenities like CD players – feature shining wooden floors, opulent Siamese furnishings and a private terrace overlooking the beach and grounds. To get the optimum picture of this amazing resort, hop aboard the Santiburi's own 59-year-old sailing junk, Tangaroa, and drop anchor offshore for a leisurely drink or sunset dinner.

Rates from: **US$ 228**
Star rating: ★ ★ ★ ★ ★
Bellhop rating: 🛎 🛎 🛎 🛎 ½

Value:	7.59	Facilities:	8.53
Staff:	8.85	Restaurants:	8.09
Location:	8.53	Families:	7.29
Cleanliness:	8.82		

Shangri-La Hotel Bangkok

89 Soi Wat Suan Plu, New Road, Bangrak, Bangkok 10500, Thailand
T: +66 2 236 7777 **F**: +66 2 236 8579
http://www.asia-hotels.com/hotelinfo/ShangriLa_Hotel_Bangkok/

If there is one thing everyone should do at the Shangri-La, it is to take an early breakfast at the Krungthep Wing's Fountain Cafe. Not that the scrambled eggs, muffins or miso soup on the buffet are so much better than anywhere else, but the tables stand right next to the Chao Praya River, in earshot of the longtails' throaty bellows and in plain view of this charismatic, aquatic super highway.

The Shangri-La is one of the largest hotels in Bangkok with 839 rooms split between two separate wings. It is rather less pricey than its neighbour, the Oriental, but with the same river vistas and much closer to the Skytrain. If your budget will stretch, grab one of the 21 River View Suites at the southern end of the Shangri-La Wing which all have an outside terrace to look down on the river traffic.

Rates from: **US$ 134**
Star rating: ★ ★ ★ ★ ★
Bellhop rating: 🛎 🛎 🛎 🛎 ½

Value:	8.15	Facilities:	8.80
Staff:	8.91	Restaurants:	8.66
Location:	8.60	Families:	6.75
Cleanliness:	9.00		

Sheraton Grande Sukhumvit

250 Sukhumvit Road, Bangkok 10110, Thailand
T: +66 2 653 0333 **F**: +66 2 653 0400
http://www.asia-hotels.com/hotelinfo/Sheraton_Grande_Sukhumvit/

The 33-storey Sheraton Grande deserves to be recognised as a truly international hotel. Hong Kong-Chinese architects took Thai culture and artistic heritage as their inspiration. A British general manager of much repute and with 30 years experience of the hospitality industry runs a very tight ship. And guests from all over the world come to dine at Rossini's, the signature Italian restaurant, and revel in this thoroughly successful 'oasis of tranquillity'. As well as the sort of 5-star comforts and facilities that are automatic in a 445-room deluxe property, a couple of extras stand out. The 1st-floor library is exceptionally well stocked, the personal butler service is on hand 24/7, the unduly masochistic can arrange for one-on-one training at the Grande Spa and Fitness Club, while Riva's brasserie is one of the hottest nightspots on the Sukhumvit Strip.

Rates from: **US$ 127**
Star rating: ★ ★ ★ ★ ★
Bellhop rating: 🛎 🛎 🛎 🛎 ½

Value:	8.00	Facilities:	8.74
Staff:	8.92	Restaurants:	8.52
Location:	8.83	Families:	6.49
Cleanliness:	9.03		

Sheraton Grande Laguna Phuket

10 Moo 4, Cherng Ta-Lay, Talang, Phuket 83110, Thailand
T: +66 76 324 101 **F:** +66 76 324 108
http://www.asia-hotels.com/hotelinfo/Sheraton_Grand_Laguna_Beach/

Everyone, whether they are a gold member at the top of the repeat guest list or a complete Sheraton Laguna virgin, should savour the thrill of arrival at this resort, one of a quintet of hotels raised on a one-time mine quarry and largely surrounded by water. Cross the canal bridge to find two ranks of imposing columns flanking a pool bedecked with lotus flowers that points straight out to the beach and sea beyond. Above is the sky and all around a respectful hush and a feeling of total peace.

The accommodation of choice here is one of the 82 two- or three-level Grande Villas accessed by motor launch and where, in what amounts to an enclave within the hotel, the tedious formality of check-in is signed away in seconds flat. While the one- and two-bedroom villas represent the acme of opulence – think king-size beds, sunken tubs, free breakfast and cocktails and a mass of other add-ons – the Sheraton's 252 regular rooms are equally appealing. Furnished with local materials, there is a choice of views over pool, lagoon or ocean.

All in all, this is an extremely amenable resort, with a full compliment of recreational facilities catering for couples or families. The shallow end of the 323-metre swimming pool that winds its way throughout the hotel is edged with a mini beach, so you can just stroll into the water. Puccini, the smart Italian restaurant, is about as haute cuisine as can be found anywhere on Phuket. Or you can don T-shirt and shorts and browse around the Asian delicacies in the open-air Market Place – in all nine restaurants and bars are on offer.

At some stage during your stay climb the observation tower above the main lobby which affords views over the property and the rest of Laguna, the shimmering waters of lake and sea, and luxuriant trees and lawns. Conclusion? Not bad for a site that UNESCO – with a certain degree of folly – declared unusable for the next 100 years.

Rates from: **US$ 134**
Star rating: ★★★★★
Bellhop rating: 🛎🛎🛎🛎 ½

Value:	7.90	Facilities:	8.83
Staff:	8.83	Restaurants:	8.43
Location:	8.52	Families:	7.52
Cleanliness:	8.80		

Sofitel Central Hua Hin Resort

1 Damnernkasem Road, Hua Hin, Prachuabkirikhan 77110, Thailand
T: +66 32 512 021 **F:** +66 32 511 014
http://www.asia-hotels.com/hotelinfo/Sofitel_Central_Hua_Hin_Resort_/

Film buffs will instantly recognise the Sofitel Central from its inclusion in *The Killing Fields* which – on celluloid at least – transferred it from the royal seaside resort in Hua Hin to the centre of Cambodia.

It is a fine looking hotel, with a glistening white facade and red tiled roofs, richly restored using the original 1923 Railway Hotel shell while incorporating the A-Z of mod cons. The main building, made up of three wings (Railway, Colonial and Garden) containing 207 rooms and suites, is shaped like an off-centered 'Y', looking out toward the beach over gardens with a weird and wonderful topiary of animals and birds. A further 41

one- and two-bedroomed bungalows (belonging to the cheaper but very cheerful sister Central Hua Hin Village hotel) are set off to one side. Prime accommodation though is in the original Railway Wing where rooms have extra-high ceilings and balconies that are a true reminder of the hotel's glory days in the roaring 20s.

The Sofitel's main swimming pool (there are three) is located down by one of the best beaches in Hua Hin, and the lawns nearby are usually carpeted with sunbathers who fancy being able to hear the waves breaking but do not want to get covered in sand.

Naturally, the Sofitel plays up its historical antecedents, but does not overdo it. The rooms are fitted out with polished hardwoods yet softened by warm Thai silks, in a manner reminiscent of pre-war days. A traditional high tea is served in the Museum, which is full

of artefacts from days when the fastest way to get to Hua Hin was by steam train. The Lobby Bar with live pianist is a mass of antiques, sweeping staircases, crystal chandeliers and freshly cut flowers. Spas are almost de rigeur in Thailand's larger hotels, and the Centara at the Sofitel provides an excellent range of on-site treatments and therapies. This is certainly the most atmospheric hotel nestling peacefully right in the heart of Hua Hin town, and all the more successful for its discreet packaging of ancient and modern.

Rates from: **US$ 98**
Star rating: ★ ★ ★ ★ ★
Bellhop rating: 🛎 🛎 🛎 🛎 🛎

Value:	8.32	Facilities:	8.69
Staff:	8.71	Restaurants:	8.51
Location:	8.73	Families:	7.49
Cleanliness:	8.94		

The Sukhothai

13/3 South Sathorn Road, Bangkok 10120, Thailand
T: +66 2 287 0222 **F**: +66 2 287 4980
http://www.asia-hotels.com/hotelinfo/Sukhothai_Bangkok_The/

Turn off Sathorn Road and suddenly you are not in Bangkok any longer. Sukhothai – meaning 'dawn of happiness' – is not so much an oasis in 'the City of Angels', as completely removed from it. Yet this thoroughly unique hotel stands right in the heart of one of Asia's most frenetic capitals, as opportune for shopping and suchlike in Patpong as it is for the business and diplomatic districts.

Low-rise and low-key, the Sukhothai discreetly turns its back on its surrounds to create its own distinctive environment on a 6-acre landscaped plot. A long marbled corridor leads from the minimalist lobby toward the restaurants and rooms, flanked by statuary and reflective pools and scented by gorgeously displayed vases of freshly cut flowers. You do not so much walk down here as glide. The

lift lobby, taking its cue from the shrines of the ancient Mon culture, is arranged in an octagon. The corridors leading to the rooms are open-air, lined with heavy wooden lattice panels. And the rooms themselves look out over the water gardens and open courtyards. In short, this is a hotel that takes a different perspective, and wonderfully so.

To reinforce this feeling, stand in the bathroom. The floor is teak, the tub hippo-sized, the tiles on the walls hand-glazed in hues of green that set off the gallery of mirrors. Now ease into the bedroom. Subtly toned silk panels, ranging through muted rust to iridescent gold to intricately patterned grey contrast restfully with solid teak furniture. And just in case it might have slipped your mind, this is primarily a business hotel, so high-speed Internet access together with all the other accoutrements of executive life are available within these four walls.

As a counter to that selfsame executive life, the Sukhothai runs the gamut of sporting options. Tennis and squash courts, saunas and whirlpools, and black and chrome exercise engines in the gym are ranked with the 25-metre swimming pool set about with deck chairs and parasols, which is buffered from the outside by the lush greenery of the hotel gardens.

Complementing the Sukhothai's exceptional architecture are its restaurants. Sunday brunch at the Colonnade has become something of a Bangkok institution – a vast Japanese, Thai and Western buffet overlaid with the aroma of freshly baked bread – that swiftly takes on the hilarity of a wedding reception or birthday party. Dinner at the Celadon is more sedate, with classic Thai dishes drawn from all over the country served in air-conditioned salas – or on the terrace outside – which are surrounded by lotus ponds. At a point midway between these two, the Bar has a lighter menu and is decorated with period artworks and classic antiques.

The Sukhothai took on a new lease of life in 2002 with the appointment of British general manager, Duncan Palmer, one of Asia's most widely respected hoteliers. His arrival dovetailed neatly with the opening of a new Italian restaurant, La Scala, while plans are in hand to launch Spa Botanica, which will open to the rear of the hotel in 2004.

The Sukhothai takes its name from the 13th-century capital of Siam, an era when art and architecture flourished, the Thai script was invented and Theravada Buddhism was codified. The hotel brings some of that much needed ethos to millennium Bangkok.

Rates from: **US$ 145**
Star rating: ★ ★ ★ ★ ★
Bellhop rating: 🛎 🛎 🛎 🛎 ½

Value:	8.18	Facilities:	8.69
Staff:	9.06	Restaurants:	8.74
Location:	8.17	Families:	6.27
Cleanliness:	9.16		

Thavorn Beach Village

6/2 Moo 6, Nakalay - Patong Beach, Phuket 83150, Thailand
T: +66 76 290 334 **F**: +66 76 340 384
http://www.asia-hotels.com/hotelinfo/Thavorn_Beach_Village/

First and foremost, the Thavorn Beach Village is a fun resort with a capital 'F', more an adventure playground than a seaside hotel. Why? The main pool, the largest free-former on the island, weaves its way around a series of mini islands that are lush with tropical foliage and decorated with crocodile sculptures and elephant-shaped showers. And the bulk of Thavorn's accommodation, rising up the hillside above Nakalay Bay, can be reached by an open-sided funicular tram. It is like Disneyland without paying for the rides. With a selection of 207 bungalows, rooms and suites here, the best choice is to go for the Ocean View Villa rooms with a balcony which also feature an ocean-view jacuzzi or the popular but very basic bungalows sitting on the beach. The rooms reflect the resort's openness, being light and airy, well furnished in a mature garden setting.

The Thavorn's Nakalay Spa occupies its own pavilion, a peaceful darkened haven where the therapists are well versed in Thai and other massage techniques, as well as a variety of other treatments. Spread over two floors with open walkways, garden showers and a Thai sala, the spa features eight private treatment rooms, two jet rooms and a relaxation area in a tranquil garden setting. However, if you want to go for the cheapo option, the hydro massage beds by the pool are free.

Three restaurants complete the picture at Thavorn. Breakfasts at the Marissa Terrace are international, with a range of Thai, Western and Japanese food laid out on the buffet. There are no prizes for guessing the cuisine or reasons behind the name of On The Sea, but the menu is certainly consistently good. And the Old Siam Nakalay has romantic, northern style 'kantoke' rooms where you can dine seated on the floor.

The only real minus at this otherwise thoroughly pleasant albeit slightly lackadaisical resort is that the beach is a bit stony – but there is no real reason to venture any further than the poolside.

Rates from: **US$ 60**
Star rating: ★ ★ ★ ★
Bellhop rating: ♘ ♘ ♘ ♘ ½

Value:	8.14	Facilities:	8.76
Staff:	8.71	Restaurants:	8.52
Location:	8.19	Families:	6.81
Cleanliness:	9.05		

The Tongsai Bay

84 Moo 5, Bophut, Koh Samui, Suratthani 84320, Thailand
T: +66 77 245 480 **F:** +66 77 245 620
http://www.asia-hotels.com/hotelinfo/Tongsai_Bay_Cottages_The/

It is an old travellers' aphorism: 'Ah, but you should have seen this place 30 years ago.' But Tongsai Bay is the Koh Samui of the 1970s – a single and very private 200-metre long beach that is removed both physically and metaphorically from the more built-up parts of the island. That said, the facilities greeting Koh Samui's pioneers rarely went beyond basic bed and board, however the Tongsai Bay has managed to combine the best of both worlds.

With just 83 rooms – divided between cottages, beachfront building suites and grand villas – spread over 25 lush acres, Tongsai retains a very intimate and natural feel. One of the swimming pools is salt water, the covered gym is enshrouded in trees and the Prana Spa massage salas open to the elements.

The rooms themselves are simple but comfortable, with seaviews, satellite TVs and a private terrace incorporating sunken bathtub. Two of the villas are especially characteristic – Mango, distinguished by the hammock slung from the fruit trees sticking up through its terrace, and Nang-gong, with fine seaviews and a private back garden.

The other very non-1970s aspect of the Tongsai Bay are the eating options, which go well beyond the old fried rice/banana pancakes of hippie days. Chef Chom's Thai Restaurant stands near the lobby with large open-air terraces overlooking the sea, while Floyd's Beach Bistro (named after the BBC chef, Keith Floyd) offers beachside dining using only the freshest ingredients. Recently opened is the Butler's Restaurant, whose European-themed menu is changed daily. There are also two regular bars, dispensing cocktails, cold beers and fine wines.

The beach is dotted with shells and umbrellas but not pestered by stray dogs and equally stray hawkers. Motorised sports are also banned. First-time visitors do not need to be told that the right-hand

end is nicknamed Lovers' Corner, for that very soon becomes blindingly obvious.

Rates from: **US$ 200**
Star rating: ★ ★ ★ ★ ★
Bellhop rating: 🐚 🐚 🐚 🐚 🐚

Value:	8.35	Facilities:	9.18
Staff:	9.55	Restaurants:	8.88
Location:	9.22	Families:	7.12
Cleanliness:	9.53		

VIETNAM

For many people Vietnam conjures up nightmarish images of combat helicopters, napalm explosions and intolerable suffering. The terrible Vietnam War was one of the great tragedies of the 20th century for all involved. The war ended in 1975 but the sad legacy still lives on in the shape of physical and mental scars. But despite everything the Vietnamese went through, visitors will find them to be a remarkably optimistic and hospitable people with little or no animosity towards foreigners. The smiles and grace of the Vietnamese are among the most lasting impressions of this beautiful country.

This patriotic nation's history of fierce resistance goes back a lot further than its battle with the United States. Before ousting the Americans, the Vietnamese repelled French colonial forces and before that, crowbarred out their Chinese rulers, not to mention seeing off the terrifying Mongol hordes.

Having spent a good millennium under the Chinese, the Middle Kingdom's influences have been heavily absorbed and are still very tangible. Much of the culture and historic architecture have strong Chinese foundations. European expansion saw the French colonising Vietnam for a century, ultimately leaving behind a splendidly romantic Gallic footprint. The Americans were to crank up the power struggle that followed the French exit, and the subsequent division of the country into north and south led to war tearing through the region and years of devastation. Revered national hero Ho Chi Minh would lead an ultimately successful effort to reunite the land under communist rule. A landmark offensive took place during the most celebrated national holiday, Tet, the Lunar New Year.

During Tet just about everything stops and it is not the best time to enjoy Vietnam. Weather may also play a part in deciding when to go if you have a particular destination in mind. This is a long gangly country straddling 30 degrees of latitude, and tucked just under the Tropic of Cancer. The climate therefore varies notably from north to south. Northern areas experience monsoons from May to September while the south basks in a typically tropical climate, although it is driest from December through April. With this see-saw of good and bad weather, generally speaking the country is accessible all year round – but be warned, it is prone to sudden and dramatic flooding, especially in the lowlands and river delta regions.

The most attractive section of the capital Hanoi is the charming French Quarter complete with flaking old buildings with delightful decaying shutters. Hanoi also boasts some proud and opulent efforts such as the exquisite Presidential Palace. The conservative city is usually slow to adapt, however it offers an excellent combination of history and cuisine as well as a more gentle insight into Vietnam developing in the 21st century.

Vietnam's narrow central regions have three sites protected by UNESCO for their heritage. The little town of Hoi An is a unique pocket of old French streets especially charming by night when gently lit by colourful lanterns. Beyond Hue's city walls the wooded environs contain dozens of imperial tombs. My Son, a little deeper into the interior, is a crumbling remnant of the fallen Cham civilisation, a pale shadow of the traditional Vietnamese enemy, the neighbouring Khmers. Back up north is the poetic rocky limestone outcrops of Halong Bay, another site protected by UNESCO, this time for its stunning natural beauty.

The country has often been polarised into north and south and to balance Hanoi is wild and energetic Ho Chi Minh City, previously known as Saigon. Vietnam's largest city and economic powerhouse, the city has traditionally been viewed as a bit of a rebel by Vietnam's frowning rulers and is certainly that today. The male of the species may have a job fending off unwanted female attentions and vice is rampant. Ho Chi Minh City also has some potent reminders of its recent troubles. Powerful war museums are grippingly absorbing and the

infamous Cu Chi tunnel network is within easy day tripping reach.

The infrastructure has quite a way to go and flying is the only practical mode of transport for long distances, unless you have plenty of time and buttocks of steel. It must be said though that Vietnamese hotels are improving rapidly. The industry is currently a blend of boring government hotels,

average hotels that tried and rather failed to be a bit fancy, and several new additions that can certainly mix it with Asia's best. The amiable Vietnamese character ensures that service is generally a delight although there are spluttering language and efficiency issues at times.

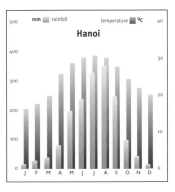

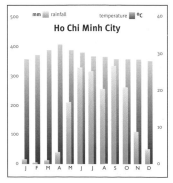

Ana Mandara Resort

Beachside Tran Phu Boulevard, Nha Trang, Vietnam
T: +84 58 829 829 **F:** +84 58 829 629
http://www.asia-hotels.com/hotelinfo/Ana_Mandara_Resort/

Vietnam's major coastal resort spot has traditionally been Nha Trang, which has perhaps the best beaches in the country. Most local hotels here cater to the domestic market, especially from Ho Chi Minh City (a 50-minute flight away). They are mostly rather functional and often dated efforts,

lagging well behind the appealing and imaginative beach accommodation in more popular countries of the region (such as beach Mecca Thailand). But the Ana Mandara, operated by the classy Six Senses Group, steadfastly bucks this trend – it is a stylish and well-designed 4-star resort, capturing that luxury resort feeling currently rare in Vietnam. Even rarer is the relative roundness of the hotel in terms of facilities, services and standards as there is almost always something missing from most hotels outside of Hanoi or Ho Chi Minh City.

The timber frame and pillars allow sunlight and the sea breeze to flood the interior, along with the gentle sounds of the rolling surf. The Ana Mandara does not have extensive facilities but it has brought all of the essential beach amenities to this relatively remote dot on the map. Their spa offers comprehensive therapies with well-trained masseurs, rather than the

semi-amateur mini-skirted gropers you often encounter in Vietnamese hotels. Loads of water sports are up for grabs on the beach just paces away, including parasailing, sailing, jet-skiing, banana boating and some reasonable diving. Other activities and tours are laid on and the restaurant is one of Nha Trang's most handsome. Note though that none of this comes particularly cheap, and the Ana Mandara is no bargain by Vietnamese standards.

Perhaps the decisive factor is that there are no anonymous corridors or packaged rooms. Its 16 palm-fringed beach villas host the 68 rooms, lending more personality, space and seclusion. All are tiled-roofed with verandahs, the majority with sea views, and all are thoughtfully put together and presented. Little if anything has been overlooked and the Ana Mandara currently has no serious competition for hundreds of kilometres.

Rates from: **US$ 165**
Star rating: ★ ★ ★ ★
Bellhop rating: 🔔🔔🔔🔔 ½

Value:	8.06	Facilities:	8.69
Staff:	8.94	Restaurants:	8.19
Location:	8.78	Families:	6.30
Cleanliness:	9.01		

The Caravelle

19 Lam Son Square, District 1, Ho Chi Minh City, Vietnam
T: +84 8 823 4999 **F:** +84 8 824 3999
http://www.asia-hotels.com/hotelinfo/Caravelle_Hotel/

The pacesetting Caravelle is widely acknowledged as Ho Chi Minh City's best hotel overall. Everything here is top rate, except the prices, which remain very reasonable. Chiefly the 24-storey towering hotel really does offer 5-star service, a challenge for a hotel of its size (335 rooms). Professional and welcoming staff are its key asset. Visually it triumphs too, with a sharp, snappy and energetic design throughout and immaculate presentation, not bad for a hotel first opened in 1959. Rooms are well appointed and warm with caramel coloured rooms, and it has some of Ho Chi Minh City's best business and leisure facilities. Absolutely indulgent dining could well have you piling on the kilos, and the trendy rooftop bar, Saigon Saigon, stands proudly above the rest in terms of both location and live entertainment. And just to make it really difficult for the competition, it is centrally located in District 1. Very hard to knock.

Rates from: **US$ 114**
Star rating: ★ ★ ★ ★ ★
Bellhop rating: 🛎 🛎 🛎 🛎 ½

Value:	8.31	Facilities:	8.60
Staff:	8.63	Restaurants:	8.33
Location:	9.01	Families:	6.85
Cleanliness:	8.91		

De Syloia

17A Tran Hung Dao Street, Hoan Kiem District, Hanoi, Vietnam
T: +84 4 824 5346 **F:** +84 4 824 1083
http://www.asia-hotels.com/hotelinfo/De_Syloia_Hotel/

Size is not everything, or so they say, it is the service. De Syloia proves this in the clearest possible way. It neither looks nor sounds like much. But this wildly popular little hotel runs rings around all the big boys when it comes to service and value for money. The modest but superbly run little property is spot on for what counts. There are few facilities beyond what is needed, and the well-maintained De Syloia is economical in more ways than one. A tidy lobby leads into a popular little local restaurant, Cay Cau, often packed with guests. The 33 guest rooms are straightforward but spacious, clean and comfortable, and the hotel is well situated only a few

minutes from the French Quarter and the city centre. Bargain hunters often have to grit their teeth in Asia – but not here – De Syloia is one of the best deals in the region.

Rates from: **US$ 55**
Star rating: ★ ★ ★
Bellhop rating: 🛎 🛎 🛎 🛎 ½

Value:	9.07	Facilities:	7.47
Staff:	9.12	Restaurants:	8.53
Location:	8.43	Families:	6.14
Cleanliness:	9.07		

The Furama Resort China Beach

68 Ho Xuan Huong Street, Da Nang, Vietnam
T: +84 511 847 888 **F:** +84 511 847 666
http://www.asia-hotels.com/hotelinfo/Furama_Resort_Danang/

The beach scene in Vietnam is in an embryonic state of development despite the thousands of kilometres of coastline of this ribbon of land. Much of the coast is rather muddy and surprisingly only pockets of decent sand exist. Presently there is only one true international class 5-star resort – the Furama Resort China Beach. Representing the future hopes of a new front of Vietnamese tourism, this stunning resort is something of an experiment. Opened in 1997, the resort is located on the best part of China Beach, famed for hosting R&R to the American GIs back in the war days. It is somewhat isolated both nationally and locally, with few attractions within

an hours drive. Luckily it has been superbly designed and constructed, to the extent that those enjoying a stay will not feel the need to leave, and crucially it is in total contrast to the rest of the developing region. It is almost as if the whole thing has been uprooted and jetted in from somewhere else.

Architecturally the experiment is a complete success. The Furama's ambience is luxuriant and tropical, and the facilities truly 5-star. It has been conceived with plenty of open space and fresh air in mind and it is set well back from the otherwise dusty industrial town of Da Nang. This is a most handsome resort and simply just fun to look at. The palm-studded

pools are magnificent oases of tropical colour and have many reaching for their camera for those jealousy-inducing holiday snaps. A horizon pool borders the excellent white sand stretch, which has choice water sports on offer including a diving school, sailing and waterskiing. The powdery beach is cleaned regularly and free of hassling vendors, a big plus in Vietnam. The hotel restaurants are also international, serving a range of excellent cuisines, a real challenge for the area. For those who know central Vietnam, where every meal is a carbon copy of the same Vietnamese buffet, this is a godsend. Instead there is a menu, and not just for show, with choices ranging from Mediterranean to

equipped gym to get chucked out of (it finishes bang on time), and some unusually large rooms to retire to. The 198 rooms flout the usual floor plan and set up, being unusually spacious and broad with split-levels and generous balconies. Highly polished teak wooden floors and lattice shutters provide a charming French colonial feel. With the inventive rooms and beautiful facilities, the Furama is picturesque resort and a superb escape.

Asian. The quality of the food on offer is the some of the best outside Hanoi or Ho Chi Minh City, for international travellers at least.

After a shaky opening the Furama's standard of service is now usually very high. Most staff members are delightful and have successfully overcome earlier teething troubles. When the sun sets there is a good and cheerful bar to relax in, and a well-

Rates from: **US$ 135**
Star rating: ★ ★ ★ ★
Bellhop rating: 🛎 🛎 🛎 🛎 ½

Value:	8.13	Facilities:	8.71
Staff:	8.67	Restaurants:	8.18
Location:	8.50	Families:	6.90
Cleanliness:	8.82		

Hilton Hanoi Opera

1 Le Thanh Tong Street, Hanoi, Vietnam
T: +84 4 933 0500 **F:** +84 4 933 0530
http://www.asia-hotels.com/hotelinfo/hilton_hanoi_opera_hotel_hanoi/

of its architectural intricacies, a single exterior window stretches between the 3rd and 4th floors, making the hotel appear smaller than it actually is.

The 269 rooms and suites enjoy two distinct designs. The executives are decorated in a restful beige and blue, the remainder in a rather sharper green and red and all the floors are distinguished by curving corridors that lend a remarkable, open air to the hotel's interiors. The 5th floor is the only one to come with balconies attached, an essential accessory for admiring the nearby scenery of tiled roofs and leafy boulevards. The rooms are wired with IDD phones and dataports, and the hotel has its own generator to back up any shortfall in the local supply.

The Hilton's 'R' floor is devoted to its restaurants – the award-winning Cantonese Turtle's Poem with its quintet of private dining rooms, the contemporary brasserie Chez Manon and JJ's Sports Bar, which offers darts, pool and big-screen events. Just outside is the swimming pool and terrace, both seemingly in touching distance of the Opera House, and the latter an unparalleled location for a party or corporate cocktails.

One of the most lovely of the many colonial-era buildings in Hanoi is the Opera House, which was built in 1911 and dominates the grand square at the end of Trang Tien Street. Its classic French exterior is happily reflected in the building just to the east, the rather more modern Hilton Hanoi Opera.

Strict government guidelines dictated that the Hilton should not be higher than the Opera House, and the architects were presented with an extremely unusual curved site. Design difficulties notwithstanding, the result – opened in 1999 – is a mini triumph, a 7-storeyed, columned crescent that blends perfectly with its historic milieu. As a neat example

Rates from: **US$ 82**
Star rating: ★ ★ ★ ★ ★
Bellhop rating: ♟ ♟ ♟ ♟ ♟

Value:	8.35	Facilities:	8.82
Staff:	9.08	Restaurants:	8.33
Location:	9.10	Families:	6.90
Cleanliness:	9.29		

Hoi An Riverside Resort

Cua Dai Road, Hoi An Town, Quang Nam Province, Vietnam
T: +84 510 864 800 **F:** +84 510 864 900
http://www.asia-hotels.com/hotelinfo/Hoi_An_Riverside_Resort/

A friendly little boutique resort on the fringes of a UNESCO-protected town, the Hoi An Riverside is a heart-warming property on the green banks of a scenic and sleepy river. The hotel comprises a series of two- and three-storey bungalows loosely sprinkled along the riverbanks and around the chilly but attractive free-form pool. Each bungalow is split into four or six rooms. The rooms are homely and warm with either ethnic Vietnamese or spotless Japanese themes, both categories thoughtfully presented with affectionate touches. On opening the curtains, many rooms look out on to the quiet river and lush paddy fields. The therapeutic effects of stooping farmers in conical hats and their munching buffalo cannot be underestimated.

There is little to do at the Hoi An Riverside, and this surely is part of its appeal. Facilities are few and low-key. A relaxing open restaurant in the small timber reception area dishes up some pleasing local food. Central Vietnam is often guilty of a tour bus factory approach, and nearly all hotel restaurants shy away from a la carte menus, churning out only monotonous Vietnamese buffets. But not here. Other facilities are few and unspectacular, but the hotel puts on a regular free shuttle to the historic town of Hoi An, which is only a few minutes away. An agreeable white sand beach lies only two minutes away in the other direction if you would like a break from lazing around the pretty pool.

Genuinely friendly staff seem to be much more involved with the guests, talking and joking freely. The combination of architecture, location and staff lends a rare warmth to this hotel. If you are not mad on big fancy hotels with reams of facilities, then this will definitely appeal. Certainly one of the most enjoyable hotels in Vietnam.

Rates from: **US$ 65**
Star rating: ★ ★ ★ ★
Bellhop rating: 🔔 🔔 🔔 🔔 🔔

Value:	8.79	Facilities:	8.68
Staff:	8.84	Restaurants:	8.68
Location:	8.58	Families:	5.79
Cleanliness:	9.42		

Hotel Majestic

1 Dong Khoi Street, District 1, Ho Chi Minh City, Vietnam
T: +84 8 829 5517 **F**: +84 8 829 5510
http://www.asia-hotels.com/hotelinfo/Hotel_Majestic_/

It is not as majestic as its name might suggest, but this is certainly a noble hotel capturing some of the romance of Indo-China. Dating from 1925 the Majestic is authentically colonial and renovators have sensibly respected it. This is certainly no Raffles Singapore or Oriental Bangkok, the standards being clearly of 4-star rank, and not immaculately presented, but the slight stuffiness of it actually works well for it. There are lots of colonial hangovers, appealingly weathered brass knobs and handles, the old ticking clocks, and high, regal ceilings and columns. The rooms are stately without being luxurious, and some counterbalance the disadvantage of noisy road traffic with open river views. Courtyard rooms overlook the inviting pool and the wonderful open sky bar on the top floor is a delight.

Rates from: **US$ 70**
Star rating: ★★★★
Bellhop rating: 🏩🏩🏩🏩 ½

Value:	8.40	Facilities:	8.03
Staff:	8.31	Restaurants:	7.59
Location:	8.93	Families:	5.81
Cleanliness:	8.54		

New World Hotel Saigon

76 Le Lai Street, District 1, Ho Chi Minh City, Vietnam
T: +84 8 822 8888 **F**: +84 8 824 3700
http://www.asia-hotels.com/hotelinfo/New_World_Hotel_Saigon/

The New World Saigon is your typical, great big anonymous hotel. It is predictable as far as towering hotels go, with everything from the design, the layout and the decor falling into stereotypical brochure outlines. The mass-produced pine rooms, the extensive list of perfectly decent facilities, plus the standards and maintenance do not stand out. This is not for bad reasons, but merely because this functional hotel is up to the job. Ironically, the New World has the distinction of being the only great big predictable hotel in Ho Chi Minh City. Its location on the fringes of District 1 is handy for business or pleasure, and the nightclub is one of the best in town. Service standards are generally good but can be a tad sloppy and casual and at times, feeling like one of Vietnam's government hotels. The rates are highly competitive for what you get, making the hotel a very popular choice.

Rates from: **US$ 75**
Star rating: ★★★★
Bellhop rating: 🏩🏩🏩🏩 ½

Value:	8.03	Facilities:	8.40
Staff:	8.50	Restaurants:	8.08
Location:	8.36	Families:	6.82
Cleanliness:	8.58		

Rex Hotel

141 Nguyen Hue Street, Ho Chi Minh City, Vietnam
T: +84 8 829 2185 **F:** +84 8 829 6536
http://www.asia-hotels.com/hotelinfo/Rex_Hotel_Vietnam/

There are few hotels anywhere that dare to be like the outlandish Rex. This is more of a time capsule than hotel. The designers of this amazing visual assault must have had no idea that their attempt to outdo rivals would result in an icon. So extroverted is it that with its prime position next to the galactic swirl of mopeds that constitute the main roundabout of District 1, it can be considered the heart of the city itself. The overdone exterior strives to be like Harrod's in London, but ends up being a cross between a Las Vegas casino and a garish Christmas tree. The excessive 1970s kitsch either works for you or it does not – oversized bamboo rattan furniture, bright gaudy woods and columns, and some interesting trimmings – this is a masterpiece of over the top, but an immensely enjoyable one. One almost expects staff to wear equally outlandish attire, sadly they do not, instead opting for traditional (but still iridescent) Vietnamese dress.

Beyond the rich character and recent war history, the Rex is more ordinary. The facilities are weathered and dated, but very functional. The Rooftop Garden bar is a popular place to down a sunset cocktail. The adjacent pool is miniscule, a width virtually being covered in a large stride. The 227 modestly proportioned and equipped rooms are decked out in that unique but slightly unforgettable style, and are great value given the location. Service is patchy, ditsy at times and some staff give the impression they can only give services on a superficial level – a few are on autopilot. The same goes for housekeeping, some areas are obviously not on the 'to do' list and are therefore neglected, especially around the inner courtyard. But services are not actually bad, just a tad disappointing for such a friendly nation. Despite the holes, the Rex is still a first-class product and at the very least has to be seen, even if it is just to raise a smile. When it comes to personality, the Rex is King.

Rates from: **US$ 57**
Star rating: ★ ★ ★ ★
Bellhop rating: ◊ ◊ ◊ ◊ ½

Value:	8.31	Facilities:	8.04
Staff:	8.27	Restaurants:	8.13
Location:	9.19	Families:	6.25
Cleanliness:	8.34		

Sofitel Dalat Palace

12 Tran Phu Street, Dalat, Vietnam
T: +84 63 825 444 **F**: +84 63 825 666
http://www.asia-hotels.com/hotelinfo/Sofitel_Dalat_Palace/

The rural mountain town of Dalat is an unlikely spot for such grandeur to say the least. The highland town is a national retreat and among the rock-bottom budget hotels, rickety theme park rides and potato patches, this sumptuous residence stands out a mile. Some hotels use the title 'palace' rather hopefully, but not the Sofitel Dalat Palace, for palatial it really is – no exaggeration.

The restored 1922 colonial mansion is an opulent example of European splendour, not the colonial cottage charm one sometimes finds lingering on, but the sort of indulgence that could have fuelled a very angry peasant revolt. It is easy to engage in brochure waffle when describing the property but, put simply, it feels too personal and too grand to be a hotel and is more like a residence of the aristocracy. Literally hundreds of European oil paintings hang off the wood-panelled walls, a magnificent chandelier hangs above the mosaic floored lobby and there are other period pieces such as podgy cherub statuettes. Surrounded by a superb park with grand lawns, the hotel faces out over the picturesque Xuan Huong Lake. It may sound a bit over the top but it is all tastefully done and is a real treat.

It is not a hotel in the usual sense and has few facilities – no pool, limited business facilities and little leisure beyond the sport courts and the well-maintained golf course opposite. There is the cosy watering hole 'Larry's Den' (named after Larry Hillblom, one of the DHL founders) and at Le Rabelais, some of the most exquisite French fine dining anywhere in Vietnam. After walking up the creaking wooden staircase one enters the quite stunning rooms. More romance awaits, with free-standing baths, honeymooners' beds and, in some of the 43 rooms and suites, crackling fireplaces to keep out the cold winter nights. There is an absence of air-conditioning due to the altitude, which is usually very temperate (but not always). The Dalat Palace has entertained royalty over the years, and it is quite unlike any other hotel in Vietnam. A hidden gem if ever there was one.

Rates from: **US$ 92**
Star rating: ★ ★ ★ ★ ★
Bellhop rating: 🛎 🛎 🛎 🛎 ½

Value:	8.31	Facilities:	8.41
Staff:	8.83	Restaurants:	8.38
Location:	8.88	Families:	6.74
Cleanliness:	9.02		

Sofitel Metropole Hanoi

15 Ngo Quyen Street, Hanoi, Vietnam
T: +84 4 826 6919 **F:** +84 4 826 6920
http://www.asia-hotels.com/hotelinfo/Sofitel_Metropole_Hanoi/

Staying at the Metropole in 1920, the noted playwright and wit Noel Coward quipped in his diary: 'We were not allowed out of the hotel as there was a revolution in progress.' Some eight decades later, there is another revolution in progress in Hanoi, but this time it is a social one. The capital of Vietnam is re-inventing itself – new buildings and businesses are springing up, and the disastrous war that finally ended in 1975 has been well and truly relegated to history.

Much of the city's new spirit has been captured by the Metropole, which first opened its doors in 1901 and was substantially renovated in 1992. The very best of the original building has been preserved, while a new wing has been built at the rear of the property. The gracious lobby, 4-metre-high bedroom ceilings, wide panelled corridors and staircases that greeted the likes of honeymooners Charlie Chaplin and Paulette Goddard in 1936 are still in situ, but nowadays they are augmented by a Clark Hatch fitness centre and high-speed Internet connections. You can take a tour of Hanoi in one of the hotel's modern fleet of Mercedes limousines, ease into the back of the Metropole's signature transport – a 1930 Citroen Traction – or climb aboard one of the pedal-powered cyclos whose drivers wait patiently outside the front entrance.

This marriage of old and new, traditional and modern, is expressed throughout the hotel. Lunch or dinner at Spices Garden is inspired by the myriad stalls selling local cuisine on Hanoi's streets. Some 40 dishes – including grilled chicken with lemon leaves, noodles with fried pork and fried rice with lotus seeds – are displayed on low tables and strung from bamboo shoulder poles. At breakfast in the art deco-style Le Beaulieu, crisp French baguettes and croissants take pride of place on the buffet, while tables by the windows look across the street to the ochre walls of the former Governor General's residence, later transformed into an official guesthouse. High tea – delicate pastries and chinaware, pots of Earl Grey and strainers – is served in Le Club Bar to the accompaniment of a grand piano. Evening cocktails at the poolside Bamboo Bar in the central courtyard are shaded by trees that must have been planted at the turn of the last century, and from here you can look around and appreciate the Metropole's classical white facade, stately green shutters and intricate wrought ironwork.

All the hotel's 232 rooms come with modern accoutrements such as satellite TV. The recently built 135-room Opera Wing duplicates the hotel's charm, but it is the original rooms that pull in the heritage guest. The timbered walls, polished floorboards that creak ever so gently, and the knowledge that perhaps Graham Greene, Bill Clinton, Jane Fonda (or any one of the scores of famous guests who have checked in over the years) may have occupied the same room are all quite unique.

The writer Edgar Snow, visiting the Metropole in 1931, wrote: 'It is all very gay and on Saturday nights, when dancing lasts until two o'clock, it even partakes of a breathless abandon.' Of course 'gay' has a rather different meaning now, but the sentiment that Snow recorded is still very much a part of this thoroughly delightful hotel.

Rates from: US$ 111
Star rating: ★ ★ ★ ★ ★
Bellhop rating: ꙮ ꙮ ꙮ ꙮ ½

Value:	8.04	Facilities:	8.25
Staff:	8.79	Restaurants:	8.54
Location:	9.11	Families:	5.99
Cleanliness:	8.85		

Victoria Hoi An Resort

Cam An Beach, Hoi An Town, Quang Nam Province, Vietnam
T: +84 510 927 040 **F:** +84 510 927 041
http://www.asia-hotels.com/hotelinfo/Victoria_Hoi_An_Resort/

Central Vietnam, a few kilometres from pretty Hoi An, is one of the last places you would expect to find a spot of the Latin Mediterranean, but here it is. Strung parallel to the beachside is a modern line of bright Spanish-style villa-apartments. Upper ones have sloping ceilings and

balconies opening out on to the road or sea. Some of these bright and airy rooms depart from the European theme and revel in highly appealing Japanese order. Facilities are limited. There are few business facilities to speak of, thankfully, but the sharp pool is a hit, and just beyond it lies a quiet beach. The

hotel continuously trumpets the talents of its French chef, and the French restaurant looks very tempting, although the food is dominated by a Vietnamese buffet. But still the resort is original and friendly with an enjoyable ambience.

Rates from: **US$ 95**
Star rating: ★ ★ ★ ★
Bellhop rating: 🐾 🐾 🐾 🐾 🐾

Value:	8.74	Facilities:	8.58
Staff:	9.45	Restaurants:	7.65
Location:	9.29	Families:	7.39
Cleanliness:	9.29		

✕® INSIGHT GUIDES Phonecard

One global card to keep travellers in touch.
Easy. Convenient. Saves you time and money.

It's a global phonecard

Save up to 70%* on international calls from over 55 countries

Free 24 hour global customer service

Recharge your card at any time via customer service or online

It's a message service

Family and friends can send you voice messages for free.

Listen to these messages using the phone* or online

Free email service - you can even listen to your email over the phone*

It's a travel assistance service

24 hour emergency travel assistance – if and when you need it.

Store important travel documents online in your own secure vault

For more information, call rates, and all Access Numbers in over 55 countries, (check your destination is covered) go to www.insightguides.ekit.com or call Customer Service.

JOIN now and receive US$ 5 bonus when you join for US$ 20 or more.

Join today at

www.insightguides.ekit.com

When requested use ref code: **INSAD0103**

OR SIMPLY FREE CALL 24 HOUR CUSTOMER SERVICE

UK	0800 376 1705
USA	1800 706 1333
Canada	1800 808 5773
Australia	1800 11 44 78
South Africa	0800 997 285

THEN PRESS ⓪

For all other countries please go to "Access Numbers" at www.insightguides.ekit.com

* Retrieval rates apply for listening to messages. Savings based on using a hotel or payphone and calling to a landline. Correct at time of printing 01.03

(INS001)

powered by ⟪ekit

"The easiest way to make calls and receive messages around the world"

Hotel ratings index

		PAGE	★	👍	Value	Staff	Location	Cleanliness
AUSTRALIA	**Area**							
ANA Harbour Grand	Sydney	9	5	4.5	7.78	8.36	8.87	8.69
Burswood	Perth	9	5	4.5	7.95	8.25	7.97	8.59
Crown Towers	Melbourne	10	5	4.5	7.90	8.32	8.85	8.85
Four Seasons	Sydney	11	5	4.5	7.88	8.78	9.21	9.07
Grand Hyatt	Melbourne	11	5	4.5	7.81	8.40	9.00	8.81
Hayman	Barrier Reef	12	5	5	8.00	9.14	9.79	9.21
Inter-Continental	Sydney	14	5	4.5	8.13	8.36	8.99	8.89
Marriott	Sydney	14	5	4.5	8.38	8.63	8.96	8.93
Marriott	Surfers Paradise	15	5	4.5	7.72	8.11	8.41	8.54
Observatory	Sydney	16	5	4.5	8.24	9.14	8.60	9.40
Park Hyatt	Melbourne	17	5	5	8.54	9.03	9.17	9.44
Park Hyatt	Sydney	18	5	4.5	7.56	8.35	9.02	8.70
Sheraton Mirage	Gold Coast	19	5	4.5	7.76	8.47	8.81	8.95
Sheraton On The Park	Sydney	20	5	4.5	7.85	8.45	8.97	8.90
Sofitel	Melbourne	21	5	4.5	7.96	8.81	9.17	9.13
W Hotel	Sydney	21	5	4	7.53	8.47	8.56	8.91
Westin	Melbourne	22	5	5	8.14	8.80	9.50	9.36
Westin	Sydney	22	5	4.5	7.73	8.33	9.08	9.04
CAMBODIA	**Area**							
Angkor Village	Siem Reap	24	3	4.5	8.35	8.81	8.64	8.73
Raffles Grand D'Angkor	Siem Reap	25	5	4.5	7.80	8.83	8.88	8.91
Raffles Le Royal	Phnom Penh	26	5	4.5	7.98	8.98	8.87	9.12
Sofitel Angkor	Siem Reap	27	5	4.5	7.79	8.72	8.88	8.95
CHINA	**Area**							
China Hotel by Marriott	Guangzhou	31	5	4.5	7.78	8.12	8.48	8.37
China World	Beijing	31	5	4.5	7.67	8.58	8.70	8.72
Grand Hyatt	Shanghai	32	5	4.5	7.79	8.35	8.32	9.04
Lu Song Yuan	Beijing	34	2	4	9.05	8.38	8.39	8.25
Palace	Beijing	35	5	5	8.27	8.69	9.16	9.14
Peace	Shanghai	36	5	4	7.76	7.67	9.23	8.05
Portman Ritz-Carlton	Shanghai	37	5	4.5	8.10	8.70	8.95	8.95
Pudong Shangri-La	Shanghai	38	5	4.5	8.02	8.53	8.31	8.91

Facilities

Facilities	Restaurants	Families	1	2	3	4	5	6	7	8	9	10	11	12	13	14	15	16	17	18	19	20
8.36	7.95	6.31			•		•			•		•		•	•	•	•			•		
8.63	8.41	7.14	•		•	•	•		•	•		•	•	•	•	•	•			•	•	•
8.78	8.69	7.03	•		•	•	•			•	•	•	•	•	•	•	•			•	•	
8.55	7.88	6.40	•		•		•			•		•		•	•	•	•			•	•	
8.68	8.42	7.39	•		•		•			•		•	•	•	•	•	•			•		
9.10	8.67	6.36	•	•				•		•		•		•	•	•	•			•	•	•
8.39	8.10	5.58			•		•			•		•		•	•	•	•			•		
8.48	8.04	7.00			•		•			•		•		•	•	•	•		•			
8.24	8.13	7.28	•		•					•		•	•	•	•	•	•		•	•		•
8.96	8.58	5.92	•		•		•			•		•		•	•	•	•		•	•		
9.12	8.88	5.98	•		•		•			•		•		•	•	•	•		•			
8.33	8.28	6.39	•		•		•			•		•		•	•	•	•		•			
8.87	8.21	7.10		•	•		•			•	•	•	•	•	•	•	•		•	•		
8.39	8.09	6.75			•		•			•		•		•	•	•	•			•		
8.57	8.53	6.40			•		•			•		•		•	•	•	•			•		
8.05	8.44	5.72			•		•			•		•		•	•	•	•					
8.64	8.14	6.88			•		•			•		•	•	•	•	•	•		•			
8.44	8.02	6.11	•		•		•			•	•	•		•	•	•	•			•		
7.98	8.21	5.65	•		•									•	•	•			•	•		
8.60	8.42	5.38	•		•					•		•		•	•	•			•	•	•	
8.65	8.29	6.48	•		•					•	•			•	•	•			•	•		
8.53	8.58	5.70			•		•			•		•		•	•	•	•			•		
8.24	8.34	7.01	•		•		•			•		•	•	•	•	•			•	•	•	
8.48	8.28	6.18	•		•		•			•		•		•	•	•		•		•	•	
8.72	8.58	6.59	•		•					•		•	•	•	•	•	•			•		
7.38	7.13	4.58			•									•	•					•		
8.69	8.54	6.80	•		•		•			•			•	•	•		•			•		
7.68	7.82	6.31	•		•					•		•	•	•	•	•				•		
8.72	8.34	6.71	•		•		•			•		•		•	•	•	•		•	•		
8.66	8.22	6.76	•		•		•			•		•		•	•	•		•		•	•	

Hotel ratings index		PAGE	★	👍	Value	Staff	Location	Cleanliness
Shangri-La	Hangzhou	38	5	4.5	7.91	8.17	8.93	8.37
Shangri-La	Shenzhen	39	5	4	7.68	8.01	8.30	8.08
Sheraton	Suzhou	39	5	4.5	8.36	8.42	8.17	8.74
St Regis	Beijing	40	5	4.5	7.70	8.57	8.70	8.99
St Regis	Shanghai	41	5	4.5	8.64	8.97	7.85	9.18
White Swan	Guangzhou	42	5	4.5	8.33	8.56	8.44	8.68
HONG KONG	**Area**							
Excelsior	Hong Kong Island	45	4	4	7.90	8.08	8.91	8.34
Grand Hyatt	Hong Kong Island	46	5	4.5	7.67	8.51	8.45	8.94
Harbour Plaza	Kowloon	47	5	4.5	8.19	8.42	7.65	8.79
Holiday Inn Golden Mile	Kowloon	47	4	4	7.80	7.95	8.71	8.22
Hyatt Regency	Kowloon	48	4	4.5	8.01	8.56	9.15	8.84
Inter-Continental	Kowloon	49	5	4.5	7.85	8.72	9.02	9.05
Island Shangri-La	Hong Kong Island	50	5	4.5	7.75	8.57	8.87	8.95
JW Marriott	Hong Kong Island	51	5	4.5	7.92	8.59	8.93	8.87
Kowloon	Kowloon	51	4	4	8.02	7.83	8.98	8.30
Mandarin Oriental	Hong Kong Island	52	5	4.5	7.78	8.81	9.08	8.96
Marco Polo	Kowloon	53	4	4.5	8.28	8.17	9.05	8.57
Novotel Century Harbourview	Hong Kong Island	53	3.5	4	8.28	7.96	7.90	8.48
Peninsula	Kowloon	54	5	5	7.76	8.91	9.09	9.20
Regal Airport	Lantau Island	56	5	4.5	8.01	8.31	8.78	8.91
Renaissance Harbour View	Hong Kong Island	57	4.5	4.5	7.88	8.15	8.68	8.72
Ritz-Carlton	Hong Kong Island	57	5	4.5	7.97	8.94	9.04	9.09
Royal Pacific	Kowloon	58	3.5	4	8.00	8.17	8.67	8.58
Sheraton	Kowloon	58	5	4.5	7.76	8.28	8.85	8.56
YMCA - The Salisbury	Kowloon	59	3.5	4.5	8.57	8.11	9.04	8.52
INDIA	**Area**							
Ajit Bhawan	Jodhpur	62	n/a	n/a	n/a	n/a	n/a	n/a
Imperial	New Delhi	63	5	4.5	8.17	8.56	8.64	8.56
Lake Palace	Udaipur	64	5	5	8.54	8.96	9.70	8.96
Leela Kempinski	Mumbai	63	5	4.5	7.78	8.36	7.93	8.33
Leela Palace	Goa	65	5	4.5	7.92	8.51	8.31	8.84
Maurya Sheraton	New Delhi	66	5	4	7.71	8.17	7.83	8.24

Facilities

Facilities	Restaurants	Families	1	2	3	4	5	6	7	8	9	10	11	12	13	14	15	16	17	18	19	20	21
8.13	7.98	6.43	•		•		•			•		•		•	•			•			•	•	
7.98	7.90	5.76	•		•		•			•		•		•	•	•				•		•	
8.41	8.12	6.49	•		•		•			•		•		•	•			•		•	•	•	
8.47	8.13	5.89	•		•		•			•		•		•	•	•			•	•		•	•
8.70	7.94	5.64	•		•		•			•		•		•	•			•	•		•	•	
8.67	8.48	7.25	•		•				•	•	•	•		•	•			•			•	•	
7.86	7.97	6.63	•		•		•			•		•		•	•						•	•	
8.56	8.66	6.85	•		•		•			•		•	•	•	•					•	•	•	
8.48	8.19	6.80	•		•		•			•		•		•	•					•		•	
7.86	7.92	6.64	•		•		•			•		•		•	•					•		•	
8.28	8.37	6.61	•		•		•		•	•		•		•	•							•	
8.77	8.72	6.81	•		•		•			•		•		•	•	•				•			
8.65	8.55	6.91	•		•		•			•		•		•	•					•			
8.52	8.43	6.97	•		•		•			•		•		•	•					•		•	
7.69	7.53	5.99			•					•				•	•	•						•	
8.32	8.72	6.63	•		•		•			•		•		•	•	•	•						
8.19	8.02	7.11	•		•			•	•	•		•		•	•					•		•	
8.04	7.04	5.94	•		•		•			•		•		•	•					•		•	
8.79	8.90	7.16			•		•			•		•		•	•	•	•						
8.46	8.10	5.93	•		•		•			•		•		•	•					•		•	
8.43	8.08	6.09	•		•		•			•				•	•					•	•	•	
8.37	8.51	6.98			•		•			•				•	•					•			
8.05	7.49	5.99	•		•					•				•	•							•	
8.18	8.06	6.50			•		•			•		•		•	•	•	•			•		•	
7.91	6.59	6.54	•				•			•		•		•	•			•				•	
n/a	n/a	n/a								•				•	•					•		•	
8.14	8.47	5.89			•					•		•		•						•			
8.34	8.56	6.61	•		•		•			•		•		•	•	•				•		•	
8.30	8.36	7.45	•		•					•		•		•	•					•			
8.65	8.45	7.75		•	•	•			•	•				•	•	•	•			•	•		•
8.21	8.55	6.71	•		•		•			•			•	•	•	•	•			•	•	•	

Hotel ratings index

		PAGE	★	👍	Value	Staff	Location	Cleanliness
								Ratings
Oberoi Grand	Kolkata	66	5	4.5	8.62	8.57	8.43	8.52
Oberoi Towers	Mumbai	67	5	4	7.15	8.19	8.44	8.39
Rajvilas	Jaipur	68	5	5	8.38	9.28	8.64	9.57
Rambagh Palace	Jaipur	70	5	5	8.59	9.19	9.33	9.11
Taj Bengal	Kolkata	71	5	4.5	7.64	8.46	7.60	8.30
Taj Mahal	New Delhi	71	5	5	8.22	8.88	8.76	8.93
Taj Mahal	Mumbai	72	5	4.5	7.54	8.27	8.52	8.32
INDONESIA	**Area**							
Alila Ubud	Bali	75	5	4.5	8.02	9.05	9.11	9.18
Amandari	Bali	76	5	4.5	7.70	9.08	8.79	9.24
Amanjiwo	Yogyakarta	78	5	4.5	7.21	9.04	8.83	9.25
Amankila	Bali	80	5	5	7.68	9.53	9.28	9.54
Amanusa	Bali	81	5	5	7.94	9.50	9.03	9.41
Balé	Bali	82	5	n/a	n/a	n/a	n/a	n/a
Bali Hyatt	Bali	82	5	4.5	8.20	8.77	8.71	8.81
Bali Inter-Continental	Bali	83	5	4.5	7.99	8.80	8.53	8.83
Bali Padma	Bali	83	5	5	8.30	8.93	8.81	8.65
Banyan Tree	Bintan	84	5	4.5	7.37	8.85	8.48	8.79
Dharmawangsa	Jakarta	85	5	4.5	8.23	9.29	7.98	9.35
Four Seasons at Jimbaran Bay	Bali	86	5	4.5	7.66	9.15	8.83	9.13
Four Seasons at Sayan	Bali	88	5	5	7.91	9.49	9.33	9.47
Gran Melia	Jakarta	89	5	4.5	8.12	8.49	8.34	8.56
Grand Hyatt	Bali	90	5	5	8.28	8.95	8.72	8.91
Grand Hyatt	Jakarta	91	5	4.5	7.72	8.42	8.81	8.58
Hard Rock	Bali	92	4	4.5	7.82	8.75	9.01	8.75
Holiday Inn	Lombok	92	4	5	8.57	9.09	8.35	9.30
Hyatt Regency	Yogyakarta	93	5	4.5	8.56	8.81	7.81	8.95
Le Meridien Nirwana	Bali	93	5	4.5	8.45	8.68	7.94	8.80
Legian	Bali	94	5	4.5	7.61	8.98	8.94	9.03
Mandarin Oriental	Jakarta	94	5	4.5	8.18	8.67	8.79	8.57
Mandarin Oriental Majapahit	Surabaya	95	5	5	8.80	9.18	8.05	9.13
Melia	Bali	96	5	4.5	8.02	8.69	8.26	8.69
Mulia	Jakarta	96	5	5	8.55	8.71	8.55	8.97

Facilities

Facilities	Restaurants	Families	F1	F2	F3	F4	F5	F6	F7	F8	F9	F10	F11	F12	F13	F14	F15	F16	F17	F18	F19	F20	F21	F22
8.41	8.67	6.62	•		•				•		•		•	•	•	•		•			•		•	
8.17	8.32	6.76	•		•				•		•		•	•	•	•		•			•			
9.20	8.80	6.90	•		•				•		•		•	•	•	•	•				•	•	•	
8.78	8.52	7.41	•		•		•		•			•	•	•	•	•		•			•	•	•	
8.26	8.46	7.68	•		•				•		•		•	•	•	•		•			•		•	
8.73	8.80	7.25	•		•				•		•		•	•	•	•		•			•		•	
8.24	8.42	7.09	•		•		•		•			•	•	•	•	•		•			•		•	
8.48	8.76	6.09	•										•	•		•			•		•		•	
8.67	8.46	6.02	•						•				•	•		•			•		•	•		
8.04	8.17	5.75	•										•	•					•		•	•		
9.19	8.99	6.18	•	•					•				•	•					•		•			•
9.03	8.81	7.28	•	•				•					•	•		•			•		•			
n/a	n/a	n/a							•		•		•	•		•			•					
8.74	8.40	7.46	•		•			•		•			•	•		•			•		•	•	•	•
8.76	8.35	6.99	•	•	•		•	•		•	•		•	•		•			•		•	•	•	•
8.54	8.52	7.86	•	•	•		•			•			•	•		•			•		•	•	•	•
8.44	8.04	6.01	•	•				•					•	•		•			•		•	•	•	
8.96	8.58	6.35	•		•				•		•	•		•	•	•	•	•			•		•	
8.96	8.60	7.03	•	•	•				•		•		•	•		•			•		•	•	•	•
9.10	8.90	5.75			•				•				•	•		•			•		•		•	
8.32	8.61	7.22			•				•		•	•		•	•	•	•				•	•	•	
9.04	8.57	7.72	•	•	•		•		•		•		•	•		•			•		•	•	•	•
8.59	8.46	7.11			•				•			•		•	•	•	•				•	•	•	
8.80	8.38	8.07	•		•			•		•			•	•		•			•		•		•	•
8.48	8.65	7.61	•	•	•		•	•		•	•		•	•	•	•			•		•	•	•	
8.73	8.07	7.32	•		•		•		•		•	•		•	•	•	•				•	•	•	
8.90	8.33	7.40	•		•		•		•		•		•	•		•			•		•	•	•	
8.56	8.28	6.72	•	•	•				•			•		•	•	•	•				•		•	
8.20	8.42	5.25			•				•		•	•		•	•	•	•				•		•	
8.75	8.60	6.85	•		•				•		•	•		•	•	•	•				•	•	•	
8.42	8.15	6.75	•	•	•			•		•			•	•		•	•		•		•	•		•
8.81	8.80	7.16	•		•				•		•	•	•	•	•	•	•				•		•	

Hotel ratings index

		PAGE	★	👍	Value	Staff	Location	Cleanliness
					Ratings			
Novotel Coralia Benoa	Bali	97	4.5	5	8.67	8.89	8.44	8.87
Novotel Coralia	Lombok	98	4	4.5	8.57	8.70	8.57	8.67
Nusa Dua	Bali	98	5	4.5	7.94	8.70	8.39	8.85
Oberoi	Bali	99	5	5	8.00	9.22	8.86	9.11
Oberoi	Lombok	100	5	4.5	8.05	9.32	8.64	9.43
Ritz-Carlton	Bali	101	5	5	8.30	9.37	8.59	9.35
Shangri-La	Jakarta	102	5	4.5	7.93	8.60	8.21	8.88
Shangri-La	Surabaya	102	5	4.5	8.15	8.57	7.83	8.72
Sheraton	Bandung	103	5	4.5	8.55	8.75	7.85	8.65
Sheraton	Lombok	103	5	4.5	8.21	9.03	8.77	8.77
Sheraton Laguna Nusa Dua	Bali	104	5	4.5	8.15	8.78	8.55	8.82
JAPAN	**Area**							
ANA	Tokyo	108	5	4	7.50	8.63	8.57	8.81
Century Hyatt	Tokyo	109	5	4.5	7.51	8.97	8.64	9.14
Four Seasons Chinzan-so	Tokyo	109	5	4.5	7.51	9.00	7.37	9.19
Hilton	Tokyo	110	5	4	7.42	8.51	8.26	8.87
Imperial	Tokyo	111	5	4.5	7.38	9.02	8.97	9.16
Keio Plaza Inter-Continental	Tokyo	112	5	4.5	7.54	8.71	8.77	8.86
New Otani	Tokyo	112	5	4.5	7.46	8.87	8.53	9.08
Okura	Tokyo	113	5	4.5	7.48	9.16	8.65	9.31
Park Hyatt	Tokyo	114	5	4.5	7.29	8.95	8.35	9.22
Prince	Tokyo	116	5	4.5	8.12	8.51	8.73	8.98
Ritz-Carlton	Osaka	116	5	5	7.60	9.48	8.82	9.60
Westin	Tokyo	117	5	4.5	7.26	9.03	8.59	9.44
Westin Miyako	Kyoto	117	5	5	8.31	9.10	9.10	9.45
KOREA (SOUTH)	**Area**							
COEX Inter-Continental	Seoul	120	5	4.5	7.53	8.39	8.63	8.73
Grand Hyatt	Seoul	121	5	4.5	7.54	8.35	8.22	8.65
Lotte	Seoul	122	5	4.5	7.82	8.29	8.67	8.62
Novotel Ambassador Kangnam	Seoul	122	4	4	7.50	7.94	8.06	8.31
Ritz-Carlton	Seoul	123	5	4	7.13	8.32	7.52	8.45
Sheraton Grande Walkerhill	Seoul	123	5	4.5	7.61	8.52	7.95	8.83
Shilla	Cheju	124	5	5	7.77	9.23	9.03	9.27

Facilities

Facilities	Restaurants	Families																				
8.67	8.21	7.86	•	•			•			•	•			•	•	•		•	•	•	•
8.40	8.07	6.77	•	•	•			•		•	•			•	•	•		•		•	•
8.66	8.52	7.51	•	•	•		•			•	•	•		•	•	•		•		•	•
8.85	8.61	7.00	•	•	•			•		•		•		•	•	•		•	•	•	•
8.71	8.64	5.75	•	•	•			•		•	•			•	•	•		•		•	•
9.15	8.83	7.37	•	•	•		•		•	•	•	•		•	•	•		•	•	•	•
8.69	8.59	6.86	•		•		•			•	•	•		•	•	•		•		•	•
8.42	8.40	6.93	•		•		•			•	•	•	•	•	•	•		•	•	•	•
8.35	8.40	8.10	•		•			•			•	•		•	•	•					
8.44	8.15	7.79	•	•	•			•		•	•	•		•	•	•		•		•	
8.74	8.20	6.96	•	•	•		•		•	•		•		•	•	•		•	•	•	•
8.20	8.14	6.13			•		•			•		•		•	•	•		•			
8.56	8.28	6.57			•		•			•		•	•	•	•	•		•		•	
8.80	8.30	7.10			•		•			•		•		•	•	•	•	•			
8.06	8.11	6.42			•		•			•		•		•	•	•		•		•	
8.29	8.37	6.55	•		•		•			•		•		•	•	•		•		•	
7.98	8.11	6.87	•		•		•			•		•		•	•	•		•	•	•	
8.52	8.31	6.76	•		•		•			•		•		•	•	•		•	•	•	
8.56	8.70	6.42			•					•		•		•	•	•		•	•		
8.68	8.75	6.70	•		•		•			•		•		•	•	•	•	•			
8.10	8.12	6.73			•					•		•		•	•	•		•	•	•	
9.18	8.80	6.88			•		•			•		•		•	•	•	•	•			
8.64	8.35	6.46			•		•		•	•		•		•	•	•					
8.76	8.72	7.48	•		•		•			•	•		•	•	•	•		•	•	•	
8.49	8.27	6.37	•		•		•			•		•		•	•	•	•		•		
8.46	8.41	7.05			•		•			•	•		•	•	•	•		•	•	•	
8.38	8.28	7.59	•		•					•		•		•	•	•		•		•	
8.03	7.69	6.83	•		•		•			•		•		•	•	•		•			
8.05	7.99	6.26			•					•		•		•	•	•		•			
8.37	8.33	7.56			•	•				•		•		•	•	•		•	•	•	
8.91	8.73	7.86	•	•	•	•		•	•			•		•	•	•		•	•	•	

Hotel ratings index		PAGE	★	👍	Value	Staff	Location	Cleanliness
					Ratings			
Shilla	Seoul	125	5	4.5	7.64	8.79	7.98	8.83
Westin Chosun	Seoul	126	5	4.5	7.71	8.78	8.99	9.03
LAOS	**Area**							
Le Calao	Luang Prabang	128	1	n/a	n/a	n/a	n/a	n/a
Lao Plaza	Vientiane	129	4	4	7.50	8.05	8.70	8.35
Novotel	Vientiane	129	4	4.5	8.00	8.52	7.95	8.43
Settha Palace	Vientiane	130	5	4.5	8.76	8.59	8.86	9.17
Villa Santi	Luang Prabang	131	3.5	4.5	7.92	8.88	8.88	8.48
MACAU	**Area**							
Hyatt Regency	Macau	133	5	4	7.98	7.94	7.83	8.10
Mandarin Oriental	Macau	133	5	4.5	7.73	8.36	8.26	8.53
Westin	Macau	134	5	4.5	7.79	8.36	7.95	8.71
MALAYSIA	**Area**							
Andaman	Langkawi	137	5	4.5	7.64	8.71	8.61	8.86
Berjaya	Langkawi	138	5	4.5	8.17	8.15	8.29	8.19
Berjaya	Redang	139	4	4.5	8.15	8.11	8.75	8.16
Berjaya	Tioman Island	140	4	4	7.51	7.95	8.67	7.87
Casa del Mar	Langkawi	140	4	4.5	7.77	8.68	8.55	8.64
Club Med	Cherating	141	3.5	5	8.38	9.23	8.15	8.81
Concorde	Kuala Lumpur	141	4	4.5	8.35	8.00	8.62	8.26
Datai	Langkawi	142	5	4.5	7.60	8.89	8.89	9.07
Eastern & Oriental	Penang	144	5	4.5	8.06	8.75	8.77	9.00
Equatorial	Kuala Lumpur	145	4	4.5	8.17	8.25	8.40	8.32
Equatorial	Melaka	145	4	4	7.91	7.88	8.45	8.22
Hilton Batang Ai Longhouse	Kuching	146	4.5	4.5	8.91	8.87	8.78	8.91
Hilton	Kuching	147	5	4.5	7.91	8.25	8.33	8.44
Hilton Petaling Jaya	Kuala Lumpur	147	4.5	4.5	8.07	8.27	8.31	8.42
Holiday Inn Damai	Kuching	148	4	4	8.52	8.39	8.52	8.42
Hyatt Regency	Kuantan	149	4.5	4.5	8.31	8.30	8.72	8.25
Hyatt Regency	Saujana	149	4.5	4	7.95	8.17	7.62	8.42
Istana	Kuala Lumpur	150	5	4.5	8.19	8.36	8.77	8.58
JW Marriott	Kuala Lumpur	150	5	4.5	8.14	8.26	9.12	8.73
Lakehouse	Cameron Highlands	151	3.5	4.5	8.06	8.75	8.75	8.56

Facilities

Facilities	Restaurants	Families	F1	F2	F3	F4	F5	F6	F7	F8	F9	F10	F11	F12	F13	F14	F15	F16	F17	F18	F19	F20	F21	F22
8.49	8.43	7.23			•		•			•			•	•	•	•	•			•		•	•	•
8.54	8.32	6.05			•					•			•		•	•	•			•			•	
n/a	n/a	n/a												•										
7.85	8.05	7.55	•		•					•			•	•	•	•		•	•			•		
8.05	8.24	6.71	•		•					•				•	•	•	•			•		•	•	
8.69	7.69	4.48			•								•		•	•	•					•		
7.44	8.28	5.68	•												•	•								•
8.22	8.10	6.99	•		•	•	•			•	•		•		•	•	•			•		•	•	
8.44	8.08	6.79	•		•	•				•	•		•	•	•	•	•			•		•	•	
8.51	8.10	7.49	•		•				•	•	•		•		•	•	•			•		•		
8.54	8.42	6.93	•	•	•				•	•					•	•	•			•		•		•
8.35	8.16	7.10	•	•	•			•		•				•	•	•	•			•		•		•
8.07	7.95	7.07	•	•				•		•				•	•	•	•			•		•		•
8.03	7.75	7.17	•	•	•			•		•				•	•	•	•			•		•		•
7.77	7.64	6.73		•						•					•	•	•			•		•		•
9.19	8.85	9.23	•	•	•		•			•	•		•		•	•				•		•		•
8.07	7.98	6.46	•		•					•					•	•	•			•		•		
8.71	8.56	6.42	•	•					•	•					•	•	•			•		•		•
8.06	8.08	6.37	•		•			•	•			•		•	•	•	•			•		•		
7.71	8.05	6.96			•			•		•	•	•			•	•	•		•			•		
7.82	7.62	6.98	•		•		•			•					•	•	•			•		•		•
8.57	7.87	7.48	•		•					•					•	•				•		•		•
8.12	7.98	6.91	•		•					•					•	•	•			•		•		
8.09	8.31	7.23	•		•					•					•	•	•			•		•		
8.19	7.52	7.16	•	•	•		•			•	•				•	•	•			•		•		
8.33	8.22	7.37	•	•	•		•			•					•	•	•			•		•		
8.10	7.75	6.67			•				•	•			•	•	•	•	•			•		•		
8.42	8.22	7.14	•		•					•				•	•	•	•		•	•		•		
8.43	8.15	7.11	•		•					•				•	•	•		•	•	•		•		
7.44	8.19	6.38	•												•	•								

Hotel ratings index

		PAGE	★	👍	Value	Staff	Location	Cleanliness
								Ratings
Langkawi Village	Langkawi	151	3	4.5	8.59	8.16	8.14	8.14
Mandarin Oriental	Kuala Lumpur	152	5	4.5	8.16	8.49	9.13	8.91
Mutiara	Penang	154	5	4.5	7.93	8.51	8.12	8.69
Mutiara Burau Bay	Langkawi	154	3	5	9.12	8.69	9.12	8.96
Palace of the Golden Horses	Kuala Lumpur	155	5	4.5	8.02	8.44	7.66	8.81
Pan Pacific KLIA	Kuala Lumpur	155	5	4.5	8.16	8.20	8.24	8.55
Pangkor Laut	Pangkor	156	5	4.5	7.75	8.83	8.73	8.83
Pelangi	Langkawi	158	4	4.5	8.21	8.51	8.63	8.55
Regent	Kuala Lumpur	159	5	4.5	8.09	8.72	8.99	8.80
Renaissance	Kuala Lumpur	159	5	4.5	8.19	8.09	8.38	8.50
Renaissance	Melaka	160	4	4	7.87	7.94	8.05	8.24
Rihga Royal	Miri	160	5	5	8.61	8.82	8.30	8.88
Ritz-Carlton	Kuala Lumpur	161	5	4.5	8.38	9.06	8.64	9.17
Shangri-La Golden Sands	Penang	162	4	4.5	8.11	8.38	8.62	8.42
Shangri-La	Kuala Lumpur	163	5	4.5	8.21	8.54	8.57	8.72
Shangri-La Rasa Ria	Kota Kinabalu	164	5	5	8.43	8.95	8.14	8.74
Shangri-La Rasa Sayang	Penang	165	5	4.5	8.04	8.52	8.56	8.59
Shangri-La Tanjung Aru	Kota Kinabalu	166	5	4.5	8.32	8.80	8.56	8.75
Sheraton	Langkawi	167	4.5	4.5	8.26	8.48	8.32	8.57
Smokehouse	Cameron Highlands	168	3	4	6.54	8.92	9.00	8.39
Sunway Lagoon	Kuala Lumpur	169	4.5	4.5	7.66	8.11	7.90	8.43
Sutera Harbour	Kota Kinabalu	169	4	5	8.42	8.75	8.92	8.81
Tanjong Jara	Terengganu	170	5	4	7.36	8.31	7.81	8.29
Tanjung Rhu	Langkawi	171	5	4.5	7.86	8.93	8.84	8.99
MALDIVES	**Area**							
Angsana	Maldives	173	5	5	8.58	8.73	9.15	8.96
Banyan Tree	Maldives	174	5	4.5	7.68	8.69	8.79	8.69
Four Seasons	Maldives	175	5	4.5	7.84	9.04	8.97	9.13
Soneva Fushi	Maldives	176	5	5	8.64	9.57	9.39	9.50
MYANMAR	**Area**							
Grand Plaza Parkroyal	Yangon	180	5	4.5	8.69	8.63	8.69	8.69
Inle Princess	Inle Lake	180	2	n/a	n/a	n/a	n/a	n/a
Pansea	Yangon	181	4	5	8.65	9.18	8.65	9.18

Facilities

Facilities	Restaurants	Families	1	2	3	4	5	6	7	8	9	10	11	12	13	14	15	16	17	18	19	20
7.69	7.86	7.04		•								•	•	•			•		•			
8.64	8.42	7.11	•		•		•		•		•		•	•	•		•	•	•			
8.60	8.34	7.64	•	•	•		•		•	•			•	•			•	•	•		•	
7.96	8.27	7.58	•	•	•					•			•	•			•	•	•		•	
8.65	8.32	7.75		•		•			•		•		•	•			•	•	•			
8.26	7.98	6.64		•		•			•		•		•	•	•		•	•	•			
8.48	8.33	6.83	•	•			•		•		•		•	•			•	•	•		•	
8.41	8.22	7.74	•	•	•		•		•	•	•		•	•			•	•	•	•	•	
8.38	8.29	6.65		•					•		•		•	•			•	•	•			
8.38	8.08	6.71		•		•			•		•	•	•	•			•	•	•			
8.04	7.11	5.87	•	•		•			•				•	•			•	•	•			
8.73	8.21	8.52		•					•			•	•	•			•	•	•			
8.37	8.10	7.02	•	•					•		•		•	•			•	•				
8.45	8.18	7.87	•	•					•	•			•	•			•	•	•			•
8.49	8.40	6.67	•		•		•		•		•		•	•			•	•	•			
8.68	8.33	7.90	•	•	•		•	•	•	•			•	•			•	•	•			•
8.65	8.46	7.78	•	•	•				•	•	•		•	•			•	•	•			•
8.71	8.41	7.43	•	•	•		•		•		•		•	•			•	•	•		•	
8.40	8.18	7.19	•	•	•				•	•	•	•	•	•			•	•	•		•	
7.46	8.85	7.15					•						•	•	•							
8.51	8.01	7.89	•	•	•		•		•		•		•	•			•	•	•		•	
8.86	8.42	7.06	•	•	•		•		•	•	•	•	•	•			•	•	•	•	•	
8.02	7.48	6.95	•	•				•		•			•	•			•	•	•			
8.66	8.47	6.63	•	•	•		•		•		•		•	•			•	•	•			
8.77	8.62	7.00			•			•					•	•			•					•
8.24	8.31	6.54		•			•		•				•	•			•			•	•	•
8.70	8.42	6.82	•	•			•		•	•			•	•	•		•					•
8.86	8.89	7.43	•	•			•		•		•		•	•	•		•			•		•
8.28	8.47	7.19	•		•				•			•	•	•	•		•	•	•	•		
n/a	n/a	n/a	•										•	•				•				
8.44	8.88	5.94	•								•		•	•	•		•					

Hotel ratings index

Facilities

Facilities	Restaurants	Families	🍼	✈	📈	🌐	♿	🌀	1	✚	🧸	⛵	♪	🍽	⛱	⛷	💧	🏠	🎿	🎾	ⓘ	z
n/a	n/a	n/a			•				•					•	•	•			•		
8.06	7.83	6.56			•					•				•	•	•			•	•	
8.59	8.41	7.69	•		•				•	•		•	•	•	•	•			•	•	•
7.56	8.13	6.07	•		•									•	•	•					•
n/a	n/a	n/a	•		•					•				•	•	•			•		
7.92	7.28	7.20	•		•		•			•				•	•	•				•	
7.80	7.98	6.28	•		•	•	•			•				•	•	•	•	•	•	•	•
8.50	8.46	6.73	•		•		•			•		•		•	•	•		•			
8.49	8.20	6.14	•		•		•			•		•		•	•	•	•		•		
9.06	8.69	7.83	•	•				•						•	•	•			•	•		•
8.62	8.31	7.96	•	•	•			•						•	•	•			•	•		•
8.77	7.96	8.27	•		•					•	•	•		•	•	•	•		•		•	
8.77	8.75	8.10	•		•		•			•		•		•	•	•	•		•		•	
8.06	8.27	6.71	•	•				•						•	•	•			•		•	•
8.47	8.44	8.45			•		•			•	•	•		•	•	•			•	•	•	•
8.40	8.20	7.63	•	•			•	•		•				•	•				•			•
8.88	8.83	8.11			•					•		•	•	•	•	•			•	•	•	
8.40	8.67	7.79	•		•		•			•				•	•	•	•		•		•	
8.66	8.71	8.19	•		•		•			•				•	•	•	•		•		•	
8.46	8.53	7.92			•		•			•				•	•	•	•		•			
8.73	7.69	7.93	•		•		•			•				•	•	•	•		•		•	
8.67	8.74	7.99	•		•		•			•				•	•	•	•		•		•	
8.85	8.48	8.20	•		•		•	•		•	•	•		•	•	•			•		•	•
9.11	8.74	8.43	•	•	•				•	•	•	•	•	•	•	•			•			•
8.29	8.02	7.08	•	•	•				•	•		•		•	•		•		•	•		
8.30	8.13	7.24	•		•		•			•		•	•	•	•	•			•		•	
8.55	8.28	7.04	•		•		•			•		•		•	•	•			•	•		
8.46	8.46	7.03			•		•			•		•		•	•	•			•		•	
8.17	8.53	7.16	•		•					•		•		•	•	•			•			

Hotel ratings index

		PAGE	★	👍	Value	Staff	Location	Cleanliness
				Ratings				
Grand Hyatt	Singapore	213	5	4.5	7.72	8.34	9.01	8.77
Holiday Inn Park View	Singapore	213	4	4.5	7.90	8.13	8.59	8.44
Inter-Continental	Singapore	214	5	4.5	7.96	8.44	8.65	8.79
Keong Saik	Singapore	215	2	4	8.16	8.28	8.31	8.28
Oriental	Singapore	215	5	4.5	7.98	8.46	8.41	8.69
Raffles	Singapore	216	5	4.5	7.62	8.89	8.99	9.14
Raffles The Plaza	Singapore	217	5	4.5	7.52	8.39	9.12	8.75
Regent	Singapore	217	5	4.5	8.05	8.83	8.45	9.04
Ritz-Carlton Millenia	Singapore	218	5	4.5	7.77	8.86	8.43	9.14
Royal Peacock	Singapore	220	3	4	8.45	8.05	8.70	8.25
Shangri-La	Singapore	220	5	4.5	7.72	8.56	8.13	8.83
Shangri-La Rasa	Sentosa	221	5	4.5	7.82	8.38	8.12	8.60
Sheraton	Singapore	222	5	4.5	8.06	8.66	8.23	8.84
Swissotel The Stamford	Singapore	222	5	4.5	7.79	8.34	8.95	8.74
SRI LANKA	**Area**							
Colombo Hilton	Colombo	225	5	4.5	7.97	8.16	8.16	8.42
Galle Face	Colombo	225	3.5	4	7.94	8.00	8.06	7.41
Kandalama	Dambulla	226	4	5	9.12	8.91	9.27	9.06
Lighthouse	Galle	228	5	4.5	8.54	8.69	8.46	8.92
Mount Lavinia	Colombo	229	4.5	4.5	8.44	8.00	8.50	8.06
TAIWAN	**Area**							
Far Eastern Plaza	Taipei	232	5	4	7.62	8.22	8.09	8.51
Grand Formosa Regent	Taipei	232	5	4.5	7.98	8.40	8.45	8.76
Grand Hyatt	Taipei	233	5	4	7.41	8.30	8.12	8.71
Landis	Taipei	235	5	4.5	7.86	8.96	8.02	8.92
Le Petit Sherwood	Taipei	234	5	4.5	7.87	8.80	8.46	8.98
Westin	Taipei	235	5	4.5	7.93	8.59	8.45	9.01
THAILAND	**Area**							
Allamanda Laguna	Phuket	238	4	4.5	8.49	8.77	8.51	8.57
Amanpuri	Phuket	239	5	4.5	7.70	9.20	9.11	9.21
Amari Palm Reef	Koh Samui	240	4	4.5	8.18	8.65	8.74	8.79
Amari Watergate	Bangkok	241	4	4.5	8.32	8.51	8.54	8.66
Baiyoke Sky	Bangkok	241	4	4	8.40	7.92	8.29	8.20

Facilities

Facilities	Restaurants	Families	1	2	3	4	5	6	7	8	9	10	11	12	13	14	15	16	17	18	19	20	21
8.41	8.44	7.17	•		•		•			•		•	•	•	•	•	•	•		•	•		
8.00	7.74	6.83	•		•		•			•			•		•	•	•	•		•		•	
8.30	8.23	6.72	•		•		•			•		•	•	•	•	•	•	•		•		•	
6.66	4.74	5.68					•						•										
8.30	8.14	6.73	•		•					•			•		•	•	•	•		•	•	•	
8.58	8.77	7.14	•		•					•			•		•	•	•	•		•	•	•	
8.44	8.40	7.35			•		•			•			•		•	•	•	•		•	•	•	
8.26	8.30	7.13	•		•					•			•		•	•		•		•			
8.77	8.45	7.20	•		•		•			•			•		•	•	•	•		•	•	•	
6.10	5.40	4.80			•		•					•	•	•	•	•	•	•					
8.61	8.42	7.26	•		•				•	•					•	•	•			•		•	
8.43	8.04	7.88	•	•	•		•		•	•			•		•	•	•	•		•			•
8.31	8.33	7.00			•					•			•		•	•		•		•		•	
8.44	8.33	7.02			•		•			•			•		•	•	•	•		•	•	•	
8.40	8.52	6.79	•		•					•	•		•		•	•	•	•		•	•	•	
6.71	7.47	5.77	•	•	•										•	•		•		•		•	
8.46	8.91	7.52								•					•	•	•	•		•			
8.08	8.00	7.92	•	•	•					•		•			•	•	•	•		•		•	
7.61	8.11	6.67	•	•	•					•				•	•	•		•		•		•	
8.26	8.03	6.45	•		•		•			•		•	•	•	•	•	•		•	•		•	
8.50	8.40	7.15	•		•					•		•	•	•	•	•		•		•		•	
8.34	8.33	6.34			•		•			•		•	•	•	•	•		•		•		•	
8.14	8.53	5.80			•		•			•			•		•	•					•		
8.02	8.14	5.82											•		•	•		•					
8.37	8.40	6.30	•		•		•		•	•	•	•	•		•	•	•		•		•		
8.24	7.74	7.80	•	•	•				•	•	•	•			•	•	•	•		•	•	•	•
8.88	8.66	6.38	•	•	•			•	•	•					•	•		•		•	•	•	•
8.29	7.94	7.02	•	•											•	•	•	•		•	•	•	
8.44	8.24	7.00	•		•		•			•					•	•	•	•		•		•	
7.84	7.79	6.60			•					•			•	•	•	•	•	•		•		•	

Hotel ratings index

		PAGE	★	👍	Value	Staff	Location	Cleanliness
				Ratings				
Marriott	Bangkok	242	5	4.5	8.40	8.69	8.19	8.88
Banyan Tree	Bangkok	243	5	4.5	8.14	8.83	8.13	9.10
Banyan Tree	Phuket	244	5	4.5	7.58	9.00	8.48	9.05
Boathouse (Mom Tri's)	Phuket	246	3.5	4.5	8.45	9.17	9.03	8.86
Cape Panwa	Phuket	246	4	4.5	8.20	8.65	9.00	8.85
Central Samui	Koh Samui	247	5	5	8.42	9.00	9.17	8.94
Chaweng Regent	Koh Samui	248	4.5	4.5	7.97	8.45	8.90	8.63
Chedi	Phuket	249	4.5	4.5	7.94	9.11	9.02	9.10
Chiva-Som International	Hua Hin	250	5	4.5	8.10	9.22	7.68	9.29
Dusit Laguna	Phuket	251	5	4.5	8.00	8.59	8.44	8.61
Dusit Polo Club	Hua Hin	252	5	5	8.43	8.98	8.67	8.93
Dusit	Pattaya	253	5	4.5	8.25	8.77	8.50	8.87
Dusit Thani	Bangkok	253	5	4.5	8.23	8.78	8.61	8.72
Grand Hyatt Erawan	Bangkok	254	5	4.5	7.98	8.69	8.77	8.82
Holiday Inn	Phuket	255	4	4.5	8.42	8.60	8.85	8.48
Hua Hin Marriott	Hua Hin	256	4	5	8.32	8.98	8.81	9.06
JW Marriott	Bangkok	257	5	4.5	8.15	8.64	8.34	8.74
Kata Thani	Phuket	257	4	5	8.81	9.06	8.72	9.16
Laguna Beach	Phuket	258	5	4.5	7.85	8.46	8.22	8.40
Le Royal Meridien	Bangkok	258	5	4.5	8.12	8.64	8.87	8.76
Le Royal Meridien Baan Taling Ngam	Koh Samui	259	5	5	8.48	9.33	8.77	9.41
Le Royal Meridien	Phuket	260	5	4.5	8.00	8.92	8.84	8.94
Majestic Suites	Bangkok	261	2	4	8.71	8.48	8.81	8.95
Marina	Phuket	262	3	5	8.64	9.04	9.14	9.07
Novotel Coralia	Phuket	262	4	4.5	8.37	8.80	8.43	8.83
Oriental	Bangkok	263	5	5	8.04	9.13	8.56	9.14
Pan Pacific	Bangkok	265	5	4.5	8.01	8.67	8.72	8.88
Pathumwan Princess	Bangkok	265	4	4.5	8.20	8.27	9.16	8.49
Peninsula	Bangkok	266	5	5	8.68	8.92	8.09	9.19
Poppies	Koh Samui	268	4	4.5	7.88	8.46	8.63	8.71
Rayavadee	Krabi	269	5	5	8.12	9.40	9.69	9.44
Regent	Bangkok	270	5	4.5	8.08	8.82	8.78	8.94
Regent	Hua Hin	270	4	5	8.46	9.18	8.61	8.96

Facilities

Facilities	Restaurants	Families
8.78	8.62	6.45
8.58	8.16	6.66
8.89	8.36	7.06
7.31	9.00	5.72
8.45	8.30	7.00
8.99	8.55	7.89
8.26	8.24	7.00
8.11	8.10	6.79
9.22	8.49	3.63
8.43	8.28	7.62
9.00	8.77	7.55
8.65	8.18	7.15
8.43	8.51	6.90
8.53	8.52	6.95
8.37	8.28	7.84
8.94	8.66	7.51
8.33	8.32	6.89
8.81	8.59	7.66
8.61	7.95	8.24
8.36	8.05	6.86
9.17	8.95	7.29
8.81	8.68	7.03
7.43	6.86	3.67
8.14	8.54	6.75
8.54	7.99	6.85
8.81	8.88	6.95
8.49	8.33	6.21
8.28	7.96	6.93
8.90	8.44	6.38
7.67	8.38	6.25
9.23	9.23	7.25
8.49	8.71	6.91
8.82	8.57	7.61

Hotel ratings index

		PAGE	★	👍	Value	Staff	Location	Cleanliness
Regent	Chiang Mai	271	5	5	7.95	9.47	8.84	9.47
Royal Cliff	Pattaya	273	5	4.5	7.88	8.32	8.13	8.47
Royal Orchid Sheraton	Bangkok	274	5	4.5	8.02	8.63	8.48	8.76
Santiburi Dusit	Koh Samui	274	5	4.5	7.59	8.85	8.53	8.82
Shangri-La	Bangkok	275	5	4.5	8.15	8.91	8.60	9.00
Sheraton Grande Sukhumvit	Bangkok	275	5	4.5	8.00	8.92	8.83	9.03
Sheraton Grande Laguna	Phuket	276	5	4.5	7.90	8.83	8.52	8.80
Sofitel Central	Hua Hin	277	5	5	8.32	8.71	8.73	8.94
Sukhothai	Bangkok	278	5	4.5	8.18	9.06	8.17	9.16
Thavorn Village	Phuket	280	4	4.5	8.14	8.71	8.19	9.05
Tongsai Bay	Koh Samui	281	5	5	8.35	9.55	9.22	9.53
VIETNAM	**Area**							
Ana Mandara	Nha Trang	284	4	4.5	8.06	8.94	8.78	9.01
Caravelle	Ho Chi Minh City	285	5	4.5	8.31	8.63	9.01	8.91
De Syloia	Hanoi	285	3	4.5	9.07	9.12	8.43	9.07
Furama China Beach	Da Nang	286	5	4.5	8.13	8.67	8.50	8.82
Hilton Hanoi Opera	Hanoi	288	5	5	8.35	9.08	9.10	9.29
Hoi An Riverside	Hoi An	289	4	5	8.79	8.84	8.58	9.42
Majestic	Ho Chi Minh City	291	4	4.5	8.40	8.31	8.93	8.54
New World	Ho Chi Minh City	291	4	4.5	8.03	8.50	8.36	8.58
Rex	Ho Chi Minh City	292	4	4.5	8.31	8.27	9.19	8.34
Sofitel Dalat Palace	Dalat	293	5	4.5	8.31	8.83	8.88	9.02
Sofitel Metropole	Hanoi	294	5	4.5	8.04	8.79	9.11	8.85
Victoria	Hoi An	296	4	5	8.74	9.45	9.29	9.29

Facilities

Facilities	Restaurants	Families	🏀	⛷	📈	🧭	♿	↩	1	✚	🐼	📓	🎵	💿	☁	✈	🎣	🏠	🏊	⚾	🏃	↪
9.08	8.69	6.52	•		•					•	•			•	•	•	•		•	•	•	
8.39	8.25	7.28	•	•	•		•			•	•	•		•	•	•			•	•	•	•
8.48	8.33	6.37	•		•		•			•		•		•	•	•	•	•	•	•	•	
8.53	8.09	7.29	•	•				•		•				•	•	•	•		•	•	•	•
8.80	8.66	6.75	•		•		•			•	•	•	•	•	•	•	•		•	•	•	
8.74	8.52	6.49	•		•		•			•		•	•	•	•	•	•		•	•	•	
8.83	8.43	7.52	•	•	•		•		•	•		•	•	•	•	•	•		•	•	•	•
8.69	8.51	7.49	•	•	•					•	•	•	•	•	•	•	•		•	•	•	•
8.69	8.74	6.27	•		•		•			•		•		•	•	•	•		•	•	•	
8.76	8.52	6.81	•	•				•		•				•	•	•	•		•	•	•	
9.18	8.88	7.12	•	•						•				•	•	•	•		•	•	•	•
8.69	8.19	6.30	•	•	•			•		•		•		•	•	•	•		•	•	•	•
8.60	8.33	6.85	•		•		•			•		•		•	•	•	•		•			
7.47	8.53	6.14			•					•		•		•	•	•						
8.71	8.18	6.90	•	•	•		•	•		•	•	•	•	•	•	•	•		•	•	•	•
8.82	8.33	6.90	•		•		•			•	•	•		•	•	•	•		•	•	•	
8.68	8.68	5.79	•		•					•		•		•	•	•	•		•	•	•	
8.03	7.59	5.81	•		•					•		•		•	•	•	•		•	•	•	
8.40	8.08	6.82	•		•		•			•		•	•	•	•	•	•		•	•	•	•
8.04	8.13	6.25			•		•			•				•	•	•	•		•	•	•	•
8.41	8.38	6.74	•		•			•		•				•	•	•				•	•	
8.25	8.54	5.99	•		•		•			•				•	•	•			•	•	•	
8.58	7.65	7.39	•	•	•		•			•	•	•		•	•	•			•	•	•	•

Hotel index